Warman's
WORLD WAR II
COLLECTIBLES

John F. Graf
Editor of
Military Trader Magazine

Identification and Price Guide

© 2007 John F. Graf

Published by

krause publications

An Imprint of F+W Publications

700 East State Street • Iola, WI 54990-0001
715-445-2214 • 888-457-2873
www.krausebooks.com

Our toll-free number to place an order or obtain a free catalog is 800-258-0929

Library of Congress Control Number: 2007923824

ISBN 13-digit: 978-089689-546-1
ISBN 10-digit: 0-89689-546-7

Designed by Sandy Kent
Edited by Dan Brownell

Printed in China

CONTENTS

ACKNOWLEDGMENTS

A work of this nature does not evolve over a short period of time. Rather, it has taken 35 years to develop the familiarity with the military material culture of World War II to even feel comfortable considering such a project. I will never fully appreciate my parent's tolerance. As a young boy, I never stopped asking my father, a World War II veteran, or my mother, a college student during the War, about their experiences and memories. They never stifled my enthusiasm. Dad let me sit with his war buddies when they got together at our family-owned grocery store to reminisce, and Mom kept me supplied with books and toys and explained photographs to me.

Perhaps, though, the moment that cemented my fascination with World War II was the day my father let his six-year-old son march alongside him and his fellow American Legion members in our city Memorial Day parade. Clad in camouflage pajamas, plastic helmet with plastic camouflage and wearing my Dad's M1936 musette bag on my back (packed with my blanket and teddy bear), I marched with the pride of knowing that these guys had been to war. They were the *true* "relics." The stories they told me, the souvenirs they showed me and the pride they demonstrated in their participation in the effort to liberate Europe and the Pacific has stuck with me to this day.

More recently, I wish to extend my gratitude to Jefferson Shrader and Anna McCoy of Advance Guard Militaria and Jody Tucker of Manion's International. They opened their business records to help me determine realistic values of military relics based on their actual sales history. Without this data, this price guide would not have been possible. The collecting hobby will benefit from this generosity for years to come. Similiarly, Ernst-Ludwig Wagner of Hermann Historica OHG, and Patrick F. Hogan of Rock Island Auction Company, graciously took time from their busy auction schedules to retrieve photos and sales data for me to use in compiling the final data and illustrations for this work.

Doug Bekke of Minnesota Military Museum, Fergus Falls, Minnesota, did not hesitate to give me access to the Museum's vast collection. His knowledge of World War II material is unsurpassed.

Likewise, lifelong friend and collector Charles D. Pautler responded to my request to photograph his collection by saying, "How soon can we do it?" His enthusiasm for collecting is contagious. I wish I had his uncanny knack for sniffing out rare items at flea markets, garage sales and forgotten antique shops was as well!

Peter Suciu took time from his own busy writing career to photograph each of his helmets for this work. His generosity has provided images of many unusual and rare examples that won't be seen in any other work (unless of course, he sits down and writes a comprehensive guide to helmet collecting...he is the one person I hope would consider such a project).

Several fine dealers and collectors of World War II memorabilia came forward and contributed past catalogs, auction and sale results, photographs, and their specialized knowledge. This group of individuals includes Fred Borch, Fred Borgmann, Collin R. Bruce II, George Cuhaj, Bill Combs, John Conway, Joseph S. Covais, Gary Harvey, Thomas R. Kailbourn, Clement V. Kelly, Denise Moss, Kelly Nelson, Dennis Piotrowski, Mary Schmidt and Judy Voss.

This book has opened my eyes to the passage of time in more than just the sense of collecting. My nephew John Lauermann helped sort out the computer data transfer problems I was having. He is no longer the little boy I remember, but an advanced college student. The bigger indicator of the passage of time, though, was when my "little girl," Trisha Graf, stepped forward to assist compiling the listings for this book. She is no longer my little girl, but obviously a competent, caring and detailed-oriented woman. Thanks, Bear. Your help was instrumental in "pushing me over the hump" on this project.

I owe a debt of gratitude to my dear friend and fellow-author David Doyle. David understands the pitfalls of authoring a book of this scope and never wavered in his encouragement to me when I felt myself falter. A friend such as David who possesses a strong professional and moral ethic is a rare thing...more valuable than any double-decal SS helmet or identified paratrooper's jacket. I am grateful for the information, vintage photographs, professional empathy and friendship he has shared with me.

And finally, the depth of thanks I owe to Diane Adams-Graf of the Minnesota Historical Society cannot be measured. She is the consummate museum professional and the finest partner I could ever imagine. I look forward to a long, caring life together so I can attempt to repay her patience for the nights and weekends that I selfishly spent writing this book.

If I have left anyone off this list, it is not out of malice, but rather, the result of a messy filing system! Thank you all, for making this book available to the thousands of World War II collectors and enthusiasts.

INTRODUCTION

During the sixty-plus years since the end of World War II, veterans, collectors and nostalgia-seekers have eagerly bought, sold and traded the "spoils of war." Actually, souvenir collecting began as soon as troops set foot on foreign soil. Whether Tommies from Great Britain, Doughboys from the United States or Fritzies from Germany, soldiers eagerly looked for trinkets and remembrances that would guarantee their place in the historic events that unfolded before them. Helmets, medals, Lugers, field gear, daggers and other pieces of war material filled parcels and duffel bags on the way back home.

As soon as hostilities ended in 1945, the population of defeated Germany and Japan quickly realized they could make money selling souvenirs to the occupation forces. The flow of war material increased. Values became well established...a Luger was worth several packs of cigarettes, a helmet, just one. A Japanese sword was worth two boxes of K-rations, while an Arisaka bayonet was valued at a Hershey's chocolate bar.

Over the years, these values have remained proportionally consistent. Today, that "two-pack" Luger might be worth $4,000 and that one-pack helmet, $1,000. The Japanese sword might fetch $1,200 and the Arisaka bayonet $85. Though values have increased dramatically, demand has not dropped off a bit. In fact, World War II collecting is the largest segment of the miltaria hobby.

Surprisingly, the values of items have been a closely guarded secret. The hobby, unfortunately, has relied on paying veterans and their families far less than a military relic is worth with the hope of selling later for a substantial profit. This attitude has given the hobby a bad reputation.

The advent of the Internet, though, has significantly leveled the playing field for sellers and buyers. No longer does a person have to blindly offer a relic for sale to a collector or dealer. Simply logging onto one of several Internet auctions will give the uninitiated an idea of value.

But, a little information can be dangerous. The value of military items is greatly affected by variation. Whether it is a difference in manufacturing technique, material or markings, the nuances of an item will determine the true value. Don't expect 20 minutes on the Internet—or even glancing through this book—to teach you these nuances. Collectors are a devoted bunch. They have spent years and hundreds, if not thousands, of dollars to establish the knowledge base that enables them to navigate the hobby. Use the basic information you can gain from this book to begin the foundation of your negotiations.

WHO NEEDS THIS BOOK?

This book was not written for the "hardened" or "veteran" collector or World War II memorabilia. Because of their years of handling objects and study, these people can pick up a piece of militaria and generally recognize its value. No, these people will not benefit from this book. In fact, they may actually *dislike* this book! Why? Because *Warman's World War II Collectibles* is for the person who is *not* an ardent collector of military objects.

Using *Warman's World War II Collectibles*, the non-collector will be able evaluate military objects that he or she may find in attics, closets, flea markets, garage sales or thrift stores. This book is also for the families who encounter a box or trunk in an attic filled with the souvenirs and remembrances of a relative's service to his or her country. Often, they just want to know what "dad's old army stuff" is worth. This book will answer those questions.

This book is not intended to be an exhaustive identification guide. The more than 1,000 photographs of artifacts don't even begin to scratch the surface of the vast mounds of World War II relics that are available. Thousands of books have been written covering a variety of subcategories ranging from bayonets and hand grenades to machine guns and Nazi Party membership badges. Thus, the scope of items is beyond what one book can cover. *Warman's World War II Collectibles* will provide pricing information for thousands of items, but readers may have to do more research to identify and price items not in this book. A variety of excellent references exist (and are listed in the bibliography) that readers can consult for more detailed information.

Warman's World War II Collectibles serves primarily as a basic introduction to help the non-collector or the novice avoid making financial mistakes while buying or selling World War II items.

WHAT IS COVERED?

Warman's World War II Collectibles lists items commonly found in antique shops, flea markets, online auctions, or long-forgotten trunks, but only those items made before the autumn of 1945 when the last of the Axis powers surrendered to the Allies. The items listed are typical of what soldiers carried or encountered daily. It does not address items primarily used by civilians from this period (such as glassware, toys, or other decorative arts or home-front items) or produced after the cessation of hostilities.

In each of the seven chapters, items from a variety of nations will be presented. The majority of the items originated in the military formations of the U.S., Great Britain, Germany and Japan, though the reader will find items from other nations as well.

IS HITLER'S CHINA LISTED?

While it is true that the occasional soldier grabbed valuable artwork or pieces of some notable's silverware to take home, they were, by far, the exception. Of the hundreds of thousands of soldiers and sailors who returned to their homes at the end of World War II, most wore their uniform and carried a duffel bag of personal belongings and, perhaps, some momentos for families and friends. They weren't art critics, looters, or investment speculators. In fact, most never considered the monetary worth of the objects they carried as souvenirs. The objects they brought home were simply reminders of—and perhaps some sort of compensation for—the extreme sacrifice they made to their country. For some veterans, the objects represented a deep, personal meaning that could never be quantified in a dollar amount.

In the following pages, the reader will find a catalogue of a wide range of World War II militaria that is typically found in veterans' estates. This book does not attempt to identify all of the great rarities or one-of-a-kind items that tend to cause a hardened collector's jaw to drop. Rather, the items described in these pages range from a soldier's own uniform and personal items to the trophies he may have carried home at the conclusion of his service.

HOW TO USE THIS BOOK

The person who will benefit the most from this book probably isn't a militaria collector. A lot of the listings may appear to be gibberish. For example, how is the uninitiated to know the difference between a "Shirt, OD, flannel, enlisted man" and a "Shirt, forest green, wool, USMC, enlisted man?"

The nomenclature used in this book tends to emulate what a particular government or army called an item. Collector-determined names will often appear in parentheses, however. For example, most collectors use the name "Model 41 jacket" or "Parsons Jacket" (a reference to the officer who popularize these garments) to refer to the khaki-colored poplin field jackets that U.S. Army soldiers commonly wore in combat in both the European and Pacific theaters. The Army's name for these garments, though, was "Jacket, field, OD (second pattern)." The listing in this book will combine both the "official" nomenclature as well as popular collector terminology. In the case of the field jacket, the listing will appear as "Jacket, field, OD, cotton poplin (second pattern—often referred to as a M1941 jacket)."

Even though both "official" and "collector" terminology are presented, the reader may not have a clue as to what a particular item might be. For example, how is a non-collector to know the difference between a "Jacket, field, OD, cotton poplin" and a "Jacket, field, lined, ETO?" Though it is hoped that this book will be used in conjunction with other photo references, more than 1,000 illustrations are included to assist the novice with item identification.

AVAILABILITY, PRICE AND REPRODUCTION ALERT

At the beginning of each chapter is a chart that provides three ratings: Availability, Price, and Reproduction Alert. Each rating is represented by one to five stars with the meaning as follows:

Availability
★★★★★ You should be able to find these items at a general antique show.
★★★★ Commonly found through online auctions or through most dealers.
★★★ Encountered with frequency at military relic shows.
★★ May find the items through private sales lists.
★ Very rare; available through advanced dealers.

Price
★★★★★ $5,001-and up
★★★★ $1,001-$5,000
★★★ $251-$1,000
★★ $51-$250
★ $50 or less

Reproduction Alert
★★★★★ Extreme care needed. You should assume that the item is a reproduction. Get proof that it isn't before making a purchase.

★★★★ Be extremely careful. Reproductions are regularly misrepresented as original.

★★★ Be careful. Reproductions are known to exist and be misrepresented.

★★ Reproductions might exist, but most often, misidentification is of more concern.

★ Items in this category are rarely, if ever, reproduced.

Several pros and cons for collecting the items represented in a particular chapter are also listed. These are not provided as a definitive list of reasons to collect or not collect that group of objects, but rather, to cause the reader to learn to consider things such as liability, storage, and fraudulent representation before making a purchase.

PRICING

Values are presented first for items "as issued," followed by listings of soldier-used items. For example, in the uniform chapter, the reader will first see listings for uniforms without any insignia. One can think of these listings as being for the "base models." These listings are followed by soldier-used or worn items with all of the insignia, markings, or accessories that show unique ownership, and therefore, affect current values. These latter items and prices are from sales of actual objects as reported by various dealers and auction houses, thereby providing the reader with a window into "real world" values.

The reader will notice that pricing is given in U.S. dollars and English pounds. Prior to the Internet dominating the hobby, there was often a huge discrepancy in prices paid for similar objects in the United States and abroad. However, in the last few years, prices have stabilized throughout the world. A U.S. Class A jacket will have approximately the same value whether found in the United States, England, Germany or Japan.

Demand, though, does vary from nation to nation. U.S. and German material is in high demand in England, throughout Europe and Japan. However, Canadian gear

is in higher demand in Canada than it is in the U.S. or Germany. The laws of supply and demand do apply in this hobby as well. Keep this in mind if you are attempting to buy or sell an English Battle Dress jacket in Texas or trying to sell a Polish order in Hawaii. Highest prices will be realized in the nation of origin or that of a direct wartime opponent.

WHERE TO DO BUSINESS

Whether you are hoping to sell some military items or to buy, chances are there is a military collector living close to you. Check your local classifieds. Advanced collectors often run "Military Items Wanted" ads in local papers and classified ad Web sites. Even if you are hoping to buy items, a call to these people may open a conversation that will lead to subsequent deals.

Militaria shows take place throughout the U.S., Europe, England and Japan. Ranging from just a dozen dealers to more than 2,000, these shows are still the best source of fresh material for the devoted collector. *Military Trader* is a monthly magazine published in the United States that contains a worldwide listing of military shows. Check the calendar of events, called the "Battle Plan," online at www.militarytrader.com.

Before you buy or sell any object, remember, you are the person who needs to be happy with the final transaction. You can only sell the object once, so be sure you are ready to sell and that you are happy with the price you are receiving. Be realistic. Don't dig a uniform out of the attic, take it to the local military dealer and expect to get top-dollar—the dealer isn't buying it for his or her own collection, but rather, to sell to a collector. Therefore, to make a profit, he will generally sell it for twice what he pays. Be aware of the basic values of items *before* you visit the dealer. Don't ask him to price your item for you. That will be uncomfortable for you and for the dealer! Likewise, don't waste a dealer's time by "shopping an item around." A dealer doesn't want to make an offer on an item only for you to take that offer somewhere else to leverage a few more dollars out of another dealer.

Finally, keep in mind that *all* of these relics represent the sacrifices of millions of men and women who fought for what they believed was a better way of life. As this generation passes on, these relics will be the only tangible links to the horror, pain, honor, and glory that engulfed our world from 1939-1945.

Currency Conversion
Need to convert U.S. dollar values to Euros, francs, lira, pesetas, marks, yen, or nearly any other world currency? Use any of the Web sites listed below to instantly convert money at current exchange rates.

http://www.oanda.com/converter/classic
http://www.xe.com/ucc/
http://www.iccfx.com/
http://www.gocurrency.com/
http://finance.yahoo.com/currency
http://www.x-rates.com/calculator.html

CHAPTER 1

UNIFORMS AND FOOTWEAR

Little evokes the sense of a soldier's personal commitment and sacrifice quite the way an original GI's field jacket or an SS officer's tunic does. After the conclusion of the war, many discharged soldiers of all nationalities were allowed to keep their dress uniforms, if not all of their issued clothing. For years after the war, surplus and used clothing stores purchased mountains of uniforms. Customers were eager to purchase the durable goods for outdoor activities, work clothes, or simply as cheap collectibles.

Uniforms, however, were not a common "trophy" piece with combat troops. Perhaps, the items were simply too personal—it is easy to imagine the individual who wore a jacket, pair of trousers or some other garment. Most likely though, it was a matter of economy—something that collectors have to deal with today as well. Combat clothing tends to be bulky. A soldier on the campaign could carry a rucksack full of medals, documents or other small trophies compared to the one tunic that would fill the same place. Collectors are faced with the same dilemna: a lot of small items can be stored in the same place as one full uniform.

Nevertheless, uniforms are very desirable. Collectors eagerly seek either entire uniforms or the various components to complete the outfit worn by a particular type of soldier. For example, a collector might begin with a German M36 combat tunic and focus on assembling the full uniform and equipment of a Wehrmacht soldier as he appeared during the 1940 campaign. Often, collectors like to display full uniforms on mannequins, thereby gaining a sense of a soldier's full load on campaign or appearance in garrison.

UNIFORMS: DRESS OR FATIGUE?

Uniforms, regardless of the nationality, can be broken into two groups: dress and fatigue. The former tends to be much more elaborate and includes the insignia and awards that a soldier had earned up to a certain time. The latter is more representative of the jobs for which soldiers were trained. Fatigue uniforms can range from a mechanic's coveralls to a combat infantryman's wool trousers.

Dress uniforms are still quite plentiful because discharged soldiers often wore their uniforms home. After changing into their civilian wardrobes, the former soldiers carefully stored their uniforms as remembrances of their service. Many of these dress uniforms haven't seen light of day since 1945. Nevertheless, as estates are settled and dispersed, these uniforms are once again emerging from trunks, attics, and closets to the delight of collectors.

The value of a dress uniform tends to come from the insignia that adorns it. Whether one is evaluating a U.S. Army Air Corps lieutenant's Class A jacket, a British Service Dress uniform, or a German Waffenrock, it is the

Collecting Hints

Pros:
- Uniforms are extremely personal and convey a direct sense of a soldier's commitment and service.
- Plentiful supply and variety available with prices in all collecting strata.
- Easy-to-find items with a known provenance.

Cons:
- Bulky! It takes plenty of space to assemble, display and store uniforms.
- Uniforms require special handling and care to preserve.
- It is quite difficult to determine if the insignia is original to a particular garment or if it has been applied after 1945 to artificially inflate the value.
- Reproductions of combat clothing abound.

Availability ★★★★

Price ★★★

Reproduction Alert ★★★

insignia and accessories that determine whether the garment is worth a few dollars or hundreds of dollars. The nuances of the insignia, however, require a great deal of study to know what patches, insignia and medals add the most value.

Conversely, the value of fatigue or "combat" uniforms is determined by function. A sailor's rain jacket doesn't evoke the strong mental images of survival in combat as does an SS soldier's camouflage smock. Even though a U.S. first pattern winter parka might be more "scarce" than a U.S. Pattern of 1941 Field Jacket because fewer were made of the former, the latter is the more desirable (and, therefore, more valuable) item. The field jacket represents the common GI in the field. Virtually every American foot soldier who saw combat wore one of these. A general rule to follow is that items worn by soldiers in combat have greater value than non-combatant worn items.

Don't Tear Off the Tag

Collectors, especially those who focus on U.S. uniforms, pay a premium for uniforms that have complete and legible tags. These tags generally detail the contract under which the garment was made, the date of the contract and pattern, the official nomenclature for the garment, and the size.

Privately purchased tags imprinted with the original owner's name can often be found sewn into garments. These help a collector to establish a provenance for the garment.

And finally, many soldiers simply used pens to write their name, serial number or other information in their garments. These markings can also add to the intrigue—if not to the value—of a uniform. No attempt should be made to obliterate or remove such markings.

Size Does Matter

It is important to remember who are buying uniforms today. Basically, there are two types of consumers: collectors and reenactors. Collectors approach the hobby with the reverence of museum curators. They handle artifacts with care. Originality and provenance command the premium prices from this group.

Reenactors, on the other hand, don't care as much about the provenance of a uniform or even the originality or the totality of insignia that is present. In fact, the less insignia the better for this group because they plan to wear the uniforms in the pursuit of their hobby. Original insignia simply drives up the price of the garment. Reenactors are looking for used clothing rather than uniforms "with a story." For this group, size is what commands the premium prices. The larger the garment, the higher the price. Scores of reenactors will pass by a mint condition, size 34 paratrooper's jacket (for which a collector would gladly pay $400-$500!/ £203-£253) but will scramble to purchase a size 46 Class A jacket with no insignia (which would be worth about $25-$35/£12-£18 to a collector).

Are Uniforms for You?

Uniform collecting is a rewarding niche in the militaria collecting hobby. A person can assemble a meaningful display with a reasonable amount of investment. Items are available and can even still be found in antique shops, estate sales, and family attics.

It should be remembered, though, that uniforms do require plenty of room for storage. If you specialize in uniforms, bear in mind that it will be the acquisition of yet another tunic, coat or other garment that will satisfy your collecting urges. But it doesn't take many uniforms to fill a closet.

Display of uniforms is difficult. Many believe that display on mannequins or clothing forms is the best way to enjoy a collection. If you thought a few uniforms filled a collecting space quickly, wait until you buy a couple of mannequins! The alternative is to "flat-display" uniforms by hanging them on walls. Again, it doesn't take too many jackets to cover all of the available vertical space in a room. Sooner or later, all uniform collectors surrender to storing the bulk of their collection out of sight in closets, attics, trunks, or boxes.

If you decide that uniform collecting is for you, do exercise caution. As with any aspect of the hobby, fakes exist. Although most fakes tend to be of expensive uniforms like those of paratroopers, SS soldiers, or Panzer troops, a lot of uniforms consist of all original period components assembled after the war. It does not take long to replace a less desireable shoulder patch or collar tab with an example from an elite unit.

Also keep in mind that people have been reenacting in an organized fashion for nearly forty years. Some early reenacting clothing, if worn hard on the campaign and put away dirty, will begin to have some convincing looking patina. Learn to recognize appropriate period construction techniques, fabrics, and styles before making your first purchase.

A Jacket's Value Is in the Detail

If you compare the listings in this book to those found on dealers' lists or Internet sales and auction sites, you might be confused. Why do dealer and auction prices seem so high?

The answer is found in the details, and specifically, the insignia. Most uniform component production ran into the hundreds of thousands, so generally speaking, the actual uniform piece is not the price determinant. Rather, the real value comes from the insignia on a particular uniform. For example, a simple U.S. Army Ike jacket with no insignia is worth about $25/£12.65. However, an identical paratrooper's jacket that still has all of its original insignia including a divisional patch, campaign and citation ribbons, paratrooper wings, special unit awards, rank chevrons, and service stripes is worth $300/£150 or more, depending on whether the name of the paratrooper is known (thereby establishing "provenance").

When trying to determine the value of your uniform jacket or tunic, first determine the price of the basic garment without any insignia. Then look at the collars, shoulders, and sleeves to determine the value that any insignia adds to the jacket or tunic. Finally, make note of any markings or oral tradition that can establish who the soldier was that originally wore the garment. Remember, the more combat a soldier saw, the higher the value of the uniform!

BELGIUM

Outerwear, Male

OFFICER'S GREATCOAT

- M1935 khaki wool double-breasted overcoat with bronze lion buttons, roll collar, side inset pockets and round cuff lined in khaki silk . . . . **$40 (£20)**

BELGIAN ARMY-IN-EXILE OFFICER'S GREATCOAT

- Khaki wool English tailor made, double-breasted overcoat for a Major of Lancers, gilt-domed, London-made Belgian lion buttons, collar with aged gold bullion embroidered crossed lances over rank insignia, shoulder straps pierced for British rank insignia now removed, right sleeve shoulder with red nationality title "BELGIUM," French cuffs and flapped side pockets. Interior lined in khaki silk twill with tailor's label named to the owner as a Lieutenant and dated "23.9.40" . . . **$140 (£70)**

Coats, Jackets, Male

1ST GUIDES REGIMENT LIEUTENANT'S TUNIC

- Khaki wool tunic with open-lapel collar with Guides regiment collar patch embroidered with two silver bullion rank stars, domed brass rampant lion buttons. Interior has Brussels tailor's label in the collar and another inside the interior pocket . . . . **$200 (£100)**

WALLONIE INTERNAL SECURITY FORCE TUNIC

- Black wool four-pocket service tunic with stand-and-fall collar with red piped black fabric collar tabs, red piped black shoulder epaulettes, embroidered badge over the right pocket comprised of white wreath and red Roman numeral "I", left sleeve with "WALLONIE" volunteer BeVo woven arm shield, and aluminum pebbled buttons. Interior lining has stenciled Gendarm "Gie/6211" markings . . . .**$600 (£300)**

Belgian carabiner's uniform and equipment, $900-$1,200 (£450-£600). www. advanceguardmilitaria.com

Tunic for Belgian "Walloon" Internal Security Force, $595-$650 (£290-£330). www.advanceguardmilitaria.com

"We received $250 in $50 bills to purchase our new officers uniforms, lieutenants gold bars and our silver wings. We bought these clothes on the base and they were of wonderful material."

LT. ROY BENSON, 9TH U.S. AIR FORCE

Belgian lieutenant's tunic, $135-$175 (£65-£90).

www.advanceguardmilitaria.com

Finnish enlisted man's Model 1936 tunic, $175-$250 (£90-£150).

www.advanceguardmilitaria.com

Bulgarian cavalry officer's tunic and breeches, $650-$750 (£325-£390). www.advanceguardmilitaria.com

Finnish infantry officer's wool tunic, $200-$375 (£100-£190).

www.advanceguardmilitaria.com

Trousers, Male

ENLISTED MAN'S TROUSERS

• Khaki wool straight-leg trousers with the metal "EQUI-PEMENTS MILITARIRES" buttons, rear with adjustment half belt, waist lined in khaki cotton, size marked, and dated "5/1933"........................**$170 (£85)**

BULGARIA

Coats, Jackets, Male

CAVALRY OFFICER'S TUNIC AND BREECHES

• Earth-brown wool tunic with Austrian pattern pleated patch pockets with scalloped pocket flaps, green-gray wool collar, pointed cuffs, and brown composition rampant lion buttons throughout, shoulders have subdued field service officer's shoulder boards with Lieutenant Colonel rank and white Cavalry branch of service piping, interior has white cotton muslin half lining with maker's ink stamp, reverse has stamped-metal rampant lion belt hooks. Breeches of earth-brown wool remain in good condition, with Austrian-style pocket detail stitching, white Cavalry branch of service side-seam piping, and a gray trimmed watch pocket, interior lining has maker's stamp matching the tunic.................**$700 (£350)**

FINLAND

Coats, Jackets, Male

ENLISTED MAN'S ARTILLERY TUNIC

• Model 1936 gray wool enlisted issue tunic with pleated breast and bellows skirt pockets, dark olive composition lion embossed buttons, shoulder straps and stand-and-fall collar with red trimmed black collar tabs. Interior with gray cotton lining with issue marks, date stamped "Int. 42," and first-aid dressing pocket ......**$200 (£100)**

INFANTRY CAPTAIN'S TUNIC

• M36 field gray wool tunic with Infantry Captain's collar tabs, infantry crossed rifles insignia on the epaulettes, Finnish lion buttons, pleated upper pockets and lower cargo pockets. Interior has gray cotton half lining and bandage pocket, well-marked with "SA" and 1943 date. ....**$330 (£165)**

FRANCE

Outerwear, Male

HUSSAR NCO GREATCOAT AND KEPI

• Enlisted mounted pattern greatcoat and service kepi of a sergeant in the 1st Hussar Regiment. Greatcoat of heavy olive drab wool, single breasted with olive drab domed buttons, collar insignia of dark blue wool with silver bullion unit designation "1" and double light blue braid, cuffs with silver braid rank insignia, lining of white cotton with numerous issue marks. Model 1935 enlisted issue kepi with red wool crown and sky blue band and piping, silvered unit numeral "1" and side buttons and black leather chinstrap and visor, interior lined in black cotton with maker . . . .**$190 (£95)**

Coats, Jackets, Male

FRENCH COLLABORATIONIST ORGANISATION TODT SCHUTZKOMMANDO INSPECTOR'S TUNIC

- Dark blue wool tunic with stand-and-fall collar, slip-on shoulder boards of dark blue wool with aluminum bullion rank insignia, pebbled aluminum buttons, and French Org. Todt *Schutzkommando* sleeve badge. Interior has white cotton pockets with "ORG. TODT/ (illegible) 40" rectangular stamp and "Magazin Kleider-lager/Westkuste BREST" stamp . . . .**$800 (£400)**

M1938 ENLISTED MAN'S ISSUE TUNIC

- M1938 olive drab wool single-breasted tunic with domed metal buttons, inset skirt pockets, and roll collar. . . . .**$170 (£85)**

Trousers, Male

INFANTRY ENLISTED FIELD TROUSERS

- Model 1938 khaki wool twill issue gaitered trousers with laced and buckled calves, white cotton waist lining with issue marks dated "40" . . . .**$70 (£35)**

Footwear, Male

MODEL 1940 HOBNAILED BOOTS

- Model 1940 ankle boots of brown rough-out leather with plain toes, soles and heels heavily hobnailed and cleated, maker marked and dated "2/42" . . . .**$130 (£65)**

Underwear, Male

FRENCH ENLISTED ISSUE UNDERWEAR

- Unissued white knit long underwear with 1924 date stamp and original paper size label. . . . .**$20 (£10)**

GERMANY

Outerwear, Male

MODEL 1935 ANTI-TANK UNIT NCO GREATCOAT

- Enlisted issue double-breasted Model 1935 field gray wool overcoat with bottle green collar, pebbled buttons, French cuffs and yellow on field gray with silver border Saddler specialist insignia on lower right sleeve, complete with wartime slip-on Oberfeldwebel shoulder straps, field gray wool with rose piping, subdued gray tresse, aluminum pips and slightly mismatched unit designation metal gothic letters "P." Gray cotton lining, maker, size and depot date stamped "H 39". . . . .**$470 (£235)**

> *The liberation of Holland cost the lives of over 50,000 Allied soldiers. 4,500 Dutch soldiers died for their country as did 258 POWs who died in German prison camps. At sea, a total of 1,500 Dutch sailors lost their lives.*

Tunic for a French collaborationist serving in the German Organization Todt, $775-$900 (£380-£450).

www.advanceguardmilitaria.com

French M1938 enlisted man's wool tunic, $150-$250 (£75-£125). Minnesota Military Museum

Model 1940 ankle boots as issued to French soldiers, $125-$150 (£65-£80). www.advanceguardmilitaria.com

MODEL 1936 GREATCOAT

- Field gray wool overcoat has bottle green collar, double-breasted front closure with aluminum pebble buttons, rolled cuffs, and inset side pockets with exterior flaps.
....**$300 (£150)**

M40 WARTIME ARMY ENLISTED GREATCOAT

- M40 issue double-breasted greatcoat of field gray wool with field gray painted pebble buttons, gray wool collar, loops for shoulder straps, round "barrel" cuffs, inset side pockets with exterior flap and rear half belt. Interior has a very well-worn gray rayon lining with size block stamp.
....**$190 (£95)**

M42 ARMY ENLISTED GREATCOAT

- M42 double breasted greatcoat of field gray wool with field gray painted pebble buttons, gray wool collar, loops for shoulder straps, round "barrel" cuffs, inset side pockets with exterior flaps, and slanted upper handwarmer pockets, reverse has rear half belt. Interior has heavy gray wool lining with sewn-in field gray wool hood attachment at the collar ....**$330 (£165)**

WAFFEN-SS ENLISTED MAN'S GREATCOAT

- Overcoat is field gray, but a very light shade of that color, wool is decent quality and with a blanket type light gray wool inner liner, coat is double breasted, with a fairly large-sized collar in the same material as the coat itself, has two vertical side pockets above the waist, with the two horizontal lower pockets (with flaps) at the waist, also has loops for a pair of slip-on shoulder boards. Insignia on this coat is a very fine example of the very rarely encountered machine woven (BeVo) style Other Ranks eagle (the standard bird for this type of coat was the machine embroidered variety). It is applied with a very fine, very tight, zig-zag border stitch with threads hardly visible past the insignia edges ....**$1,750 (£875)**

COLD WEATHER RABBIT FUR JACKET

- Waist-length overcoat with exterior of natural white leather has clear button and loop front closure, underarm vents, and white leather tape seam edging. Interior has thick natural gray and white rabbit fur lining. Front of jacket has German Army property stamp with maker and an additional paper tag still attached ...**$200 (£100)**

German Model 1936 overcoat for enlisted men, $295-$395 (£150-£200). www.advanceguardmilitaria.com

German Model 1940 overcoat for enlisted soldiers, $185-$295 (£90-£150). www.advanceguardmilitaria.com

German Model 1942 overcoat for enlisted troops, $225-$350 (£100-£180). www.advanceguardmilitaria.com

EXTREME COLD WEATHER SHEEPSKIN COAT

- Knee-length sheepskin coat with grayish natural side on the exterior, thick fleece on the interior, with white flannel hood sewn to the collar, gray horn buttons on the cuffs and elsewhere except for the front, which closes with the toggle bars and loops system. One of a large variety of ersatz overcoats employed by Hitler's armed forces on the Eastern Front when winter caught them without the proper gear . . . .**$230 (£115)**

SPLINTER CAMOUFLAGE REVERSIBLE WINTER JACKET

- 1942 pattern Army splinter camouflage hooded winter service jacket, double-breasted front closure with pebble-grained buttons. Reversible interior of white cotton. . . . .**$450 (£225)**

OFFICER'S RUBBERIZED GREATCOAT

- Full-length, double-breasted greatcoat of field gray rubberized fabric with inset flapped waist pockets, shoulder yoke, rear half belt, gray pebbled metal buttons, and field gray wool collar. . . . .**$300 (£150)**

KRIEGSMARINE OFFICER'S RAINCOAT

- Blue rubberized material with double row of six gold anchor buttons down the front, plus three more on each of the two rear flaps, marked "Kriegsmarine 1940," has the maker's logo on reverse and set of slip-on shoulder boards. . . . .**$450 (£225)**

LUFTWAFFE MECHANIC'S COVERALL

- Blue denim HBT coverall with stamped aluminum general service buttons, Technical Aviation Personnel sleeve badge placed over right breast where the Luftwaffe breast eagle would normally be found. Piece shows heavy wear, soiling, and some repairs in the elbow, cuff and upper thigh area, as would be expected of a work garment. . . . .**$390 (£195)**

LUFTWAFFE FIGHTER PILOT'S ELECTRICALLY-WIRED "CHANNEL" FLYING SUIT

- Intermediate-weight flying suit comprised of Luftwaffe blue-gray cotton jacket and trousers. Jacket has blue-violet synthetic fur short-pile lining and outer collar, right breast with hand-applied embroidered Luftwaffe eagle insignia, brown leather adjustment tabs and electronic fitting covers. Matching wired "channel trousers" have large flare pistol cartridge pockets with interior bandoleer loops filled with original fired inert aluminum Signalpatrone flare pistol cartridge casings, and several fitted with the simple yet very rare lanyard cord for use with accouterments such as the "gravity" knife, top has loops for attachment to suspenders, which are lacking, but trousers are complete with leather-covered heating system snap cords that are usually missing from the trousers and almost always removed from surviving "Channel Suit" flight jackets. . . . .**$1,850 (£925)**

Sheepskin coat typical of those worn by German soldiers on the Eastern Front, $225-$275 (£105-£140).
www.advanceguardmilitaria.com

German Army reversible camouflage winter jacket, $400-$500 (£200-£250). Charles D. Pautler

First pattern SS camouflage smock, $3,500-$5,000 (£1,800-£2,500). Hermann Historica OHG

German paratrooper's camouflage jump smock, $5,500-$6,000 (£2,800-£3,000). Hermann Historica OHG

LUFTWAFFE PILOT'S LEATHER
ONE-PIECE FLIGHT SUIT

- Black leather flight suit with side slash pockets, turned collar with additional straps, functional zipper front, sleeve and leg cuff closures. Interior has gray blanket wool lining, Dresden manufacturer label, and "Mai 1943" date tag..................................**$490 (£245)**

Coats, Jackets, Male

INFANTRY NCO'S WAFFENROCK

- Enlisted Waffenrock of field gray wool with bottle green epaulettes, collar, and Swedish cuffs, white infantry piping throughout, collar has bullion litzen on white wool collar tabs and NCO rank braid, shoulders with white piped Feldwebel rank NCO straps, and cuffs with white wool backed Ärmelpatten, tunic has Army breast eagle, all aluminum pebble-grain buttons, loops for one medal ribbon bar and three other awards, reverse has piped false skirt pockets........................**$480 (£240)**

ARMY ADMINISTRATIVE
OFFICIAL'S WAFFENROCK

- Waffenrock of field gray wool with bottle green epaulettes, collar, and Swedish cuffs, green official's piping throughout, collar is piped in green with bullion litzen on green wool backing piped in white and has a clip-in starched white cotton collar liner, shoulders with officer's straps with single gold-colored rank pip, aluminum bullion dress aiguillette, and cuffs with green wool backed "ärmelpatten" piped in white, reverse has piped false skirt pockets..................................**$480 (£240)**

PANZER GRENADIER'S REED GREEN
SUMMER COMBAT TUNIC

- Reed green HBT combat tunic with four unpleated patch pockets with pointed flaps, general service embroidered collar litzen, soldat shoulder straps with grass green Panzer Grenadier Waffenfarbe piping and field gray rayon underside facing material, field gray woven Army breast eagle, and gray pebble-grained buttons. Interior has field gray rayon wound dressing pocket and reinforcements. .... **$800 (£400)**

ARMY CAMOUFLAGE FIELD-MADE
ARMOR SOLDIER'S "WRAP" TUNIC

- Panzer or assault-gun-style wrap tunic field made of Army Zeltbahn splinter camouflage cotton material that has brown composition buttons and shows ghost stitch outline where an Army breast eagle and sleeve rank chevron were once worn but were subsequently removed. ....**$950 (£475)**

EARLY ISSUE INFANTRY ENLISTED
MAN'S MODEL 35 TUNIC

- Four-pocket tunic of early war high-quality field gray wool with green collar as used on WWI and Reichswehr tunics, infantry enlisted collar Litzen on dark-green wool field and early slip-on dark-green unpinned shoulder straps with pointed ends, complete with pebbled buttons and four sets of three sewn grommet holes for belt hooks front and rear. Interior half lining of gray cotton with maker and size markings as well as a Munich Depot issue date stamp "M 35," showing issue of this tunic during the first year of production...................**$850 (£425)**

Waffenrock for an artillery soldier, $475-$600 (£250-£300). Charles D. Pautler

German rural police general's tunic, $2,000-$2,500 (£1,000-£1,250). Rock Island Auction Company

Uniform of an identified Major General in the ROA, $12,000-$15,000 (£6,000-£7,700).
Hermann Historica OHG

Allied losses in Italy amounted to 31,886 killed; 19,471 of them were Americans.

ARMY MODEL 1935 ENLISTED
ISSUE COMBAT TUNIC

- Four-pocket early war tunic of early war field gray wool has bottle green collar, pebble-grained aluminum buttons, and pleated patch pockets, upper left with vertical award loops, interior has 1938-dated size and depot stamp on brown cotton lining, interior belt supports lacking . . . .**$630 (£315)**

ENLISTED SERVICE TUNIC

- Enlisted third-pattern tropical service tunic has Afrika-korps enlisted collar litzen of woven blue-gray cotton with golden-khaki piping, tropical pattern enlisted BeVo Army breast eagle, gray pebble finished buttons, and distinctive third-pattern straight pocket flaps over unpleated exterior pockets, has loops and buttons but lacks unit shoulder straps, perhaps because it was never issued, interior has good size stamps and RBN number. . . . . **$890 (£445)**

ARMY INFANTRY CAPTAIN'S UNIFORM
COMPLETE WITH VISOR HAT

- Army officer's field service uniform has field gray wool tunic with infantry Hauptmann subdued silver shoulder straps and bottle green wool collar with officer's embroidered litzen, bullion embroidered breast eagle, olive painted pebble-grained buttons, and sewn loops for award on the upper left pocket, as well as loops for medal bar above. Interior gray twill lining has Memmingen tailor's label. Uniform is complete with matching breeches. Visor cap is of good quality field gray wool with white crown piping and white piping flanking the bottle green band, obverse has metal Reichscockade with embroidered wreath and embroidered Army eagle insignia, pebble-grained side buttons retain aluminum bullion officer's chinstrap and pressed Vulkanfiber visor. . . . . **$2,300 (£1,150)**

M44 ARMY PANZER GRENADIER NCO TUNIC

- 1944 pattern field service tunic of brownish gray Erdgrau M44 wool with open lapel collar and Litzen with rose lights and subdued white NCO tresse, slip-on shoulder boards with subdued silver NCO tresse and rose Waffenfarbe, right breast has a gray BeVo woven Army eagle on field gray triangular field, pebble grain buttons throughout. Interior with olive cotton partial lining stamped with maker's size marks and date "44" . . . . **$890 (£445)**

GROSSDEUTSCHLAND PANZER UNIFORM GROUP

- Post-1942-style black wool panzer wrap jacket has rose piped collar patches with gray metal death's head insignias, black wool shoulder boards with rose piping and officer-style gray metal intertwined "GD"cyphers and BeVo gray Army breast eagle woven on black Panzer background, tunic has black composition buttons, Iron Cross 2nd Class ribbon in the buttonhole, and scarce

Field-made wrap-around tunic in splinter camouflage, $850-$1,200 (£425-£700).
www.advanceguardmilitaria.com

Open collar tropical tunic (without accouterments), $850-$1,100 (£425-£550). Charles D. Pautler

Field tunic for a First Lieutenant in the Grossdeutschland Regiment, $2,000-$2,250 (£1,000-£1,300). Hermann Historica OHG

Early Model 1935 German tunic with no insignia, $650-$800 (£325-£400). www.advanceguardmilitaria.com

Field tunic for an SS-Obersturmführer, $4,500-$5,000 (£2,250-£2,500).
Hermann Historica OHG

Panzer uniform and decorations for an officer, $2,600-$3,000 (£1,300-£1,500).
Hermann Historica OHG

final pattern Grossdeutschland cuff title, lot includes black wool Army Panzer trousers with integral waist-belt, distinctive Panzer pattern angled inset side pockets with rear mounted flaps, watch pocket, one flapped rear pocket, and blousing ties at cuffs, uniform is complete with the correct field gray Panzer issue shirt with pointed stand-and-fall collar, also included is a black leather waistbelt with Army enlisted buckle, and a example of the Doppelfernhorer Model G headphones with rubber cushions, complete "Y" cord assembly with three prong jack attachment, and adjustable leather head strap.
. . . . **$7,450 (£3,725)**

PANZER JÄGER HAUPTMANN'S ASSAULT GUN WRAP

- Field gray wool M43 Assault Gun wrap with Hauptmann rank Panzer rose piped shoulder straps with Gothic "P" cypher on gray subdued silver bullion shoulder straps, matching panzer rose piped black wool collar tabs have "death's-heads" with 40% silvered finish remaining and rose piping visible through the skull eyes and nose, aluminum bullion Army breast eagle, sleeve with Krim shield, and left breast has medal ribbon bar with Iron Cross Second Class and Winter Campaign in Russia rib-bons, reverse complete with aluminum interior suspend-ed belt supports, interior has gray rayon lining with RB number, "BII 43" clothing office stamp, size block stamp, as well as Russian capture, museum, and inventory mark-ings, insignia has age patina throughout.
. . . . **$2,500 (£1,250)**

Panzer wool wrap-around and trousers, $5,000-$5,500 (£2,500-£2,800).
Hermann Historica OHG

Model 1940 tunic for enlisted soldier, $950-$1,150 (£475-£600). Charles D. Pautler

Model 1936 tunic for enlisted ranks, $975-$1,250 (£460-£625). Charles D. Pautler

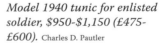

By D-Day, 35% of all German soldiers had been wounded at least once, 11% twice, 6% three times, 2% four times and 2% more than 4 times.

LATE WAR ARMY/SS FIELD SERVICE JACKET

- Model 1944 short battle dress jacket of requisitioned Italian army field gray wool with pebble finish buttons, patchbreast pockets with flaps and loops for shoulder straps, lacks insignia and one shoulder strap button, lining of gray rayon herringbone twill, unmarked.
....**$600 (£300)**

LUFTWAFFE SIGNALS NCO REED GREEN SUMMER COMBAT TUNIC

- Reed green herringbone twill combat tunic with four unpleated patch pockets with pointed flaps, Feldwebel shoulder straps with brown signals waffenfarbe piping factory-applied embroidered Luftwaffe breast eagle, and Luftwaffe dark blue pebble-grained buttons, interior has olive rayon reinforcements and wound dressing pocket with accountability number stamp, interior of button stand has size block stamp ....**$850 (£425)**

LUFTWAFFE FLIGHT PERSONNEL NCO BLOUSE

- Luftwaffe blue-gray wool issue blouse, Unterfeldwebel rank, collar has aluminum tresse border and yellow wool tabs with two gulls, embroidered Luftwaffe breast eagle, and pebbled buttons, lacks shoulder straps, interior has gray cotton lining stamped with maker and size markings, as well as European costume house property stamp.
....**$830 (£415)**

ENLISTED FLAK ARTILLERY TUNIC

- Luftwaffe blue-gray wool four-pocket enlisted issue tunic with red twisted cord collar piping, plain red wool collar patches, silver-gray pebble uniform buttons, and Luftwaffe breast eagle. Interior has 1939-dated size block stamp and still retains the printed paper version attached to the interior lining bandage pocket, shoulders have buttons for shoulder straps but none have been installed, wool is in excellent shape with no visible mothing.
....**$890 (£445)**

LUFTWAFFE FLIGHT/FALLSCHIRMJÄGER UNTEROFFIZIER TUNIC

- Four-pocket dress tunic of Luftwaffe blue-gray wool with Unteroffizier rank collar insignia and shoulder tabs with Flight or Fallschirmjäger golden yellow Waffenfarbe, embroidered Luftwaffe eagle and swastika insignia, three-award medal ribbon bar and Iron Cross First Class ribbon in button loop, as well as loops for the award on the upper left pocket pleat. Shoulder straps appear to have once been pierced for cypher or numeral. Interior lining has 1942 date and Luftwaffe clothing office acceptance stamp, lacks belt support hooks but retains the cloth tabs, and interior breast pocket has label with soldier's name ....**$830 (£415)**

LUFTWAFFE FLIGHT LIEUTENANT COLONEL'S UNIFORM

- Luftwaffe blue-gray wool officer's tunic with Oberstleutnant rank shoulder straps and collar tabs on golden yellow waffenfarbe, attractive bullion embroidered early pattern Luftwaffe breast eagle, Iron Cross, First Class ribbon in button hole loop, and embroidered DLV Glider Pilot Level "C" Proficiency badge, tunic has loops for two awards or badges on upper left pocket and loops for medal bar above. Interior blue-gray silk lining has pocket with Lille, France, tailor's label inscribed faintly with this officer's name. Uniform includes matching trousers complete with correct period suspenders, subdued pebble-grained buttons throughout............**$1,250 (£625)**

KRIEGSMARINE TROPICAL OFFICER'S TUNIC

- Khaki tropical twill tunic with machine-applied gold BeVo woven Navy breast eagle on triangular background, painted anchor buttons retaining 99% finish, barrel cuffs, and Oberfänrich shoulder cords with Engineering career insignia. Interior has white cotton upper lining and still retains the original tack-stitched maker's paper size label, near mint condition.....................**$630 (£315)**

Luftwaffe four-pcket tunic for a flak soldier, $785-$950 (£375-£500). www.advanceguardmilitaria.com

Luftwaffe Fliegerbluse for a paratrooper, $1,100- $1,500 (£550-£750). Charles D. Pautler

Panzer wrap-around tunic in black-dyed cotton fabric, $2,400-$2,600 (£1,200-£1,800). Minnesota Military Museum

KRIEGSMARINE KAPITÄN ZUR SEE WHITE SERVICE DRESS UNIFORM

• 1937 pattern, white cotton-twill summer service uniform has Kapitän zur See rank shoulder boards, gilt metal removable breast eagle, removable Navy buttons, and loops for a medal ribbon bar. Interior has Offizierkleiderklasse Der Kriegsmarine tailor's label from Kiel, with faint inscription noting the date "1939," this officer's name, which is faint but legible and rank "K. Kpt." indicating that owner purchased this tunic while a Korvetten-kaptiän, includes matching trousers, which have some discoloration and stains, tunic also has the normal light stains and age toning shared by all antique white cotton military uniforms . . . . **$900 (£450)**

RURAL POLICE DUESSELDORF DISTRICT NCO'S TUNIC

• Police gray wool tunic with orange piped brown collar and cuffs, Meister of the Gendarmerie (Rural Police) shoulder straps, Enlisted/NCO Rural Police collar litzen, police embroidered arm shield with "Aachen" embroidered above the eagle, and aluminum pebble-grained buttons. Interior has unmarked dark brown cotton lining. . . . .**$530 (£265)**

Shirts, Male

ISSUE KNIT SHIRT

• Gray green machine knit shirt with pointed collar and gray metal utility buttons, pre-1943 style produced without breast pockets . . . . **$90 (£45)**

TROPICAL ISSUE KNIT SHIRT

• Tropical tan machine knit shirt with pointed collar and pressed paper buttons, pre-1943 style produced without breast pockets. . . . .**$140 (£70)**

Trousers, Male

ARMY TROPICAL TROUSERS

• Tropical olive cotton trousers of the same style and cut as the field gray wool trousers, with integral adjustment belt, dish utility buttons, slant side pockets, watch pockets with sewn watch ring, suspender button tabs and blue-gray twill lining . . . .**$470 (£235)**

ARMY INFANTRY OFFICER'S DRESS TROUSERS

• Fine quality field gray wool with white seam piping, side pockets, watch pocket and ring, interior with gray cotton lining. . . . .**$170 (£85)**

ARMY TROPICAL SHORTS

• Olive green cotton shorts with slash side and watch pocket, waistband with interior olive web belt and three-prong metal buckle, reverse with one hip pocket, and stamped metal utility buttons throughout. . . . .**$380 (£190)**

PANZER ENLISTED ISSUE TROUSERS

• Black wool Army Panzer trousers with integral waist-belt, distinctive Panzer pattern angled inset side pockets with rear mounted flaps, watch pocket, one flapped rear pocket, and blousing ties at cuffs. Interior with black cotton button facing and white cotton waistband lining with "RB" number and size stamps, Depot marked and dated "St 43". . . . .**$1,170 (£585)**

LUFTWAFFE ENLISTED BREECHES

• Luftwaffe blue-gray wool breeches have inset welted side pockets, inset back pocket with exterior flap, front with watch pocket, and reverse with suspender tabs. Interior has white cotton and Luftwaffe blue-gray herringbone twill cotton pockets, size stamps and maker stamp. . . . .**$270 (£135)**

Reichsarbeitsdienst tunic, $400-$500 (£200-£260). www.advanceguardmilitaria.com

Rural police tunic, $650-$800 (£320-£400). Minnesota Military Museum

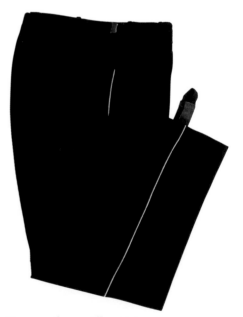

Trousers for an Allegemeine SS officer, $850-$1,000 (£425-£500). Minnesota Military Museum

FIELD POLICE SERVICE TROUSERS

- Police blue-gray wool trousers with welted side pockets, reverse with back adjustment belt and one rear pocket, obverse has watch pocket sewn closed, complete with green and white cotton elastic period suspenders. Interior has field gray cotton and rayon lining. . . . **$150 (£75)**

Underclothing, Male

KRIEGSMARINE ISSUE UNDERSHIRT

- Off-white knit cotton short sleeve shirt of Navy collarless pattern, issue marked . . . . **$40 (£20)**

Footwear, Male

GERMAN ENLISTED SOLDIER'S JACKBOOTS

- Black leather issue jackboots have hobnails, heel rims, and toe plates. Interior with heavy twill tape pulls. . . . . **$330 (£165)**

GERMAN LUFTWAFFE / POLICE ENLISTED SOLDIER'S BROWN LEATHER JACKBOOTS

- Brown leather issue jackboots have hobnails, heel rims, and toe plates. Interior with heavy twill tape pulls, and soles with stamp "44". **$450 (£225)**

MOTORCYCLE BOOTS

- 16" tall black leather boots, lined, stitched leather soles with metal toe plates and two buckle adjustment at the top of the shaft. Non-issue pattern but typical of the variations seen in period photos . . . . **$100 (£50)**

LUFTWAFFE PILOT'S FLYING BOOTS

- Double side zip pattern of black leather and black exterior dyed shearling, with single black leather tightening strap at the top, interior with 1/4" thick shearling pile lining. . . . . **$290 (£145)**

EASTERN FRONT WINTER BOOTS

- 16-1/2" tall with brown leather bases and gray thick felt upper portions. Interiors have pull straps . . . **$200 (£100)**

HUNGARY

Coats, Jackets, Male

LIEUTENANT'S SERVICE TUNIC

- Field brown wool lieutenant's field service tunic has hunter green wool felt collar tabs with bullion embroidered star insignias, brown flecked bullion shoulder straps with hunter green wool underlay, four pleated pockets with flaps cut in the traditional Austro-Hungarian pattern, and gilt Hungarian helmet buttons, ... **$300 (£150)**

ITALY

Outerwear, Male

M1929 CAMOUFLAGE SHELTER HALF / RAIN CAPE

- Shelter half that was also designed to be worn as a rain cape. Has Bakelite buttons and sewn grommet holes. . . . . **$150 (£75)**

Coats, Jackets, Male

ITALIAN MVSN BLACKSHIRT OFFICER'S TUNIC

- Model 1931 green-gray wool tunic, Sotto capomanipolo (2nd Lt.) rank, brass buttons mixed with coat size fascio buttons and pocket size eagle buttons, open lapel collar with black velvet "flames" embroidered with gold fascios, gold and black rank insignia on cuffs, complete with removable GIL youth Leader shoulder boards of black wool piped purple and yellow with gold bullion embroidered GIL branch insignia. . . . . **$300 (£150)**

Brown leather jackboots for Luftwaffe soldiers, $375-$475 (£175-£250).
www.advanceguardmilitaria.com

Hobnailed "jackboots," $300-$400 (£150-£200). www.advanceguardmilitaria.com

Hungarian officer's service tunic, $295-$350 (£150-£180).
www.advanceguardmilitaria.com

Luftwaffe pilot's boots, $250-$300 (£125-£150). Charles D. Pautler

BERSAGLIERI COLONEL'S TUNIC

* Officer's gray wool service dress tunic has Colonel rank epaulettes with bullion stars, crimson Bersaglieri "flame" collar badges, two bullion wound stripes, and 11 award medal ribbon bar, single-breasted front closure with khaki painted buttons. Interior with quilted gray lining. ....**$240 (£120)**

Trousers, Male

TROPICAL BREECHES

* Issue khaki cotton tropical enlisted breeches with olive composition Italian pattern utility buttons and rear half belt ....**$250 (£125)**

ARMY OFFICER'S BREECHES

* Field gray wool breeches with red piped black wool side seam trim, appropriate for Infantry, Granatieri, and Tanks officers, buttons, back belt buckle, and interior waistband all marked with "Union Militare" trademark. ....**$180 (£90)**

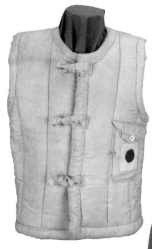

Japanese Army cold weather vest, $300-$375 (£150-£175).

www.advanceguardmilitaria.com

Japanese tanker's coveralls, $250-$300 (£125-£150).

www.advanceguardmilitaria.com

JAPAN

Outwear, Male

MODEL 1938 ENLISTED GREATCOAT

* Wartime Type 98 olive drab wool issue single breasted overcoat has wooden buttons and inset waist pockets with exterior flaps. Unlined, interior with clear issue markings ....**$100 (£50)**

COLD CLIMATE COMBAT GREATCOAT

* Cold climate greatcoat with olive cotton exterior, olive pile faux fur roll collar, quilted upper interior lining and skirt portion lined in olive pile, as are the lower sleeves, upper sleeves with fur lining, features include removable sleeves, double-breasted front closure with olive composition buttons, shoulders with mitten string guides, waist with "J" hook belt supports, reverse with button closing skirt vent. Interior with Japanese issue stamps dated 1944....................................**$290 (£145)**

ARMY COLD WEATHER VEST

* White silk insulated vest with four silk cloth ties to close it in the front, left chest has single exterior patch pocket with 3" square screen printed on silk Army style national flag attached ....**$330 (£165)**

TANKER COVERALLS

* Olive cotton twill coveralls have concealed button front closure, waist with olive twill tape adjustment tie. Interior with issue and size stamp, and tie-adjust cuffs. Collar has Private First Class rank insignias........**$300 (£150)**

TANKER'S JACKET

* Heavy olive cotton short-waisted jacket has quilted interior lining, olive synthetic pile collar, button closure with olive composition buttons, waistband with tie adjustment, and cuffs with button tabs. Exterior has single left chest pleated patch pocket with Private Second Class rank insignia above. Interior has Japanese issue stamps. ....**$430 (£215)**

NAVAL AVIATOR'S TWO-PIECE FLIGHT SUIT

* Dark khaki cotton heavy twill flight suit is comprised of jacket and trousers. Jacket has concealed button front closure, zippers at the wrists, waistband with interior belt and heavy aluminum frame buckle, and front with two large kidney pockets. Trousers are of matching material, zipper cuffs, olive painted fly buttons, gray twill tape waist adjustment ties, open-top knee pockets, and interior white cotton waistband well-marked with Japanese issue stamps.........................**$400 (£200)**

Coats, Jackets, Male

TYPE 98 COTTON TUNIC

* 1938 pattern (Type 98) olive cotton combat tunic with four inset pockets with exterior flaps, dark olive composition buttons, under arm vents, left side with belt support loop (missing the small button), waist vents on either side. Interior has bandage pocket and Japanese stamp ....**$230 (£115)**

ENLISTED TROPICAL COMBAT TUNIC, THIRD PATTERN

- Olive cotton tunic is similar to the Type 98 cotton tunic but with of button closure side ventilation openings. This example has Private First Class collar insignia, brown bakelite buttons. Tunic has inset pockets with exterior flaps identifying it as the "third pattern" tropical tunic. Unlined interior has bandage pocket and faint issue stamp listing size (medium) and date (1944). . . . . **$290 (£145)**

TYPE 98 WOOL TUNIC

- Type 98 olive drab wool combat tunic has four inset pockets with exterior flaps, brass buttons, under arm vents, left side with belt support loop, waist vents on either side. Interior has white cotton lining with bandage pocket and Japanese issue stamp. . . . . **$190 (£95)**

Japanese infantry sergeant's cotton tunic, $275-$350 (£135-£180). www.advanceguardmilitaria.com

The 81-day battle for the island in the Ryukyus caused losses totalling 107,500 among the Japanese garrison.

Japanese tanker's jacket, $400-$475 (£200-£245).
www.advanceguardmilitaria.com

The 1938 pattern cotton tunic was also known as the Type 98, $200-$300 (£100-£150).
www.advanceguardmilitaria.com

Japanese Type 98 wool combat tunic intended for cold climates, $175-$250 (£80-£125). www.advanceguardmilitaria.com

Japanese aviator's lightweight jacket, $300-$400 (£150-£200). Minnesota Military Museum

Japanese third-pattern summer weight combat tunic, $250-$350 (£120-£180). Minnesota Military Museum

Japanese military police tropical tunic, $275-$300 (£135-£150).

www.advanceguardmilitaria.com

INFANTRY SERGEANT MAJOR'S COTTON TUNIC

- Type 98 olive cotton combat tunic with four inset pockets with exterior flaps, brown composition buttons, under arm vents, left side with belt support loop, waist vents in the skirt. Interior has bandage pocket and Japanese issue stamp. Collar has Sergeant Major rank insignia, and the left chest has Infantry branch of service insignia above the upper left pocket........**$300 (£150)**

LATE WAR COTTON COMBAT TUNIC

- Late war simplified combat tunic of olive cotton with collar showing Private First Class rank insignia, two upper patch pockets, lower pockets are completely on the inside of the tunic, sides with vertical ventilation openings, and left side with belt support loop. Tunic has olive painted wood buttons and Japanese issue stamp dated 1945 ....**$230 (£115)**

NAVAL LANDING FORCE ENLISTED UNIFORM

- Olive cotton twill tunic and trousers. Tunic has notched lapel collar, pleated upper pockets and inset lower pockets with exterior flaps, stamped brass buttons with chrysanthemum on anchor insignia. NLF issue olive cotton trousers have olive composition buttons, waist with belt loop but lacks the twill tape waistbelt. Interior has issue stamp ....**$650 (£325)**

Simplified late-war Japanese cotton tunic, $250-$275 (£130-£140).

www.advanceguardmilitaria.com

Japanese Naval Landing Force cotton tunic, $350-$400 (£180-£200).

www.advanceguardmilitaria.com

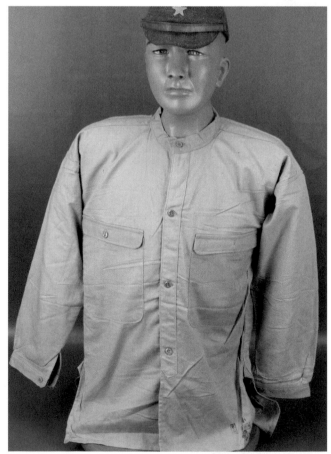

Japanese enlisted man's flannel-lined shirt, $150-$175 (£70-£90). www.advanceguardmilitaria.com

Shirts, Male

ENLISTED MAN'S SHIRT

• Enlisted man's issue shirt of light olive canton flannel (cotton on the outside, flannel on the inside) with short standing collar, olive glass buttons, and two chest pockets. Tail is nicely marked with Japanese issue stamps and Showa 17 (1942) date. . . . . **$170 (£85)**

ARMY TROPICAL COMBAT ISSUE SHIRT

• Light olive cotton three-quarter length sleeve issue shirt has dark olive composition buttons, side ventilation openings under the arms, and interior with clear issue stamp dated 1945 . . . . **$240 (£120)**

NAVY SUMMER ISSUE SHIRT

• Khaki cotton twill short sleeved summer issue shirt with brown composition buttons and one exterior patch pocket on the left breast . . . . **$150 (£75)**

NAVY SEAMAN'S WHITE JUMPER AND TROUSERS

• Enlisted seaman's white cotton uniform with blue cotton neck cape with white trim, blue trim along the bottom edge of the jumper and on the sleeve cuffs, Japanese issue tag under the neck cape. Includes matching fall-front trousers with bone buttons and Japanese issue tag inside the waistband . . . .**$400 (£200)**

Jackets, Dresses, Female

ARMY NURSE DRESS

• Olive cotton one piece dress has gathered shoulder details, turned cuffs, olive composition buttons, collar complete with the snap-in necktie, self fabric waistbelt, one breast pocket, two skirt pockets, and right chest with octagonal sewn reinforce and loops for a badge or award. Collar has white cotton tag with Japanese name stamp. . . . .**$230 (£115)**

Japanese Army nurse's dress, $200-$250 (£100-£180).
www.advanceguardmilitaria.com

Japanese Navy seaman's white jumper, $200-$250 (£100-£125).
www.advanceguardmilitaria.com

Japanese Army tropical combat shirt, $200-$250 (£100-£135). www.advanceguardmilitaria.com

Trousers, Male

TROPICAL LIGHTWEIGHT TROUSERS

* Lightweight olive cotton tropical service trousers have maker's stamp with 1945 date, olive wood buttons, and cotton tie waistbelt.......................**$180 (£90)**

TYPE 3 COTTON ISSUE FIELD TROUSERS

* Light olive cotton trousers are nearly identical to the Type 98 trousers, but have a button waistband fastener instead of the clip and socket system used before, cuffs have tie closures, waistband lining is white cotton with 1944-dated issue stamp...................**$190 (£95)**

> *"Have a few souvenirs I'll try to send home... You probably won't think much of them as one is a Jap Nambo [sic] machine gun but it will be good for Stinky to play with."*
>
> LT. BOB GREEN, 763RD TANK BN.

Underwear, Male

FUNDOSHI (LOINCLOTH)

* Traditional loincloth of lightweight linen with white cotton twill tape ties ....**$30 (£15)**

Footwear, Male

EARLY WAR HOBNAILED FIELD SHOES

* Model 1930 ankle-high issue shoes, brown rough-out leather that has been oiled, five aluminum eyelets, leather double soles with metal hobnails, and clear embossed issue stamp. Heels have inlayed metal rims that protect two-thirds of the leather..................**$330 (£165)**

ERSATZ PIGSKIN FIELD SHOES

* Early Class B pattern brown pigskin hobnailed field shoes. The square style stitching on the heel counter was changed to a horseshoe pattern in early March, 1942. The Army found these light, durable, and breathable pigskin ersatz shoes particularly suitable to combat in tropical climates........................**$250 (£125)**

Early Japanese field shoes had five pairs of eyelets, $295-$350 (£150-£180). Minnesota Military Museum

Japanese pigskin field shoes were best-suited for tropic areas, $200-$250 (£1100-£125). www.advanceguardmilitaria.com

Lightweight trousers for Japanese troops stationed in tropical areas, $150-$200 (£80-£100). www.advanceguardmilitaria.com

Japanese type 3 cotton trousers have a button waistband fastener, $175-$225 (£90-£120). www.advanceguardmilitaria.com

Japanese Tabi toe shoes, $150-$200 (£75-£100). Minnesota Military Museum

TABI TOE SHOES
- Dark blue wool shoes have tabi toe split, heavy woven soles, and white cotton lining. Tops have the same metal tab closures seen on the field cap havelock . . . **$180 (£90)**

POLAND

Coats, Jackets, Male

BATTLE DRESS TUNIC
- Enlisted khaki wool battle dress tunic may be private production, left sleeve with printed white on red "PO-LAND" shoulder title and red cloth shield with white female mythological figure insignia, right sleeve with embroidered "POLAND" shoulder title and embroidered gold cross on white shield with black background insignia, four award very well worn ribbon bar above left pocket. Interior with issue stamp . . . . **$130 (£65)**

1ST ARMORED DIVISION BATTLE DRESS JACKET
- First issue Pattern 1940 British battle dress jacket, corporal rank, of khaki wool with blue over yellow regimental collar insignia, shoulder straps with silver and red braid rank insignia, left strap of black wool, red and white printed "POLAND" shoulder titles on both sleeves, embroidered Winged Hussar helmet divisional insignia on left sleeve. Interior with two inside pockets and issue label marked large "Size No. 15" and dated 1942. . . . . **$370 (£185)**

SOVIET UNION

Outerwear, Male

INFANTRY GREATCOAT
- Pattern prescribed on December 18, 1926, heavy coarse khaki-gray wool full length overcoat with concealed hooked front, side welted pockets, roll collar with crimson infantry collar tabs piped in black, cuffs with rear seam point, left cuff with opening for a wound dressing, rear half belt with crimson wool lining. Interior lined in coarse natural linen and burlap. . . . . **$370 (£185)**

TELOGREIKA
- Cotton insulated winter combat jacket has dark gray exterior, light gray interior, and cotton batting sewn between in long vertical "sausages," with loop and button closure, simple stamped steel buttons that are original to the coat. . . . . **$390 (£195)**

Coats, Jackets, Male

ENLISTED INFANTRY GYMNASTIORKA
- Model 1943 issue shirt/tunic of dark olive green wool with brass buttons and olive green wool shoulder boards with crimson piping. . . . . **$220 (£110)**

CAVALRY OFFICER'S DRESS COAT
- Model 1943 single breasted coat of olive drab wool with standing collar and no pockets. Senior command collar tabs of black wool with two gold bullion rank bars and cuffs each have two gold bullion "column" tabs, no shoulder boards, two-piece stamped brass buttons have a hammer and sickle in a stippled star on smooth field. Collar, cuffs, front opening and false tail pockets are piped in blue. Interior lined in a heavy gray twilled fabric. . . . .**$330 (£165)**

Shirts, Male

NAVY FATIGUE SHIRT
- Tan linen gymnastiorka style pullover shirt with stand collar, one button placket, steel buttons and breast patch pocket, issue marks in the rear skirt. . . . . **$80 (£40)**

Footwear, Male

ENLISTED MAN'S ISSUE ANKLE SHOES
- Black leather ankle boots with black enameled lace eyelets, steel rivet at the vamp, original blue gray cotton laces, and pegged leather soles with rubber heels. . . . .**$230 (£115)**

ENLISTED MAN'S BOOTS
- 15" tall boots of black pebble grained leather with flared shafts, square toes . . . . **$150 (£75)**

SPAIN

Outerwear, Male

FALANGE ERA OVERCOAT
- Black wool overcoat has bullion bordered shoulder straps with red embroidered yoke and arrows insignias, double-breasted front closure with gilt domed Falange insignia buttons, and back adjustment belt . . . .**$300 (£150)**

The Soviet's padded Telogreika was well-suited for the winter campaign in Russia, $375-$450 (£190-£230). www.advanceguardmilitaria.com

REPUBLICAN ARMY MONO

- Republican Army issue pattern garment as worn by the elite assault guards and the Popular Army's medical services, khaki cotton, double breasted, one piece overall with four pocket front, open lapel collar, pointed cuff decoration, self-fabric belt with friction buckle, brown, four holed composition buttons, and cuffed legs. ....**$450 (£225)**

Coats, Jackets, Male

CIVIL WAR ENLISTED ISSUE
TUNIC AND GRANADEROS

- Wartime issue Model 1926 enlisted tunic was dark olive and has faded to an olive-khaki on the exterior, front has two pleated patch pockets, wooden wartime economy buttons, and sides with belt support loops. Breeches are olive cotton granaderos with button calves and instep straps, paper backed stamped metal utility buttons and small back adjustment belt. The granaderos are more commonly associated with Nationalist troops, but with the exception of the colorful armed militias, the regular forces of both sides wore the same issue uniform during most of the conflict ....**$380 (£190)**

EARLY CIVIL WAR ERA COLONEL
OF GENERAL STAFF TUNIC

- A 1914 pattern field service coat that has been altered to conform to 1926 regulations, with General Staff insignia on the collar, Colonel metal star rank insignias on the cuffs, stamped leather "knot" buttons, five award medal ribbon bar with sewn loops above for when the actual medals were worn, and sewn loops on the upper left pocket for the General Staff badge, which is lacking, ribbon bar includes the Philippine Campaign medal, indicating that this officer was a Spanish-American War veteran ....**$330 (£165)**

REPUBLICAN PRE-CIVIL WAR ENGINEER'S TUNIC

- Olive cotton field service 1926 pattern tunic has collar with early Republican Era unit insignia comprised of silver Engineer castles on both collar ends, with silver regimental numeral "2" on the right and "F" company designation on the left. Has two pleated upper patch pockets, brown composition faux stamped leather buttons, collar with white neck stock, and Madrid military dealer's woven label ....**$280 (£140)**

Shirts, Male

CIVIL WAR ISSUE SHIRT

- Standard Spanish Army issue shirt of the period, olive cotton with brown composition buttons, pointed shoulder yoke, square pleated patch pockets, and pointed collar...................................**$150 (£75)**

The Spanish Civil War began after parts of the army attempted a coup d'état against the Second Spanish Republic. It lasted from July 17, 1936 to April 1, 1939, ending in a rebel victory and the establishment of National General Francisco Franco as dictator.

Spanish Model 1926 enlisted tunic, $225-$275 (£100-£150).
www.advanceguardmilitaria.com

This Spanish colonel's 1914 pattern tunic has been altered to conform to the 1926 regulations, $300-$375 (£150-£190). www.advanceguardmilitaria.com

Republican cotton field service tunic, $250-$300 (£130-£150).
www.advanceguardmilitaria.com

UNITED KINGDOM

Outerwear, Male

BRITISH ENLISTED OVERCOAT

- Dark khaki wool enlisted overcoat has interior tag with Broad Arrow proof, "Overcoat, Dismounted, 1940 Pattern" and size "Height 5' 9" to 5' 10", Breast 41" to 43". Dated 1944. . . . .**$100 (£50)**

BRITISH INFANTRY GREATCOAT

- Heavy khaki wool overcoat has British general service buttons; interior with maker's label "Great Coat/Dismounted 1940 Patt. Size No. 5" (37" to 39" chest), and date "1944". . . . .**$80 (£40)**

CANADIAN COLD WEATHER FLEECE OVERCOAT

- Knee-length khaki canvas overcoat has fleece shawl collar, double-breasted front closure with large brown composition buttons, khaki canvas wide waistbelt, and two inset front pockets. Interior has white fleece lining and is well marked near the end of the skirt with "C" / Broad Arrow proof, "SIZE 42 / L 47" and maker "S.S. HOLDEN LTD. / 1943" . . . .**$330 (£165)**

MOTORCYCLE RIDER'S RUBBERIZED COAT

- Pattern 1942 waterproof coat of heavy rubberized khaki canvas with angled chest and inset skirt flapped pockets. Interior maker and Broad Arrow marked, and dated 1943. . . . .**$100 (£50)**

BRITISH PARA DENISON SMOCK

- Second wartime pattern Airborne Denison smock of heavy cotton twill with printed camouflage pattern, zipper neck closure, two interior pockets, four exterior front cargo pockets, cuff bands with tab adjustment, skirt has "ape tail" complete with securing snaps on front and rear, marked with white contractor label "SMOCKS, DENISON / AIRBORNE TROOPS / SIZE 3," Broad Arrow proofed and dated 1945 . . . .**$650 (£325)**

BRITISH PARACHUTIST'S JACKET

- 1942 pattern parachutist's olive denim overalls jacket, sleeveless design with short turned collar, two skirt pockets with elastic gathered tops, "ape tail" securing flap has several snaps pulled through the material. Interior has label with Broad Arrow proof listing size "No. 2" and 1945 date. These were designed to be worn over the equipment, producing a more aerodynamic parachutist, and helping to keep everything in place until the landing. . . . .**$250 (£125)**

BRITISH SNOW CAMOUFLAGE SET

- Three-piece set of lightweight white duck outerwear to be worn over the regular OD wool battledress consists of a pullover smock with hood, bib trousers, and leather over mittens with windproof gauntlets, Broad Arrow proof marked in smock and mittens. . . . .**$190 (£95)**

BRITISH RAF AIRCREW HARNESSUIT

- Heavy olive cotton armless and legless suit which doubles as a parachute harness and flotation bladder has fittings for attaching a chest parachute. Exterior has two zipper pockets and two zipper front closure. Interior has

Spanish Army issue shirt, $125-$175 (£60-£90).

www.advanceguardmilitaria.com

Canadian cold weather fleece overcoat, $300-$350 (£150-£180).

www.advanceguardmilitaria.com

British paratrooper "Denison" smock, $550-$700 (£300-£400).

Minnesota Military Museum

has Air Ministry nomenclature stamp listing maker
"G.Q. Parachute Co. Ltd.," size "Small," and date "2 August. 1940"................................**$700 (£350)**

BRITISH DENIM TANKER COVERALLS

* Pattern introduced before D-Day in 1944, khaki one-piece garment with patch breast and leg pockets, wound dressing pocket, self fabric belt and olive plastic buttons. Interior with integral suspenders and data label marked "Tank Suit Denim / size No. 4" and dated "1944".
....**$260 (£130)**

BRITISH LEATHER JERKIN

* Brown leather sleeveless over garment designed to protect the wearer's uniform, and to some degree the wearer too, from the hazards of battle, complete with khaki composition buttons, one slightly mismatched. ......**$100 (£50)**

Outerwear, Female

BRITISH WOMEN'S LAND ARMY OVERALL COAT

* Three-quarter length brown denim smock with patch pockets at the hip and integral waistbelt. Interior with 1944-dated contractor tag that reads, "OVERALLS, COAT, DRILL/WOMEN'S LAND ARMY". . .**$140 (£70)**

BRITISH ATS OVERALL SMOCK

* First pattern, one-piece wrap-over of olive drab denim with long sleeves, two patch pockets and integral self fabric ties. Interior tag reads "OVERALLS Women Workers A.T.S." Cooks, ordnance workers, shopkeepers etc. wore these over their uniforms to keep them clean. . **$70 (£35)**

BRITISH LAND ARMY OVERALLS FROCK

* Tan canvas frock comes to below the knee and has a stand and fall collar, integral belt and button down front, similar to the ATS second pattern Working Overalls.

Interior tag has 1943 date. Worn over the clothes to keep them clean when at work, unissued, but there is a large darkened area covering the shoulders and upper back.
....**$100 (£50)**

Coats, Jackets, Male

AUSTRALIAN RAAF SERVICE DRESS TUNIC

* Royal Australian Air Force Sergeant's service dress tunic dated 1941, all RAAF buttons intact, complete with all insignia including AUSTRALIA cloth shoulder tabs, with RAAF eagle underneath each, Sergeant rank chevrons, right sleeve has five service chevrons on cuff . . **$150 (£75)**

AUSTRALIAN 39TH INFANTRY BATTALION TUNIC

* WWI pattern enlisted four pocket khaki wool tunic with bronze "AUSTRALIAN MILITARY FORCES" buttons, false belt, roll collar and button cuffs, 39th Battalion "Colour Patch," a copper toned brown and rose colored divided wool oblong oval, sewn on both shoulders. Interior with khaki cotton dressing pocket and maker's label dated "1941" ....**$190 (£95)**

BRITISH ENLISTED SERVICE DRESS TUNIC

* Khaki wool "Jacket, Service Dress, O.R." has stand-and-fall collar, rifle patch shoulders, upper patch pockets and inset lower pockets with exterior flaps, and olive plastic Commonwealth general service buttons. Interior has khaki facing and pocket material with "WD Broad Arrow" stamp, issue tag has 1943 date and lists "Size No. 14 (breast 40" to 41")........................**$190 (£95)**

BRITISH ENLISTED BATTLE DRESS TUNIC

* 1940 pattern battle dress blouse of khaki wool has brown composition buttons and waist adjustment belt. Interior has "June 1943" dated label.................**$150 (£75)**

British Land Army frock, $75-$125 (£50-£125). www.advanceguardmilitaria.com

British Service Dress jacket, $175-$225 (£100-£125). www.advanceguardmilitaria.com

British enlisted man's Model 1940 Battle Dress Tunic, $100-$150 (£50-£75). www.advanceguardmilitaria.com

BRITISH AUSTRALIAN-MADE BATTLE DRESS

- Olive drab short battle dress jacket with dark blue and red shoulder titles "No 3 COMMANDO" over inverted black triangle with red embroidered sword, Australian contract tag with 43 date . . . .**$170 (£85)**

BRITISH ENLISTED BATTLE DRESS TUNIC AND TROUSERS

- 1940 pattern khaki wool battle dress blouse has label with Broad Arrow stamp and date "1943," maker's size information "No. 13 / Height 5 ft. 11 ins to 6 ft. 0 ins. / Breast 38 to 39 ins / Waist 33 to 34 ins." 1940 pattern khaki wool battle dress trousers have 1942-dated maker's label listing size "No. 16 / Height 6 ft. 1 in. to 6 ft. 2 in. / Waist 34 in. to 35 in."; olive brown composition and metal utility buttons throughout including interior suspender buttons, one rear pocket, left front patch pocket, and exterior wound dressing pocket. . . . .**$230 (£115)**

BRITISH BOMB DISPOSAL SOLDIER'S BATTLE DRESS TUNIC

- 1945-dated khaki wool battle dress has RAF eagle shoulder badges, single blade propeller Leading Aircraftman rank badges, and wreathed "BD" bomb disposal specialty badge, right cuff with four red service chevrons. Left chest has four medal ribbon bar including 1939-45 Star, France and Germany Star, Defence Medal, and War Medal . . . .**$130 (£65)**

BRITISH GURKHA COLONEL'S BATTLE DRESS TUNIC

- Fine officer quality wool battle dress has green felt backed metal Colonel rank pips and crowns on the epaulettes, wine red field grade officer's collar tabs, white crossed Gurkha knives on red square formation patches, and six row medal ribbon bar including Military Cross, India General Service Medal 1938-39, 1939-45 Star, Burma Star, War Medal 1939-45, and India Independence Medal . . . .**$180 (£90)**

BRITISH 12TH ARMY JUNGLE GREEN BUSH JACKET AND TROUSERS

- Jungle green bush jacket has Burmese dragon embroidered 12th Army shoulder sleeve insignia on the right sleeve and epaulettes with Major's embroidered crown slip-on rank insignias. Tunic has handsewn button holes, brown composition buttons (the two cuff buttons lacking), self fabric waistbelt with button closure and frame buckle adjustment, and two medal ribbon bar with 1939-45 Star and Burma Star. Jungle green battledress trousers have bandage pockets, a single large front patch pocket on the left thigh, and a single patch pocket on the right rear. The 12th Army was raised in Burma in May 1945. The 12th and 14th Army were charged with recapturing Burma and Malaya from the Japanese . . . . . **$290 (£145)**

BRITISH ARTILLERY LT. COLONEL'S BATTLE DRESS UNIFORM

- 1940 pattern khaki wool battle dress tunic has Lieutenant Colonel's cloth rank insignia, "ROYAL ARTILLERY" shoulder titles, white cypher letters on black wool square formation badges, and two red service chevrons. 1940 pattern battledress trousers of khaki wool have large front cargo pocket and bandage pocket, side seam pockets, single rear pocket, and khaki cotton lining. . . . .**$300 (£150)**

BRITISH RAF ENLISTED PILOT'S UNIFORM

- RAF blue wool battle dress tunic with RAF pilot embroidered badge, RAF eagle printed shoulder insignia, and Corporal rank chevrons, interior with Broad Arrow proof and number code, "1944" date on sewn cotton label. Uniform includes mid-war production 1937 pattern issue trousers of RAF blue wool with open top wound dressing pocket and composition buttons, and is further complete with an issue side cap, matching RAF blue wool with eagle cape closure buttons and an RAF cap badge with rich dark patina. Interior with Broad Arrow proof and 1945 Glasgow maker's stamp . . . .**$300 (£150)**

BRITISH RAF ENLISTED TROPICAL SERVICE TUNIC

- Khaki cotton "Frock, Khaki Drill, Airmen" has red embroidered eagle on tan cotton shoulder patches, Corporal rank chevrons, and RAF crown and eagle buttons throughout. Interior has undated contract tag. **$80 (£45)**

BRITISH NAVY JUMPER

- Dark blue wool serge jumper with worn three medal ribbon bar with 1914-1915 Star, 1914-1920 War Medal and Mercantile Marine Medal 1914-1918, jumper has issue tag with "1943" date. . . . .**$70 (£35)**

CANADIAN ISSUE BATTLE DRESS UNIFORM

- Pattern 1940 Canadian manufactured jacket and trousers of dark khaki wool serge; jacket with concealed button front, pleated breast pockets, metal frame waist buckle

British jungle bush jacket with the insignia of the 12th Army, $175-$250 (£100-£150).

www.advanceguardmilitaria.com

Canadian battle dress jacket, $185-$250 (£100-£150). Minnesota Military Museum

and khaki painted metal buttons, those at the cuffs now lacking; half lined in olive cotton with two interior pockets, ink stamped with "C" Broad Arrow and maker's label marked "SIZE No. 9" (size 40) and dated "1945". Closely matching trousers with metal buttons, cargo and dressing pockets, belt loops and cuff tabs, olive cotton lining marked with "C" Broad Arrow and size stamps for a 36" to 37" waist, dated "1943" . . . . **$200 (£100)**

CANADIAN 2ND CORPS LIEUTENANT'S BATTLE DRESS TUNIC

• Khaki wool battle dress has embroidered sew-on Lieutenant rank pips, embroidered "Royal Canadian Army Service Corps" shoulder titles, Canadian 2nd Corps flashes, and three award medal ribbon bar including Defence Medal, Canadian Volunteer Service, and 1939-45 War Medal. Interior dated "1943" . . . . **$100 (£50)**

CANADIAN WARRANT OFFICER'S BATTLE DRESS TUNIC

• Khaki wool battle dress has "CANADA" embroidered shoulder titles, Warrant Officer 2nd Class sleeve insignia and four-award medal ribbon bar indicating that this man was also a WWI veteran. Interior has 1942 date stamp . . . . **$90 (£45)**

CANADIAN RCAF CORPORAL'S TROPICAL BUSH JACKET

• Olive khaki cotton bush jacket has pleated upper pockets and inset waist pockets, self-material waistbelt with frame buckle, RCAF buttons, red on green RCAF eagle shoulder badges, and Corporal rank chevrons. Interior has size label, C-Broad Arrow stamp, and 1941 date. . . . . **$90 (£45)**

Coats, Jackets, Female

BRITISH ATS TROPICAL TUNIC

• 1942 "austerity pattern" service dress jacket of khaki cotton has pleated upper pockets and internal lower pockets, Senior Commandant (Major) rank badges, ATS shoulder titles, Royal Electrical and Mechanical Engineers breast badge, and ATS shoulder cord. . . . . **$200 (£100)**

CANADIAN CWAC UNIFORM

• Tan wool barathea tunic with CWAC buttons throughout, brown wool epaulettes have applied C.W.A.C. embroidered shoulder titles and yellow and brown CANADA sleeve titles. Collar with enlisted CWAC collar badges and each cuff has a trade or proficiency badge, right has an olive drab wool disc with red embroidered circle and arrow, left has a dark blue disc with red embroidered "GS" $300 (£150)

CANADIAN CWAC UNIFORM GROUP

• Uniform and accessories of Canadian Women's Army Corps Corporal E.A. Reeve consists of tunic, visor cap, shoes, PT shorts, some accessories, and duffle bag, many items with Reeve's ID in ink or on her embroidered nametags. Tan wool barathea tunic has three exterior pockets, CWAC buttons, brown wool epaulettes with embroidered and applied C.W.A.C. shoulder titles, brown and gold embroidered CANADA sleeve titles, Corporal rank badges, and CWAC collar badges. Tan wool visor cap has fold-down ear flaps, six enameled ventilation grommets at the edge of the crown, leather chinstrap and CWAC cap badge, no mothing and little signs of wear.

British Auxiliary Territorial Service bush jacket, $175-$250 (£100-£150). www.advanceguardmilitaria.com

British officer's shirt, $50-$65 (£25-£35). www.advanceguardmilitaria.com

Canadian Women's Army Corps tan wool barathea tunic, $150-$175 (£75-£125).

www.advanceguardmilitaria.com

Low quarter shoes are olive canvas with brown leather toe caps and original laces. White cotton PT shorts have a fall front opening and are dated 1942. Accessories include a pair of C-Broad Arrow marked cotton panties with heavy wear near the rear waistband and in the seat, a pair of khaki cotton hose, ribbed cotton socks, a brown knit wool scarf, brown necktie, khaki canvas toiletry hold all with brown leather strap . . . .**$650 (£325)**

Shirts, Male

BRITISH ARMY ENLISTED ISSUE SHIRT, FIRST PATTERN

* Khaki wool flannel first pattern issue shirt with short khaki twill standing collar, with Belfast factory markings, and olive drab composition buttons. This was superseded by the second pattern with stand-fall collar introduced in 1944. . . . .**$100 (£50)**

BRITISH ARMY ENLISTED ISSUE SHIRT, SECOND PATTERN

* Khaki wool flannel second pattern pullover shirt with attached collar, Belfast maker marked and dated 1944, with khaki composition buttons. . . . .**$60 (£30)**

BRITISH OFFICER'S SHIRT

* Olive light wool flannel shirt has shoulder epaulettes, pleated patch pockets, pull-over style with top button placket, pleated back shoulder panel, and interior with woven labels "Viyella (Regd) 15" and "This Garment Must Not Be Sold Except To Members of H.M. Forces". . . . . **$70 (£35)**

This grouping belonging to a Canadian Women's Army Corps corporal sold for $650 (£325). www.advanceguardmilitaria.com

Trousers, Male

BRITISH BATTLEDRESS TROUSERS

* Khaki wool twill trousers with buttoning belt loops, wound dressing pocket on right thigh, left leg with exterior flap pocket, reverse with one pocket and label "Battledress / Trousers, 1940 Pattern / Size No. 18". . . . .**$230 (£115)**

BRITISH BATTLEDRESS TROUSERS

* Pattern 1940 "Economy Issue" khaki serge wool trousers with thigh and dressing pockets, brown plastic buttons used throughout, moderate mothing. Lined in khaki cotton with illegible markings. . . . .**$120 (£60)**

BRITISH CAMOUFLAGE JUNGLE TROUSERS

* Camouflage printed cotton trousers have two-buckle front closure, waistbelt loops, wound dressing pocket and one cargo pocket on the front of the legs, bloused cuffs, two rear pockets, and label with Broad Arrow proof and 1944 date, "Trousers (Jungle) Size No. 8". . . . .**$230 (£115)**

Trousers, Skirts, Female

BRITISH ATS WOMEN'S PT SHORTS

* "Skirts Divided. P.T. A.T.S," chocolate brown shorts with a side button closure. Interior with label, dated 1942. This pair is unissued but the hem of the right leg has some frayed damage in the back. Scarce item used during training but withdrawn once ATS members were assigned a post . . . . **$20 (£10)**

Footwear, Male

BRITISH "AMMUNITION BOOTS"

* Pair, black pebbled leather Ammunition Boots with typical British heel and sole plates, cap toe, hobnailed soles, size 8, and complete with worn leather laces. Soles are stamped with Broad Arrow proof, no date visible. . . . .**$140 (£70)**

MOTORCYCLE RIDER'S HIGH BOOTS

* Black leather 3/4 height front lace boots with attached three- buckle gaiter, soles with hobnails . . . . .**$140 (£70)**

BRITISH OFFICER'S ANKLE BOOTS

* Pebble-grained russet brown leather shoes, 3/4 height with capped toe and pull tab on the heel counter. Interior marked with 1944 date, War Department Broad Arrow acceptance proof, and Northampton manufacturer's stamp on the insole . . . .**$190 (£95)**

BRITISH RAF 1936 PATTERN FLYING BOOTS

* Black leather boots with felt cushion interior soles and thick pile fleece linings have V-shaped openings at the tops with black leather billet and buckle adjustment closure, and leather soles with rubber heels. Underside of interior pull-tabs has embossed brown leather Air Ministry label listing size "11" and date "39". . . . .**$400 (£200)**

CANADIAN ANKLE BOOTS

* Pair of black pebble finish leather Ammunition Boots, with hobnails as well as toe and heel irons, soles marked

British ATS physical training shorts, $25-$35 (£25-£35).

www.advanceguardmilitaria.com

British Women's Auxiliary ankle shoes, $65-$95 (£30-£50).

www.advanceguardmilitaria.com

Commonly known as the "tanker's jacket," the official designation noted that it was a "winter combat jacket," $250-$350 (£130-£195).

Charles D. Pautler

USMC overcoat with shoulder insignia for the 6th Marine Division, $75-$100 (£40-£50).

www.advanceguardmilitaria.com

with the "C" Broad Arrow proof, interior marked by contractor and dated "1943" . . . . **$140 (£70)**

Footwear, Female

BRITISH WAAF ANKLE SHOES

* Black pebble grained ankle boots have a decorative stitched Broad Arrow above the toe cap. Soles stamped with Arabic numeral "5" and Roman numeral "VIII," insoles stamped "JOHN WHITE 1942." Interior of the tongue is ink stamped with a "W" over an "&" (ampersand) . . . .**$100 (£50)**

Underwear, Male

BRITISH STRING VEST

* Knotted white cotton cord undergarment intended as winter insulation . . . . **$18 (£9)**

BRITISH ARMY ISSUE UNDERWEAR

* White wool flannel long drawers with button closure waistband and sewn loops, wartime dated proof stamp. . . . . **$40 (£20)**

UNITED STATES

Outerwear, Male

MODEL 1926 OFFICER'S OVERCOAT

* Long, double-breasted olive drab wool M1926 overcoat with notched lapel collar and two vertical inset waist pockets. Interior has tag that reads "Overcoat, Officer's and Warrant Officer's / Dated August 11, 1942." Has back adjustment belt . . . . **$70 (£35)**

MODEL 1942 ARMY OFFICER'S OVERCOAT WITH LINER

* Two-ply water-resistant olive drab cotton poplin overcoat with a self-fabric belt with brown frame buckle. Includes the optional button-in wool liner . . . . **$50 (£25)**

1942 PATTERN MACKINAW

* Olive drab cotton duck Mackinaw has the distinctive 1942 pattern shawl collar, double-breasted front closure with olive composition buttons and matching waistbelt. Interior has olive drab blanket wool lining . . . . **$80 (£40)**

1943 PATTERN MACKINAW

* Double breasted olive drab cotton coat with composition buttons and notched collar. Interior has lining cotton and wool . . . . **$70 (£35)**

ARMY ENLISTED MAN'S OVERCOAT

* Heavy olive drab wool enlisted issue overcoat with olive plastic eagle buttons . . . . **$60 (£30)**

USMC ENLISTED MAN'S OVERCOAT

* Forest green wool overcoat with rear belt loops . . . . **$70 (£35)**

USMC 6TH MARINE DIVISION OVERCOAT

* Forest green wool overcoat with 6th Marine Division shoulder insignia and bronze Marine buttons . **$80 (£40)**

WINTER COMBAT JACKET

* Issue pattern khaki cotton jacket with olive drab knit collar, cuffs and waistband. Front opening with inset side

pockets. Popularly referred to as a "tanker's jacket," was officially known as the Winter Combat Jacket.

....**$300 (£150)**

COLD WEATHER PARKA/OVERCOAT

* Olive drab wool overcoat with integral hood, two inset slash upper pockets with flaps, two lower skirt cargo pockets with a G.I. khaki web waistbelt that passes through several wide belt loops around the sides and reverse. Front closes with zipper and large olive drab composition buttons over the zipper windscreen. Interior has brown alpaca pile lining, one pocket with contract tag "Overcoat, Parka Type / With Pile Liner / Medium / September 1943." Knitted interior wool sleeve cuffs.

....**$140 (£70)**

REVERSIBLE PARKA, FUR-TRIMMED HOOD AND CUFFS

* Light olive drab and white reversible cotton poplin pull-over parka, fur trimmed hood and cuffs with drawstring adjustment, flapped slash pockets, long, calf length designed for use by snowshoe troops, also used by the First Special Service Force......................**$140 (£70)**

ARMY ENLISTED MAN'S RAINCOAT

* Olive drab synthetic resin coated enlisted dismounted pattern raincoat ....**$80 (£40)**

ARMY WET WEATHER PARKA

* Pullover olive drab waterproofed cotton parka with laced front closure, hood, and drawstring at waist... **$70 (£35)**

ARMY PONCHO

* Olive drab rubber coated canvas poncho with high drawstring neck opening and snaps along edges.... **$60 (£30)**

This style of parka could be worn with or without a pile liner, $95-$150 (£50-£75). Author's collection

The cold weather parka for snowshoe troops had fur-trimmed hood and cuffs, $125-$165 (£60-£80). Author's collection

U.S. enlisted man's synthetic raincoat, $75-$135 (£35-£60). Author's collection

The Army wet weather parka was similar to the Navy's pattern, $50-$75 (£20-£30). Author's collection

The World War II poncho did not have a hood, but rather, a gathered neck opening, $50-$75 (£25-£40). Author's collection

The A-2 flight jacket was one of the most popular leather jackets during the war, $400-$1,200 (£300-£750).
www.advanceguardmilitaria.com

An A-2 jacket with a painted squadron insignia immediately skyrockets in value. A jacket such as this one could easily sell for $1,500-$2,500 (£750-£1,300). www.advanceguardmilitaria.com

The AN-J-2 was a lightweight summer flight jacket, $175-$300 (£90-£150).
www.advanceguardmilitaria.com

USMC CAMOUFLAGE PONCHO

* Rubberized fabric poncho with neck opening, printed in reversible green to brown camouflage patterns, bronze snaps along edges. . . . . **$120 (£60)**

A-2 LEATHER FLIGHT JACKET

* Rich chocolate brown goatskin leather A-2 flight jacket has aviator's leather nametag stitch lines on the epaulettes indicating where Lieutenant rank insignia once was, and normal wear and tear on the knit cuffs and waistband. Interior has original brown cotton lining with "TYPE A-2" AAF woven nomenclature label listing the maker as "ROUGH WEAR CLOTHING CO. / MIDDLETOWN, PA." and size "36." Leather remains in excellent pliable condition. . . . . **$530 (£265)**

8TH AIR FORCE GUNNER'S PAINTED A2 JACKET GROUPING

* Extensive group from 571st Bomb Squadron, 390th Bomb Group waist gunner. The paperwork with the group indicates that the Staff Sergeant was drafted in 1943, trained in South Dakota, and his diary notes that he flew his first mission in February 1945. His brown leather A2 jacket has reverse with faded but still very visible painted B-17 aircraft detailed down to the unit markings on the tail; silver outlined fancy script motto above "EPSOM SALTS / 'Just Passin' Thru'" and 20 mission bombs below. Cuffs and waistband are old

AAF P-51 Ace's identified group that included the flyer's A-2 jacket, flight gear, documents, and even his gun camera sold for $9,975 (~£5,000). www.advanceguardmilitaria.com

replacements. Front of the jacket has leather name badge with embossed Aerial Gunner wings, stitch line below indicates where a squadron patch was on the jacket but is no longer. Pocket contains silver Aerial Gunner wrist bracelet. Enlisted issue shirt has 8th Air Force shoulder insignia, S/Sgt. rank chevrons and a white embroidered on padded blue wool felt Air Crew wing badge.
.... **$2,750 (£1,375)**

424TH BOMB SQUADRON PAINTED AN-J-3A FLIGHT JACKET

- AN-J-3a brown leather flight jacket with fur collar and worsted knit cuffs and waistband, obverse with painted 424th Bombardment Squadron insignia depicting black aerial bomb on 4" diameter black piped white disc with red sun setting behind blue waterline. Left shoulder has painted 13th Air Force winged star insignia The right front pocket bears a 2- 1/4" diameter black disc and 307th Bomb Group stylistic intertwined "LR" Long Rangers insignia. Reverse painted with 9" x 8" B-24 Liberator in flight, tail with "LR" group insignia, blue and white clouds in background, and block printed inscription in red trimmed white 1-1/2" letters "LONG RANGERS." Specification label lacking, cuffs heavily worn, nice original waistband, leather is in excellent shape, 70-80% of insignias remain, and zipper is functional
.... **$1,900 (£950)**

A-9 WINTER FLIGHT JACKET

- Type A-9 of olive drab gabardine with down-filled quilted satin lining, mouton-lined hood and knitted cuffs. Interior with Eddie Bauer contract tag labeled size 38. Has little wear, and a good zipper. ...... **$330 (£165)**

AN-J-2 FLIGHT JACKET, PBM-5 RADIO/GUNNER'S GROUP

- Uniforms, flight jacket, and photos from a Radio Technician Third Class, USNR. Includes the AN-J-2 lightweight summer flight jacket of khaki cotton poplin with roll collar, black leather name tag with gilt embossed Aviation Radio Technician winged lightning bolts insignia. Left sleeve has red, white, and blue leather CBI insignia over the pen and implement pockets. Reverse has applied leather CBI "blood chit" insignia with U.S. and Chinese flags over printed anchor and "USN" designation with Chinese character inscriptions. Other parts of the grouping includes one pair of dark blue wool Navy enlisted bell bottom trousers and two dark blue wool jumpers. Both of these have Aerial Gunner sleeve insignias and Aviation Radio Technician Third Class Petty Officer's rating badges. .... **$695 (£350)**

AN-J-3A FLIGHT JACKET

- Almost identical to the Navy G-1 flight jacket but much more rare, this wartime production brown goatskin leather flight jacket has a mouton fur collar, reverse of collar with silver "U.S.N." stencil, scalloped pocket flaps and bi-directional weave knit waistband. Interior has the original maroon synthetic lining with woven manufacturer's nomenclature label identifying the jacket as an AN-J-3a .... **$210 (£105)**

AN-J-4 FLEECE FLIGHT JACKET AND FLYING TROUSERS

- Brown shearling jacket has turned golden fleece collar with button tab, left shoulder with 70% AAF multicolor insignia decal remaining, zipper front closure with AAF winged star logo decal on wind screen panel. Iinterior with fleece pile, and woven label with size "40R" and designation "AN-6553 / AN-J-4", supple condition. Flying trousers are AN-T-35, of brown finished fleece with functional zippers, brown elastic suspenders, three exterior pockets with snap closures, windscreen panel with AAF winged star insignia, and interior with woven nomenclature label listing size "40" .... **$495 (£250)**

AN-S-31A SUMMER FLYING SUIT

- Olive drab gabardine coveralls with zipper front, chest and lower leg pockets and matching fabric belt. Has chest and shin pockets .... **$145 (£75)**

B-3 FLIGHT JACKET

- Thick fleece sheepskin flying jacket has brown poly-acrylate exterior finish with normal scuffs and wear, functional zipper, implement pocket, waist adjustment tabs, and two buckle collar tabs; interior has AAF woven nomenclature label listing type "B-3", maker "WERBER SPORTSWEAR CO.", and size "38R" .... **$495 (£250)**

B-6 FLIGHT JACKET

- AAF short pile shearling with brown exterior finish, turned sheepskin collar with single buckle closure, brown leather epaulettes, front with two inset slant pockets, sides have short zipper adjustment with zippers that no longer function, front has good functional Lightning zipper closure. Interior with AAF woven nomenclature label "TYPE B-6 / AERO LEATHER CLO. CO." and size "42R." The B-6 was quite popular with fighter pilots who had to deal with the constraints of a small cockpit.
.... **$375 (£190)**

The AN-J-F fleece flight jacket was issued to high-altitude flyers, $250-$350 (£125-£180).
Charles D. Pautler

B-7 EXTREME COLD WEATHER SHEARLING FLYING PARKA

♦ Type B-7 flight parka of natural colored shearling with brown leather pockets and trim has AAF winged star shoulder decal, fur-trimmed shearling hood, functional zipper covered by shearling flap with button and cord loop closure, zipper inset side pockets and brown leather open-top patch pockets. Interior has "B-7" woven nomenclature label with size "42R"..........**$495 (£250)**

B-9 WINTER FLYING COAT

♦ Scarce AAF coat, the Type B-9 has an alpaca lined hood, olive poplin exterior with slanted upper and lower pockets, reinforced sleeves, and the down-filled quilted satin interior lining that distinguishes it from the B-11.
....**$195 (£100)**

B-11 WINTER FLYING JACKET

♦ Olive drab cotton gabardine parka with alpaca lining and sheepskin bordered hood, has black and gold tag "JACKET; WINTER, FLYING TYPE-B-11-(ALPACA & WOOL LINING) SIZE 36" and faint silk screened AAF shoulder sleeve insignia .... **$90 (£45)**

D-1 FLEECE FLIGHT JACKET AND AN-6554 TROUSERS

♦ Brown shearling leather flight jacket as designed for use by flight mechanics, but actively used by flight crews, especially fighter pilots who valued the fact that it was warm shearling, but was not as thick as the B-3 and so allowed much more maneuverability in the cockpit. Interior has AAF woven contract tag "JACKET, MECHANICS / TYPE D-1 / SIZE LARGE." AAF AN-6554 fleece flying trousers complete with suspenders.
....**$395 (£200)**

F-1 "BLUE BUNNY" HEATED FLYING SUIT

♦ Type F-1 horizon blue wool felt flying suit with electrical heating element wires, olive drab knit cuffs and collar, and plug receptacles mounted at the chest, wrists, and ankles. Interior has brown wool felt lining and woven contract tag. These were worn under the fleece flying trousers and jackets and plugged into temperature rheostats mounted in the aircraft at the various duty stations. Mint condition ....**$395 (£200)**

F-2 HEATED FLYING SUIT OUTER COAT

♦ Dark olive drab wool elastique jacket buttons on to the F-2 heated flying suit top, which gives it the appearance of an Ike jacket. These came in several flavors, including one with a partial fur lined collar. This is the one in dark OD wool elastique with brown composition buttons, two upper patch pockets, one lower inset pocket, and interior with button tabs for attaching to the electrically heated F2 jacket. Has woven nomenclature label "JACKET, OUTER / For Type F-2 Electrically Heated Flying Suit," listing size "36" ....**$125 (£65)**

K-1 LIGHT SUMMER FLYING SUIT

♦ Khaki cotton flying suit with pockets with zipper closure and map retaining clip on the left thigh, waist with button tab adjustment, and interior with AAF nomenclature label "Suit, Flying, Very Light, Cotton Twill / Type K-1".
....**$85 (£45)**

L-1 FLYING SUIT

♦ Olive drab gabardine flying suit with button tab side adjustment, zipper pockets, sleeve with instrument pockets, left thigh with leather covered metal notepad clip. The interior has AAF woven nomenclature label listing size "Medium-Short," and maker "Sigmund Eisner Co." ....**$65 (£33)**

M-422A NAVY FLIGHT JACKET

♦ The brown goatskin leather M-422A flight jacket has brown mouton fur collar with pointed ends and silver "U.S.N." designation stenciled on the back underside of the collar ....**$425 (£215)**

The B-9 winter flying coat had a down-filled quilted satin lining, $175-$200 (£90-£100). www.advanceguardmilitaria.com

The F-2 heated flying suit outer jacket resembled the "Ike" jacket in outward appearance only, $100-$150 (£50-£75). www.advanceguardmilitaria.com

The Navy's M-422A flight jacket had a brown mouton fur collar, $400-$500 (£200-£275). www.advanceguardmilitaria.com

NAVY PATROL BOMBER SQUADRON M-422A FLIGHT JACKET WITH PAINTED INSIGNIA

* Navy M-422A pilot's brown goatskin leather flight jacket with brown mouton collar and original wovenwaistband and period replacement cuffs. Left chest has blue-green painted canvas disc with VPB 102 squadron insignia depicting a a winged dragon hurling a bomb from a cloud. The jacket interior has worn but intact maroon fabric lining. . . . . **$1,275 (£640)**

M-444 FLIGHT JACKET

* Lightweight winter flying jacket made of of pile sheepskin with chocolate brown finish, large diamond-shaped elbow reinforcement patches, two flapped waist pockets, and adjustment tabs and buckles at sides . . .**$325 (£165)**

M-445A NAVY FLEECE FLYING JACKET

* M-445A fleece flying jacket has rich chocolate brown color exterior and thick golden fleece pile interior and turned collar, underside of collar stenciled "USN" in black, cuffs turned with fleece edges and interior knit attachments, two front patch pockets, and sides with adjustment tabs . . . .**$315 (£160)**

Outerwear Female

WAAC RAINCOAT

* Single breasted, rubberized cotton poplin coat, complete with hood, has vents under the arms and beneath the rear yoke. Contract label read "RAINCOAT, WAAC, MEMBERS". . . . .**$125 (£65)**

9TH AIR FORCE WAC OFFICER'S UTILITY OVERCOAT

* Olive drab cotton poplin overcoat with belt and removable liner has 9th AAF shoulder sleeve insignia and 1st Lieutenant rank insignia on the epaulettes . . . . **$85 (£45)**

ARMY NURSE CORPS OVERCOAT

* Early war nurse's overcoat of dark blue wool, open lapel with epaulettes, matching belt with rectangular brass frame buckle, two welted front pockets, and removable interior lining. Hem has a distinctive triple stitched edge. . . . .**$125 (£65)**

Like any piece of flight gear, the presence of squadron insignia adds significantly to the garment's value. This Navy M-422A jacket with a patch for bomber squadron VPB 102 sold for $1,275 (~£640). www.advanceguardmilitaria.com

This WAC officer's utility overcoat with 9th Air Force insignia sold for $85 (~£42). www.advanceguardmilitaria.com

Single breasted WAAC rubberized cotton poplin raincoat, $100-$150 (£50-£75). www.advanceguardmilitaria.com

U.S. Army Nurse's overcoat in blue wool, $100-$125 (£50-£65). www.advanceguardmilitaria.com

USMC WOMEN'S RESERVE RAINCOAT

- Raincoat, Lightweight, U.S. Marine Corps, Womens' Reserve. Unlined double-breasted trench coat, olive green with dark green composition buttons throughout. $135 (£70)

Coats, Jackets, Male

1ST PATTERN HERRINGBONE TWILL JACKET

- 1938 pattern oive drab HBT short jacket with pleated patch pockets and waistband, 13 Star buttons throughout. $95 (£50)

2ND PATTERN HERRINGBONE TWILL JACKET

- Second Pattern HBT jacket with large unpleated cargo pockets on chest. Faded from use and washing, all 13 Star buttons and gas flap intact. Has ghost of shoulder patch as well as name and US Army tapes above pockets. $65 (£35)

HERRINGBONE TWILL JACKET , OD #7

- Olive drab shade #7 HBT jacket with Army 13 Star metal utility buttons, two large chest cargo pockets and interior gas flap $40 (£20)

ARMY CAMOUFLAGE HERRINGBONE TWILL JACKET

- Issue HBT camouflage jacket with concealed button front, patch pockets with flaps, and composition buttons. Fabric printed on both sides but not reversible. Interior has gas protection flap. Sleeves have elbow reinforcement patches $395 (£200)

ARMY MODEL 1942 CAMOUFLAGE HERRINGBONE TWILL TWO-PIECE CAMOUFLAGE SUIT

- Trousers and jacket in Army camouflage with brown composition buttons, cargo pockets, gas flaps, and all correct details. Trousers have size label "32 / 33" and 1943-dated contract label $1,150 (£575)

This P1941 Jacket was worn by both Navy and USMC troops, $65-$95 (£35-£50). Charles D. Pautler

The presence of original insignia can elevate a Model 1941 Field Jacket's value from $150-$200 (£75-£100) to as much as $400-$500 (£200-£250). Author's collection

The Arctic Field Jacket was a longer version of the Model 1941 Field Jacket. It was worn by troops in the Aleutians, United States and European theater, $100-$165 (£50-£80). Author's collection

USMC Women's Reserve raincoat, $125-$150 (£60-£75). www.advanceguardmilitaria.com

The Model 1943 Field Jacket was first issued in 1943. By the end of the war, it was widely distributed and remained in service through the Korean War. World War II-dated examples will sell for $95-$165 (£40-£80). Charles D. Pautler

Australian-made Ike jacket with insignia for a 5th Air Force aerial gunner, $225-$275 (£125-£150). www.advanceguardmilitaria.com

USMC 1941 PATTERN HERRINGBONE TWILL COMBAT UTILITY COAT

- 1941 Pattern olive drab HBT combat utility coat with breast pocket marked with a dark stenciled Marine EGA emblem with "USMC" above. Two waist pockets and Marine Corps buttons . . . . **$65 (£35)**

USMC 1944 PATTERN HERRINGBONE TWILL UTILITY JACKET

- Sage green HBT cotton jacket with two large inset pockets and one flapped patch pocket stenciled with "USMC" and EGA stenciled in black. Bronze USMC utility rivet set buttons used throughout . . . . **$65 (£35)**

PATTERN OF 1938 FIELD JACKET

- First pattern field jacket of olive drab cotton poplin with flapped side pockets, shoulders without epaulettes, functional zipper, size approximately 42, shows mild wear to cuffs . . . . **$185 (£95)**

M1941 FIELD JACKET

- Model 1941 field jacket of olive drab cotton poplin with epaulettes, inset side pockets and front closing zipper. . . . . **$165 (£85)**

MODEL 1941 ARCTIC FIELD JACKET

- Light olive drab cotton jacket with the same features as a model 1941 field jacket but longer in length with buckle adjustment tabs at waist and wrist. Fully lined with olive drab blanket weight wool . . . . **$110 (£55)**

M1943 FIELD JACKET

- Olive drab field jacket with detachable hood. Interior lining has waist drawstring . . . . **$125 (£65)**

M1942 PARATROOPER JUMP JACKET

- Khaki cotton jump jacket has blackened zinc snap fittings, crown zipper closure, throat with knife pocket, and cloth waistbelt. Left shoulder has 82nd Airborne Division shoulder sleeve insignia . . . . **$1,125 (£565)**

BRITISH MADE ETO JACKET

- Enlisted ETO jacket of olive drab wool with turned collar, exposed khaki composition button front closure, shoulder epaulettes. 1943-dated British maker's label present. . . . . **$185 (£95)**

1ST CAVALRY DIVISION COMBAT MEDIC'S UNIFORM

- Enlisted issue OD wool Ike jacket has U.S. and Medical Corps collar discs, 1st Cavalry Division shoulder insignia, wreathed silver Combat Medic's badge, honorable discharge, four medal ribbon bars including Silver Star and Philippine Liberation, Technician 5th Grade rank chevrons, and two overseas service bars. Uniform includes issue shirt and khaki tie. . . . . **$125 (£65)**

5TH RANGER BATTALION INFANTRY CAPTAIN'S OFFICER PATTERN IKE JACKET

- Dark olive drab wool elastique Ike jacket has Captain's rank insignia, U.S. and Infantry lapel insignia, 5th Ranger Battalion shoulder insignia, Combat Infantryman Badge, Army Presidential Unit Citation bar, three bullion service bars, and eight-place medal ribbon bar including Silver Star, Bronze Star, and Purple Heart . . . . **$225 (£115)**

Model 1942 Paratrooper Jump Jacket with no insignia, $450-$695 (£250-£375). Charles D. Pautler

Mountain Trooper's jacket, $400-$550 (£200-£265). Author's collection

9th Air Force Senior Pilot's Ike jacket with bullion insignia, $385-$400 (£200-£250). www.advanceguardmilitaria.com

8TH AIR FORCE NAVIGATOR'S SERVICE COAT

- Four-pocket olive drab wool elastique service coat with 8th Air Force shoulder sleeve insignia, 1st Lieutenant bars, officer's US and Aviation collar insignia, frosted Navigator's wing pinback marked "VANGUARD N.Y." Three-medal ribbon bar includes Air Medal, American Campaign and ETO Campaign, cuff with one bullion overseas service bar . . . .**$200 (£100)**

9TH AIR FORCE SENIOR PILOT'S IKE JACKET AND TROUSERS

- Army officer's olive drab wool Eisenhower jacket has bullion embroidered Colonel rank eagles, gilt brass U.S. and AAF winged prop collar devices, bullion embroidered Senior Pilot wing badge, bullion 9th Air Force shoulder insignia, four service bars, and six-medal ribbon bar including Bronze Star, WWI Victory and ETO Campaign with five campaign stars. Includes a pair of light OD "pink" wool elastique trousers . . . .**$485 (£245)**

11TH AIR FORCE PILOT'S B-13 FLIGHT JACKET AND UNIFORM SET

- Includes B-13 Officer's Flight Jacket in olive drab wool elastique with U.S. and AAF winged prop lapel devices, 11th Air Force shoulder sleeve insignia, and three gilt bullion embroidered overseas service bars. Complete with olive drab wool elastique trousers. Flight jacket has silver clutch-back pilot wing badge. Ghost appears to show where Captain's rank insignia was on the epaulettes. Four-pocket dark olive drab wool elastique service dress tunic has matching waistbelt, 11th Air Force shoulder insignia, and three bullion overseas bars. Includes light olive drab 'pink' service dress trousers. . . . .**$325 (£115)**

13TH AIR FORCE AERIAL PHOTOGRAPHER'S IKE JACKET

- Enlisted issue olive drab wool Ike jacket has U.S. and Air Corps discs, left sleeve with 13th Air Force shoulder insignia and four service bars, right sleeve with Far East Air Forces shoulder insignia, "Official U.S. Army Photographer" rectangular shoulder insignia, and AAF Photography specialist cuff badge. Obverse has Sterling pinback Aircrew wing badge, Presidential Unit Citation ribbon bar, and five medal ribbon bar including Good Conduct, Asia/Pacific Campaign with three stars, Victory, Philippine Liberation, and Occupation. Interior has 1944-dated contract tag . . . .**$165 (£85)**

14TH AIR FORCE/CBI AERIAL GUNNER'S TUNIC

Enlisted four-pocket OD wool service dress tunic has bullion embroidered U.S. and Air Corps winged prop collar devices, regular issue 14th Air Force and bullion CBI shoulder insignias. Left chest has Sterling hallmarked clutch-back Aerial Gunner wing badge and five medal ribbon bars. . . . .**$195 (£100)**

15TH AIR FORCE PILOT'S TUNIC WITH BULLION INSIGNIA

- Officer's olive drab wool four-pocket service coat has silver First Lieutenant rank insignias, AAF Air Materiel Command distinctive insignias, bullion embroidered 15th Air Force shoulder sleeve insignia, officer's U.S. lapel devices with early "top hat" style clutches, one AAF winged prop device present, other one is missing. Also has silver pinback pilot wing badge with "STERLING" hallmark, Good Conduct and ETO Campaign medal ribbon bars. Left cuff has three bullion service bars, right cuff has Meritorious Service cuff badge. Interior has 1942-dated Quartermaster tag . . . .**$225 (£115)**

13th Air Force Aerial Photographer's Ike jacket, $150-$175 (£75-£90). www.advanceguardmilitaria.com

The B-13 Flight Jacket was essentially an Ike jacket, $85-$125 (£40-£65). www.advanceguardmilitaria.com

15th Air Force pilot's Class A tunic with bullion insignia, $200-$250 (£100-£125). www.advanceguardmilitaria.com

17TH AIRBORNE DIVISION LIEUTENANT'S DRESS TUNIC

- Dark olive drab wool elastique four pocket service tunic has bullion embroidered 1st Lt. rank insignias, U.S. and Infantry collar devices, 17th Airborne shoulder insignia, Presidential Unit Citation ribbon, silver Parachutist qualification wing badge on Airborne Command white, red, and blue oval, pinback Combat Infantryman Badge, five-place medal ribbon bar including Bronze Star ribbon with silver (five award) oakleaf cluster, and cuff with two overseas service bars, complete with matching waistbelt. Interior has 1943-dated tailor's label with this officer's name inscribed . . . .**$325 (£165)**

24TH DIVISION NCO'S IKE JACKET

- Enlisted issue olive drab wool Ike jacket with U.S. and Signal Corps collar discs, 24th Division shoulder insignia, T/5 rank chevrons, three overseas bars and one service stripe. Interior has 1946-dated contract tag and size tag "36L" . . . . **$40 (£20)**

36TH DIVISION FIRST SERGEANT'S FOUR-POCKET TUNIC

- Enlisted man's olive drab wool four-pocket tunic has U.S. and Armor screwback collar devices, 36th Division shoulder insignia, First Sergeant rank chevrons, three overseas service bars and two service stripes. Has 1941-dated contract tag, and interior lining has size stencil "38S" . . . . **$40 (£20)**

37TH DIVISION LIEUTENANT'S AUSTRALIAN-MADE "PINKS AND GREENS" UNIFORM

- Dark olive drab wool officer's four-pocket service dress tunic has silver 1st Lieutenant rank insignias, U.S. and Infantry officer's lapel devices, 37th Division shoulder insignia, Bronze Star and Pacific Theater medal ribbon bars, and five bullion overseas service bars. Complete with waistbelt; interior has Brisbane tailor's label. Uniform is complete with matching light olive drab "pink" wool issue trousers with Brisbane tailor's label in waistband, complete with a waistbelt made from the same material. Also includes an officer's overseas cap. . . . .**$135 (£70)**

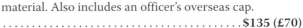

> "My pay was raised from $50 a month to $54...I squandered the $4 buying extra chevrons, a sewing kit and a necktie more suitable for weekend passes..."
>
> PFC. JOHN BABCOCK, 78TH U.S. INFANTRY DIVISION

40th Division Sergeant's Ike jacket with bullion patch and Combat Artilleryman Badge, $75-$100 (£40-£55).
www.advanceguardmilitaria.com

24th Division T/5's Ike jacket, $35-$50 (£15-£25). www.advanceguardmilitaria.com

82nd Airborne Division PFC's Ike jacket, $450-$575 (£250-£300).
www.advanceguardmilitaria.com

36th Division First Sergeant's Class A tunic, $25-$40 (£15-£25). www.advanceguardmilitaria.com

40TH DIVISION SERGEANT'S UNIFORM WITH COMBAT ARTILLERYMAN BADGE

• 1944-dated Ike jacket has U.S. and Artillery enlisted collar devices, epaulettes with 143rd Field Artillery SB distinctive insignias, one with a bit of enamel damage. Sleeves have Technical Sergeant rank chevrons, left shoulder with gilt bullion on blue wool felt 40th Division shoulder insignia that has four eraser size moth holes but remains an attractive patch, also three overseas service bars on the left cuff. Has unofficial "Combat Artilleryman" badge. Shoulder insignia and Combat Artilleryman badge are both most likely German made. Includes enlisted issue olive drab wool flannel shirt, and olive drab wool field trousers . . . . **$125 (£65)**

82ND AIRBORNE, 505TH PARACHUTE INFANTRY REGIMENT SOLDIER'S IKE JACKET

• Enlisted issue olive drab wool Ike jacket has 82nd Airborne Division shoulder sleeve insignia, U.S. and Infantry collar discs, French and Belgian Croix-de-Guerre fourragere cords, pinback Parachutist qualification wing badge on 505th Parachute Infantry Regiment oval, with medal ribbon bars comprised of Silver Star, Purple Heart, Good Conduct, and ETO Campaign with two campaign stars. Tunic also has Combat Infantryman badge, Expert Marksmanship badge with "RIFLE" and "CARBINE" bars, PFC rank chevrons, honorable discharge insignia, and four overseas service bars. Interior has contract tag dated 1944. All of the insignia that is clutch-back has the proper period flat-face clutches. . . . .**$495 (£250)**

82ND AIRBORNE, GENERAL MATTHEW RIDGEWAY UNIFORM

• Khaki wool summer service tunic and trousers, tunic has four silver General rank stars, U.S. lapel insignias, Distinguished Unit Citation ribbon, cuff with six overseas service bars, silver pinback Parachutist wing badge with combat jump star, and nine-award medal ribbon bar including Distinguished Service Cross with oakleaf, Distinguished Service Medal with two oakleaves, Silver Star with oakleaf, Legion of Merit, Bronze Star with "V" and oakleaf, Purple Heart, ETO with Invasion arrowhead and five campaign stars, Korean Service with arrowhead, bronze and silver star, and UN Korean Service. Includes khaki officer's shirt and matching trousers. Coat and trousers both have "Gen. Ridgeway" laundry stencils visible inside. The fourth star on each epaulette is darker than the other three, likely a personal gift in Army tradition by the officer who promoted him. Though most of General Ridgeway's medals and uniforms were donated to museums, this uniform and other interesting items were auctioned by the estate in 1997 following the passing of his wife. The uniform is unaltered and remains exactly as it was when originally obtained from Mrs. Ridgeway's estate . . . . **$6,500 (£3,250)**

100TH CHEMICAL MORTAR BATTALION SERGEANT'S UNIFORM

• Ike jacket, shirt, trousers, and Chemical Corps piped overseas cap of a Technician, 4th Grade. Jacket has U.S. and Chemical Corps collar discs, beautiful silk and

The U.S. had the lowest casualty rates of the major powers in WWII.

Navy Amphibious Petty Officer's Jumper, $25-$50 (£10-£25). www.advanceguardmilitaria.com

Navy Shore Patrolman's Jumper, belt, holster and cap, $125-$175 (£50-£90). Charles D. Pautler

USMC Sergeant's Dress Blues, $200-$250 (£100-£125). www. advanceguardmilitaria.com

bullion embroidered 100th Cml Bn. shoulder insignia consisting of dark blue background with red embroidered Chemical Corps insignia outline and "4.2" for the 4.2 mortars used by this unit, with "100" embroidered in bullion across the insignia, 5th Army insignia on right shoulder. Nice group with one of the scarcest and most highly-sought shoulder sleeve insignias. . . . . **$685 (£345)**

701ST TANK DESTROYER BN. CORPORAL'S UNIFORM GROUPING

- Uniform, loose insignia, ID tags, photos, and papers from a corporal of the 701st Tank Destroyer Battalion. Four-pocket OD wool service dress tunic has U.S. and Artillery collar discs, Tank Destroyer and 1st Armored Division shoulder insignia, Corporal rank chevrons, honorable discharge insignia, and five overseas service bars. Loose insignia includes 1st Armored Division, Tank Destroyer patches and a 5th Army shoulder patch. Documents include the soldier's discharge copy, a photograph of the corporal in uniform and several snapshots of other 1st Armor soldiers, 5th Army sheet music by Irving Berlin, and several other small items . . . . **$275 (£140)**

NAVY N-1 FIELD JACKET

- Similar in pattern to the Army's Model 41 field jacket, but of a darker shade of olive drab and made without epaulets or cuff tabs. Left breast stenciled "U.S.N." in black. . . . . **$85 (£45)**

NAVY AMPHIBIOUS FORCES PETTY OFFICER'S JUMPER

- Dark blue wool jumper has red Amphibious Forces shoulder sleeve insignia, Yeoman Second Class rating badge, and one four-year service stripe . . . . **$30 (£15)**

NAVY RADIOMAN FIRST CLASS' WHITE ENLISTED JUMPER

- White cotton enlisted jumper with white trimmed blue wool neck cape and cuffs, Radioman First Class Petty Officer's rating badge with left-facing eagle, and three service chevrons. . . . . **$40 (£20)**

NAVY U.S.S. YORKTOWN SAILOR'S JUMPER WITH "LIBERTY" EMBROIDERY

- Dark blue wool dress jumper has post- "U.S.S. YORKTOWN" ship shoulder title and Medical Third Class Petty Officer ratings. Interior black silk lining with silk embroidered mermaid figure. . . . . **$40 (£20)**

NAVY AVIATOR CAPTAIN'S TUNIC

- Dark olive green wool twill service dress tunic has bronze Navy buttons, one epaulette button broken, cuffs with black mohair Captain rank insignia and line star, left chest with mellow patina gold Naval Aviator wings with clutch back attachment. **$115 (£60)**

> *"I had flown ten missions and was entitled to receive the Air Medal. At a ceremony at the base, we were presented with the medal by General Whelan."*
>
> LT. ROY BENSON, 9TH U.S. AIR FORCE

NAVY CHIEF PETTY OFFICER WHITE SERVICE COAT

- Double-breasted white cotton jacket with Chief Ship Writer's rate and three service stripes . . . . **$30 (£15)**

NAVY CAPTAIN'S DRESS BLUE JACKET

- Double-breasted, open lapel black wool jacket with six-place ribbon bar including ETO, Victory, and Reserve Special Commendation ribbon. Cuffs with four rows of gold bullion tape and bullion Line Officer's star, bullion wire is worn on the points of the stars . . . . **$40 (£20)**

NAVY REAR ADMIRAL'S SERVICE COAT

- Double-breasted coat with Rear Admiral gilt cuff braid and line officer star, gilt Navy buttons, and eight-award medal ribbon bar including Legion of Merit, Navy Commendation by SECNAV ribbon with second award star, WWI Victory Medal with bronze campaign star, Second Nicaraguan Campaign Medal, American Defense Medal with bronze star, American Campaign Medal, ETO Campaign Medal, and Victory Medal. Interior with tailor's tag inscribed "L. McKee". . . . . **$395 (£200)**

USMC SERGEANT'S DRESS BLUE UNIFORM

- Set of dress blues from a Marine Sergeant who most likely served in the Navy prior to the Marine Corps. Dark blue wool tunic has collar with gilt EGA devices, Line Sergeant rank chevrons, eight years service stripes, and left sleeve with Navy Gun Captain and "E" Excellence in Gunnery distinguishing marks. Interior sleeve lining has "1938-39" USMC date stamp. Includes red piped blue USMC dress trousers with no markings in the waistband, possibly private purchase. Also includes the white web waistbelt with brass belt buckle. . . . . **$225 (£115)**

USMC 1ST DIVISION TUNIC AND TROUSERS

- Model 1927 enlisted forest green wool tunic and trousers, Private First Class rank four-pocket tunic with bronze plastic buttons, EGA's on collar with good finish and two-place ribbon bar including Philippine Liberation and U.S.C.G. Expert Rifleman. Left sleeve with 1st Marine Division shoulder insignia and both sleeves with rank chevrons. Lined in green cotton. Complete with forest green wool trousers . . . . **$75 (£40)**

USMC 2ND DIVISION CORPORAL'S VANDEGRIFT JACKET

- Khaki cotton Vandegrift jacket, the Marine version of the Army Ike with blackened bronze EGA lapel insignia, green Corporal chevrons, and 2nd Marine Division Coral Snake insignia . . . . **$55 (£30)**

Jackets, Female

ARMY AIR FORCE WAC SERGEANT'S UNIFORM

- Women's Army Corps enlisted jacket, shirt and tie. Olive drab wool jacket with embroidered wool AAF shoulder sleeve insignia, Sergeant chevrons, two overseas service bars, and ruptured duck . . . . **$155 (£80)**

FAR EAST AIR FORCES WAC UNIFORM

- "Air Wac" uniform consisting of jacket, skirt, shirt, and tie. Women's Army Corps olive drab wool jacket with U.S. and Air Corps enlisted collar discs, Australian made

Far East Air Forces shoulder sleeve insignia, Honorable Discharge lozenge, two overseas service bars, and the early plastic WAAC buttons throughout. Complete with matching olive drab wool skirt, khaki cotton shirt, and khaki neck tie . . . .**$275 (£140)**

4TH AIR FORCE WAC SERGEANT'S UNIFORM

- Uniform consists of WAC pattern OD wool enlisted service tunic with 4th Air Force shoulder insignia, Sergeant rank chevrons, meritorious unit citation insignia, U.S. and WAC collar discs, and small enameled 4th Air Force distinctive insignias, matching issue skirt, and tan women's issue shirt with mothing around the bottom edges. . . . .**$285 (£145)**

8TH AIR FORCE WAC UNIFORM

- Olive drab enlisted wool tunic, skirt, and overseas cap. Olive drab wool tunic with US and WAC collar discs, right sleeve British-made 8th AAF insignia, left with US Strategic Air Forces in Europe insignia. Corporal chevrons and three bullion tape overseas service bars. Three-medal ribbon bar includes Good Conduct, WAC Service, and ETO campaign with one star. . .**$195 (£100)**

9TH AIR FORCE ARMY NURSE TUNIC AND CAP

- Army Nurse Corps officer's 1943 pattern service jacket of dark olive drab wool elastique has U.S. and Medical Corps caduceus insignias with "N" designations, gilt eagle buttons, silver pinback First Lieutenant rank insignias, and ETO Campaign medal ribbon bar with four campaign stars. Left shoulder has English-made embroidered 9th Air Force shoulder sleeve insignia decoratively sewn to the tunic and cuff with three overseas service

bars. ANC officer's sidecap has gold and black trim and 1st Lt. rank insignia . . . .**$125 (£65)**

9TH AIR FORCE WAC OFFICER'S "PINKS AND GREENS"

- Dark olive drab WAC officer's shirt has AAF shoulder sleeve insignia, interior with maker's tag "Miss Apollo" and content "20% virgin wool, 80% spun rayon." Accompanied by a contrasting pink wool necktie and pink wool elastique skirt . . . .**$145 (£75)**

ARMY NURSE CORPS LIEUTENANT'S UNIFORM

- Olive drab worsted wool tunic and matching skirt. Tunic has 2nd Lieutenant rank insignia, U.S. and ANC collar insignia, U.S. Army Forces in the Pacific Areas shoulder sleeve insignia, two overseas service bars and officer's cuff . . . .**$145 (£75)**

ARMY NURSE CORPS CAPTAIN'S SUMMER SERVICE UNIFORM

- Second pattern (1943) off-white service jacket with maroon piped epaulettes, mismatched Captain rank insignia, Sixth Service Command shoulder sleeve insignia, U.S. and Army Nurse Corps collar insignia, and maroon cuff braid . . . .**$195 (£100)**

ARMY NURSE CORPS CAPTAIN'S UNIFORM

- Olive drab wool barathea tunic with Captain rank insignia, US and Army Nurse Corps collar insignia, ETO ribbon bar with one star plus American Campaign and American Defense bars, three overseas service bars, and officer's cuff braid. Matching skirt, khaki wool issue shirt and khaki wool necktie completes the uniform. . . . .**$325 (£165)**

WAC sergeant's Ike jacket, $150-$175 (£75-£100). Charles D. Pautler

WAC uniform with 8th Air Force insignia, $175-$225 (£75-£100). www.advanceguardmilitaria.com

WAC officer's "pinks and greens," $125-$150 (£50-£75). www.advanceguardmilitaria.com

ARMY NURSE CORPS THEATER-MADE BUSH JACKET AND SLACKS

• Khaki cotton belted shirt weight jacket, long sleeved with two bellowed hip pockets, five-button front, and epaulettes. Interior has tag "MADE IN AUSTRALIA 1944." Matching khaki cotton trousers have side button closure and two bellows pockets in the front like the ones on the jacket. They are marked in the waistband with a broad arrow. These uniforms were ordered by the theater commander in Australia when it became apparent that there were going to be delays in supplying U.S. Army nurses stationed there with adequate clothing . . . . . **$250 (£125)**

NAVY WAVE'S UNIFORM AND HEADGEAR GROUP

• Group from a woman who served her country as a communications specialist/cryptographer includes dark blue wool WAVES pattern tunic and skirt, tunic with WAVES collar insignia and Petty Officer First Class rating badge with "Q" communications specialist/cryptographer designation. Headgear includes the WAVES sidecap, the dark blue soft brimmed hat with snap-in (interchangeable) crown, "U.S. NAVY" tall; and the scarce dark blue rubberized fabric rain cover with WAVES woven label. . . . .**$275 (£140)**

USMC WOMEN'S RESERVE SERGEANT'S TUNIC

• Forest green wool USMCWR winter service tunic with EGA lapel insignia, Sergeant rank chevron, four-place ribbon bar including Marine Good Conduct and Asiatic-Pacific Campaign . . . . **$135 (£70)**

Shirts, Male

A-1 ARMY AIR FORCE AIRCREW SHIRT

• Lightweight khaki wool gabardine shirt with AAF shoulder sleeve insignia, white embroidered Aircrew wing badge, four medal ribbons sewn directly to the shirt including Air Medal, Purple Heart, and ETO with one star, Staff Sergeant chevrons and flight engineer cuff tab. . . . .**$35 (£20)**

Army Nurse Corps theater-made bush jacket, $175-$200 (£80-£100). www.advanceguardmilitaria.com

A-1 Army Air Force shirt, $25-$35 (£10-£20). www.advanceguardmilitaria.com

Navy WAVE's uniform, $200-$275 (£100-£150).
www.advanceguardmilitaria.com

Army Nurse Corps captain's summer service uniform, $175-$235 (£80-£125).
www.advanceguardmilitaria.com

Army Nurse Corps captain's uniform complete with matching skirt, shirt and necktie, $300-$350 (£150-£180). www.advanceguardmilitaria.com

Army Nurse Corps lieutenant's uniform, $125-$175 (£55-£90).
www.advanceguardmilitaria.com

A-1 ARMY AIR FORCE SWEATER
- Type A-1 Mechanic's sweater of olive drab knit wool, heavy shaker knit with V-neck. . . . . **$65 (£35)**

ARMY ENLISTED ISSUE SHIRT
- OD wool flannel issue shirt . . . . **$15 (£7.50)**

ARMY OFFICER'S SHIRT
- Olive drab lightweight wool officer's shirt. . . . . **$25 (£15)**

ARMY ISSUE FIVE-BUTTON SWEATER
- Oive drab wool knit sweater with five-button front placket and standing collar. . . . . **$65 (£35)**

ARMY ISSUE V-NECK SWEATER
- Olive drab wool knit pullover sweater . . . . **$48 (£25)**

Dresses, Shirts, Female

ARMY NURSE CORPS OFF-DUTY DRESS
- One-piece dress of olive drab rayon crepe with self fabric belt, officer's cuff braid, and olive drab piped epaulettes. Has 6th Service Command and Persian Gulf Service Command shoulder sleeve insignia. Interior has woven label: "AUTHORIZED REGULATION U.S. ARMY NURSE CORPS UNIFORM". . . . . **$150 (£75)**

ARMY NURSE CORPS SEERSUCKER HOSPITAL DUTY DRESS
- Brown and white seersucker dress originally designed for Army nurses serving overseas. Wrapper-style dress has an interior tie and a seersucker fabric belt, no insignia. Complete with the matching seersucker nurse's cap with tie fastener. . . . . **$125 (£65)**

ARMY NURSE CORPS ISSUE SHIRT
- Khaki cotton female cut WAC/ANC issue shirt with brown composition buttons. . . . . **$28 (£15)**

ANC/WAC HBT UTILITY SHIRT
- Women's pattern fatigue shirt of olive drab herringbone twill. . . . . **$55 (£30)**

ARMY AIR FORCE "AIR WAC" SHIRT
- Private purchase or officer's shirt, rayon blend in a dark shade of khaki resembling the "pink" shade (olive drab No. 54). Quality shirt with epaulettes, box pleated pockets, and AAF shoulder sleeve insignia with an Air Technical Service Command tab. Complete with a dark olive drab wool necktie . . . . **$45 (£25)**

Trousers, Male

1942 PATTERN HBT TROUSERS, OD #7
- Large size 1942 Pattern HBT trousers updated to 1943 color specs (SPEC. No. 42C) in mint, unissued condition. These have contract tag listing maker, size "40 x 33" and 1945 production date. . . . . **$80 (£40)**

SECOND PATTERN HBT TROUSERS
- Second Pattern HBT trousers with cargo pockets. This is an evenly faded pair of trousers that has a sewn in size tag of 38W x 33L . . . . **$85 (£45)**

ARMY CAMOUFLAGE HERRINGBONE TWILL TROUSERS
- HBT camouflage trousers with two side cargo pockets, belt loops, knee reinforcement panels, and olive composition suspender and fly buttons . . . . **$395 (£200)**

Army Nurse Corps off-duty dress, $150-$175 (£75-£90). www.advanceguardmilitaria.com

Army enlisted man's shirt, $15-$25 (£8-£15).
Author's collection

Army five-button sweater, $50-$75 (£25-£40). Author's collection

USMC HERRINGBONE TWILL UTILITY TROUSERS, FIRST PATTERN

- Model 1941 first type herringbone twill fatigue trousers. Olive drab with bronze "U.S. MARINE CORPS" riveted buttons and watch pocket detail . . . . **$195 (£100)**

USMC HERRINGBONE TWILL UTILITY TROUSERS, SECOND PATTERN

- Model 1941, second type trousers of olive drab HBT with "U.S. MARINE CORPS" riveted buttons . . . . . . **$95 (£50)**

USMC P1942 CAMOUFLAGE HERRINGBONE TWILL TROUSERS

- Reversible green and brown dominant pattern sides, waistband has sewn belt loops, domed snap button fly closure, and a single front and rear pocket for each side. . . . . **$475 (£240)**

USMC P1944 REVERSIBLE CAMOUFLAGE TROUSERS, FIRST PATTERN

- Reversible green and brown HBT camouflage trousers have exterior belt loops, grommets for use with the P1941 suspenders, side pockets with domed snap closures, large seat pocket, fly closure with blackened plain riveted utility buttons, and cuffs with integral blousing tie cord . . . . **$385 (£195)**

USMC P1944 CAMOUFLAGE HERRINGBONE TWILL TROUSERS, SECOND PATTERN

- Second pattern P1944 reversible green and brown HBT camouflage trousers have sewn openings for lacing a waistbelt, grommets for use with the P1941 suspenders, side pockets with domed snap closures, large seat pocket, fly closure with black "USMC" riveted utility buttons, and cuffs with integral blousing tie cord . . . . **$325 (£165)**

WINTER COMBAT TROUSERS

- Bib-front olive drab cotton overalls with olive drab wool lining and cotton adjustable suspender system. Front and sides with zipper closures, groin with short relief zipper access. Popularly referred to as "Tanker Bibs" . **$100 (£50)**

Army Nurse Corps herringbone twill shirt, $50-$65 (£25-£35).
www.advanceguardmilitaria.com

Woman's Army Air Force shirt with necktie, $35-$50 (£20-£25). www.advanceguardmilitaria.com

USMC P1942 camouflage herringbone twill trousers, $450-$500 (£200-£250). www.advanceguardmilitaria.com

USMC P1944 camouflage herringbone twill trousers, $300-$375 (£150-£190). www.advanceguardmilitaria.com

Winter trousers with kersey lining, $35-$75 (£20-£35). Author's collection

1942 pattern "Jungle" boots, $275-$325 (£140-£160).
www.advanceguardmilitaria.com

Army service shoes, $125-$150 (£65-£75). Author's collection

Army "double-buckle" combat boots, $125-$175 (£65-£90). Author's collection

WAC low quarter ankle boots, $65-$85 (£35-£45).
www.advanceguardmilitaria.com

WAC brown leather shoes, $25-$50 (£10-£35). Charles D. Pautler

PACIFIC THEATER JUNGLE BOOTS

- 1942 pattern "Jungle" boots are made of light olive canvas with black rubber soles, blackened metal lace eyelets and light olive laces . . . . **$295 (£150)**

ARMY PARATROOPER BOOTS

- Brown leather lace-up paratrooper boots with cap toes. . . . .**$225 (£115)**

USMC PARATROOPER BOOTS

- Black leather high-top parachutist boots with brown laces in instep grommets with speed-lace fittings above, black composition rubber soles with chamfered heels. . . . .**$685 (£345)**

ARMY SERVICE SHOES

- Brown leather service shoes with cap toes, brown painted eyelets, and gray-green shoelaces with brown painted end tabs . . . . **$125 (£65)**

ARMY FIELD SHOES

- Three-quarter ankle height, cap-toed shoes of rough-out brown leather with black composition soles and khaki laces . . . . **$225 (£115)**

ARMY "DOUBLE BUCKLE" COMBAT BOOTS

- Brown rough-out leather double-buckle pattern combat boots have original laces . . . . **$125 (£65)**

USMC COMBAT SHOES

- Brown rough-out leather boondockers with brown composition soles, marked. . . . . **$165 (£85)**

TYPE A-6A FLYING BOOTS

- Type A-6A flying boots have black rubber traction soles, brown sheepskin uppers with Army Air Forces winged star insignia decal, and and thick pile white fleece interiors . . . . **$185 (£95)**

TYPE A-10 FLEECE FLIGHT BOOTS

- Pair of early war fleece-lined shearing winter boots, exterior in natural finish with brown seam covers, upper arch strap with buckle, drawstring top and rubber soles and heels. Rare component of the "Alaskan Suit" adopted in 1941 . . . . **$225 (£115)**

M-380B NAVY AVIATOR'S FLEECE BOOTS

- Brown sheepskin fleece flyer's boots have black rubber soles, double zipper front closure, tongue has black and gold woven nomenclature label "BOOTS - FLIGHT / MEDIUM / Bu Aero-Navy / Spec. No. M380B". . . . . **$155 (£80)**

Footwear, Female

WAC FIELD BOOTS

- Brown leather, double buckle closure . . . . **$85 (£45)**

WAC ROUGH-OUT LOW QUARTERS

- Ankle shoes of brown rough-out leather . . . . . . **$65 (£35)**

WASP OR WAVE SHOES

- Ankle-height black leather shoes with black cotton laces that would conform to the regs for either a WASP or WAVE. Interior with faint "ADDISON FOOTWEAR , INC." manufacturer's stamp and QM information. . . . . **$95 (£50)**

CHAPTER 2

HEADGEAR

One of the most popular, focused areas of World War II collectibles is headgear. Whether German helmets, fatigue "boonie" hats, or dress visor caps, nothing seems to connect with collectors more than a soldier's head covering.

Headgear collectors can be divided into three groups: helmet collectors, visor cap collectors, and a mixture of the two. The first group, helmet collectors, are, by far, the most numerous.

HELMETS

Probably the most sought-after souvenir among British Tommies and American GIs (after Luger pistols) were German helmets. Images of jackboots and the steel-curtained helmets of the German soldier had permeated news reels, magazines, and newspapers since 1934. Prior to World War II, the boys (who would later serve as the soldiers in the global conflict) had played with the helmet trophies that their dads, brothers, and uncles brought home as souvenirs of the Great War. People recognized the basic shape. So, it was no wonder that soldiers clamored to bring home the Teutonic helmets.

It has only been during the last few years, however, that helmets of other participant nations have gained popularity. The steadily increasing prices of German helmets has directed many collectors to consider the headgear of Allied and Axis nations. Helmets of Japan, Bulgaria, and eastern European nations have all gained value in recent years.

Though German helmet prices have steadily increased since World War II, the meteoric rise has been in the prices of U.S. helmets. Surplus stocks of American M1 helmets kept prices low for years following the end of World War II. Only as collectors sifted through the piles of surplus helmets to find the rare examples with some sort of camouflage or painted insignia did the hobby take notice of GI helmets.

The key to the value of any helmet is two-fold: relative rarity and markings. An un-marked, Model 36 Soviet helmet is rare because so few survived the war, having been mostly replaced by Models 39 and 40. On the other hand, an American M1 helmet with a chinstrap on non-swiveling loops, is relatively common. With liner, such a helmet will sell for $100-$175 (in 1999, it was not uncommon to purchase one for $20!). However, the same helmet with the small, painted insignia of the 2nd Infantry Division will jump to $800-$1,000. Why? Because very few U.S. helmets were decorated with any sort of insignia. And those that were usually received a layer of

Collecting Hints

Pros:

- Headgear is extremely personal. The collector can determine some of a soldier's history from a single piece.
- Supply is plentiful. It is easy for a collector to find a level that is both affordable and enjoyable.
- Display is not difficult. A few shelves and hat stands will allow a collector to adequately and safely exhibit their items.
- Items are small enough that shipping is not a big issue, enabling a collector to buy from any source in the world.

Cons:

- Fakes abound, so if a helmet displays any sort of decal or painted insignia, it is best to be suspicious.
- Helmets are prone to shifts in humidity. Rust is the biggest threat to a helmet collection.
- It is easy to get carried away and acquire more than one can enjoy or even afford. Supply is high, so collectors should exercise discipline and purchase wisely rather than wildly.
- If you decide to collect either helmets or visor caps, rare examples will run into the thousands of dollars.

Availability ★★★★

Price ★★

Reproduction Alert ★★★

paint when they were reissued during or after the War. This phenomenon is not limited to U.S. helmets. It didn't take long for collectors to realize that the value of German helmets was not in the shell but rather, the markings on the shell. A simple M40 steel helmet with liner and no decals or other insignia will sell for around $185-$285. But, if that same helmet has a single Army decal, add $300 to the price. If it has a single SS decal, add about $1,500. Same shell, three different configurations for three widely disparate prices.

Value based on markings, however, has lead to a serious pitfall within the hobby. Unscrupulous dealers can't resist the temptation to "upgrade" a German helmet or paint something on an American shell. If you are fortunate enough to obtain a helmet with a trusted provenance, you will have a hard time convincing others of its validity. Similarly, if you want to buy a special helmet, you should buy only from a source that you trust and who offers a return policy should you later learn that the helmet is fake.

Visor Caps

When military collectors or dealers describe themselves as "visor cap collectors," they usually mean they collect Third Reich visor caps. The term could apply to the headgear worn by a variety of nationalities, but usually, within the hobby, the term "visor cap" refers to a peaked cap worn by German military and paramilitary personnel.

Collectors of German visor caps approach their hobby with the same intensity that dagger collec-

tors do. They study and know the nuances of maker marks, celluloid plakets, lining material, and fabric samples. They talk among themselves with a level of jargon that seems to purposefully exclude the "non-headgear" collector. Don't let that intimidate you, however. They have simply specialized in order to navigate a section of the hobby that is fraught with fakes.

Visor caps from the principal combatant nations are quite plentiful. Why? In simplest terms, visor caps were part of dress uniforms. As such, they survived the war in the closets and trunks of the veterans.

Visor caps celebrate a soldier's military nature. Wearing one announces to others, "Here is a warrior. He walks erect and is smart in his bearing, decisions and prowess." Visor caps usually display some sort of national insignia and often convey (through colored piping or special insignia), the wearer's branch of service. This is the sort of stuff a collector loves...variety of material and enough clues to piece together some sort of understanding about the soldier who wore it. For example, a gray wool cap with a dark green band with a cockade in a wreath on the front, an eagle with a swastika in its talons above the wreath, and white piping around the crown tells the collector that this cap was intended for a German infantry soldier. Without knowing the soldier's name, the collector knows something about him. The collector, through the cap, is able to bond with history.

Every branch of service in the German military had its own unique color and insignia combina-

tions, which creates the other lure to a collector: variety. German visor caps are seemingly endless, so a collector can devote an entire career to this one form.

Visor caps of other nationalities have not been as quick to rise in value as German caps, though. The prices of American visor caps have remained stagnant for many years, although several attempts have been made to divide two basic cap forms (enlisted man's and officer's) into many groups. Other than the national seal on the front of either form, differences are limited to manufacturer, body color (basically, olive drab or khaki) and shape (the most desirable being the romantic "crusher" cap often associated with flight crews or other personnel who wore headphones over their caps). It doesn't take long for the collector to become bored and expand into different areas.

Whatever the cap, condition plays a big role in its relative value. You might pull a Japanese Type 45 visor cap out of grandpa's war trunk, but if it is moth damaged, crushed and smelly, you will have a hard time selling it to a collector. Likewise, if you are going to try to sell a U.S. enlisted man's visor, condition is about the only thing that will set it apart from the thousands of other examples on the market.

UTILITY HEADGEAR

"Utility" is a catch-all word to describe all the fatigue caps and hats, winter hoods, and other non-dress coverings. Not many collectors specialize in just utility headgear, but rather, obtain examples as parts of larger groupings. Utility headgear, by its very nature, generally does not display a variety of insignia, so collecting it usually is based on types of headgear—a single example of a particular variety sufficing the need to fill a "hole" in a collection. Therefore, the demand for utility headgear is not as high as it is for helmets or visor caps.

Values for utility headgear tends to be determined by function. An American GI's herringbone twill fatigue cap will run about $35-$55 because so many were made, quite a few survived, and the demand is low. A ski trooper's mountain cap, on the other hand, will run $285-$350 because few were made and they were intended for a small group of "elite" soldiers and were not available to masses of U.S. soldiers.

SIZE MATTERS

When it comes to headgear (and uniforms, for that matter), size matters. If you have two German helmets with the same markings but one is a size 56 and the other a 64, the latter is going to command about a 30 percent higher price. How could size possibly matter, if it is the insignia on the helmet that is the primary price determinant? It is fact of which the hobby should not be proud. Size influencing price means only one thing: People intend to put these on their heads. The bigger the size, the higher the price. It is a dark fact of the hobby.

CAMOUFLAGE IS AN AESTHETIC THING

Evaluating camouflaged helmets is a very difficult area. Because most camouflage was applied to helmets in the field and not at the factory, no two camouflaged helmets are alike. Therefore, one has to develop the sense of an art critic to be able to recognize a "pleasing" (that is, a desirable and expensive) camo job as opposed to a more "pedestrian" paint job. Whereas a mud-splattered M1 German M35 helmet is probably a good representative of camouflage helmets of the Eastern front, a four-colored, spray painted example has a lot more eye appeal, and therefore, will command a higher price.

Consider camouflaged helmets carefully. It is just as easy to splatter paint on a helmet today as it was in 1944. The lure of high profit has pried open many paint cans in the last 20 years. Know your source before you hand over cash for any camouflaged helmets. A good rule to follow: "It is fake until the dealer can convince me that it is not."

Belgian artillery enlisted man's side cap with tassel, $25-$50 (£15-£25).
www.advanceguardmilitaria.com

Belgian Service Corps enlisted man's side cap, $25-$50 (£15-£25).
www.advanceguardmilitaria.com

When Germany invaded Belgium, the defenders were wearing Model 26/32 steel helmets, $95-$150 (£50-£75). Peter Suciu

The Bulgarian Model 36/A steel helmet has a rolled edge, two vent holes and six rivets, $50-$125 (£25-£60). Peter Suciu

The Bulgarian Model 36/C steel helmet has an unrolled edge and small crest on dome. Two versions were made: one with a long-visor and this short-visor helmet, $75-$150 (£40-£75). Peter Suciu

BELGIUM

Caps, Visor, Officer

VISOR CAP, ARTILLERY OFFICER

- Model 1930 junior officer cap of dark blue wool with red piping around the crown and top of the band, obverse with gold and silver multi-toned bullion and red silk crown over an oval black velvet badge with gold bullion "A" cypher for King Albert I, bordered in gold bullion and red silk, complete with gold bullion chin cord with gilt rampant lion side buttons and bound black composition visor . . . . **$85 (£45)**

Caps, Visor, Enlisted

VISOR CAP, ORDNANCE ENLISTED

- Khaki wool visor cap with matching cloth covered visor and chinstrap, gilt side buttons, obverse with with enamel national cockade and silvered crossed cannon on a wheel Royal Army Ordnance Corps insignia, light purple cord branch piping around the top of the band, lined in light purple cotton with celluloid sweat shield and Brugge maker's label . . . . **$65 (£35)**

MODEL 43 CAP, FLEMISH COLLABORATIONIST VLAAMISCHE WACHT

- Black wool M43 field cap with cloth covered visor and folding neck cape with button closure. White machine embroidered oak leaf wreath on black wool field on the front. Pebbled buttons retain black finish; lined in dark blue rayon . . . . **$475 (£240)**

Caps, Visorless, Enlisted

SIDE CAP, ARTILLERY ENLISTED

- Khaki wool twill cap with scalloped side band piped in orange-crimson with royal blue tassel and brass crown and crossed cannon on left side, lined in khaki cotton. . . . . **$40 (£20)**

SIDE CAP, SERVICE CORPS ENLISTED

- Khaki wool cap with scalloped side band piped in dark blue with dark blue tassel and brass initials "SA," lined in khaki cotton. . . . . **$25 (£15)**

Helmets

MODEL 1926/32 COMBAT HELMET

- French manufactured Model 1926 Adrian helmet with dark khaki finish, obverse with pronounced lion's face front plate . . . . **$95 (£50)**

MODEL 1935 TANKER HELMET

- Model 35 tanker's helmet with dark khaki finish, Belgian lion badge and leather crash bumper, crown with comb. Interior has black leather liner and adjustable chinstrap. . . . . **$295 (£150)**

PRO-NAZI INTERNAL SECURITY TROOPS HELMET

- Dutch M.34 helmet with dark midnight blue finish, obverse with the blue and silver oak leaf wreath oval decal used by both the Vlaamsche Wacht (Flemish Watch) and

Garde Wallonne Belgian pro-German internal security troops . . . .**$465 (£235)**

BULGARIA

M36/A COMBAT HELMET

* Steel helmet with a rolled edge, two vent holes, and six rivets. This model was the first type of the Model 36 produced and was manufactured in Brno, Czechoslovakia. This helmet features the tri-color transfer of Bulgaria. . . . .**$85 (£45)**

BULGARIAN M36/C COMBAT HELMET

* Model 36/C steel helmet with unrolled edge and small crest on dome. This is one of three patterns of helmets produced for the Bulgarian army before WWII. This particular model was German-produced . . . .**$175 (£90)**

M36/C "SHORT VISOR" COMBAT HELMET

* Steel helmet with unrolled edge and small crest on dome. This is a variation of the M-36/C with a shorter visor than the standard version . . . .**$75 (£40)**

MODEL 1938 "LUFTSCHUTZ" HELMET

* Produced in Germany for the air defense personnel , this helmet design is often called the "Gladiator" style. These helmets were supplied to Bulgaria for air and civil defense use. Has Bulgarian Air Defense multi-colored shield and rampant lion . . . .**$250 (£125)**

CHINA

FIELD CAP, NATIONALIST ARMY

* Khaki rough corded cotton field cap resembling the German M43 in cut and style, with blue and white enameled Chinese sun badge and two stamped brass buttons, interior with rough loosely woven blue and white cotton lining and the remains of a brown leather sweatband . . . .**$525 (£265)**

CZECHOSLOVAKIA

MODEL 1932 COMBAT HELMET

* Known as the "last pattern" because the Czechs had gone through many models of steel helmet before finally deciding upon this on design. This pattern helmet was produced in large numbers from the early thirties until the German takeover in 1938. Brown-gray finish with white leather five-pad liner system and chinstrap. Marked on the inside rear skirt with Czech lion and "38" date. . . . .**$375 (£190)**

MODEL 1932 COMBAT HELMET WITH SLOVAK INSIGNIA

* The Slovak army fought alongside the Germans during the Soviet campaign. During this campaign the Slovaks painted the rim blue and added the Slovak cross to both sides. This was reportedly done to avoid confusion with the Soviet helmet . . . .**$675 (£340)**

The Model 1938 "Luftschutz" helmet was produced in Germany and supplied to Bulgaria for air defense personnel, $250-$350 (£125-£175). Peter Suciu

Nationalist Chinese Army field cap, $450-$650 (£225-£325). Minnesota Military Museum

Nationalist Chinese Army with hand-painted insignia, $1,200-$2,500 (£600-£1,250). Minnesota Military Museum

Czech Model 32 steel helmet, $300-$450 (£150-£225). Peter Suciu

The Slovak Army marked its helmets with crosses so its German allies would not confuse them with Russian soldiers, $500-$750 (£250-£375). Peter Suciu

Danish Model 1923 combat helmet, $300-$400 (£150-£200). Peter Suciu

Finnish officer's Model 1936 wool field cap, $175-$300 (£90-£150). www.advanceguardmilitaria.com

Finland's Model 1936 wool field cap for enlisted soldiers, $375-$450 (£190-£225). www.advanceguardmilitaria.com

This Finnish M35 helmet was actually produced by Hungary, $200-$350 (£100-£175). Peter Suciu

French Model 26 "Adrian" combat helmet, $125-$275 (£65-£140). Peter Suciu

DENMARK

MODEL 1923 COMBAT HELMET

- Model 1923 steel helmet with arsenal repainted olive drab finish. Model 1927 bronze national emblem on the front. Carrying strap loop pierced in rear skirt, interior with brown leather liner and chinstrap . . . . . **$350 (£175)**

MODEL 1939 POLICE HELMET

- Danish reserve police force helmet, first used from 1942 until 1944. These helmets were called the "Amalienborg Helmet," as they were used by the police units that protected the Amalienborg Palace . . . . **$100 (£50)**

FINLAND

Caps, Officer

FIELD CAP, ARTILLERY OFFICER

- Model 1936 field cap of fine quality gray wool twill, folding neck cape with red wool branch of service piping and gray rampant lion buttons, cloth visor, and obverse with enameled white and blue officer's cockade. Interior has gray oilcloth sweatband and purple-gray silk lining. . . . . **$465 (£235)**

SIDE CAP, OFFICER

- Model 1922 side cap construction style cap of field gray wool twill with fur side capes, obverse with enameled officer's cockades, and interior has blue-green cotton covered quilted lining over fleece felt insulation. . . . . **$325 (£165)**

FUR CAP, OFFICER

- Model 1939 fur cap of gray wool twill with gray fur front and folding side panels semi-permanently retained by stitches to the crown. Front has gilt and enameled officer's cockade. Interior has quilted gray rayon lining. . . . . **$475 (£240)**

Caps, Enlisted

FIELD CAP, ENLISTED

- Model 1936 gray and brown mixed wool field cap has neck curtain that buttons in the front with two small pressed wood buttons, obverse has early style 1918-1922 period cockade, and fabric covered stiffened short visor. Interior has brown quilted cotton lining . . . . **$375 (£190)**

Helmets

COMBAT HELMET, HUNGARIAN REISSUE

- One of the 75,000 reworked Hungarian Model 35/38 helmets sent to Finland for the war with Russia. Helmet has field gray finish. Interior has brown leather liner and chinstrap . . . . **$385 (£190)**

The Soviet Union invaded Finland on November 30, 1939. When the armistice finally came on March 13, 1940, the Finns counted 25,000 dead, 55,000 wounded and 450,000 homeless.

FRANCE

Caps

SIDE CAP, CORPORAL
- Model 1918 enlisted side cap of olive drab wool with double red wool braid Corporal rank chevron on obverse. Interior has white cotton sweatband with "1938" date on the underside . . . . **$55 (£30)**

SIDE CAP, FOREIGN LEGION NCO
- Model 1918 enlisted side cap of olive drab wool with single gold bullion braid Sergeant rank chevron with green Legion branch color border on obverse. White cotton sweatband with faint issue mark . . . . **$75 (£40)**

SIDE CAP, CAPTAIN
- Brown wool twill side cap with Captain rank insignia on front. Interior with green embossed maker's stamp on brown leather sweatband . . . . **$40 (£20)**

BERET, CHASSEUR
- Classic large midnight blue wool chasseur beret with yellow embroidered hunting horn insignia and interior lining with maker's label and size "58" . . . . . . **$125 (£65)**

NAVY CAP, LE HARDI
- Red piped blue wool flat hat has "LE HARDI" ship's tally. Silver bullion fouled anchor insignia on the front. Interior has black leather sweatband . . . . **$65 (£35)**

Helmets

MODEL 1919 TANKER HELMET
- Adrian helmet with horizon blue finish. This pattern helmet was a modification of the Model 1915 helmet to fit the needs of France's new armored force, the Artillerie Speciale. "Flaming bomb" badge and padded black leather crash guard on the front. Interior complete with brown second model Adrian liner and dark brown leather chinstrap. . . . . **$400 (£200)**

MODEL 1926 INFANTRY COMBAT HELMET
- Dark olive painted finish with 1937 pattern round badge featuring the Infantry flaming bomb insignia. Brown leather liner and chinstrap . . . . **$125 (£65)**

MODEL 1935 TANKER HELMET
- First pattern Model 1935 Tanker helmet with dark horizon blue finish. Obverse has 1915 pattern Artillery badge. Front brim has padded leather crash bumper and interior has grained black leather suspension liner with a wide harness chinstrap assembly. These were issued to tankers, motorcyclists, and specially equipped motorized cavalry troops . . . . **$325 (£165)**

GERMANY

Visor Caps, Officer

VISOR CAP, ARMY ARTILLERY OFFICER
- Gray wool twill peaked visor cap with wartime pattern aluminum Army eagle and wreathed cockade on obverse, red artillery/ordnance Waffenfarbe piping around crown and flanking the bottle green band, aluminum bullion chinstrap and pebbled side buttons, and black Vulkanfiber visor . . . . **$585 (£295)**

VISOR CAP, ARMY CHAPLAIN
- Superior quality cap of fine field gray wool with bottle green wool band and violet piping, obverse with silvered eagle, wreath and national cockade, silver Gothic cross positioned between the eagle and wreath. Interior with cream silk lining and celluloid sweat shield with gold leaf maker's mark, brown leather sweatband, shows light service wear. . . . . **$2,250 (£1,125)**

VISOR CAP, ARMY INFANTRY OFFICER
- Field gray wool twill cap with black Vulkanfiber visor and bottle green wool band with white Infantry Waffenfarbe piping, aluminum two-piece eagle and wreath, Army eagle insignia and subdued officer's braid chinstrap. . . . .**$565 (£285)**

VISOR CAP, ARMY MEDICAL OFFICER
- Field gray wool twill Sattelform profile cap has black Vulkanfiber visor, bottle green wool band, blue Medical Waffenfarbe piping, aluminum two-piece cockade and wreath, and Army eagle insignia, and aluminum bullion officer's braid chinstrap. . . . . **$675 (£340)**

VISOR CAP, ARMY MOUNTAIN TROOPS OFFICER
- Field gray wool visor cap has light green crown and band piping, dark green band with wreathed cockade insignia, crown with aluminum Army eagle over bi-color Edelweiss mountain troops insignia, aluminum bullion chinstrap, and black lacquered Vulkanfiber visor. Interior has gold silk lining with silver embossed Vienna maker's logo under celluloid sweat protector, pierced tan leather sweatband stamped with "'Erel' Stirnschutz / D.R.G.M." . . . . **$945 (£475)**

far right: German Army officer's cap, $875-$1,200 (£440-£600).

www.advanceguardmilitaria.com

right: Army medical officer's visor cap, $650-$900 (£325-£450). www.advanceguardmilitaria.com

Waffen SS visor cap for a medical officer, $3,000-$3,650 (£1,500-£1,825). Hermann Historica OHG

Luftwaffe officer's visor cap, $675-$900 (£340-£450). Minnesota Military Museum

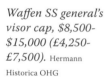

Waffen SS general's visor cap, $8,500-$15,000 (£4,250-£7,500). Hermann Historica OHG

German political leader's cap, $600-$1,200 (£300-£600). Minnesota Military Museum

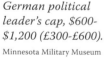

Germany Army infantry enlisted man's visor cap, $450-$650 (£225-£325). www.advanceguardmilitaria.com

VISOR CAP, ARMY MOUNTAIN TROOPS MEDICAL OFFICER

- Field gray wool visor cap with peak front profile has "bottle green" band with cornflower blue Medical Waffenfarbe band and crown piping; obverse with subdued aluminum oak leaf wreath and cockade, aluminum Army eagle over bi-color Edelweiss mountain troops insignia, black lacquered visor, and aluminum bullion officer's chinstrap . . . . **$925 (£465)**

VISOR CAP, ARMY PANZER OFFICER

- Field gray wool twill with dark green band and rose piping, metal eagle, cockade and wreath with soft gray patina to finish, aluminum bullion chin cord and pebbled side buttons, and black fiber visor. . . . . **$945 (£475)**

VISOR CAP, LUFTWAFFE OFFICER

- Field gray wool twill visored cap with the classic Sattelform profile, aluminum bullion crown and band piping, black mohair band, aluminum bullion officer's chin cord with pebble-grained side buttons, and bound edge black lacquered visor with green checkered reverse; obverse of cap complete with bullion embroidered Luftwaffe eagle and Luftwaffe pattern bullion embroidered wreathed national cockade. . . . . **$700 (£350)**

Visor Caps, Enlisted

VISOR CAP, ALLGEMEINE SS ENLISTED

- Black wool twill visor cap in the Sattelform profile, with white wool piping, black wool band and black lacquered Vulkanfiber visor. Obverse has silvered finish SS Totenkopf insignia and black leather chinstrap, lacks eagle device. Interior has maker embossed brown leather sweatband and heavily worn ochre brown oilcloth lining lacking celluloid sweat shield but retaining imprinted "SS" runes insignia. Visor interior has brown finish, retains a faint but legible "SS/RZM" ink stamp. A rare SS issue cap in need of a few simple restorations.
  . . . . **$3,850 (£1,925)**

VISOR CAP, ARMY INFANTRY ENLISTED

- Field gray wool twill has bottle green band and Infantry white Waffenfarbe piping, aluminum two-piece wreath and cockade set, Army eagle, adjustable black leather chinstrap, and black Vulkanfiber visor. . . . . . **$485 (£245)**

VISOR CAP, ARMY JÄGER ENLISTED

- Field gray wool crown has bottle green wool band and light green corded piping, aluminum Army cap eagle and wreathed cockade insignia, adjustable black leather chinstrap, and black visor . . . . **$445 (£225)**

VISOR CAP, ARMY PANZER ENLISTED

- Field gray wool twill visor cap has rose Panzer crown and band piping, bottle green band with gray aluminum wreath and cockade and eagle. Black Vulkanfiber visor and black lacquered leather adjustable chinstrap.
  . . . . **$750 (£375)**

VISOR CAP, KRIEGSMARINE ENLISTED WHITE TOP

- Navy blue wool cap body has black mohair band with embroidered Navy wreath and cockade insignia, ad-

justable black leather chinstrap secured by anchor side buttons, and obverse with black Vulkanfiber visor; removable white heavy cotton crown has gilt embroidered Kriegsmarine eagle on navy blue wool backing.
....**$595 (£300)**

VISOR CAP, LUFTWAFFE FLAK ARTILLERY ENLISTED

- Sattelform Schirmütze of Luftwaffe blue-gray twill with red Artillery branch of service piping, later pattern aluminum Luftwaffe eagle and winged oak leaf wreath with national cockade, black mohair band, black adjustable chinstrap, and black composition visor .....**$415 (£210)**

VISOR CAP, LUFTWAFFE CIVILIAN EMPLOYEE

- Luftwaffe blue-gray wool visor cap has Bordeaux red colored band and piping, aluminum political eagle and winged wreathed swastika cap insignia identical to that worn by Luftwaffe airfield fire brigades, bound black Vulkanfiber visor, and adjustable black leather chinstrap.
....**$825 (£415)**

VISOR CAP, LUFTWAFFE FLIGHT/ FALLSCHIRMJÄGER NCO

- Luftwaffe blue-gray wool visor cap with aluminum Luftwaffe eagle emblem and winged national cockade and wreath insignia, yellow Waffenfarbe piping around crown and black mohair band, bound black composition visor, and black leather chinstrap ....**$795 (£400)**

Field Caps

FELDMÜTZE, ARMY MODEL 1934 ENLISTED

- Field gray wool M34 field cap with machine-sewn woven Army eagle and national cockade insignias, obverse without branch of service insignia as that became officially out of fashion in mid-1942...............**$385 (£195)**

FELDMÜTZE, PANZER MODEL 1934 PANZER ENLISTED

- Cap of field gray wool with rose Panzer soutache branch of service braid on obverse with BeVo woven Army eagle and national cockade; interior has field gray and tan cotton lining with size stamp "57" ....**$865 (£435)**

FELDMÜTZE, ARMY M1938 ENLISTED TROPICAL

- Model 1938 field cap of olive cotton twill, obverse with BeVo woven blue Army national eagle and cockade. Interior has red cotton lining stamped with maker's name.
....**$650 (£325)**

FELDMÜTZE, PANZER MODEL 1942 PANZER ENLISTED

- 1934 enlisted pattern field cap of black wool with machine-sewn cockade and Army eagle emblem woven on black backgrounds, sides with reinforced ventilation grommets, and interior with black cotton twill lining printed with maker's stamp. Absence of soutache Waffenfarbe conforms with 1942 regulations
....**$1,095 (£550)**

FELDMÜTZE, PANZER ENLISTED TROPICAL

- Unissued condition with pink soutache. Maker marked, size 60....................................**$1,675 (£840)**

Army police enlisted man's visor cap, $550-$800 (£275-£400).
Minnesota Military Museum

Luftwaffe civilian employee's visor cap, $750-$900 (£375-£450).
www.advanceguardmilitaria.com

Luftwaffe enlisted man's visor cap, $450-$795 (£225-£400).
Charles D. Pautler

Very early SA visor cap, $1,800-$2,500 (£900-£1,250).
Minnesota Military Museum

Model 1934 enlisted Army field cap, $350-$550 (£175-£275). www.advanceguardmilitaria.com

Privately purchased German Army wool cap, $275-$350 (£140-£375).

Charles D. Pautler

Luftwaffe tropical issue field cap, $850-$1,300 (£425-£650).

Minnesota Military Museum

Luftwaffe enlisted man's field cap, $275-$395 (£140-£200).

Minnesota Military Museum

Black wool NSD-Studentenbund (indoctrination service) side cap with RZM sealed pattern control tag still attached, $500-$650 (£250-£325).

www.advanceguardmilitaria.com

Black wool German Motor Corps (NSKK) field cap, $450-$600 (£225-£300). www.advanceguardmilitaria.com

Army Model 1938 medical officer's field cap, $700-$900 (£340-£450). www.advanceguardmilitaria.com

FELDMÜTZE, LUFTWAFFE ENLISTED

- Enlisted issue cap of blue-gray wool with eagle and cockade insignia, gray rayon lining . . . . **$295 (£150)**

FELDMÜTZE, NSDAP/NSD OFFICIAL

- Black wool NSD-Studentenbund (indoctrination service) side cap has white cord piping, obverse has RZM sealed pattern control number tag. Interior black twill lining has large brown and white RZM tag with control numbers
. . . . **$525 (£265)**

FELDMÜTZE, ARMY MODEL
1934 MEDICAL OFFICER

- Wehrmacht officer's M34 field cap with Medical soutache . . . . **$875 (£440)**

FELDMÜTZE, ARMY MODEL
1938 MEDICAL OFFICER

- Officer's Model 1938 Feldmütze of field gray wool has aluminum bullion cord piping; obverse has woven Army eagle insignia and national cockade with blue Medical Waffenfarbe piping in an inverted V above the cockade. Sides each have a single field gray painted metal ventilation grommet. Interior has gray cotton twill lining with maker's stamp, size stamp "57", and issue stamp "St. / A.R.36" . . . . **$725 (£365)**

FELDMÜTZE, ARMY PANZER OFFICER

- Black wool field cap with aluminum bullion crown seam and side panel piping, obverse with Panzer rose Waffenfarbe soutache piping, BeVo woven cockade and Army eagle insignia. Interior has dark gray rayon lining and backed blackened metal side vent grommets **$800 (£400)**

FIELD CAP, HITLER YOUTH
LUFTWAFFE FLAK HELPER

- Blue gray wool Flakhelfer service cap similar to the Luftwaffe 44 pattern, obverse with cloth visor, single button neck cape closure and embroidered blue, white, and black diamond Hitler Youth insignia . . . . **$325 (£165)**

FIELD CAP, ARMY MODEL 1943
MOUNTAIN TROOPS ENLISTED

- Field gray wool M43 cap with BeVo woven Army eagle and cockade emblem, ear cape with buttons made to resemble leather knots as was a popular non-regulation substitution for the small pebble buttons, left side has a gray metal Edelweiss cap insignia. Cap interior has gray synthetic lining. Side cape interior has short tape pulls
. . . . **$600 (£300)**

FIELD CAP, AUXILIARY FORCES MODEL 1943

- Regulation pattern issue cap of dark blue wool with gray pebbled metal buttons closing the folding neck cape, lining of dark blue rayon. Variation used by many auxiliary and foreign volunteer units . . . . **$275 (£140)**

FIELD CAP, LUFTWAFFE MODEL 1943 ENLISTED

- Enlisted issue cap of lightweight blue-gray wool with eagle and cockade on trapezoid wool field, gray rayon lining with size stamp "56" . . . . **$360 (£180)**

FIELD CAP, RAD REED GREEN HBT

- Model 1942 Sommermütze summer field service cap made of reed green herringbone twill material with cloth covered visor, side panels and stitching to simulate a folding ear cape, and obverse with woven RAD insignia; interior has brown cotton twill lining with size "59" and "RBNr. 0/0390/0377" stamp . . . .**$395 (£200)**

FIELD CAP, SA M1943

• SA brown wool M43 field cap has folding side curtain with two brown composition button front closure, obverse with silver SA cap eagle on brown background, and RZM sealed pattern control number metal tag. Interior has vented brown leather sweatband and brown cotton twill lining with size stamp "56." The cloth RZM tag is loose but still with the hat, with control numbers, "RZM" logo, and printed inscription "Feldmütze nach Vorschrift" (Field cap according to regulation).
. . . .**$895 (£450)**

FIELD CAP, WAFFEN SS MODEL 1943 ENLISTED

• Waffen SS M43 enlisted man's cap made from Italian gabardine wool with trapezoid insignia . . . **$1,675 (£840)**

FIELD CAP, LUFTWAFFE MODEL 1943 OFFICER

• Luftwaffe blue-gray wool officer/NCO private purchase M43 pattern cap has aluminum bullion crown piping, and reinforced front visor, obverse with embroidered Luftwaffe eagle and swastika over National cockade, aluminum pebble-grained button closure. Interior has white cotton lining nicely marked with Hamburg maker stamp and size "57" . . . .**$675 (£340)**

Helmets

M16 HELMET, ARMY, SINGLE DECAL

• Model 1916 steel helmet retains 85% arsenal refurbished gray finish, left side with 80% Army eagle decal. Interior has brown leather M31 liner and 1920s Austrian/Czech/Hungarian style brown leather adjustable chinstrap with blackened roller buckle . . . .**$600 (£300)**

Army tropical issue M43 cap, $895-$1,350 (£450-£675).
Charles D. Pautler

Army enlisted man's M43 cap, $450-$650 (£225-£325). Charles D. Pautler

Waffen SS enlisted man's Model 43 cap, $1,200-$1,750 (£600-£875).
Charles D. Pautler

Luftwaffe enlisted man's M43 cap, $375-$550 (£190-£275).
Minnesota Military Museum

Waffen SS Model 43 officer's cap, $2,000-$3,500 (£1,000-£1,750).
Hermann Historica OHG

Reichsarbeitsdienst reed green Model 1942 summer cap, $350-$550 (£175-£275).
www.advanceguardmilitaria.com

Referred to as "transitional," this German Model 1916 helmet has a single Army decal, $450-$650 (£225-£325).
Charles D. Pautler

Sturmabteilung Model 43 cap with RZM sealed pattern control tag still attached, $800-$1,250 (£400-£625).
www.advanceguardmilitaria.com

German Army Model 35 double decal helmet, $1,000-$1,450 (£500-£725).

Charles D. Pautler

Double decal M35 Luftwaffe helmet, $795-$950 (£400-£475).

www.advanceguardmilitaria.com

Waffen SS double decal helmet, $3,850-$5,000 (£1,925-£2,500).

private collector

Model 40 Army helmet with a subtle gray camouflage, $675-$850 (£340-£425).

www.advanceguardmilitaria.com

German Army Model 40 helmet with what collectors call the "Normandy" style camouflage paint, $950-$1,400 (£475-£700).

Charles D. Pautler

M35 HELMET, ARMY, DOUBLE DECAL

- M35 helmet retains 60% apple green finish with approximately 70% national shield decal and 50% Army eagle decals remaining. Interior has worn but intact M31 liner with broken chinstrap . . . . **$1,295 (£650)**

M35 HELMET, ARMY, SINGLE DECAL

- Model 1935 steel helmet retains 90% glare resistant dark army green painted finish, side with Army eagle and swastika decal, and two piece air vents. Interior has M1931 brown leather liner complete with chinstrap. . . . . **$535 (£270)**

M35 HELMET, LUFTWAFFE, DOUBLE DECAL

- Model 1935 steel helmet, maker and size marked "ET 62," with inserted air vent bushing, retaining 85% rough blue-gray finish as ordered in March, 1940. Early style flying eagle insignia with thick swastika 75% complete, 80% of national color shield remaining. Interior with M31 brown leather liner dated 1937 . . . . **$895 (£450)**

M35 HELMET, LUFTWAFFE, SINGLE DECAL

- Model 1935 single decal steel helmet, size and maker marked "Q 62," retaining over 85% blue-gray painted finish, 85% of the decal remains . . . . **$585 (£295)**

M35 HELMET, LUFTWAFFE, SINGLE DECAL, TROPICAL CAMOUFLAGE

- M35 steel helmet has 70% finish overall, with two layers of Luftwaffe blue-gray and blue-gray textured finish showing through the 30% tropical tan finish that remains, Luftwaffe eagle still visible beneath the tan finish on the left side. . . . . **$950 (£475)**

M35 HELMET, SS, DOUBLE-DECAL

- Model 35 steel helmet retains 95% textured gray finish, left side with NSDAP Party decal, right side with SS decal, both of the first pattern with more pointed bases than their later counterparts . . . . **$3,850 (£1,925)**

M40 HELMET, ARMY, SINGLE DECAL

- Model 1940, exterior retains 50% Army green finish turned dark from age, side with 70% decal, and interior with brown leather liner and partial chinstrap. . . . . **$450 (£225)**

M40 HELMET, ARMY, SINGLE DECAL, CAMOUFLAGED

- Model 1940 steel combat helmet retains 50% dark green and ordnance tan camouflaged finish with Army decal visible on left side. Interior has M31 brown leather liner, lacks chinstrap . . . . **$785 (£395)**

M40 HELMET, ARMY, SINGLE DECAL, WINTER CAMOUFLAGE

- M40 helmet retains 40% striped white camouflaged finish, half of the Army decal is visible on the left side. Interior brown leather M31 liner . . . . **$895 (£450)**

M40 HELMET, ARMY, CAMOUFLAGED

- M40 helmet retains 90%+ ordnance tan with field gray and red-brown foliage camouflage finish applied in large feather edge brushstrokes. Interior has M31 liner. . . . . **$895 (£450)**

M40 HELMET, ARMY, CAMOUFLAGED

- Model 1940 helmet retains 50% dark and light green

brushstroke camouflage finish. The crown of the helmet from the side vents up is rusty, having likely been up-side-down in water for an extended period. Interior has brown leather M31 liner with chinstrap . . . . **$965 (£485)**

M40 HELMET, KRIEGSMARINE, SINGLE DECAL

• Model 40 steel helmet retains 80% rough texture dark 'midnight' blue finish, side with 30% gold Kreigsmarine eagle decal remaining, gray finish visible where the decal has been worn away. Interior has M31 liner . **$685 (£345)**

M40 HELMET, LUFTWAFFE, SINGLE DECAL

• Model 1940 steel combat helmet retains 85% Luftwaffe dark blue-gray finish, left side with 80% Luftwaffe decal remaining. Interior has brown leather M31 liner with size stamp "57" . . . .**$550 (£275)**

M40 HELMET, LUFTWAFFE, CAMOUFLAGED

• Model 40 helmet with khaki tan "smoke" meandering camouflage bands over Luftwaffe blue finish. Brown leather Model 31 liner inscribed on reverse with soldier's name and maker's size stamp "ET64" . . . . . . **$825 (£415)**

M40 HELMET, POLICE, DOUBLE DECAL

• Model 40 helmet retains 80% glare resistant dark field gray painted finish, right side with national swastika on white circle in red shield decal and left side has bordered police eagle decal. Interior has Model 31 leather liner. . . . .**$665 (£335)**

M40 HELMET, SS, DOUBLE DECAL

• Model 1940 helmet retaining 90% dark field gray finish. 90% of the SS shield insignia and 80% Party shield decals remain. Leather liner in poor condition. . . . . **$3,000 (£1,500)**

M40 HELMET, SS, SINGLE DECAL, CAMOUFLAGED

• M40 combat helmet retains 85% textured panzer yellow Zimmerit camouflaged finish. Brown leather M31 liner, lacks chinstrap. Right side has SS decal visible through the Zimmerit. . . . . **$3,750 (£1,875)**

M42 HELMET, ARMY, SINGLE DECAL

• Model 42 helmet retains 60% dark Army green textured finish, almost black from age and use, left side with 80% of the decal remaining. Interior complete with brown leather M31 liner. Lacks chinstrap . . . .**$595 (£300)**

M42 HELMET, ARMY, SINGLE DECAL, CAMOUFLAGE

• Model 1942 steel helmet retains 60% green camouflaged finish with 70% Army eagle decal remaining on the left side. Interior has well-worn but pliable and intact M31 leather liner . . . .**$850 (£425)**

M42 HELMET, ARMY, SINGLE DECAL, FULL CHICKEN WIRE

• M42 helmet retains 80% gray finish and Army decal, dusty from storage with a pattern of white residue from the oxidation of the chicken wire camouflage that covers the entire exterior. Interior has brown leather M31 liner with original draw cord. . . . .**$1,350 (£675)**

M42 HELMET, LUFTWAFFE, SINGLE DECAL

• M42 helmet retains 95% Luftwaffe blue-gray finish and intact Luftwaffe eagle decal. Interior retains M31 liner. . . . .**$450 (£225)**

German Army Model 40 camouflage helmet, $800-$1,350 (£400-£675).
Charles D. Pautler

Germany Army Model 40 tropical camouflage helmet, $1,000-$1,500 (£500-£750).
Charles D. Pautler

German Luftwaffe Model 40 single decal helmet, $400-$650 (£200-£325).
Minnesota Military Museum

The Model 42 with no decal was probably the most common German Army combat helmet, but today is somewhat hard to find (as a result of many unscrupulous dealers who can't resist the temptation to "upgrade" the helmet with the addition of a decal or two), $200-$350 (£100-£175). Charles D. Pautler

Germany Army Model 42 helmet with chicken wire camouflage, $850-$1,400 (£425-£700). Charles D. Pautler

Waffen SS Model 42 single decal helmet, $2,000-$3,500 (£1,000-£1,750). Charles D. Pautler

"Gladiator" style German Luftschutz helmet, $275-$350 (£140-£175).
Charles D. Pautler

Civil Air Defense (Luftschutz) helmet, $285-$400 (£145-£200). Charles D. Pautler

NSKK crash helmet, $450-$650 (£225-£325).

www.advanceguardmilitaria.com

1st Model NSKK crash helmet, $800-$1,200 (£400-£600).

Rock Island Auction Company

M42 HELMET, SS, SINGLE DECAL

- M42 steel combat helmet retains 85% dark field gray finish. Right side retains 95% SS decal .... **$2,500 (£1,250)**

M42 HELMET, ARMY, SINGLE DECAL, TROPICAL CAMOUFLAGE

- M42 helmet has 85% tropical tan finish painted around single Army decal, camouflage holding field gray breadbag strap is attached to the helmet with its own snaps and wire, which has rusted through, staining both the breadbag strap and the helmet where it makes contact. . . . .**$975 (£490)**

FALLSCHIRMJÄGER HELMET WITH ROUGH TEXTURED FINISH

- Second Pattern Type III helmet body with slotted bolts, and 95% heavy textured gray finish. . . . . **$3,250 (£1,625)**

CIVIL PATTERN HELMET, POLICE, DOUBLE DECAL

- Third Reich civil pattern helmet with flat black finish, star punched vents in pairs on either side, interior with brown leather liner and crown pad and leather tabs for attaching neck cape. Sides of the helmet retain Police and National decals . . . .**$450 (£225)**

LUFTSCHUTZ HELMET

- Gladiator style steel helmet has 85% Luftwaffe blue finish, obverse retains 95% "LUFTSCHUTZ" winged decal. . . . .**$235 (£120)**

M35 LUFTSCHUTZ HELMET

- 1935 pattern Luftschutz helmet with beaded band has 85% Luftwaffe blue finish, obverse with large Luftschutz decal which has unfortunately been "de-nazified" with the swastika removed. Interior complete with brown leather liner and size stamp "ET 64." This style was worn by the SHD (Security and Assistance Service) and the LSW (Air Warning Service) . . . .**$290 (£145)**

M42 LUFTSCHUTZ COMBAT HELMET

- M42 Luftschutz helmet has bead between the crown and the rim, retains 65% dark blue painted finish, obverse with 85% Luftschutz decal . . . .**$365 (£185)**

NSKK CRASH HELMET

- Black leather padded NSKK crash helmet with black pebble-grained ear and neck capes with blackened iron adjustment buckle. Interior has light brown leather liner and cushion. Interior of liner has NSKK RZM tag dated 1936 and size stamp "57" . . . .**$485 (£245)**

RURAL POLICE MOTORCYCLE CRASH HELMET

- Brown leather crash helmet has front visor and leather covered padded bumper strip, obverse with large aluminum wreathed eagle insignia. Interior has green visor facing, brown leather neck cape with ear holes, tan leather drawstring liner, black painted fabric crown with "EREL" woven maker's label . . . .**$465 (£235)**

ARMY TROPICAL PITH HELMET

- Olive twill cotton covered cork pith helmet with National shield and Army national eagle insignias. Interior with dark green grained leather sweatband, red cotton lining stamped with size "57," and complete with olive painted leather chinstrap. . . . .**$395 (£200)**

ARMY POLICE SHAKO

- Stiffened Jäger green gray wool body with brown lacquered front and rear visor, crown, and lower band. Large finished aluminum wreathed Police eagle and swastika insignia, national field badge, brown leather chinstrap with aluminum fittings, and green gray finished double pair side vents . . . . **$645 (£325)**

Flight Helmets

LUFTWAFFE FK34 SUMMER FLIGHT HELMET

- Model FK34 summer flight helmet of brown reed fabric with brown leather double chinstrap arrangement, top with loop and side with metal hooks for attaching the oxygen mask; interior has brown linen lining with rayon size and RBNr. Tag . . . . **$260 (£130)**

LUFTWAFFE K33 LEATHER FLIGHT HELMET

- Brown leather K33 flight helmet with studs and hooks for the oxygen mask, ear cups but no electronics. . . . . **$275 (£140)**

LUFTWAFFE LKPN 101 SUMMER FLIGHT HELMET, EARPHONES AND THROAT MICROPHONE

- LKpN 101 Netzkopfhaube flying helmet with dark brown open weave mesh crown. Sides have hard dark brown earphone cups with slots along the top to catch the goggles strap, elastic rear band fitted with wiring loom holding a complete "Mi 4b" throat microphone rig and earphone communication attachment socket. Interior has white sheepskin lining surrounding the earphones. . . . . **$475 (£240)**

Hoods and Helmet Covers

SPLINTER CAMOUFLAGE HELMET COVER

- Army splinter pattern camouflage material helmet cover with foliage loops. Interior with drawstring. . . . . **$335 (£170)**

ARMY WINTER HOOD

- Reversible field gray wool and white cotton winter hood with neck cape and ties . . . . **$150 (£75)**

ARMY CAMOUFLAGE REVERSIBLE WINTER HOOD

- Padded cotton Kopfhaube in "Splinter B" pattern camouflage on one side, white on the other, and ear areas have loose weave field gray wool to facilitate better hearing. Interior has accountability number stamp, size "55" and date . . . . **$265 (£135)**

ARMY CAMOUFLAGE REVERSIBLE WINTER HOOD

- Padded cotton Kopfhaube in "Tan Water A" pattern camouflage on one side, white on the other. Interior has Rb-nr. accountability number stamp but is otherwise unmarked. . . . . **$225 (£115)**

ARMY WINTER FUR CAP

- Field gray wool cap with brown rabbit fur turned front visor and fold-up ear flaps with field gray tape ties, obverse with Army eagle insignia . . . . **$285 (£145)**

German rural police motorcycle crash helmet, $450-$700 (£225-£350).
www.advanceguardmilitaria.com

The German Army tropical pith helmet was a favorite with General Rommel's Afrikakorps, $350-$600 (£175-£300). Charles D. Pautler

Prototype of the Model SSK 90 flying helmet made by Siemens, $20,000-$23,500 (£10,000-£11,750).
Hermann Historica OHG

Waffen SS dot-pattern camouflage cover, $650-$900 (£325-£450).
Charles D. Pautler

German Army reversible camouflage hood, $200-$300 (£100-£150). Charles D. Pautler

This particular Greek Model 34 helmet was repainted dark green and likely used by the Italians during the occupation until 1944, $125-$250 (£65-£125). Peter Suciu

Holland's Model 23/27 was known as the Nieuw Model helmet $150-$225 (£75-£115). Peter Suciu

Dutch Model 34 steel combat helmet, $50-$75 (£25-£40). Peter Suciu

Model 35/38 Hungarian combat helmet, $800-$1,200 (£400-£600). Peter Suciu

GREECE

MODEL 1934/39 COMBAT HELMET

- Many Greek helmets ended up being reissued to Italian troops during the 1944 occupation . . . . **$200 (£100)**

HOLLAND

Helmets

MODEL 23/27 COMBAT HELMET

- Nieuw Model helmet in field gray finish with bronze oval rampant lion crest on obverse, rear skirt pierced with loop for carrying strap. Interior complete with black leather liner chinstrap . . . . **$175 (£90)**

MODEL 23/27 DUTCH COLLABORATIONIST TENO DOUBLE DECAL COMBAT HELMET

- Nieuw Model reissued army helmet with black painted finish, oval rampant lion plate attached to obverse, left side with a black and silver "TN" on cogged wheel TeNo shield emblem and on the opposite side, the Dutch national tricolor shield decal . . . . **$895 (£450)**

MODEL 34 COMBAT HELMET

- Model 34 steel helmet with distinctive sloping profile and oblong slot at the edge of the rear visor. Interior complete with chinstrap, three piece leather liner, wool pads and the small flap at the nape with leather strap used for attaching a leather neck cover . . . . **$75 (£40)**

HUNGARY

Helmets

MODEL 1935/38 COMBAT HELMET

- Helmet with dark olive finish, complete with strap loop riveted to the rear of the skirt. Interior has brown leather three-pad liner and chin strap . . . . **$795 (£400)**

MODEL 1935/38 ANTI-AIRCRAFT DEFENSE FIRE BRIGADE HELMET

- Helmet as worn by members of the Anti-Aircraft Defense Fire Brigades with a very distinctive cruciform aluminum comb. Horizon blue painted finish. Interior has brown leather liner with drawstring adjustment, large crown cushion, and chinstrap with elastic "Y" side harness . . . . **$950 (£475)**

ITALY

Caps, Visor

VISOR CAP, ARMY ARTILLERY OFFICER

- Captain of Artillery rank, green-gray wool crown with three gold bullion rank braids around the band, obverse with gold bullion branch of service insignia with unit number "1," gilt Artillery side buttons with black leather chinstrap and bound visor. Interior with pale yellow silk lining marked with the Savoy eagle and maker's name

"UNIONE MILITARE / TORINO," celluloid sweat shield and brown leather sweatband . . . . **$250 (£125)**

Caps, Visorless

BUSTINA, BRIGADE GENERAL
- Model 1934/35 berretto a busta of field gray wool twill has obverse with silver embroidered on red background Generals and Staff badge, side with silver bullion rank patch on red wool background mounted by General of Brigade vaulted rank star. Interior has gray fabric lining and brown leather sweatband . . . . **$495 (£250)**

BUSTINA, ARTILLERY OFFICER
- Enlisted issue field gray green wool bustina with officer's quality First Artillery Regiment bullion embroidered insignia. Interior with black leather chinstrap and liner with 1938-dated issue stamp . . . . **$195 (£100)**

BUSTINA, MVSN BLACK SHIRT MILITIA
- Reinforced black silk grosgrain bustina with gilt embroidered fascio. Interior has black silk lining and sweatband with worn Italian maker's stamp . . . . **$275 (£140)**

BERET, PARATROOPER
- Field gray wool beret with crown tab, lining of gray cotton with size stamp. Pattern used by paratroops and the elite San Marcos Marine assault units and some of the RSI Black Brigades . . . . **$175 (£90)**

Helmets

MODEL 1933 COMBAT HELMET WITH CAMOUFLAGE COVER
- Steel helmet with no stencil. Camouflage cover of standard Italian shelter half material with a row of six foliage loops ringing the liner about three inches from the lower edge and a rayon drawstring . . . . **$295 (£150)**

MODEL 1933 ALPINI COMBAT HELMET
- Model 1933 helmet with the stencil insignia of alpine (mountain) troops . . . . **$375 (£190)**

MODEL 1933 ARDITI COMBAT HELMET
- Model 1933 steel helmet with gray-green finish, obverse with black stenciled crossed Roman swords within a crowned wreath insignia used by the Arditi, the special assault units of the Italian Royal Army before 1942. . . . . **$375 (£190)**

MODEL 1933 BERSAGLIERI COMBAT HELMET
- Model 1933 helmet with early light field gray finish, obverse stenciled with Bersaglieri branch of service insignia in black with unit number "6," interior complete with brown leather liner and olive gray leather chinstrap. . . . . **$375 (£190)**

MODEL 1933 GRENADIERS COMBAT HELMET
- Helmet with field green finish; obverse has clear stenciled Granatieri flaming bomb insignia with "11" unit numeral. Interior has brown leather liner and chinstrap. . . . . **$295 (£150)**

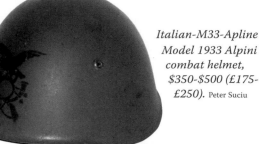

Italian-M33-Apline Model 1933 Alpini combat helmet, $350-$500 (£175-£250). Peter Suciu

Most Model 33 Italian helmets were painted a green-gray color until 1940, when a darker shade of green was used. In 1934, stenciled emblems were adopted for all the various units of the Italian military. This helmet bears the insignia of the Savoy Cavalry, $400-$600 (£200-£300). Peter Suciu

Italian Model 1933 combat helmet with the insignia of the "Blackshirts" (Voluntary Militia for Nation Security), $400-$675 (£200-£340). www.advanceguardmilitaria.com

Italian Model 35 tanker's helmet, $175-$250 (£90-£125). www.advanceguardmilitaria.com

This Italian Model 28 features the insignia of the 10th Granatieri (Grenadier) Division, $200-$450 (£100-£225). Peter Suciu

"*Telegraph poles, blocks, all sorts sticking out of the sand, each with a mine on top.*"
LT. GEOFFREY GIDDINGS, 9TH FIELD SQUADRON, ROYAL ENGINEERS, DESCRIBING GOLD BEACH ON JUNE 6, 1944

Japanese Naval officer's visor cap, $400-$600 (£200-£300).
www.advanceguardmilitaria.com

Type 45 Japanese Army visor cap. These were not worn in combat zones, but rather, in rear areas, $275-375 (£140-£190).
www.advanceguardmilitaria.com

Type 45 Imperial Guard visor cap, $350-$400 (£175-£200).
www.advanceguardmilitaria.com

Model 1937 Army field cap, $275-$350 (£140-£180).
www.advanceguardmilitaria.com

Japanese Navy cotton field cap, $300-$450 (£150-£225). Minnesota Military Museum

Naval Landing Force field cap, $350-$500 (£175-£250).
www.advanceguardmilitaria.com

MODEL 1933 MSVN COMBAT HELMET
* Helmet in field green finish. Obverse has clear stenciled black M.S.V.N. wreathed fasces with crossed gladiator swords insignia. Interior has brown leather liner and chinstrap .... **$450 (£225)**

MODEL 35 TANKER'S HELMET
* Model 35 tank helmet of padded black leather, which has a neck cape, rim bumper cushion, and is stenciled with a white Tank insignia. Interior has black leather finger and drawstring liner system, chinstrap panels with ear holes and buckle attachment .... **$195 (£100)**

MODEL 1928 PITH HEMET
* The Italian Model 1928 was first introduced in 1935 and remained in service until the end of World War II.
.... **$300 (£150)**

JAPAN

Caps, Officer

VISOR CAP, ARMY OFFICER
* Officer quality Army pattern visor cap of olive wool twill with red band and piping, bound black fiber visor, obverse band with brass vaulted star insignia, and sides with chrysanthemum gilt buttons securing adjustable black fiber chinstrap. Interior has dark green silk lining with embroidered Japanese characters, painted fabric sweatband .... **$245 (£125)**

VISOR CAP, NAVY OFFICER'S
* Extra quality dark blue wool visor hat has welted crown seam, bound black lacquered leather visor, obverse with gilt bullion Navy officer's wreathed cap badge, and black leather chinstrap with Japanese mum side buttons. Interior has black painted fabric sweatband and violet silk lining provided with white label for officer's name.
.... **$425 (£215)**

FIELD CAP, ARMY OFFICER
* Officer's lightweight olive drab wool field cap with stitch reinforced visor, obverse with applied Army yellow wool and thread star insignia, olive painted leather adjustable chinstrap with gilt chrysanthemum side buttons, brown painted side vent grommets and rear lace adjustment. Interior has brown synthetic lining and brown finished split pigskin sweatband printed with maker's stamp on the inside .... **$365 (£185)**

Caps, Enlisted

VISOR CAP, ARMY TYPE 45 ENLISTED
* Fine quality olive wool crown with red band and piping; obverse with vaulted Army star insignia, unbound multi-layered black leather visor, and adjustable black leather chinstrap secured by gilt brass side buttons. Interior has brown pigskin visor facing and sweatband with loose weave cheesecloth lining. .... **$295 (£150)**

VISOR CAP, TYPE 45 IMPERIAL GUARD ENLISTED
* Type 45 enlisted visor cap with olive twill wool crown with red wool band and crown piping, band with gilt

wreathed star Imperial guard insignia, black lacquered fabric chinstrap secured by chrysanthemum side buttons, and bound black lacquered fiber visor. Interior has black silk lining and thin black leather sweatband.
· ·**$365 (£185)**

FIELD CAP, MODEL 1937 ARMY ENLISTED

- Olive wool field cap with stitch reinforced visor and obverse with yellow embroidered star, brown painted fabric chinstrap, and reverse with adjustment tie. Interior has brown painted fabric sweatband and paper cloth lining.
· ·**$295 (£150)**

FIELD CAP, NAVY

- Olive heavy cotton fatigue cap with stitch reinforced visor of the same material, obverse with yellow Japanese Navy anchor insignia woven on olive oval disc, adjustable chinstrap, and reverse has tie adjustment with original lace. Interior has olive cotton sweatband and Japanese character issue stamp dated 1945 and listing size (2)**$335 (£170)**

FIELD CAP, NAVAL LANDING FORCE

- Olive cotton Navy field cap has stitch reinforced visor, obverse with yellow woven Navy anchor insignia on olive oval background, adjustable chinstrap, sides with three sewn ventilation grommets, and reverse with tape tie closure. Interior has nice clear issue stamp dated 1944 listing size 1 and identifies it as having come from the Shanghai Depot ·**$350 (£175)**

FIELD CAP, NAVY NCO'S TROPICAL

- Olive cotton field cap has black NCO stripe around the base and obverse with BeVo woven Navy NCO cap badge, adjustable cloth chinstrap, stitch reinforced visor, sewn side ventilation grommets, and reverse with adjustment ties. Interior is well marked with Japanese issue stamp listing 1944 date and marked to the Shanghai Depot ·**$375 (£190)**

SEAMAN'S HAT, NAVY ENLISTED

- Blue wool "Donald Duck" service hat, reverse has thread guides ready to attach a tally. Interior has black cotton sweatband and lining with kana script issue label, complete with black ribbon chinstrap · · · · · · · · · ·**$385 (£190)**

SEAMAN'S HAT, NAVY ENLISTED

- Dark blue wool Navy service hat has tally with gilt Japanese kana inscription, properly affixed by threading through the guides at the reverse. Interior has printed issue label, black cotton lining, and is complete with black ribbon chinstrap ·**$475 (£240)**

FUR CAP, WINTER COMBAT

- Olive wool cap with white fur ear flaps, neck cape, yellow star insignia on olive wool disc. Interior white fur lining has dark violet rayon crown lining with white cotton cover, issue tag lacking. Hat is complete with olive tape neck ties and the seldom-seen padded removable face mask piece ·**$350 (£175)**

BOONIE HAT, ARMY FATIGUE

- Olive cotton fatigue hat with stitch reinforced brim and band with false ribbon detail. Interior has light olive facing material ·**$225 (£115)**

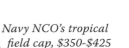

Navy NCO's tropical field cap, $350-$425 (£175-£215).
www.advanceguardmilitaria.com

Japanesee Navy seaman's cap with "Imperial Japanese Navy" katana, $400-$550 (£200-£275).
www.advanceguardmilitaria.com

Japanese Navy seaman's cap, $400-$550 (£200-£275). Minnesota Military Museum

Winter Japanese combat fur cap, $325-$400 (£165-£200).
www.advanceguardmilitaria.com

Japanese Army fatigue "boonie" hat, $200-$275 (£100-£140).
www.advanceguardmilitaria.com

"Nearly all American soldiers were inveterate souvenir hunters, even at the risk of their own lives..."
LT. BOB GREEN, 763RD TANK BN.

Japanese tropical combat headnet, $175-$225 (£90-£115).

www.advanceguardmilitaria.com

Japanese Kamikaze headband, $300-$450 (£150-£225).

www.advanceguardmilitaria.com

Leather Japanese Army winter flight helmet, $450-$550 (£225-£275).

www.advanceguardmilitaria.com

Leather Japanese Army summer flight helmet, $400-$500 (£200-£250). www.advanceguardmilitaria.com

HEADNET, TROPICAL COMBAT

- Olive and green tropical headnet designed to be worn over the steel combat or pith helmet, base with drawstring closure and Japanese issue stamp . . . . **$195 (£100)**

HEADBAND, KAMIKAZE

- White cotton cloth printed in the center with the red national emblem flanked by Japanese script, unfolds to reveal verses about falling cherry blossoms, etc. These were worn by Kamikaze pilots as well as war industry workers in Japan to show solidarity with the "never surrender" Bushido code during the national emergency. . . . . **$300 (£150)**

Flight Helmets

FLIGHT HELMET, ARMY WINTER HELMET

- Brown leather flight helmet with olive synthetic fur interior lining, back with adjustment tab, sides with formed earphone compartments, and goggle guide straps secured to the earphone compartments by blackened snap fittings. Chinstrap with double ring securing system. Obverse crown has leather star insignia . . . . **$450 (£225)**

FLIGHT HELMET, ARMY SUMMER

- Brown leather flight helmet has leather sewn star insignia on the obverse, sides with ear cups for communications equipment and goggle guide straps with brown painted snap closures, reverse has billet and buckle size adjustment strap. Interior has olive fabric lining. Interior of ear cups well marked with 1944-dated issue stamps. Helmet fastens with strap and double ring system. . . . . **$425 (£215)**

Helmets

TYPE 90 ARMY COMBAT HELMET

- Model 30/32 steel helmet with field khaki finish, obverse has Army five pointed star badge. Interior has three-pad brown pigskin liner and full uncut olive web chin tie cord, with size and 1941 date stamp on the cotton side of the front liner pad . . . . **$625 (£315)**

TYPE 90 ARMY COMBAT HELMET

- Steel helmet with field khaki finish and a band of olive paint randomly applied in a 1-1/2" to 2-1/2" wide band along the bottom edge. Obverse has Army five-pointed star badge, interior has complete three-pad brown pigskin liner and full uncut olive web chin tie cord. Interior of helmet has white painted Japanese character indicating size (large), 1943 date, and name "Kawashima". . . . . **$695 (£350)**

TYPE 90 ARMY COMBAT HELMET WITH FIELD COVER

- Khaki painted finish, obverse with Army star insignia and proof stamp. Interior has complete and supple brown leather liner with original drawcord and tie straps, reverse of brim with Japanese character stamp indicating large size. Field cover of olive cotton has yellow wool felt star insignia on olive cotton disc and rim with draw cord. . . . . **$675 (£340)**

TYPE 90 NAVAL LANDING FORCE COMBAT HELMET WITH CAMO NET

- Steel helmet with field khaki finish. Navy anchor, star, and chrysanthemum badge on the front. Complete with 2" square tied mesh cord camouflage net with remains of original plant fiber camouflage material. Interior has three-pad cushioned brown pigskin liner and khaki web chin tie cords. . . . .**$975 (£490)**

M32 TANKER HELMET

- M32 protective tanker's helmet with brown cotton exterior and red star insignia on the obverse, vented crown, and sides with grommets and ties. Interior has black painted fabric front and rear panels with brown leather liner suspension and off-white cotton fabric crown lining marked with 1945-dated issue stamp. Sides have lined brown leather "Y" straps with billet and dual ring buckle system. . . . .**$645 (£325)**

ARMY TROPICAL HELMET

- Light olive-khaki cotton covered cork tropical pith helmet, obverse with yellow BeVo woven Army star insignia, and olive-khaki cloth chinstrap looped over the brim. Interior has dark olive cotton lining with tie-adjust web suspension, white cotton issue labels with Japanese kana character stamps, and interior of front brim with painted Japanese size symbol . . . .**$465 (£235)**

ARMY COLONEL'S PITH HELMET

- British style khaki cloth covered pith helmet with puggaree and crown vent. Obverse has brass vaulted Army star insignia, and left side has Army Colonel rank collar tab affixed to the puggaree . . . .**$325 (£165)**

PERU

MODEL 1934 COMBAT HELMET

- Model 1934 (French M26) Adrian helmet with olive painted finish and radiant sun badge . . . .**$125 (£65)**

POLAND

FIELD CAP, ENLISTED

- Olive khaki wool field cap has stitch reinforced visor and the distinctive Polish square cornered crown, obverse with embroidered Polish eagle and Amazon shield insignia, sides with folding neck curtains secured with a khaki Bakelite buckle in the front. Crown has a pair of olive painted vent grommets on either side. Interior has black cotton lining with Warsaw maker stamps dated 1938. . . . .**$1,200 (£600)**

COMBAT HELMET, SOVIET REISSUE

- Soviet Model 40 steel helmet with olive finish heavily worn and revealing previous regulation black painted finish with traces of red and white Polish insignias on both sides, obverse with white painted 1943 pattern Polish Eagle insignia, applied over the olive finish. . . . .**$400 (£200)**

Type 90 combat helmet, also referred to as the "Type 30/32," $595-$750 (£300-£375).

www.advanceguardmilitaria.com

Type 90 Army helmet with a painted band around brim, $650-$795 (£325-£400).

www.advanceguardmilitaria.com

Japanese Type 90 Army helmet with cover and camouflage net, $700-$1,100 (£350-£550).

Minnesota Military Museum

Japanese Type 90 Naval Landing Force steel helmet, $700-$1,200 (£350-£600). Peter Suciu

Japanese-tanker Japanese M32 tanker helmet, $500-$800 (£250-£400). Peter Suciu

Japanese Army "two-tone" pith helmet, $550-$750 (£275-£375).
www.advanceguardmilitaria.com

Japanese Army officer's pith helmet with colonel's insignia sewn on the side, $300-$375 (£150-£190).
www.advanceguardmilitaria.com

Peru's Model 1934 Adrian helmet, $100-$300 (£100-£150). Peter Suciu

Polish Army enlisted man's wool field cap with an old tag noting that a German soldier took it as a souvenir during the 1939 campaign, $1,200-$1,400 (£600-£700). www.advanceguardmilitaria.com

Poland first issued the Model 31 (Wz.) helmet in 1936, $800-$2,000 (£400-£1,000). Peter Suciu

MODEL 1931 COMBAT HELMET

• Wz 31 steel helmet with heavily textured olive drab finish. Interior has three-pad brown leather liner on metal band similar to the WWI German pattern. Interior crown has arsenal marks, complete with black leather chinstrap with distinctive catch. . . . .**$950 (£475)**

PORTUGAL

MK I PATTERN COMBAT HELMET

• Portuguese production rimless Brodies pattern steel helmet retaining olive drab finish. Defensa Civil Territorial decal on front . . . .**$350 (£175)**

MODEL 1940 HELMET

• Model 40 steel helmet with olive finish. Interior has brown leather cushioned three pad liner on steel band with brown leather chinstrap and double buckle adjustment . . . .**$175 (£90)**

MOTORIZED TROOPS CRASH HELMET

• Black grained leather skull cap with padded band and three padded bars running front to back on the crown, complete with padded black leather "Y" yoke chinstrap, lined in brown leather . . . .**$155 (£80)**

ROMANIA

MODEL 1928 COMBAT HELMET

• Romania used a variety of Dutch-produced steel helmets during World War II including the Dutch M28 helmet with a distinctive King Carol badge. After King Carol II went into exile, the use of this emblem was discontinued. . . . .**$950 (£475)**

MODEL 1938 COMBAT HELMET

• Romanian M38 (Dutch M34) combat helmet as supplied to Romanian forces by the Germans until 1942. Olive with black camouflage finish; interior has M23/27 pattern black leather three-pad liner, brown leather band and mustard felt crown pad, and is complete with its black leather chinstrap . . . .**$895 (£450)**

RUSSIA

Caps

MODEL 1922 BUDENOVKA, SUMMER PATTERN

• Model 1922 "Budenovka" of khaki cotton with distinctive pointed crown, stitched visor and skirt, and matching fabric chinstrap with leather side buttons, Infantry cranberry red wool star on obverse. Khaki cotton lining, clearly issue marked and dated "1922" . . . . . .**$435 (£220)**

MODEL 1927 BUDENOVKA, WINTER PATTERN

• Model 1927 "Budenovka" of gray wool with distinctive pointed crown, stitched visor, and folding neck cape retained by stamped brass Soviet star buttons, obverse with brass and red enameled star on attractive red wool flannel star Infantry branch of service field. Interior lin-

ing of blue quilted cotton with 1939-dated issue stamp.
....**$465 (£235)**

WINTER FUR CAP

• Gray faux fur winter cap with gray wool crown, upturned front visor with red enameled Soviet star insignia, sides with ear flaps tied at the top of the crown. Interior with quilted gray cotton lining ....**$185 (£90)**

WINTER CAP, FIELD-MADE

• Winter cap with folding ear cape appears to be hand-assembled from material salvaged from a discarded telogreika (padded winter jacket). Obverse has two piece brass and enamel star with hammer and sickle insignia.
....**$150 (£75)**

Helmets

SHVARTZ EXPERIMENTAL HELMET

• This Soviet experimental helmet dates back to the early 1930s. It was designed by Senior Lieutenant Aleksandr Abramovich Shvartz of the Red Army's Department of Supply. It has the liner system that was later used in the SSh-36 helmets......................**$4,000 (£2,000)**

MODEL 1936 COMBAT HELMET

• Soviet combat helmet with short comb crown reinforcement with dark olive finish. Front has stenciled star insignia. Interior has gray painted fabric sweatband, olive cotton twill drawstring adjusted lining, corrugated metal reinforcement side panels intact and complete, lacks chinstrap ....**$650 (£325)**

MODEL 1939 COMBAT HELMET

• "Ssh39" helmet with olive finish, interior with very clear issue marks and date "41r." Complete with khaki cotton liner, worn gray oilcloth sweatband and khaki web chinstrap ....**$500 (£250)**

MODEL 1940 COMBAT HELMET

• Olive finish with three-pad liner of black synthetic oil-cloth ....**$350 (£175)**

ARMOR CREWMAN HELMET

• Black cotton armor crewman helmet with padded ridges, reverse skirt has issue stamp with 1944 date.
....**$395 (£200)**

ROMANIA

MODEL 1928 COMBAT HELMET

• Romania used a variety of Dutch-produced steel helmets during World War II including the Dutch M28 helmet with a distinctive King Carol badge. After King Carol II went into exile, the use of this emblem was discontinued.
....**$950 (£475)**

MODEL 1938 COMBAT HELMET

• Romanian M38 (Dutch M34) combat helmet as supplied to Romanian forces by the Germans until 1942. Olive with black camouflage finish; interior has M23/27 pattern black leather three-pad liner, brown leather band and mustard felt crown pad, and is complete with its black leather chinstrap ....**$895 (£450)**

Portuguese MK I combat helmet, $300-$500 (£150-£250). Peter Suciu

Romania used a variety of Dutch-produced steel helmets during World War II, including the Dutch M-28 helmet, $800-$2,000 (£400-£1,000). Peter Suciu

Romanian Model 38 combat helmet was derived from a Dutch pattern, $800-$1,500 (£400-£750). Peter Suciu

Model 1922 Budenovka in the khaki summer pattern, $400-$650 (£200-£325).
www.advanceguardmilitaria.com

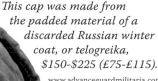

This cap was made from the padded material of a discarded Russian winter coat, or telogreika, $150-$225 (£75-£115).
www.advanceguardmilitaria.com

Soviet shvartz Soviet "Shvartz" experimental helmet, $3,500-$5,000 (£1,750-£2,500). Peter Suciu

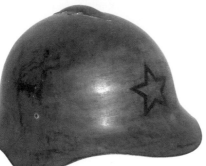

The Soviet SSh-36 steel helmet was first issued in 1936, $400-$800 (£200-£400). Peter Suciu

Soviet SSh-39 steel helmet, introduced in 1939 and featuring a liner to the German Model 31 system, $450-$600 (£225-£300). Peter Suciu

The Model 40 helmet was produced from 1940 and remained in Soviet service into the 1960s, $300-$450 (£150-£225). Peter Suciu

A Leningrad pan factory made these civil defense helmets during the 900-day siege, $850-$1,500 (£425-£750).
Peter Suciu

RUSSIA

Caps

MODEL 1922 BUDENOVKA, SUMMER PATTERN

- Model 1922 "Budenovka" of khaki cotton with distinctive pointed crown, stitched visor and skirt, and matching fabric chinstrap with leather side buttons, Infantry cranberry red wool star on obverse. Khaki cotton lining, clearly issue marked and dated "1922"......**$435 (£220)**

MODEL 1927 BUDENOVKA, WINTER PATTERN

- Model 1927 "Budenovka" of gray wool with distinctive pointed crown, stitched visor, and folding neck cape retained by stamped brass Soviet star buttons, obverse with brass and red enameled star on attractive red wool flannel star Infantry branch of service field. Interior lining of blue quilted cotton with 1939-dated issue stamp.
...................................**$465 (£235)**

WINTER FUR CAP

- Gray faux fur winter cap with gray wool crown, upturned front visor with red enameled Soviet star insignia, sides with ear flaps tied at the top of the crown. Interior with quilted gray cotton lining ....**$185 (£90)**

WINTER CAP, FIELD-MADE

- Winter cap with folding ear cape appears to be hand-assembled from material salvaged from a discarded telogreika (padded winter jacket). Obverse has two piece brass and enamel star with hammer and sickle insignia.
...................................**$150 (£75)**

Helmets

SHVARTZ EXPERIMENTAL HELMET

- This Soviet experimental helmet dates back to the early 1930s. It was designed by Senior Lieutenant Aleksandr Abramovich Shvartz of the Red Army's Department of Supply. It has the liner system that was later used in the SSh-36 helmets.....................**$4,000 (£2,000)**

MODEL 1936 COMBAT HELMET

- Soviet combat helmet with short comb crown reinforcement with dark olive finish. Front has stenciled star insignia. Interior has gray painted fabric sweatband, olive cotton twill drawstring adjusted lining, corrugated metal reinforcement side panels intact and complete, lacks chinstrap ....**$650 (£325)**

MODEL 1939 COMBAT HELMET

- "Ssh39" helmet with olive finish, interior with very clear issue marks and date "41r." Complete with khaki cotton liner, worn gray oilcloth sweatband and khaki web chinstrap ....**$500 (£250)**

MODEL 1940 COMBAT HELMET

- Olive finish with three-pad liner of black synthetic oilcloth ....**$350 (£175)**

ARMOR CREWMAN HELMET

- Black cotton armor crewman helmet with padded ridges, reverse skirt has issue stamp with 1944 date.
...................................**$395 (£200)**

SPAIN

Caps, Officer

VISOR CAP, ARTILLERY OFFICER, NATIONALIST ARMY

- M1931 olive wool cap, Comandante (Major) rank, with matching cloth covered visor, band with olive silk cord top border and obverse with gold bullion rank star on red wool field, crown obverse has gold bullion flaming bomb insignia. Brown leather chinstrap has brass buckle and pressed olive leather false knot side buttons. Interior has silk lining and eagle embossed brown leather sweatband. $225 (£115)

Caps and Hats, Enlisted

SIDE CAP, FALANGE, NATIONALIST ARMY

- Blue cotton side cap has crown with red and black tassel, red embroidered trim on the sides, and interior with fabric sweatband. $125 (£65)

MODEL 1933 SIDE CAP, INFANTRY, NATIONALIST ARMY

- Model 1933 pre-war quality Infantry "Isabellino" of olive drab cotton with red trim and tassel, interior Madrid maker marked. $85 (£45)

MODEL 1937 SIDE CAP, INFANTRY, REPUBLICAN ARMY

- Model 1937 side cap of khaki cotton with red cord infantry piping, manufactured without the traditional tassel to make them distinct from those worn by Nationalist troops, complete with red painted brass star insignia. $115 (£60)

PASAMONTANA KNIT CAP, REPUBLICAN ARMY

- Dark brown wool, converts from cap with short cloth visor to a balaclava $185 (£95)

"AMERICAN" HAT

- Named for the campaign hats that the American forces wore in battle against them during the War of 1898, this olive cotton campaign hat was worn from 1914 to the Civil War period. Olive cotton hat has stitch reinforced brim, crown with brown painted metal ventilation grommets, and interior with adjustable leather chinstrap and brown leather sweatband with maker stamp. $250 (£125)

Helmets

MODEL 1926/32 COMBAT HELMET, REPUBLICAN ARMY

- French production Adrian helmet under contract for the Spanish Republican Government. Khaki painted finish, obverse never pierced for a badge. Interior has one of the brown leather liners particular to this contract, and complete with brown leather chinstrap $150 (£75)

MODEL 1935 TANKER HELMET

- Introduced in the 1930s by Italy and used in large numbers in Lybia and Ethiopia, these tanker helmets were

The dark blue cotton side cap was worn by the Spanish Nationalist Army, $100-$150 (£50-£75).
www.advanceguardmilitaria.com

Commonly referred to as "American Hats" because of their similarity to U.S. soldier's campaign hats during the Spanish-American War, these olive cotton hats are quite rare today, $225-$300 (£130-£150). www.advanceguardmilitaria.com

Spanish tanker Introduced by Italy, the Spanish Model 35 tanker helmet was used in large numbers in Lybia and Ethiopia, $100-$200 (£50-£100). Peter Suciu

Spanish Modelo Z Spain adopted a German-style helmet in 1942 that it termed the "Modelo Z," $100-$250 (£50-£125). Peter Suciu

Swedish-M21 Swedish Model 21 combat helmet, $50-$100 (£25-£50). Peter Suciu

Swedish Model 26 combat helmet did not have a rolled rim or the royal crest, $50-$100 (£25-£50). Peter Suciu

Swiss Model 18/40 helmet with a federal silver cross, $75-$125 (£40-£65). Peter Suciu

Pattern 1943 General Service Cap for the Canadian Lake Superior Regiment, $85-$125 (£45-£65). Minnesota Military Museum

Australian jungle hat, $350-$450 (£175-£225). Charles D. Pautler collection

later adopted by the Franco's army following the Spanish Civil War. Black leather helmet padded with felt and cardboard. .... **$150 (£75)**

MODEL 1942 "MODELO Z" COMBAT HELMET

• The Spanish adopted a German-styled helmet in 1942. It has a three-pad liner attached by seven bolts.
.... **$175 (£90)**

SWEDEN

MODEL 1921 COMBAT HELMET

• The Swedish Model 1921 helmet has a rounded bowl shell. The front of the helmet features the royal steel crest .... **$75 (£40)**

MODEL 1926 COMBAT HELMET

• The Swedish Model 1926 helmet has the same basic shape of the Model 1921 but without the royal crest or rolled rim................................. **$65 (£35)**

SWITZERLAND

MODEL 1918/40 COMBAT HELMET

• This Swiss helmet, which is similar in shape to the German M18 helmet, was introduced in 1918 and modified in 1940 .... **$75 (£40)**

UNITED KINGDOM

Caps, Visor, Officer

VISOR CAP, SERVICE DRESS, OFFICER

• Khaki wool officer's Service Dress cap with matching wool covered visor and brown leather chinstrap with bronze side buttons. Obverse with wartime emergency brown plastic "Royal Engineers" badge. Lining of gray quilted silk with Covent Garden maker's label and brown leather sweatband. .... **$135 (£70)**

VISOR CAP, SERVICE DRESS, OFFICER, CANADIAN

• Khaki wool General Service cap with cloth cover visor, obverse with brass and nickel bimetal "Le Regiment de Maisonneuve" badge and brown leather chinstrap.
.... **$125 (£65)**

Canadian summer WAC cap, $95-$175 (£50-£90). www.advanceguardmilitaria.com

British ATS wool Service Dress cap, first pattern, $175-$225 (£90-£115). www.advanceguardmilitaria.com

VISOR CAP, SERVICE DRESS, OFFICER, CANADIAN MEDICAL

- Khaki wool cap and matching cloth covered visor with green leather underside. Obverse has brass Medical Corps badge and brown leather chinstrap with brass RAMC side buttons. Lined in rayon with full crown sweat shield and leather sweatband embossed with a Toronto maker's label . . . . **$125 (£65)**

VISOR CAP, RAF OFFICER

- RAF blue wool cap with sides worn into the classic crusher style, obverse has gilt officer's badge with King's crown device, black mohair crown band, black lacquered leather chinstrap, and stiffened blue wool cloth visor. Interior with green wool felt lining and brown leather sweatband printed with a London hatter's maker stamp. . . . . **$185 (£95)**

VISOR CAP, RCAF OFFICER

- RAF blue wool visor cap with black mohair braid, gilt embroidered Air Force badge with red velvet crown and bronze eagle, and black leather chinstrap. Interior with gray leather sweatband and red lining printed with Toronto maker's stamp . . . . **$165 (£85)**

Caps, Visor, Enlisted

VISOR CAP, SERVICE DRESS, ENLISTED

- Rigid visor cap of khaki wool with cloth covered visor, bi-metal Suffolk Regiment badge and general service side buttons . . . . **$85 (£45)**

Caps, Visorless, Enlisted

SIDE CAP, FIELD SERVICE ENLISTED

- Pattern 1937, khaki wool twill side cap with General Service buttons, side pierced for cap badge. White cotton lining with large Broad Arrow proof and maker's 1941-dated size stamp . . . . **$45 (£25)**

SIDE CAP, FIELD SERVICE ENLISTED, CANADA

- Pattern 1937 khaki wool twill side cap with folding neck cape closed by two brown snaps. Black cotton lining marked with "C" Broad Arrow, maker stamp and date "1944," cotton sweatband . . . . **$50 (£25)**

SIDE CAP, FIELD SERVICE ENLISTED, NAVY

- Pattern 1937 side cap of khaki wool twill with Navy pattern service buttons front closure, never pierced for badge. Khaki cotton lining with Broad Arrow proof and "1938" stamp . . . . **$30 (£15)**

SIDE CAP, RAF ENLISTED

- RAF blue wool side cap with crown over wing front closure buttons and bronze "RAF" badge on side. Interior has 1942-dated contract stamp with Broad Arrow proof. . . . . **$55 (£30)**

FLAT HAT, ROYAL NAVY

- Dark blue wool hat with woven wool tape chinstrap and H.M.S. ARK ROYAL tally. Interior with adjustable silk lining with leather sweatband . . . . **$275 (£140)**

FLAT HAT, ROYAL NAVY, AUSTRALIA

- White weatherproof body with black wool band, woven tape chinstrap, and black silk "H.M.A.S. CERBERUS" cap tally. Interior has red silk lining, a white sweat guard and a panel of green silk to resemble the Italian tri-color flag. Stamped with maker's name "C.H. BERNARD & SONS... MALTA / GIBRALTAR" . . . . **$250 (£125)**

PATTERN 1943 GENERAL SERVICE CAP

- Beret style khaki wool cap with nickel Cameron Highlander's cap badge on obverse. Lined in khaki quilted cotton with Glasgow maker's stamp and Broad Arrow, dated "1944" . . . . **$75 (£40)**

PATTERN 1943 GENERAL SERVICE CAP, CANADA

- Khaki wool beret style cap with Canadian gilt general service badge. Lining made of waterproofed khaki quilted cotton and marked "7 1/8 / J. COLLETT Ltd. / LONDON / 1944" with the Broad Arrow . . . . . **$85 (£45)**

BERET, ARMORED FORCES

- Black wool beret has Royal Tank Regiment "Fear Naught" badge, black leather edge binding and adjustment ties. Interior lining with 1944 date, Broad Arrow proof, and maker's stamp . . . . **$165 (£85)**

Hats, Enlisted

JUNGLE HAT

- Australian style khaki wool felt bush hat with snap-up brim, light moth tracking to nap, khaki cotton pleated puggaree, battle flash on the upturned brim and silk ribbon orange square with two vertical black lines. Interior with brown leather sweatband embossed "Ball & Phillips Ltd. / 7 / 1942," reverse ink-stamped with "WD" and Broad Arrow. Complete brown leather chinstrap. . . . . **$200 (£100)**

JUNGLE HAT, AUSTRALIA

- Olive drab fur felt slouch hat with plain olive wool puggaree with red and blue wool felt Army insignia on the obverse. Left side snapped up with bronze "Australian Commonwealth Military Forces" badge. Interior has has brown leather sweatband with silver embossed inscription "N. 196 / SYDNEY AUST / SIZE 7 1/8 / 1944 / FUR FELT HAT" . . . . **$385 (£190)**

Caps, Female

CAP, ARMY CORPS SERVICE DRESS, CANADIAN

- Khaki cotton service cap with stitch reinforced visor and permanently turned-up neck cape, each side with three brown enameled vent grommets, obverse with brown leather chinstrap and "CANADIAN WOMEN'S ARMY CORPS" triangular cap badge. Interior has brown leather sweatband and olive satin twill lining stamped with "C" Broad Arrow proof and 1944-dated maker's stamp. . . . . **$95 (£50)**

CAP, ATS SERVICE DRESS, FIRST PATTERN

- First pattern khaki wool Service Dress cap. This earlier "soft" pattern had rows of reinforcing stitches on the visor, band, and curtain to give some substance to the cap. Interior is lined in an iridescent red/green rayon. . . . . **$195 (£100)**

The British MK II helmet was the standard headgear of the UK soldier in World War II, $75-$150 (£40-£75).

www.advanceguardmilitaria.com

Because of its distinctive shape, the MK III combat helmet was called the "turtle shell," $100-$175 (£50-£90).

www.advanceguardmilitaria.com

The MK IV was introduced in 1945. Very few actually were worn in combat, $50-$125 (£25-£65). Peter Suciu

The second-pattern British paratrooper helmet drew inspiration from the German M38 helmet, $800-$1,000 (£400-£500). Peter Suciu

The British dispatch rider's helmet was made of steel, $100-$200 (£50-£100). Peter Suciu

Caps and Hats, Miscellaneous

GLENGARRY, CAMERON HIGHLANDERS
- Midnight blue wool cap has black grosgrain edge band and tails, left side with stamped metal "CAMERON" badge. Interior has black cotton lining........ **$60 (£30)**

SCOTTISH ATHOLL BONNET, BLACK WATCH
- Dark blue traditional Highland side cap with red wool tuft and black silk ribbon tail, lined in black with Broad Arrow mark, lacks badge. As worn by the Black Watch and Queen's Own Cameron Highlanders ..... **$65 (£35)**

TAM O'SHANTER, KING'S OWN SCOTTISH BORDERERS
- Khaki wool bonnet with decorative bow on reverse of band, left side displaying a silvered King's Own Scottish Borderers regimental badge on tartan wool background and a white feather hackle, lined in khaki cotton.
....**$75 (£40)**

Flight Helmets

FLIGHT TEST HELMET
- Heavy khaki cotton twill flight helmet has interior lining of off-white wool flannel, brow with adjustable strap, reinforced ear port coverings, and stiffened chinstrap. Interior has "W / Broad Arrow / D" stamp and 1940-dated paper label............................**$125 (£65)**

FLIGHT HELMET, CANADA
- Sheepskin fleece helmet with brown finished exterior, sides with zipper closure earphone housings, and single buckle chinstrap with sliding fleece chin pad. Earphone housings are complete with "C-Broad Arrow" marked earphones with cloth covered cord and plug fitting.
....**$365 (£185)**

TYPE B FLYING HELMET, CANADA
- Canadian flight helmet of brown leather, pattern nearly identical to the RAF Type "B" flying helmet but without snaps and a bit different pattern chin buckle. Sides have zipper closure domed earphone housings and goggle strap guides. Reverse has sizing adjustment strap and buckle assembly. Interior lined with chamois and corded cloth brow sweat band...................**$275 (£140)**

TYPE C FLIGHT HELMET
- Type "C" leather flying helmet, as used by both RAF and American AAF pilots and aircrew. Made of supple brown leather with chamois lining, khaki web chinstrap, and complete with Air Ministry stamped electronics with fabric covered cord ....**$295 (£150)**

Helmets

MK I COASTAL DEFENSE HELMET
- British Mk I steel helmet with an elaborate spring-loaded flip down protective visor, obverse of helmet is stenciled "COASTAL DEFENCE" ....**$595 (£300)**

MK II CIVIL DEFENSE HELMET
- British MKII steel helmet with brown rubberized anti gas fireproof cover and neck cape, interior complete with suspension liner and khaki web chinstrap.....**$75 (£40)**

MK II COMBAT HELMET

- Mark II steel helmet with khaki finish, complete with liner and khaki web chinstrap . . . . **$95 (£50)**

MK II COMBAT HELMET, CANADIAN MANUFACTURE

- Canadian Manufactured Mark II helmet with olive drab finish. Interior rear brim maker marked "C.L./C." for the Canadian Motorlamp Company and dated "1940." Has black rubber and oilcloth liner, and early khaki web and spring chinstrap . . . . **$115 (£60)**

MK II COMBAT HELMET, DESERT CAMOUFLAGE

- WWI Brodies helmet refitted and repainted with khaki tan finish. Obverse has three small, evenly spaced holes presumably for attaching camouflage or splinter mask. Oilskin liner and elasticized chin strap present. . . . . **$285 (£145)**

MK II COMBAT HELMET, SOUTH AFRICA MANUFACTURE

- WWI Brodies helmet refitted and repainted with khaki tan finish. Liner band has "U" Broad Arrow South African proof, "1943" and "1942" dates . . . . **$125 (£65)**

MK II TANKER'S HELMET

- Mark II Tanker's helmet with olive drab finish, complete with black rubber and oilcloth liner dated 1941 and early khaki web and spring chinstrap . . . . **$175 (£90)**

MK III COMBAT HELMET

- "Turtle" shell shaped helmet with darkened khaki finish. Interior has black rubber bolstered MK II liner with cruciform pad, complete with adjustable web chinstrap. . . . . **$125 (£65)**

MK IV COMBAT STEEL HELMET

- Introduced in 1945, this pattern features the "lift the dot" liner that allows the helmet to remain watertight (for use as a wash basin in the field, etc.) . . . . **$85 (£45)**

MK I AIRBORNE HELMET

- Helmet has khaki finish, right side with red painted triangle and left side with vertical green stripe unit insignia, rim with the characteristic first pattern hard rubber edge reinforcement, and interior with padded liner and the unique first pattern black leather chin cup harness assembly. Brown leather sweatband has maker's stamp with war department proof and "1942" date . . . **$1,100 (£550)**

MK II SECOND PATTERN AIRBORNE HELMET

- Based on the design of the German M38, this helmet features a canvas chinstrap and special padded liner. The shell was also used by dispatch riders and tank personnel during and after World War II. . . . . **$850 (£425)**

DISPATCH RIDER'S HELMET

- Steel crash helmet with rough khaki finish. Interior has felt and leather padding, complete with wool lined leather ear flaps. Maker marked and dated "1942". . . . . **$195 (£100)**

> *"We learned to use our helmets for all kind of things."*
>
> PVT. HARRY HEINLEIN, 29TH U.S. INFANTRY DIVISION

UNITED STATES

Caps and Hats, Dress, Male

CAMPAIGN HAT, ENLISTED

- Olive drab heavy fur felt with khaki hat band and interior with brown leather sweatband. . . . . **$50 (£25)**

VISOR CAP, PRE-WWII ARMY AIR CORPS AVIATION CADET, SLATE BLUE

- Cap has bound black lacquered composition visor and adjustable chinstrap with gilt eagle side buttons. The slate blue crown, as worn between 1928 and 1940, has large winged propeller Aviation Cadet insignia badge. . . . . **$90 (£45)**

VISOR CAP, ARMY ENLISTED

- Enlisted pattern olive drab wool visor cap with gilt two-piece enlisted eagle device, brown lacquered leather chinstrap and visor. . . . . **$65 (£35)**

VISOR CAP, ARMY ENLISTED SUMMER

- Khaki cotton cap with brown leather front and rear chinstraps, and bound visor, obverse with gilt enlisted eagle badge . . . . **$55 (£30)**

Pre-World War II Army Air Corps Aviation Cadet cap in slate blue, $75-$100 (£40-£50). www.advanceguardmilitaria.com

U.S. Army enlisted visor cap, $45-$65 (£25-£35).
Author's collection

U.S. Army enlisted man's summer khaki visor cap, $45-$75 (£25-£40).
Charles D. Pautler

U.S. Army officer's visor cap, $85-$195 (£45-£100).

Charles D. Pautler

Army officer's wool elastique visor cap, $175-$250 (£90-£125).

www.advanceguardmilitaria.com

Army Air Force's officer's khaki summer visor cap formed into "crusher" shape, $225-$275 (£115-£140).

Charles D. Pautler

USMC officer's visor cap with white removable cover, $275-$325 (£140-£165).

www.advanceguardmilitaria.com

U.S. Navy field grade officer's cap with tropical cover, $100-$150 (£50-£75).

www.advanceguardmilitaria.com

VISOR CAP, AAF ENLISTED "CRUSHER"

- Khaki summer weight wool enlisted service cap with soft brown leather visor, chinstrap and back strap secured by gilt commercial eagle buttons, obverse with gilded enlisted eagle insignia, interior with full crown sweat shield, "Society Brand" maker's label. . . . .**$110 (£55)**

VISOR CAP, ARMY OFFICER

- Service dress visored cap of olive drab felted wool with mohair crown braid, gilt officer's eagle device, eagle side buttons, brown leather chinstrap, and bound brown leather visor. . . . .**$95 (£50)**

VISOR CAP, ARMY OFFICER, "PINK"

- Light olive drab wool elastique officer's visor cap with olive drab mohair band, gilt officer's eagle device and side buttons. . . . .**$225 (£115)**

VISOR CAP, ARMY OFFICER KHAKI SUMMER

- Khaki visor cap with adjustable brown lacquered leather chinstrap secured by gilt eagle side buttons, brown lacquered leather visor and gilt Army officer's eagle device. . . . .**$115 (£60)**

VISOR CAP, AAF OFFICER "CRUSHER"

- Soft, two-ply, very thin brown leather visor and brown leather adjustable chinstrap, khaki lightweight wool crown with gilt officer's eagle device . . . .**$250 (£125)**

VISOR CAP, USMC OFFICER

- Marine Corps officer's visor cap with white removable crown with internal stiffener and quatrefoil crown braid, silver and gilt USMC officer's cap emblem, red piped gilt adjustable chinstrap secured by gilt Marine eagle side buttons, and bright lacquered visor. Interior has basket weave crown band, sweat guard with "Berkshire Caps" logo and "Jos. A. Wilner Co. / Uniform Shop / Washington, D.C." dealer's information with blank identification name tag. . . . .**$295 (£150)**

VISOR CAP, NAVY OFFICER

- Visor cap has white cotton cover, black mohair band, obverse has Navy officer's eagle device, gilt chinstrap secured by two Navy eagle side buttons. Interior has brown leather sweatband and crown strap both printed with maker's stamp "The ALOHA Cap / Service Center, Ltd. / Honolulu, T.H." . . . . **$95 (£50)**

VISOR CAP, NAVY COMMANDER

- Officer's visor cap has white cotton crown, deluxe quality bound leather and velvet visor with gold embroidered oak leaf and acorn visor trim, bullion chinstrap, and black mohair band with gold and silver bullion embroidered commissioned officer's cap device. . . . .**$135 (£70)**

OVERSEAS CAP, AIRBORNE INFANTRY ENLISTED

- Olive drab wool garrison cap with infantry piping and enlisted airborne personnel embroidered insignia. . . . . **$85 (£45)**

OVERSEAS CAP, AIRBORNE ARTILLERY ENLISTED

- Officer quality dark olive drab wool elastique sidecap with red Artillery piping and Airborne Personnel insignia on the left side of the cap . . . . **$85 (£45)**

OVERSEAS CAP, INFANTRY ENLISTED

- Officer quality dark OD wool elastique with bright bold blue Infantry piping. Interior with black synthetic lining and brown leather sweatband . . . . **$25 (£15)**

OVERSEAS CAP, ARMY ENLISTED, AUSTRALIAN-MADE

- Khaki wool overseas cap with "US" disc. Interior with olive cotton lining, gray cotton sweatband, and Brisbane, Australia maker's label. . . . . **$25 (£15)**

OVERSEAS CAP, USMC ENLISTED

- Forest green wool sidecap with bronze EGA emblem, ... **$55 (£30)**

OVERSEAS CAP, ARMY FIRST LIEUTENANT

- Olive drab wool elastique overseas cap has gold and black officer's piping and silver pinback first lieutenant's rank insignia . . . . **$25 (£15)**

OVERSEAS CAP, ARMY SECOND LIEUTENANT, BRITISH MADE

- Dark olive drab elastique overseas cap with officer's gilt and black edge piping and pinback second lieutenant's rank insignia. Interior has chocolate brown twill lining and London maker's name . . . . **$35 (£20)**

Caps and Hats, Utility, Male

FATIGUE HAT, ARMY BLUE DENIM HAT

- Hat has stitch reinforced brim and interior with contract tag dated 1937 . . . . **$50 (£25)**

FATIGUE HAT, ARMY OLIVE DRAB

- Olive drab cotton "Daisy Mae" hat with stitched brim. . . . . **$45 (£25)**

ARMY 1941 PATTERN HBT CAP

- Olive drab HBT cotton cap with bound stitch reinforced visor and two olive enameled side grommet vents. . . . . **$55 (£30)**

ARMY M1943 FIELD CAP

- Olive drab cotton M43 visored field cap with two side grommets, bound cloth covered visor, and interior with fold-up ear flaps and 1944-dated Philadelphia Quartermaster Depot tag . . . . **$35 (£20)**

ARMY MOUNTAIN TROOPS SKI CAP

- 1942 pattern olive drab cotton poplin cap has olive drab wool flannel lining, turned ear cape with adjustable chinstrap that pivots on its attachment points, and olive poplin covered reinforced visor. . . . . **$325 (£165)**

AAF A3 MECHANIC'S BALL CAP

- Sage green HBT ball cap has stitch reinforced visor, side with "ARMY AIR FORCE" winged star logo, and interior. . . . . **$85 (£45)**

AAF A4 KNIT CAP

- Olive drab wool knit cap has silver and black woven nomenclature label "TYPE A-4" with specification data and contractor below . . . . **$95 (£50)**

AAF B-2 FLEECE CAP

- Brown finished exterior and white fleece interior with turned ear and neck cape, front with large bound brown leather visor. . . . . **$175 (£90)**

U.S. Navy officer's khaki cap, $145-$295 (£775-£300).
www.advanceguardmilitaria.com

Overseas cap for an enlisted para-glider infantryman, $85-$150 (£45-£125).
Minnesota Military Museum

Overseas cap for an enlisted airborne artillery soldier, $65-$125 (£35-£65).
www.advanceguardmilitaria.com

Artillery enlisted man's overseas cap, $10-$15 (£5-£8).
Minnesota Military Museum

Para-glider officer's overseas cap, $100-$175 (£50-£90).
www.advanceguardmilitaria.com

U.S. Army blue denim "Daisy Mae" fatigue hat, $35-$65 (£20-£35). Charles D. Pautler

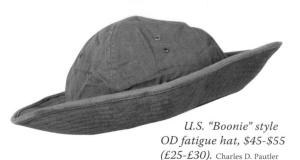

U.S. "Boonie" style OD fatigue hat, $45-$55 (£25-£30). Charles D. Pautler

Herringbone twill fatigue cap in OD #7, ca. 1944, $25-$45 (£15-£25).
Charles D. Pautler

The Model 1943 field cap was introduced in 1943 and worn well into the late 1950s, $25-$45 (£15-£25). Author's collection

1942 pattern ski cap for mountain troops, $300-$365 (£150-£185). Author's collection

The Model 1943 Winter Cap, Fur, was issued to troops in the Italian and southern France campaigns, $55-$95 (£30-£50).
Author's collection

Army Air Force Type A3 mechanic's cap, $65-$95 (£35-£50).
Charles D. Pautler

Army Air Force Type B-2 winter flying cap, $150-$225 (£75-£115). Charles D. Pautler

USMC PATTERN OF 1941 HBT UTILITY CAP
- P1941 sage green herringbone twill fatigue cap with black stenciled EGA on obverse and stitched visor.
.... **$65 (£35)**

FATIGUE HAT, NAVY, WHITE
- White cotton hat with stitched brim. Interior with white cotton lining and size stamp................... **$5 (£2)**

M1941 KNIT CAP
- M1941 "jeep cap" of olive drab wool with narrow, pasteboard stiffened visor and fold down ear flaps.. **$85 (£45)**

CAP, WINTER
- WWII version of the M1907 winter cap. Olive drab cotton canvas with OD wool lining, obverse with strap and buckle securing neck flap, and stitch reinforced visor.
.... **$40 (£20)**

WWII LAMBSKIN LINED WINTER CAP
- Oive drab wool serge with lambskin lined folding neck cape fitted with bronze buckles and snap closures. Interior has quilted olive drab cotton lining....... **$85 (£45)**

M41 CLOTH HOOD
- Water and wind resistant olive poplin hood with integral cap bill, as worn over the wool knit toque during cold weather.................................... **$20 (£10)**

M43 JACKET HOOD
- Detachable hood for the M1943 Field Jacket ... **$10 (£5)**

NAVY DECK HELMET, OLIVE DRAB
- Heavy olive drab cotton twill visored cloth helmet with neck cape has olive gray wool lining, "U.S.N." stencil on the cape, adjustable chinstrap, and reverse with strap guides for goggles. Interior has Navy contract tag listing size "7" .... **$30 (£15)**

MARINE TROPICAL FIBER PITH HELMET
- Model 1940 helmet with khaki fabric covered molded fiber with green fabric covered interior, brown cloth chinstrap, and brown painted fabric sweatband suspension. Obverse with Marine EGA insignia .... **$135 (£70)**

Hats and Caps, Female

VISOR CAP, AMERICAN RED CROSS
- Oxford gray whipcord wool ARC female pattern visor cap with blue and white enameled Red Cross insignia on the front................................. **$45 (£25)**

VISOR CAP, WAAC/WAC SUMMER
- "Hobby Hat" (so named after the first director of the WAC, Col. Oveta Hobby) in khaki tropical worsted wool. Cap has straight semi-stiff sides and a flat crown with a cloth covered visor, cloth chinstrap and plastic WAC crest buttons .... **$145 (£75)**

VISOR CAP, WAAC/WAC WINTER
- Olive drab wool "Hobby Hat." Cap has straight sides and a flat crown with a cloth covered visor, cloth chinstrap and plastic WAC crest buttons, no badge applied. Interior lined in bronze colored rayon with a plastic sweat shield.................................. **$145 (£75)**

The white fatigue hat is probably the most recognizable of U.S. World War II naval headgear, $5-$10 (£2-£5). Charles D. Pautler

The M1941 knit cap was made to be worn under the M1 helmet, $65-$95 (£35-£50). www.advanceguardmilitaria.com

Existing stocks of M1907 winter caps were issued to U.S. troops in cold climates in the first few years of World War II, $25-$65 (£15-£35). Author's collection

U.S. Army enlisted man's winter cap, third pattern, $25-$45 (£15-£25). Author's collection

The "Cap, Winter, Lambskin Lined" was a favorite with troops in Alaska, $65-$95 (£35-£50). Author's collection

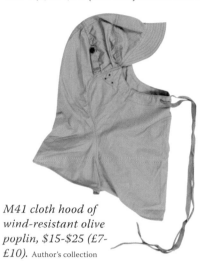

M41 cloth hood of wind-resistant olive poplin, $15-$25 (£7-£10). Author's collection

The M43 hood was made to worn alone or buttoned to the M43 field jacket, $5-$15 (£2-£5). Author's collection

U.S. Navy deck helmet in olive drab, $25-$30 (£10-£15). www.advanceguardmilitaria.com

Marine Corps Model 1940 tropical fiber pith helmet, $100-$165 (£50-£85). www.advanceguardmilitaria.com

WAAC/WAC Summer "Hobby Hat," $125-$165 (£65-£85). www.advanceguardmilitaria.com

Women's Army Corps winter issue cap, $125-$175 (£65-£90). Mary Schmidt

USMC Women's Relief service cap, $100-$150 (£50-£75).
www.advanceguardmilitaria.com

Navy enlisted WAVES summer cap, $65-$95 (£35-£50). www.advanceguardmilitaria.com

U.S. Navy WAVE soft-brimmed cap with "NAVY" tally, $65-$95 (£35-£50).
www.advanceguardmilitaria.com

Women's Army Corps enlisted overseas cap, $35-$55 (£20-£30). Mary Schmidt

WAC summer enlisted overseas cap, $25-$50 (£15-£25).
www.advanceguardmilitaria.com

VISOR CAP, ANC OFFICER

- Model 1943 olive drab wool barathea Army Nurse pattern visor cap with semi soft, round sloped crown and brass officer's cap device . . . . **$85 (£45)**

SERVICE CAP, USMCWR WOMAN'S WOOL

- Forest green wool women's pattern service cap with red hat cord Marine eagle side buttons, and crown with bronze EGA device . . . . **$125 (£65)**

SERVICE CAP, NAVY ENLISTED WAVES

- Soft, brimmed cap with blue and white seersucker crown and navy blue brim with US NAVY black silk tally. Interior has light blue woven WAVES tag. . . . . **$85 (£45)**

CAP, NAVY ENLISTED WAVES

- Soft brimmed WAVES cap, two piece with a dark blue brim and snap on crown. Lacks the US NAVY tally. Interior has the light blue woven WAVES clothing label. . . . . **$55 (£30)**

OVERSEAS CAP, WAC ENLISTED

- Olive drab wool side cap with distinctive WAC profile has green and gold enlisted piping. Lined in light olive rayon . . . . **$45 (£25)**

OVERSEAS CAP, WAC SUMMER ENLISTED

- Khaki cotton side cap with distinctive WAC profile has green and gold enlisted piping . . . . **$30 (£15)**

OVERSEAS CAP, WAC ENLISTED OFF-DUTY

- Off white or "Military-Beige" side cap of shantung rayon has green and gold enlisted WAC piping. Interior is lined in dark taupe rayon . . . . **$65 (£35)**

OVERSEAS CAP, NAVY WAVES

- Gray and white pinstriped cloth sidecap. Contract tag marked "MADE AND SOLD UNDER THE AUTHORITY OF U.S. NAVY W.A.V.E.S." . . . . **$85 (£45)**

WINTER CAP (BERET), CADET NURSE CORPS

- "Montgomery beret" made of three sections of gray wool with silvered Cadet Nurse badge on the front. Interior with grosgrain sweatband . . . . **$195 (£100)**

Caps and Hats, Utility, Female

UTILITY CAP, WAC

- White cotton lawn cap worn by cooks, bakers, and laundresses has a wide folded band and a loose, pleated crown to cover the hair. It is adjusted by means of a drawstring at the nape of the neck . . . . **$25 (£15)**

Flight Helmets

A-9 FLIGHT HELMET

- Type A-9 helmet fitted with the Gosport tube communication system used for intracockpit communication. Heavy olive cotton with printed Army Air Forces emblem, shearling padded chinstrap, and leather reinforced openings for the plated copper Gosport receivers. Interior with woven nomenclature tag and pink "powder puff" ear cushions. Gosport communication system is complete with the ear pieces, flexible red/orange rubber hose, olive drab plastic "V" tube splitter and mouthpiece. . . . . **$175 (£90)**

A-11 LEATHER FLIGHT HELMET

- Brown leather A-11 flight helmet has AAF winged star insignia decal on the left side, ear ports complete with ANB-H-1 receivers and wiring harness with cord and plug attachment . . . . **$200 (£100)**

AN-H-15 FLIGHT HELMET

- Khaki cotton flight helmet with black rubber earphone cups, with ANB-H-1 avionics and extension cord, AAF winged star insignia, brown leather fittings and cushioned chinstrap. . . . . **$155 (£80)**

AN6540 FLIGHT HELMET

- Brown leather flight helmet with chamois lining, ANB-H-1 earphones complete with cord and plug, padded chin strap and buckles for attaching oxygen mask. Has Slote & Klein woven contract tag and size label. . . . . **$175 (£80)**

B-6 FLEECE FLIGHT HELMET AND EARPHONES

- Sheepskin fleece flying helmet with brown polyacrylate finish with brown leather trim and blackened metal fit-

tings. Interior has Army Air Force woven label "TYPE B-6" with contract data and size "Medium." Earphones are complete with ANB-H-1 receivers, wiring loom, and plug . . . . **$285 (£145)**

NAF-1092 FLIGHT HELMET

- Brown leather flight helmet. Interior chamois lining has contract tag and size label. . . . . **$110 (£55)**

D-1 FLYER'S COLD WEATHER FACE MASK

- Thick olive drab felt face mask with open eyes and nose, with light olive edge binding and elastic head strap system. Interior with gray felt lining and AAF printed nomenclature label. Has AAF winged star insignia faintly stamped on one side . . . . **$50 (£25)**

M-450 FLIGHT HELMET

- M-450 khaki cotton flight helmet with tan/gray painted leather ear cups and TH37 receivers complete with the very scarce extension cord attachment that fits the TH37 receiver wiring loom. Has matching tan/gray painted leather lined chin cup with the top of the oval trimmed

WAC enlisted "off-duty" cap, $50-$75 (£25-£40). www.advanceguardmilitaria.com

Cadet Nurse Corps' winter cap, $175-$225 (£90-£130). www.advanceguardmilitaria.com

WAC white cotton lawn utility cap, $20-$30 (£10-£15). www.advanceguardmilitaria.com

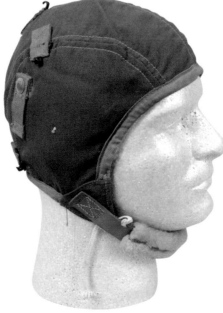

A-11 Intermediate flight helmet (leather fleece lined) with B-8 goggles, and A-14 oxygen mask, $495-$595 (£250-£300). Charles D. Pautler

A-9 flying helmet was made of unlined gabardine, $150-$200 (£75-£100). Charles D. Pautler

AN-H-15 summer weight flying helmet, $145-$175 (£75-£90). Charles D. Pautler

Operation Overlord, the code name of the Normady landings, began on June 6, 1944. By June 12, 1944, 326,000 troops and 54,000 vehicles were on the beaches of Normandy. By July 2, another 929,000 men and 177,000 vehicles were put ashore. The ship armada at Normandy totalled 6,939 vessels of all kinds. In the 10 days after D-Day (June 6 to June 16) a total of 5,287 Allied soldiers were killed. With the massive amount of men and equipment involved, the Normandy invasion was, and still is, the largest naval landing in history.

M1 HELMET, SWIVEL BAIL, NAVY
7TH BEACH BATTALION
- Mid-war M1 helmet with front weld seam and flexible chinstrap loops lacking chinstraps. Exterior has olive drab painted finish, base with light blue band, and obverse with red arc over "USN" with unit numeral "7" below. The 7th Navy Beach Battalion went ashore with and ahead of the 29th Division on Omaha Beach.
.... **$4,275 (£2,140)**

M1 HELMET, SWIVEL BAIL WITH SECOND
MARINE CAMOUFLAGED COVER
- Mid- to late-war M1 helmet has flexible chinstrap loops with olive web chinstrap and front brim weld seam. Covered with Marine second pattern camouflage cover, obverse with faded but still quite visible Marine eagle, globe and anchor insignia. Has WWII Firestone liner with light olive web suspension............**$550 (£275)**

Helmet Liners

M1 HELMET LINER, HAWLEY
- Cloth covered fiber helmet liner complete with early style leather chinstrap with permanent side post attachments and metal frame buckle.............**$295 (£150)**

M1 helmet, fixed bail with first pattern USMC cover, $650-$850 (£325-£425). www.advanceguardmilitaria.com

M1 helmet with swivel bails and liner, $75-$100 (£40-£50). www.advanceguardmilitaria.com

29th Infantry Division painted rough texture M1 helmet with swivel bails, $895-$1,400 (£450-£700). Charles D. Pautler

1st Army swivel bail helmet, $750-$950 (£375-£475). www.advanceguardmilitaria.com

M1 helmet, swivel bail, painted with combat medic's insignia, $500-$950 (£250-£475). Charles D. Pautler

M1 helmet, swivel bail, U.S. Navy, 7th Beach Battalion, $4,000-$5,000 (£2,000-£2,500). www.advanceguardmilitaria.com

HAWLEY HELMET LINER, CIVIL DEFENSE AIR RAID WARDEN

- Hawley helmet liner produced as a stand-alone item painted white with the CD Air Raid Warden's decal on the front . . . . **$185 (£90)**

M1 HELMET LINER, WESTINGHOUSE

- Westinghouse contract composition liner with olive drab finish, interior with khaki suspension and leather sweatband, complete with leather chinstrap . . . . **$75 (£40)**

HELMET LINER, 5TH ARMY CAPTAIN

- M1 helmet liner with olive finish. Captain's bars insignia on obverse, and 5th Army insignia on left side. Interior is complete. . . . . **$110 (£55)**

HELMET LINER, MAJOR

- M1 helmet composition liner with olive drab finish, obverse with detailed Major's gilt oak-leaf painted insignia and silver name inscription . . . . **$95 (£50)**

PARATROOPER HELMET LINER

- Westinghouse airborne helmet liner with olive drab exterior finish. Interior has light olive web suspension with brown leather sweatband and liner chinstrap. Sides have darker olive web "A" straps properly fitted under the triangular web suspension retaining pieces as can only be properly done during manufacture of the liner, not later by someone trying to make an airborne liner out of a standard one. Sides have snap fittings for attaching the chinstrap tabs from the helmet itself . . . . **$450 (£225)**

Helmets, Flak

NAVY MKII "TALKER" HELMET

- Navy "sea blue" textured finish, interior complete with permanent cloth covered padding liner system and detachable leather chin cup assembly, interior reverse of helmet stenciled "U.S.N.", obverse "MK-2" . . . . . **$95 (£50)**

M3 FLAK HELMET

- Olive drab finish with flock coating, hinged ear armored ear flap, khaki web chinstrap with snap closure, and interior with khaki web suspension . . . . **$185 (£95)**

M4A2 FLAK HELMET

- The M4A2 was standardized in June 1942. Olive drab cloth covered Hadfield steel plate helmet has attached side ear flaps and leather chinstrap. . . . . **$175 (£90)**

M5 FLAK HELMET

- Olive drab flocked finish, armored ear flaps with leather strap and buckle, and interior with khaki web and leather suspension system . . . . **$135 (£70)**

M1 helmet, swivel bail, with second pattern USMC camouflage cover, $450-$795 (£225-£400). Charles D. Pautler

The Hawley pattern liner for the U.S. M1 helmet is the most desirable of all the various liner manufacturers, $250-$375 (£125-£190). Charles D. Pautler

Hawley also manufactured liners that were used for Civil Defense personnel, $150-$200 (£75-£100). www.advanceguardmilitaria.com

Composition M1 helmet liner for a two-star general, $200-$350 (£100-£175). www.advanceguardmilitaria.com

Composition helmet liner with major's insignia, $85-$100 (£45-£50). www.advanceguardmilitaria.com

The MK II "talker's" helmet was large enough to allow to wear a headset underneath it, $75-$135 (£40-£70). Minnesota Military Museum

M3 flak helmet, $175-$225 (£90-£115).

www.advanceguardmilitaria.com

Helmets, Tanker

M1930 INFANTRY-STYLE "DOUGHNUT" TANKER HELMET

* This early tanker helmet was developed by the Army in 1930. Resin impregnated fiber crown has ventilation holes and a light olive painted finish. It is encircled by a crash "bumper" covered in tan doeskin leather. Cushioned sides have olive leather exteriors with ear cups for headphones and leather neck strap. Reverse has rear neck guard with goggle retaining straps.
. . . . **$3,850 (£1,925)**

M1942 ARMORED CREWMAN HELMET

* "Tanker" helmet of olive drab hardened composition fiber material. Interior has padded brown leather liner marked with "RAWLINGS / 7" maker's size stamp.
. . . .**$185 (£95)**

M4A2 flak helmet, $150-$200 (£75-£100). www.advanceguardmilitaria.com

The M5 flak helmet was one of the last flak helmets to be authorized during World War II, $125-$150 (£65-£75). Minnesota Military Museum

M1942 "Tanker's" helmet, $150-$275 (£75-£14). Charles D. Pautler

CHAPTER 3

ACCOUTERMENTS

After World War II, many soldiers brought home pieces of their "field gear." Often, the intent was to continue to use their war materials in the pursuit of hobbies or careers. Today, it is not uncommon to find an old Army shovel, pair of wire cutters, or some form of haversack or pouch amidst a stash of tools or outdoor gear.

Collecting and displaying accouterments provide the World War II enthusiast with a feeling of direct connection to the soldier. These were, after all, the tools of the soldier's trade—the very trappings that he or she wore on campaign, in battle, on the drill field, and finally, the souvenirs to remind him of his or her time in the service.

Nearly every World War II combatant was issued some form of cartridge belt or carrier, a pack for his belongings, mess gear and canteen and some form of tent or shelter. Nevertheless, all accouterments have not survived at the same rate and one doesn't find the same proportion of these items today. While cartridge belts, first-aid pouches, and even knapsacks have survived by the hundreds of thousands, specialty items such as gas detection brassards or special "paratrooper" first-aid pouches are exceedingly rare.

Once sold as surplus material, a lot of accouterments are still seeing hard service today. Reenacting the lives of the World War II soldier is a popular hobby in the United States, Great Britain, most of Europe, and even Japan and Australia. The demand for the common trappings has driven up prices and even given birth to a widespread reproduction market. Some caution should be exercised when considering rare accouterments, especially those designed for elite troops such as paratroopers, commandos or SS soldiers. However, the mass of material that survived the war has kept prices affordable for many of the more common pieces.

The abundance of some items (like cartridge belts, canteens, and shovels) enables collectors to specialize in one particular accouterment by seeking out variations and various makers' marks. Others find it satisfying to amass all the trappings worn by typical officers or enlisted men of various nations. Whatever the angle, though, there is plenty of material that survived the war to keep a collector busy for years.

Collecting Hints

Pros:

- Fakes of common items are not as prevalent.
- Due to the volume of equipment produced, a wide variety of variations and manufacturers exists for most accouterments.
- Accouterments, by their very nature, have a "personal" feel to them. By collecting the complete trappings of a soldier, a collector can develop a keen sense of a typical World War II soldier's burden.

Cons:

- Leather and metal accouterments can be hard to store properly. Leather requires special treatment and is prone to flaking and dryness. Ideally, it is stored in a slightly humid environment. Metal items, especially tin-dipped iron such as canteens, are prone to rust, and must be kept dry.
- Different types of accouterments survived at disproportionate rates. As an example, U.S. cartridge belts have survived by the hundreds of thousands, but very few U.S. paratrooper first-aid pouches have survived. Therefore, assembling a complete soldier's kit is costly, especially if one is depicting an "elite" soldier such as a paratrooper or British Commando.
- Because the bulk of accouterments have entered the market through surplus channels, very few items have a known provenance. This can give accouterments a "bland" feel, since they do not have the same sorts of associated war stories as, for example, a soldier's uniform with all of his medals displayed on it.

Availability ★★★★

Price ★★

Reproduction Alert ★

BELGIUM

Belts, Buckles and Plates

INFANTRY WAIST BELT AND BUCKLE

• Dark brown leather belt with brass catch, maker marked, complete with brass frame buckle. . . . . **$40 (£20)**

Bread Bags

BREAD BAG

• Khaki canvas bread bag, similar in style to the pattern used in WWI but updated with adjustable belt loops and double canteen holder band on flap. Complete with adjustable web sling, both marked "ARMEE BELGE" in purple ink. . . . . **$80 (£40)**

Canteens and Mess Equipment

CANTEEN

• Spun aluminum single spout canteen, similar to the German pattern, with stopper on khaki web strap with buckle, olive drab wool felt cover with Prym snap closure and web loops to hold Mills type khaki web shoulder sling with buckle, marked "ARMEE BELGE" . . **$35 (£20)**

ARMY MESS KIT

• Kidney-shaped aluminum mess kit retaining olive drab finish, with friction lid and loop for equipment strap. Complete with folding wire bail, maker marked.
. . . . **$45 (£25)**

Belgian Sacic pattern gas mask, $65-$95 (£35-£50).

www.advanceguardmilitaria.com

Chemical Warfare Equipment

GAS MASK AND CARRIER

• Belgian Sacic pattern gas mask has brown rubber facemask with 1934 date. Mask is complete good pliable brown rubber hose, metal box filter, and khaki canvas and web rectangular carrier . . . . **$85 (£45)**

Entrenching Equipment

ENTRENCHING SHOVEL AND CARRIER

• Flat-bladed soldier's entrenching shovel with French style ringed socket riveted to mildly curved square blade, turned oak handle with "T" grip, and reverse of blade with 1920 maker's date stamp. Cover/carrier is made of brown leather, open-face style similar in pattern to both the Belgian and French WWI patterns, with loops for attachment to the combat waist belt. Stamped with Brussels maker stamp . . . . **$65 (£35)**

Holsters

BROWNING HI-POWER PISTOL HOLSTER

• British-style khaki web holster with breakaway flap secured by web strap and D-ring through metal escutcheon, reverse with belt loop and wire belt securing attachments. Interior has a place for a spare magazine and retains the original cleaning rod. Unmarked. . . **$35 (£20)**

PISTOL AND SHOULDER STOCK HOLSTER

• Model 1935 Browning automatic pistol holster of dark brown leather, pistol holster sewn directly to the obverse of the larger holster for the wooden shoulder stock. Both share a single flap and closure strap, double belt loops on reverse with brass "D" ring to attach a shoulder sling.
. . . .**$225 (£115)**

Packs

INFANTRY KNAPSACK

• Olive cotton webbing box knapsack with web loops on flap and sides to attach the mess kit and blanket roll. Interior with bamboo frame and issue marked "J.D.V." Complete with adjustable brown leather shoulder straps.
. . . . **$50 (£25)**

Belgian Browning Hi-Power pistol holster, $25-$50 (£15-£25).

www.advanceguardmilitaria.com

Finland

Belts, Buckles and Plates

COMBAT WAIST BELT

- Brown leather waist belt with integral brass roller buckle. Chape stamped with issue date "INT 39". . . . . **$125 (£65)**

ENLISTED WAIST BELT PLATE

- German-style stamped metal, bold relief wreathed rampant lion Finnish insignia. Reverse has two-prong roller bar attachment . . . . **$55 (£30)**

OFFICER'S BROCADE BELT

- Silver bullion flecked with blue silk brocade belt on sky blue wool backing complete with silvered metal two-piece rampant lion officer's belt buckle, catch, interior leather adjustment belt, and sliding keeper. . . **$185 (£95)**

Bread Bag

BREAD BAG AND STRAP

- Slightly larger than, but similar in pattern to, the German WWI bread bag. Made of field gray canvas with gray leather fittings and matching field gray strap.. **$135 (£70)**

Canteens and Mess Kits

CANTEEN

- German-style aluminum flask canteen with brown leather strap assembly and lace-up closure, brown wool cover, screw cap marked with White Guards stamp and "31" date. . . . . **$95 (£50)**

Russian shovel captured and reissued by the Finnish Army, with hanger, $100-$150 (£50-£75).
www.advanceguardmilitaria.com

Norwegian shovel reissued by Finnish Army, $100-$125 (£50-£65). www.advanceguardmilitaria.com

MESS KIT

- German-style aluminum mess kit with blackened finish (from use). Lit marked "INT 43". . . . . **$65 (£35)**

Chemical Warfare Equipment

GAS MASK BAG

- Field gray cotton divided rectangular carrier with two-button flap closure and carrying strap. Interior has tie-down cord and a maker's stamp, "Kss". . . . . **$55 (£30)**

HORSE GAS MASK

- Complete horse gas mask comprised of padded gray rubberized fabric enclosed muzzle cover with large field gray metal exhalation valve on front, brown leather straps for attaching the mask to the horse's bridle, heavily cushioned top band to help create a good gas seal around the horse's muzzle, and side connection to a very large ribbed gray cloth covered air intake hose. The hose disappears into an olive and field gray padded carrier that attaches to the horse's harness with gray cloth tie straps. Inside the carrier and connected to the hose is the massive 8" diameter metal gas filter that is dated "27.10.1941". . . . .**$465 (£235)**

Entrenching Equipment

SHOVEL, SOVIET REISSUE, WITH BELT HOOK

- Russian Linneman pattern entrenching tool with olive painted finish. Blade has an "SA" rectangular Finnish cartouche, and is pierced for the belt hanger. This shovel is complete with the blackened metal hook system that has thumb-release locking cam latch to keep the shovel in place. Brown harness leather belt hook is secured by two rivets and has rectangular Finnish "SA." stamp. The shovels are fairly common, but the hook is quite scarce. . . . .**$125 (£65)**

SHOVEL

- 26" long Norwegian style soldier's issue entrenching spade with rectangular "SA" Finnish Army cartouche and metal framed wood "D" handle. Side of the blade is pierced for the Finnish issue belt hook carrying assembly. . . . .**$115 (£60)**

SHOVEL BELT HOOK

- Blackened metal hook system has thumb-release locking cam latch to keep the shovel in place, brown harness leather belt hook is secured by two rivets and has rectangular Finnish "SA" stamp. . . . . **$75 (£40)**

Finnish shovel belt hook rarer than the shovels, $65-$85 (£35-£45). www.advanceguardmilitaria.com

Holsters

LAHTI HOLSTER

• Olive green leather clamshell holster for the Finnish Lahti automatic pistol. Flap has Finnish army "SA" proof. Reverse of holster has belt loop and 3" wide loop at top and narrow 3/4" leather loop at muzzle end used to retain the shoulder stock attachment . . . .**$215 (£110)**

FRANCE

Canteens and Mess Kits

MODEL 1935 CANTEEN

• Single spout 2-liter canteen with stopper and olive drab wool cover. Complete with brown leather suspension straps with snap hooks, cork stopper, and stopper cord. . . . . **$80 (£40)**

CANTEEN, DOUBLE SPOUT

• Two-liter, double spout canteen with khaki wool cover and stoppers . . . . **$85 (£45)**

MESS KIT

• Model 1935 aluminum mess kit with folding bail handle and closure, complete with interior tray, base maker marked and dated 1936 . . . . **$45 (£25)**

Chemical Warfare Equipment

ANP 31 GAS MASK

• 1939-dated mask with flexible face piece, hose and filter, complete with olive canvas bag with web sling. Issue marked and dated "1935" . . . . **$75 (£40)**

French risque trench art, German canteen with etched inscription "TOURNADRE JEAN / SOUVENIR DE L' HOTEL CAFARD / EAU SANS VIN." Reverse has depiction of a nude female figure seated on a bench, $60-$80 (£30-£40). www.advanceguardmilitaria.com

TC 38 GAS MASK

• Civilian protection gas mask, which is very similar to the military ANP T 31 mask. Has khaki rubberized face mask and clear celluloid lenses with 1939-dated filter. These were issued to the French civilian population at the beginning of WWII. Includes the original metal reinforced pasteboard cylindrical carrier with broken lid and base. These were issued to the French civilian population at the beginning of WWII . . . . **$45 (£25)**

Pouches, Ammunition

AMMUNITION POUCH SET

• Matching left and right pair of Model 1935 ammunition pouches of brown leather . . . . **$135 (£70)**

Pouches and Packs, Personal Equipment

AMMUNITION HAVERSACK

• Model 1935 olive drab canvas single bag haversack with brown leather trim and straps, metal fittings painted black, complete with pockets on body front, attaches to rings on the belt set. This was intended to hold a soldier's reserve ammunition . . . . **$45 (£25)**

AUXILIARY HAVERSACK

• M1861 olive canvas side bag with flap closed by two "EQUIPEMENTS MILITAIRES" buttons and adjustable web shoulder sling with steel buckle and two attached spring clips so it can be worn alone or as an auxiliary haversack on the M1935 equipment . . . . **$35 (£20)**

INFANTRY KNAPSACK

• Model 1935 olive drab canvas single bag knapsack with brown leather trim and straps, metal fittings painted black, complete with side pockets . . . . **$65 (£35)**

Tents

SHELTER HALF

• Khaki canvas shelter half with aluminum corner grommets. Unmarked . . . . **$50 (£25)**

French shelter half with aluminum grommets, $50-$65 (£25-£35).

www.advanceguardmilitaria.com

Wire Cutters

LONG HANDLE WIRE CUTTERS

* 20" overall, iron with steel cutter teeth and integral wire guides. Iron handles terminate into wood grips. Maker marked and dated "PEUGEOT FRERES 1940" . . . . **$65 (£35)**

WIRE CUTTER CARRIER

* Brown leather frame with A-shaped cap for the cutter nose. Reverse has loops for attaching to other equipment. Stamped "34" . . . . **$35 (£20)**

GERMANY

Bayonet Frogs

BAYONET FROG, MAUSER

* Brown rough-out leather bayonet frog with sewn construction with aluminum reinforcement rivets. Reverse side has indistinct maker's stamp . . . . **$65 (£35)**

TROPICAL BAYONET FROG

* Light olive heavy canvas with retaining strap **$135 (£70**

Belts, Belt Plates and Buckles

ARMY BELT PLATE

* Pebbled aluminum buckle painted army green . . . . **$45 (£25)**

ARMY WARTIME BELT PLATE

* Stamped steel plate with army eagle, late war dark gray finish, reverse maker marked . . . . **$55 (£30)**

ARMY COMBAT WAIST BELT AND PLATE

* Black leather combat waist belt with Army buckle in field gray painted finish with "1940" dated maker's tab . . . . **$125 (£65)**

ARMY OFFICER'S COMBAT WAIST BELT
WITH PEBBLED FRAME BUCKLE

* Leather officer's field service equipment belt with gray pebble-grained metal double-prong frame buckle . . . . **$165 (£85)**

ARMY TROPICAL BELT AND PLATE

* Olive tropical web belt has Army buckle with olive-gray tropical finish. Interior of belt has brown leather adjustment strap and is stamped with accountability number . . . . **$165 (£85)**

ARMY TROPICAL WEB BELT

* Web and leather belt with faint markings, paint on clasp worn with some oxidation . . . . **$75 (£40)**

ARMY OFFICER'S BELT AND BUCKLE

* Double-pronged, open frame buckle of dull pebbled aluminum, RZM marked . . . . **$85 (£45)**

> *"We broke out our combination GI shovels and picks. With slow deliberation, we began digging shallow excavations just long enough to sleep in."*
>
> PRIVATE GENE GARRISON, 87TH U.S. INFANTRY DIVISION

Brown leather bayonet frog for Mauser bayonet, $50-$75 (£25-£40). www.advanceguardmilitaria.com

Stamped steel Heere enlisted man's belt plate, $55-$85 (£30-£45).
Charles D. Pautler

Stamped steel Heere belt plate on dated leather tab, $75-$100 (£40-£50). Minnesota Military Museum

Stamped steel Heere belt plate on black leather belt, $100-$175 (£50-£90). Minnesota Military Museum

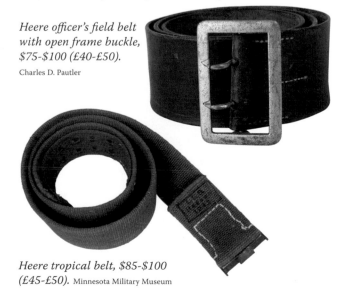

Heere officer's field belt with open frame buckle, $75-$100 (£40-£50).
Charles D. Pautler

Heere tropical belt, $85-$100 (£45-£50). Minnesota Military Museum

Heere officer's belt and buckle, $450-$525 (£225-£265). Charles D. Pautler

Luftwaffe tropical web belt, $350-$400 (£175-£200). www.advanceguardmilitaria.com

Luftwaffe painted belt plate on black leather belt, $100-$150 (£50-£75). Charles D. Pautler

Luftwaffe belt plate with dated leather tap, $65-$95 (£35-£50). Charles D. Pautler

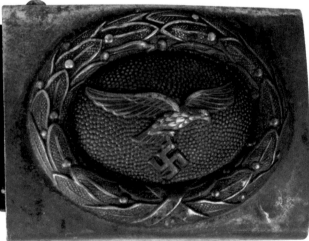

Luftwaffe pebble-surface enlisted belt plate, $55-$75 (£30-£40). Minnesota Military Museum

ARMY OFFICER'S BROCADE BELT
- Green and silver brocade on a field gray wool backing. Has the aluminum keeper but no buckle.....**$150 (£75)**

LUFTWAFFE ENLISTED BELT PLATE
- Matte pebble-grained aluminum buckle for the combat waist belt ....**$65 (£35)**

LUFTWAFFE BELT BUCKLE WITH DATED TAB
- Stamped steel buckle with wreathed Luftwaffe eagle insignia and dark blue finish. Brown leather tab has Dresden maker's stamp with 1941 date ....**$85 (£45)**

LUFTWAFFE TROPICAL WEB
WAIST BELT AND PLATE
- Blue tropical web belt with Luftwaffe stamped metal buckle retaining 85% dark blue finish.......**$695 (£350)**

LUFTWAFFE OFFICER'S BUCKLE

- Two-piece aluminum buckle with brass early style eagle fastened by one rivet, reverse with Overhoff and Cie. maker's mark. Buckle and prongs only, lacks keeper. $265 (£135)

LUFTWAFFE EARLY PATTERN TYPE I OFFICER'S BELT AND PLATE

- Silvered aluminum plate has gilt "tail down" 1935-style Luftwaffe eagle and swastika insignia. Complete with catch and mounted on the original brown leather belt $575 (£290)

KRIEGSMARINE ENLISTED BELT PLATE

- Steel buckle with gilt finish and roller with attachment prongs and belt catch, maker "BandN - 43" (Berge and Nolte) $235 (£120)

HITLER YOUTH BELT AND PLATE

- Brown leather waist belt with silvered stamped metal Hitler Youth plate. Interior embossed with RZM cartouche and "M4/38" date stamp $95 (£50)

REICHSLUFTSCHUTZBUND ENLISTED BELT PLATE

- Second pattern, one piece steel plate with silver painted finish and oval roundel on a plain field $85 (£45)

SA SMALL SIZE BELT PLATE

- Two-piece all-brass buckle for use on the 35mm wide trouser size belt, reverse with catch and prongs $55 (£30)

Two-piece Luftwaffe officer's plate with early style "droop-wing" eagle, $250-$375 (£125-£190). www.advanceguardmilitaria.com

Luftwaffe tropical web belt, $350-$400 (£175-£200). www.advanceguardmilitaria.com

Small-sized SA belt plate, $50-$85 (£25-£45). Charles D. Pautler

Luftwaffe officer's brocade dress belt with early style "droop-wing" eagle belt plate, $575-$700 (£290-£350).

www.advanceguardmilitaria.com

Stamped aluminum Hitler Youth belt plate, $55-$85 (£30-£45). Minnesota Military Museum

*SS enlisted
man's
belt and plate,
$375-$500
(£190-£250).*
www.advanceguardmilitaria.com

*SS enlisted
man's plate
on a Luftwaffe
unit-marked belt sold for
$395 (~£200).* www.advanceguardmilitaria.com

*Luftwaffe bread bag, $50-$75
(£25-£40).* Charles D. Pautler

*Tropical Heere issue bread bag,
$75-$100 (£40-£50).* Charles D. Pautler

*Tropical bread
bag strap, $35-
$65 (£20-£35).*

Charles D. Pautler

SS ENLISTED BELT AND PLATE

- Black leather waist belt with nickel-finished, metal-riveted tab and buckle catch. Silvered stamped metal SS buckle has SS eagle and motto. Interior marked "OandC / ges.gesch" $375 (£190)

SS OFFICER'S BELT PLATE

- Gray metal subdued finish SS officer's plate has stamped proof marks on reverse, and is complete with its opposite side catch.............................$785 (£395)

Bread Bags

ARMY BREAD BAG, GRAY

- Field gray canvas bread bag with brown leather fittings and gray pebbled buttons $45 (£25)

LUFTWAFFE BREAD BAG

- Luftwaffe blue canvas with black leather fittings $50 (£25)

TROPICAL BREAD BAG

- Olive canvas and web bread bag with gray painted metal fittings. Interior has stamped "RB" number ...$85 (£45)

TROPICAL BREAD BAG STRAP

- Olive cotton with web ends, gray painted metal fittings, dated "1942" $50 (£25)

Canteens

ARMY CANTEEN WITH CUP

- M31 aluminum flask canteen with cap that is marked "RFI 38." Brown felt cover with Prym snap. Black leather harness secures aluminum cup with folding handles and "JSD 38" maker's stamp. Snap hook assembly marked "Ritter Aluminum" and "DRGM" $95 (£50)

LUFTWAFFE CANTEEN

- M31 canteen has aluminum body with 1938 maker's date and aluminum cap, Luftwaffe blue-gray wool felt cover has black enameled Prym snaps and black leather harness with snap hook. Lacks cup..............$95 (£50)

MEDICAL CANTEEN

- Larger capacity than the M31, oval aluminum flask with black Bakelite screw cap, brown wool cover and black leather black leather harness with gray snaphook. Neck of the canteen marked "41." Complete with black plastic cup $70 (£35)

TROPICAL CANTEEN SET

- Brown composition tropical canteen with 1942 maker's date stamp on reverse. Tropical canteen harness has thumb release with roller bar that secures 1943-dated olive painted canteen cup...................$95 (£50)

> *"On the beach, an officer was yelling, 'There are only two sorts of people on this beach: those who are dead and those who are going to die. So get off it now.'"*
>
> STANLEY BURROWS, 2ND BN ROYAL ULSTER RIFLES

Chemical Warfare Equipment

MODEL 1930 GAS MASK AND CANISTER

* Gasmaske 30, of treated olive canvas with rubberized interior and all head straps. Filter is stamped "FE 42." Ribbed metal canister has pull-style latch closure, retains field gray painted finish. Complete with shoulder sling and belt hook . . . . **$150 (£75)**

MODEL 1938 GAS MASK AND CANISTER

* Gasmaske 38, field gray rubber face mask with all head straps, filter attachment socket with "bmw 41" maker's date. Filter stamped "FE 41" with 1944 maker's date code, complete with base plug. Second pattern can has elastic pull style latch closure. Complete with original belt hook . . . . **$135 (£70)**

REISSUED CZECH GAS MASK

* 1938-dated Czech regulation gas mask with Waffenamt stamped 1940-dated filter, complete with carrier . . . . **$50 (£25)**

GAS SHEET AND POUCH

* Tan chemically treated paper gas protection sheet with field gray cotton carrier. **$60 (£30)**

HORSE GAS MASK AND CASE

* Black rubber mask, Waffenamt marked and dated "40", has three filters and attaches to horse's head with russet leather harness. Comes in field gray canvas case marked the same that has leather straps with blackened fittings. . . . . **$325 (£165)**

TROPICAL GAS SHEET BAG

* Rubberized tan bag with double snap flap and tan web tabs and loops, interior marked "gdn / Tp" . . . **$160 (£80)**

ANTI-DIMMING STICK

* Brown Bakelite container, wartime dated . . . . . . **$15 (£7)**

Communications Gear

THROAT MICROPHONE FROM LKP101 FLIGHT HELMET

* Mi4b throat mic of brown Bakelite on brown leather strap with snaps and adjustment buckles. Retains some internal wiring but lacks plug and cord. Removed from a Luftwaffe LKp101 series flight helmet . . . . **$65 (£35)**

ARMY COMMUNICATIONS HEADPHONES

* Headset has "Dfh.a" stamped marking for Doppelfernhörer A (double headphones, model a), with white eagle and swastika stamp and date "42." Cloth covered cord terminating in double plug and headband retains black leather covering . . . . **$125 (£65)**

ARMORED CREWMAN EARPHONE HEADSET

* Armored crewman noise insulating Dfh.b headphones with black rubber earcups dated "45." Complete with black leather covered headband and brown cord with black Bakelite plug . . . . **$165 (£85)**

FIELD TELEPHONE, PAIR

* Field signals units housed in a brown Bakelite case with hinged covers, German military alphabet code on affixed cover label. Complete with hand set, hand crank and interior with "TN" monogram insignia . . . . . . **$150 (£75)**

M31 canteen with aluminum cup, $75-$95 (£40-£50).
Minnesota Military Museum

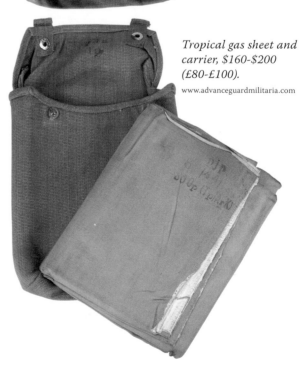

Tropical canteen with black plastic cup, $85-$125 (£45-£65). Charles D. Pautler

Gas sheet and carrier, $50-$75 (£25-£40).

Charles D. Pautler

Tropical gas sheet and carrier, $160-$200 (£80-£100).

www.advanceguardmilitaria.com

Compasses

ARMY COMPASS

• Black metal and Bakelite case with maker's code "clk" with adjustable internal graduated bezel and side with scale markings. . . . . **$85 (£45)**

ARMY COMPASS

• Black thermoplastic compass with map scale rule along one edge, face with adjustable degree dial, face marked "D.R.G.M. / Busch / Rathenow," top with mirrored surface and peep sight, complete with black cord and protective. . . . . **$85 (£45)**

LUFTWAFFE AK 39 WRIST COMPASS

• Black and clear composition large wrist compass retains the liquid suspension filler, adjustable dial, black leather wrist strap, and reverse with nomenclature "AK 39 / FL 23235-1". . . . . **$225 (£115)**

Entrenching Tools, Axes and Hammers

LINNEMANN PATTERN ENTRENCHING SHOVEL

• German Linneman pattern entrenching shovel with turned wood handle and blackened-finish blade. Marked with Waffen eagle and 1939 date stamp. Shovels are plentiful, but a nice marked one is scarce . . . . **$175 (£90)**

1938 PATTERN FOLDING ENTRENCHING SHOVEL WITH CARRIER

• Klappspaten M1938 with turned oak handle and Bakelite locking nut. Shovel is complete with a second pattern 1941-dated carrier . . . . **$375 (£190)**

MOUNTAIN TROOP'S PITON HAMMER

• Square steel head with a pointed "beak" on a 10-1/2" wooden handle with 3" long metal reinforcing plates to protect the wood in case the user misses the striking surface. Head is marked "STUBAI AUSTRIA" and the handle retains the gray leather thong . . . . **$135 (£70)**

PIONEER AXE CARRIER

• Black pigskin leather carrier for the pioneer axe with closure tab and exterior closure implement pouch. Reverse has tab with roller buckle for attaching to other equipment. Interior has maker's three letter code and date stamp "hlv / 42" . . . . **$65 (£35)**

Eyewear

MODEL 295 FLYING GOGGLES

• Field gray painted metal frames with pierced air vents, convex clear lenses, "OW" O.W. Wagener maker's stamp and brown, one-piece rubber pad. Complete with field gray elastic headband . . . . **$195 (£100)**

MODEL 306 FLYING GOGGLES AND CASE

• Model 306 Flight Goggles with field gray painted adjustable metal frames with clear glass lenses, "SuG" maker's stamp, field gray rubber eyepads, and wide gray elastic headband. Complete with metal carrying case and gray rayon sleeve for extra lenses. . . . . **$295 (£150)**

Mountain troop's piton hammer, $125-$150 (£65-£75).
www.advanceguardmilitaria.com

"Daimon" brand soldier's tunic flashlight, $35-$50 (£20-£25).
Minnesota Military Museum

Black metal marching compass, $75-$95 (£40-£50). www.advanceguardmilitaria.com

German folding map compass made by Breithaupt, Kassel, $75-$95 (£40-£50). www.advanceguardmilitaria.com

SNOW AND SKI GOGGLES

- Aluminum oval eye covers pierced with slits to allow clear vision, tan leather binding with elastic head band .... **$45 (£25)**

MASKENBRILLE GAS MASK EYEGLASSES

- Unissued gray metal frames have flexible short temple leads attached to gray twill tape ear loops..... **$25 (£10)**

SERVICE GLASSES METAL CASE

- Gray finished hinged metal case with script stencil "DIENST-BRILLE," interior with Army eagle stamped lining cushion. No glasses .... **$15 (£7)**

Flashlights

FIELD FLASHLIGHT

- Rectangular metal battery box stamped "DAIMON" with a hinged cover and a beveled glass lens. Turns on and off by means of a knurled knob and has a leather tab at the top and bottom for attaching to a uniform button. One of many private purchase styles in use in the field .... **$35 (£20)**

Gloves, Mittens

ARMY LEATHER GLOVES

- Black leather gloves have wrist closure with pebbled snap fitting; olive wool linings with accountability number tags .... **$40 (£20)**

ARMY WOOLEN GLOVES

- Gray wool machine-knit issue gloves with two white woven bands around the wrist indicating size "2" .... **$55 (£30)**

FIELD GRAY WOOL TRIGGER FINGER MITTENS

- Soldier's trigger finger mittens of field gray wool have gray blanket wool lining and gray leather tab and toggle arrangement at the cuff to keep the pair together .... **$45 (£25)**

ARMY CAMOUFLAGE REVERSIBLE MITTENS

- 1942 pattern reversible splinter camouflage/white padded gauntlet mittens with connecting tape attachment. Stamped with 1943 date and accountability number .... **$125 (£65)**

LUFTWAFFE PILOT'S FLYING GAUNTLETS

- Brown goatskin leather flying gauntlets with two wrist adjustment straps with metal and brown figured composition Prym snaps. Interiors have a light white felt body lining and unlined wrist portions .... **$275 (£140)**

MOTORCYCLISTS/DRIVER'S GAUNTLETS

- Olive waterproof cotton gauntlets with field gray leather thumb reinforcements, elastic wrist panel and adjustment tape with metal friction buckle. Opening ends have olive tape straps, one with a loop and the other with a wood toggle bar .... **$40 (£20)**

By D-Day, the Germans had 1.5 million railway workers operating 988,000 freight cars.

Heere leather gloves, $35-$50 (£20-£25).
www.advanceguardmilitaria.com

Luftwaffe pilot's gauntlets, $250-$300 (£125-£150).
www.advanceguardmilitaria.com

Leather motorcyclist's gloves, $35-$50 (£20-£25).
Minnesota Military Museum

Holsters

P-08 LUGER AUTOMATIC PISTOL HOLSTER

* Hardshell pattern P08 holster of smooth finished black leather with leather closure billet and black painted roller buckle, side with spare magazine pouch, interior with pistol lift tab, implement pouch, and unit stamp. Reverse marked with Waffenamt, maker stamp, and "1940" maker date stamp . . . .**$225 (£115)**

P-38 AUTOMATIC PISTOL HOLSTER

* Second model breakaway holster of black pebble-grained leather. Has standard military style attachment strap mounted on the top flap, spare magazine pouch, and reverse marked with large "P38" stamp, maker's code, and "4" 1944 issue stamp . . . .**$195 (£100)**

MODEL PPK HOLSTER

* Black leather with aluminum stud on the flap, complete with closure billet, magazine pouch and belt loop, marked . . . . **$80 (£40)**

BROWNING HI-POWER HOLSTER

* Black leather break-away holster for the Browning Hi-Power automatic pistol. Has extra magazine pouch and a "dla 44" Third Reich maker's stamp . . . .**$125 (£65)**

M1935 RADOM AUTOMATIC HOLSTER

* German manufactured black leather holster for the Polish M35 Radom pistol. Obverse has spare magazine pouch and flap billet. Reverse has two belt loops. Interior of flap marked "P35(p)" . . . . **$145 (£75)**

Horse Equipment

OFFICER'S SPURS

* Pair of mounted spurs with blackened finish. Interior marked "ERN" . . . . **$45 (£25)**

ISSUE MILITARY SADDLE

* Brown leather English-style military saddle built on iron tree interior canvas covered pads. Rear of seat marked with a Reichswehr eagle Waffenamt proof, size stamp "3" and maker's mark with date "1935." Iron fittings used throughout. Complete with iron stirrups on adjustable straps, as well as a gray and white striped woven girth . . . .**$375 (£190)**

Leggings

ARMY CANVAS GAITERS

* M1940 Gamaschen for wear with the issue ankle boots. Olive canvas with brown leather straps and reinforcements, marked and dated "44." Unissued. . . . . . . **$85 (£45)**

Map Cases

OFFICER'S MAP CASE AND CONTENTS

* Brown pebble-grained leather map case with two adjustable belt loops on reverse, front with seven pen/pencil sleeves, pull-release eraser pocket, ruler pocket, and implement pocket complete with folding metal rule fitted with a magnifier. Other original contents include eraser, five pencils, leather cased military marching compass, and 1937-dated leather-bound map pouch . . .**$135 (£70)**

P-38 pistol holster, $175-$225 (£90-£115). www.advanceguardmilitaria.com

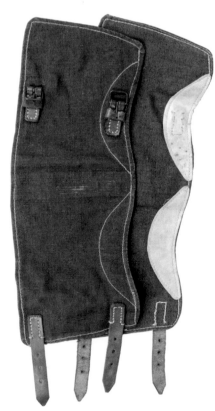

German canvas gaiters, $50-$85 (£25-£45). Minnesota Military Museum

Officer's map case, $95-$150 (£50-£75). Minnesota Military Museum

LUFTWAFFE LEATHER MAP CASE

- Brown leather two-compartment map case has flap closure, pencil holder pockets and shoulder sling, Luftwaffe issue stamped "L.B.A. (S.)" . . . . **$95 (£50)**

Medical Gear

RED CROSS MEDIC'S BELT POUCH

- Black leather box type pouch with gray metal fittings, front hinged lid marked on the interior with purple ink-stamped Red Cross eagle and swastika and inscription "Deutsches Rotes Kreuz / Bereitschaft m. / Wiener-Neustadt 4." Interior divided and retains one 1944-dated first-aid dressing . . . . **$60 (£30)**

MEDICAL ORDERLIES LEATHER POUCHES

- Unmatched pair of brown leather pouches with hinged leather lid and two belt loops . . . . **$55 (£30)**

WOUND TOURNIQUET

- Issue black rubber tourniquet in olive cotton individual item bag from a larger medical kit . . . . **$17 (£8)**

FIELD DRESSING

- 8" x 6" combine field dressing in original paper wrapping with stamped markings . . . . **$25 (£15)**

Mess Kits and Utensils

ARMY MESS KIT

- M31 mess kit with green painted finish. Lid and body by the same maker. Complete with black leather attachment strap . . . . **$75 (£40)**

TROPICAL MESS KIT

- Aluminum mess kit with 1941-dated maker stamp and olive finish. Fitted with tropical olive web and leather strap . . . . **$85 (£45)**

FOLDING SPOON AND FORK COMBINATION

- Aluminum fork and spoon joined at the handle by pivoting pin, reverse marked "HMZ39" . . . . **$35 (£20)**

KRIEGSMARINE ISSUE SPOON-FORK COMBINATION

- Very similar to the Army pattern, but with more robust locking divots and a nice "Eagle / M" proof . . . **$45 (£25)**

Optics

6 X 30 BINOCULARS, TROPICAL

- 6 x 30 service binoculars with ordnance tan painted finish with black plastic eyepieces, stamped "Dienstglas / 6x30 / 351546 / ddx." Includes black leather neck strap, lacks carrying case . . . . **$250 (£125)**

10 X 50 FIELD BINOCULARS

- Porro prism binoculars have field gray finish, stamped with "beh" maker's code for Ernst Leitz GmbH of Wetzlar, with adjustable focus eyepieces . . . . **$135 (£70)**

M31 Heere mess kit, $55-$85 (£30-£45).
Minnesota Military Museum

7 x 58 binoculars made by Hensoldt-Wetzlar, $125-$175 (£65-£90).
Charles D. Pautler

Tropical 6 x 30 service binoculars with ordnance tan painted finish, $250-$300 (£125-£150). www.advanceguardmilitaria.com

COMMANDER KRIEGSMARINE BINOCULARS

- Classic rounded profile porro prism 7 x 50 binoculars with blackened metal frames and black crackle texture finish. Maker marked "beh / 453774" with accountability number, complete with black rubber armored objective lenses and form-fitting black rubber armor for the complete eyepiece mount, with flip-up caps for use without having to remove the rubber. Complete with chinstrap and black leather carrying case well-marked with 'Eagle / M' and swastika on the lid . . . . **$1,250 (£625)**

LUFTWAFFE FLAK 10 X 80 BINOCULARS WITH TRIPOD, TRANSIT CHEST, AND ACCESSORIES

- Flakfernrohr 10 x 80 binoculars with Waffenamt-stamped black metal adjustable tripod, graduated turntable tripod head with bubble level and dovetail mortise to accommodate the binoculars and their elevation cradle. Left side of cradle has brown Bakelite elevation knob and graduated elevation degree guage, and right side has fold-down traversing handle. The binoculars have shielded objective lenses, 45° adjustable focus eyepieces, gray rubber forehead cushion, knob that activates several different degrees of drop-in light filters, optional electrical reticule light attachment (lacks bulb and switch), and top with dovetail tenon for attaching the auxiliary sight loop. Side has "cxn" maker code for Emil Busch AG, Optische Industrie, Rathenow. Includes olive painted wood transit chest with dividers and storage blocks to accomodate the binoculars, cradle, forehead cushion, auxiliary sight loop, and is complete with a metal battery box for the reticule light . . . . **$2,450 (£1,225)**

Pare of 7 x 50 binoculars that are marked with an NSKK eagle over "M26," $800-$1,000 (£400-£500). Rock Island Auction Company

RANGEFINDER

- 31-1/2" long rangefinder with textured gray painted finish. Binocular viewfinder with flexible one-piece rubber eyepiece. Nomenclature tags with maker's code "dow" (Waffenwerke Brünn AG, later Opticotechna GmbH), M IV/5. Waffenamt, and specs. "0.7 RI Vergr. 7.8x Lattenastand 1650 cm" . . . . **$450 (£225)**

Parachutes

FALLSCHIRMJÄGER PARACHUTE MODEL RZ20

- Fallschirmjäger parachute includes white heavy web harness and olive pack with sewn accountability number label "Sprungschirm Fallschirmtruppen / 10-481-B1 / 3312486," quick-release buckle mechanism, camouflaged silk parachute, and carrying bag. Chute is complete with the olive woven fiber storage/carrying bag . . . . **$1,900 (£950)**

Pouches, Ammunition

RIFLE THREE-POCKET AMMUNITION POUCHES, SET

- Service matching pair of black pebbled leather three pocket pouches, complete with all straps and gray metal fittings, reverse with "RB" numbers . . . . **$85 (£45)**

MG-13 AMMUNITION POUCH SET

- Pair of field gray canvas half-moon shaped pouches designed to hold four magazines each, trimmed in brown leather with gray metal fittings, complete with a matching field gray web and brown leather connecting neck strap . . . . **$155 (£80)**

MP 38/40 MAGAZINE POUCH FIELD SET

- Right side and left side pouches of heavy olive canvas with black leather fittings. Right side pouch has implement pouch that still retains clip loader. Maker stamped and dated 1943 on the belt loops. Each pouch with the metal "D" ring for attachment to load-bearing straps . . . . **$395 (£200)**

K98 RIFLE AMMUNITION POUCH

- Black pebble-grained leather three-pocket rifle ammunition pouch has blackened hardware, sewn and riveted construction; reverse has maker stamp, date stamp . . . . **$45 (£25)**

LUFTWAFFE AMMUNITION POUCH SET

- Brown pebble-grained leather three-pocket rifle ammunition pouches as used by Police and Luftwaffe forces. Maker date stamps present. . . . . **$185 (£95)**

LUFTWAFFE MP 38/40 MAGAZINE POUCH

- Right side pouch of blue heavy canvas. Has metal tipped closure straps and black leather fittings with gray metal finials. Reverse has angled belt loops of blue-gray woven material and metal "D" ring for attachment to load-bearing straps . . . . **$295 (£150)**

RIFLE GRENADE LAUNCHER CARRYING CASE

- Black leather carrier for the rifle grenade launcher kit. Reverse has Waffenamt and 1942 maker's date stamp, complete with adjustable shoulder sling . . . . . . **$65 (£35)**

Pouches, Packs and Bags, Personal Gear

TORNISTER PACK
• Field gray cotton knapsack with black leather hardware, steer-hide, hair-on, back panel complete with straps. "1943" maker date stamp. Interior has early style sewn mess kit pouch with black leather closure strap.
. . . . **$100 (£50)**

TROPICAL RUCKSACK
• M31 rucksack of olive canvas with olive web fittings and gray painted metal closure buckles drawstring interior closure and hooks for attaching to the "Y" strap combat gear . . . . **$85 (£45)**

PACK FOR "A" FRAME ASSAULT RIG
• Olive canvas with olive web and brown leather fittings. "Carl Vogel" maker's stamp . . . . **$195 (£100)**

LUFTWAFFE RUCKSACK
• Luftwaffe blue canvas with black leather fittings, reverse with rings for attaching to the combat suspenders, 1940 date . . . . **$65 (£35)**

MOUNTAIN RUCKSACK
• M1931 mountain troops rucksack, olive green canvas rucksack with black leather straps and fittings, front closure straps and exterior pocket straps. . . . . . **$85 (£45)**

Black leather three-pocket rifle ammunition pouch, $35-$50 (£20-£25). Minnesota Military Museum

"A-frame" for the assault pack, $150-$175 (£75-£90). Charles D. Pautler

Small size Heere rucksack, $85-$125 (£45-£65). Charles D. Pautler

Slings, Weapons

MP40 MACHINE PISTOL SLING

* Brown leather sling with crosshatch embossed pattern, sliding loop, friction buckle and metal double button . . . . **$95 (£50)**

MG 34/42 LEATHER SLING

* Brown leather double strap sling with reinforced handle section, rectangular attachment clip and snap hook . . . . **$85 (£45)**

Suspenders, Combat

ARMY COMBAT "Y"-STRAPS

* Black leather with gray finished iron hardware, all buckles and tabs intact. Reverse marked with RB number stamp . . . . **$250 (£125)**

LUFTWAFFE COMBAT "Y"-STRAPS

* Brown leather lightweight "Y"-straps with stamped aluminum ammunition pouch and belt supports, rear strap marked with 1938-dated manufacture stamp and "L.B.A. (S)" Luftwaffe equipment office issue stamp. . . . . **$200 (£100)**

KRIEGSMARINE MARKED LIGHTWEIGHT COMBAT "Y"-STRAPS

* Identical to the Luftwaffe Field Division or Fallschirm-jäger lightweight "Y"-straps but clearly marked with Marine "Eagle / M" and 1938 Berlin maker date stamp. Brown leather with aluminum fittings . . . . . . **$225 (£115)**

Tents

ARMY SHELTER HALF

* Army splinter camouflage shelter tent section/rain cape. Large stamp "RB Nr. 0/0573/0134" present. . . **$150 (£75)**

SS SHELTER HALF

* Reversible SS dot pattern camouflage Zeltbahn with its original cord anchor loops . . . . **$575 (£290)**

BAKELITE TENT PEG SET

* Set of five reddish brown Bakelite tent pegs dated 1942 . . . . **$45 (£25)**

Weapon Accessories

98K MUZZLE COVER

* Snap-on steel cover with hinged muzzle cap . . **$25 (£15)**

MAUSER RIFLE CLEANING KIT

* Standard issue cleaning kit with dark green non-reflective finish, interior contents that remain include the pull-through chain, a brown Bakelite oiler, and two cleaning brushes. . . . . **$50 (£25)**

SS dot-pattern shelter half, $550-$650 (£275-£325). Charles D. Pautler

"Splinter" pattern camouflaged shelter half, $100-$150 (£50-£75). Minnesota Military Museum

Mauser rifle cleaning kit, $35-$50 (£20-£25). Minnesota Military Museum

HUNGARY

Canteens

CANTEEN

• Aluminum fluted body complete with stopper and chain
.... **$50 (£25)**

Chemical Warfare

GAS MASK AND CARRYING CANISTER

• Khaki rubberized canvas mask with dark khaki painted fittings and filter, complete with all field gray web head straps. Interior stamped with an Hungarian crest issue mark. The metal carrying can is similar to the German can but larger in size. Dark khaki finish with adjustable sling and hook strap. Lid interior has spare lenses and the can is lined in pasteboard............**$175 (£90)**

Tents

SHELTER HALF

• Issue camouflage shelter quarter, marked and dated "1940"...............................**$95 (£50)**

*Lot3473
Holster for Hungarian Femaru M1937 (P.37u) pistol, $130-$200 (£65-£100).* Rock Island Auction Company

Cloth-covered Japanese infantry belt, $75-$85 (£40-£45). Minnesota Military Museum

Officer's field service saber belt, $175-$225 (£90-£115). www.advanceguardmilitaria.com

ITALY

Belts, Buckles and Plates

OFFICER'S BROCADE BELT

• Gilt spoon and wreath buckle with eagle perched on fascis and marked "S.A.F.S. NAPOLI" on the reverse. Belt is made of black grosgrain silk and gold bullion on white kid backing ....**$150 (£75)**

Canteen, Mess Equipment

CANTEEN

• Pre-1939 style canteen as used in Ethiopia and Spain in conjunction with the WWI style haversack. Aluminum body with gray-green wool cover fitted with web and leather securing strap ....**$65 (£35)**

MESS KIT, ALPINI TROOPS

• Large-size mountain troop mess kit. Aluminum kidney shape with wire bail and friction lid with folding handle
....**$40 (£20)**

Chemical Warfare Equipment

GAS MASK

• Model 1935 gas mask with rubberized face piece and detachable filter, complete with olive canvas carrier with filter cap and lens reinforcement wires in implement pouch ....**$55 (£30)**

GAS MASK CARRIER

• Olive canvas carrier with gray leather closure tab for the Model 1935 gas mask. Reverse has pocket for gas cape. Interior has pockets for extra lenses and anti-dimming compound. Sides have cloth shoulder strap ... **$20 (£10)**

Pouches, Ammunition

INFANTRY ACCOUTERMENT SET

• Complete set of basic olive green leather equipment for an Italian infantryman including two-pocket ammunition pouch, waist belt with black iron frame buckle, neck support strap with two black iron hooks and bayonet frog ....**$225 (£115)**

JAPAN

Belts, Buckles and Plates

COMBAT WAIST BELT

• Thick natural undyed brown leather waist belt with blackened metal frame buckle. Markings are barely visible on the reverse side behind the tab where the buckle is stitched on...........................**$85 (£45)**

OFFICER'S FIELD SERVICE SABER BELT

• 7.5 cm wide khaki web waist belt with brown leather adjustment belt with iron roller double buckle, leather chape and iron hook for attaching the saber hanger. Unmarked................................**$195 (£100)**

Pattern of 1940 bread bag with shoulder sling, $100-$150 (£50-£75).

www.advanceguardmilitaria.com

Wartime "economy" issue bread bag was a simplified version of the Pattern of 1940 bag, $100-$145 (£50-£75). www.advanceguardmilitaria.com

Bread Bag

BREAD BAG, PATTERN OF 1940

* 1940 pattern haversack made of olive cotton canvas with web shoulder strap with adjustment frame buckle and plain aluminum fittings as was standard after May 1941. Interior has divided compartment, tape tie closures fixed in the pattern differentiating the 1937 and 1940 patterns, with 1944 date stamp and name inscription . . **$125 (£65)**

BREAD BAG, ECONOMY ISSUE

* Wartime economy issue olive canvas bread bag that has a shoulder strap without adjustment and an interior without divided compartment to save materials and production time. Central attachment strap is olive twill, as are the two closure straps. Interior has clear issue stamps with 1941 date . . . . **$110 (£55)**

Canteens and Mess Equipment

CANTEEN

* Flask-style canteen with khaki finish and aluminum capped cork stopper . . . . **$45 (£25)**

CANTEEN, TYPE 94, FIRST MODEL

* Aluminum flask canteen with khaki painted finish. Base has Japanese 1940 date stamp. Has olive web strap harness and adjustable strap, which is also marked. Canteen is complete with standard pattern stopper and first model leather retaining strap with adjustment buckles on both sides . . . . **$115 (£60)**

CANTEEN, TYPE 94, SECOND MODEL

* Aluminum flask canteen with khaki painted finish. Base has Japanese stamp. Complete with olive web strap harness and adjustable strap, which is also marked. Canteen has standard pattern stopper retained by cloth loop and tie strap . . . . **$115 (£60)**

The stopper of the second model of the Type 94 canteen has a cloth strap, $100-$150 (£50-£75).

www.advanceguardmilitaria.com

Aluminum flask-style canteen with leather carrier, $65-$85 (£35-£45).

Minnesota Military Museum

Souvenir Type 94 canteen decorated by American GI of the 33rd Division, $100-$150 (£50-£75).

Minnesota Military Museum

CANTEEN, NAVY

- Aluminum oval flask canteen with olive canvas lace-on cover with Japanese character inscription, complete with cap fitted with retaining chain and adjustable khaki web shoulder sling . . . . **$125 (£65)**

COLD WEATHER CANTEEN COVER

- Heavily insulated canteen cover made with an olive cotton exterior and white flannel interior. Has cap cover and olive twill tie tapes. Interior has issue stamp dated 1940 . . . . **$135 (£70)**

MESS KIT

- Tall pattern three-piece darkened aluminum mess kit with internal tea strainer, locking wire bail handle and lid with Japanese character inscription . . . . **$85 (£45)**

OFFICER'S PATTERN MESS KIT

- 17.5 cm x 9 cm x 10 cm rectangular aluminum mess kit with wire bail handle. Interior tray has maker's logo and "Made in Japan" in English as one commonly sees on period private purchase/private sale items . . . **$110 (£55)**

Chemical Warfare Equipment

GAS MASK, TYPE 99

- Orange-khaki rubberized face mask with elastic head harness and neck strap. Base complete with well-marked filter . . . . **$65 (£35)**

GAS MASK CARRIER, TYPE 99

- Olive cotton carrier for the Type 99 Gas Mask with olive painted metal closure and shoulder strap adjustment buttons that mate with olive rubber adjustment tabs. Interior has accouterment pockets. Base marked with 1944 date and faint issue stamp. . . . . **$110 (£55)**

Entrenching Equipment

ENTRENCHING SHOVEL

- 28-1/2" overall including the blade and helve. Blade has light olive painted finish. Helve and blade both have a pierced hole for the carrying cord. . . . . **$425 (£215)**

Japanese Navy pattern canteen with adjustable sling, $100-$135 (£50-£70). Minnesota Military Museum

Cold weather cover for the Type 94 canteen, $100-$125 (£50-£65).
www.advanceguardmilitaria.com

German-style mess kit used by Japanese troops, $65-$85 (£35-£45). Minnesota Military Museum

Type 99 gas mask carrier, $100-$125 (£50-£65).
www.advanceguardmilitaria.com

Japanese officer's pattern mess kit, $100-$125 (£50-£65).
www.advanceguardmilitaria.com

Aviator goggles, $300-$350 (£150-175). www.advanceguardmilitaria.com

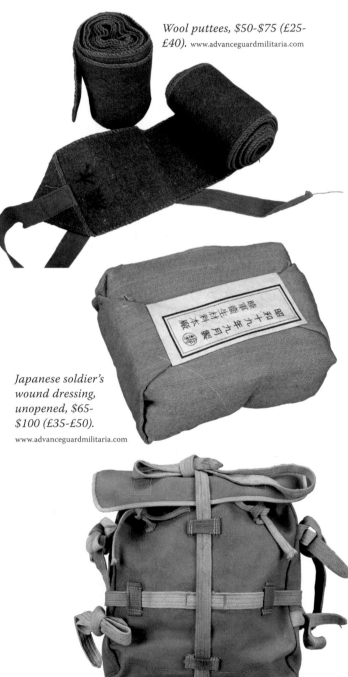

Wool puttees, $50-$75 (£25-£40). www.advanceguardmilitaria.com

Japanese soldier's wound dressing, unopened, $65-$100 (£35-£50).

www.advanceguardmilitaria.com

The Type 99 knapsack was standardized in 1940, $175-$225 (£90-£115). www.advanceguardmilitaria.com

Eyewear

AVIATOR'S GOGGLES
- "Cat-eye" goggles used by Army and Navy pilots. Goggles have maroon metal frames with clear lenses on a brown padded backing and an adjustable wide brown elastic band . . . . **$325 (£165)**

Gloves

COLD WEATHER TRIGGER FINGER MITTENS
- Olive wool and cotton trigger finger mittens with synthetic olive tape tie wrist adjustment . . . . **$45 (£25)**

MOSQUITO GLOVES
- Olive cotton mittens with exit ports for both thumb and fingers so that they could be easily exposed when needed, then tucked back in safety from mosquitoes. Mittens have wide gauntlet wrists and olive twill tape string. Interiors have Japanese issue stamp dated 1945 . . . . **$65 (£35)**

Holsters

NAMBU PISTOL HOLSTER
- Leather trimmed, waterproofed, ocher fabric hardshell Nambu pistol holster. Interior with extra ammunition pouch, reverse with blackened metal rings for shoulder strap and single belt loop. Interior of flap with Japanese maker issue stamp . . . . **$155 (£80)**

1904 NAMBU HOLSTER AND SLING
- Brown leather holster for the 1904 "Papa" Nambu automatic pistol. Early production with all brass hardware, hard clamshell flap and extra ammunition pocket containing bullet loops . . . . **$175 (£90)**

TYPE 14 NAMBU HOLSTER, SECOND PATTERN
- Brown leather holster for the 8 mm Type 14 Nambu automatic pistol. Second pattern with all brass hardware, hard clamshell flap with spring closure billet and extra ammunition pouch. Reverse has a belt loop and rings for a shoulder sling . . . . **$200 (£100)**

Leggings

PUTTEES, WOOL
- Pair of olive wool wrap puttees with cotton tape ties, white cotton labels with Japanese inscription . . **$65 (£35)**

PUTTEES, COTTON
- Olive cotton twill variant puttees with olive twill tape ties. Unmarked . . . . **$35 (£20)**

Medical Equipment

WOUND DRESSING
- Soldier's individual wound dressing as carried in the small interior pocket of the tunic. Unissued, wrapped in olive cotton with printed instructions on one side and sealed with a paper label on the other . . . . **$80 (£40)**

Optics

4 X 10 BINOCULARS AND FIELD CARRYING CASE

• 4 x 10 roof prism binoculars with adjustable focus ring, black textured finish and leather carrying strap. Complete with thick, stiffened, khaki-painted web carrier fitted with khaki web carrying strap with sewn Japanese characters and brown leather closure strap. . . **$150 (£75)**

7 X 50 NAVY BINOCULARS

• Standard Navy binoculars with Japanese character inscription. Complete with gray laminated fiber carrying case with khaki web strap and yellow Japanese character inscription . . . . **$225 (£115)**

"RABBIT EARS" OPTICS WITH TRIPOD AND CASE

• Gray painted wood carrying case has Japanese character script on the lid. Interior contains 10 x 45 "rabbit ears" optics with field brown finish, adjustable eyepieces and adjustment knobs. Includes original folding wood tripod . . . .**$650 (£325)**

Pouches, Ammunition

NAVAL AND MARINE 30-YEAR CARTRIDGE POUCH

• Single brown leather front cartridge pouch of unique Naval and Marine pattern, retaining all straps and belt loops . . . . **$95 (£50)**

Pouches and Packs, Personal Equipment

KNAPSACK, FIRST PATTERN

• First pattern olive cotton frameless pack with white cotton interior lining with pocket divider and issue stamps. Exterior has drawstring and button flap top closure, attachment rings and tie system and reinforced shoulder straps . . . .**$225 (£115)**

TYPE 99 KNAPSACK

• Standardized in 1940, the thick olive canvas Type 99 knapsack featured a stable tie system for securing a mess kit to the exterior reverse, sides with blanket tie straps and a closure flap with tie fasteners . . . .**$195 (£100)**

ASSAULT PACK

• Type 93 "Tube Holdall" made of white lined olive cotton with tie ends and olive synthetic tie tapes. Interior has Japanese issue and Showa 19 (1944) date stamp . . . . **$95 (£50)**

Tents

SHELTER HALF

• Olive canvas shelter half with aluminum corner grommets and brown leather reinforces. Marked with Japanese issue stamps dated Showa 19 (1944) . . .**$235 (£120)**

Carrier for Japanese NCO binoculars, $65-$95 (£35-£50).
Minnesota Military Museum

Rifle oiler, $15-$25 (£7-£10).
Minnesota Military Museum

Army Type 30 rifle ammunition pouch, $65-$85 (£35-£45).
Minnesota Military Museum

Rubberized fabric-covered 50-round rifle ammunition pouch, $65-$95 (£35-£50).
Minnesota Military Museum

POLAND

Bayonet Frogs

POLISH/THIRD REICH 88/95 BAYONET FROG

* Polish bayonet frog designed to carry the Austrian M1895 bayonet, with blackened finish that was most likely applied by German forces to reuse captured equipment after the success of the 1939 invasion . . . **$65 (£35)**

Canteens

CANTEEN, MODEL 1931

* Aluminum flask canteen with brown wool felt cover and German Prym snap side closure, complete with cork stopper and collar with slot for equipment strap. An interesting early pattern combining a WWI German style body and cover and Belgian style spout with the unique Polish metal spout collar mounted with loop for the equipment strap . . . . **$65 (£35)**

Chemical Warfare

GAS MASK

* "Wz. 32" gas mask with dark khaki rubber face mask ink-stamped " wz. 32 / S / w.s.p. / IV-38." Black elastic web head straps. Complete with a screw-in, French-made khaki painted filter dated "39" . . . . **$85 (£45)**

Entrenching Equipment

ENTRENCHING TOOL COVER

* Brown leather frame cover for the pointed blade entrenching tool, and central belt loop with closure stud. The handle retaining strap is marked with a Polish eagle, Warsaw maker's mark and date stamp "33". . . . **$75 (£40)**

SOVIET UNION

Belts, Buckles and Plates

ACCOUTERMENT BELT

* 1-3/4" wide brown leather belt with heavy single prong roller buckle . . . . **$45 (£25)**

ENLISTED WAIST BELT

* Wartime ersatz pattern olive web belt with leather reinforcement strip and single prong buckle . . . . . . **$45 (£25)**

BELT AND BELT PLATE

* Brass frame buckle has rayed Soviet star, hammer and sickle in the center have worn off. Adapted during the period to a Soviet Sam Browne belt . . . . **$65 (£35)**

NAVAL ENLISTED BELT PLATE

* Early production rectangular heavy brass belt buckle has embossed Soviet rayed star over anchor insignia, reverse with double-loop attachment system and tongue catch . . . . **$35 (£20)**

Canteens and Mess Equipment

CANTEEN AND COVER

* Oval aluminum canteen with cork stopper, maker marked on the neck, in gray cotton flannel cover with matching fabric belt and closure strap with steel button. . . . . **$85 (£45)**

MESS KIT

* 6-1/2" x 4-1/2" galvanized tin kettle in ordnance olive green painted finish with wire bail handle. Unmarked. Simple wartime production model that replaced the German style M1936 mess kit . . . . **$135 (£70)**

Entrenching Equipment

ENTRENCHING TOOL

* Pointed blade Linnemann pattern entrenching tool in dark finish, with straight turned wood handle. Blade marked with Cyrillic maker's mark and "1940r" date. . . . . **$65 (£35)**

Pouches, Ammunition

AMMUNITION POUCHES, ERSATZ

* Wartime ersatz rifle ammunition pouches of olive canvas with natural linen lining and olive web belt loops. Obverse has loop and button closure. Pouches dated "1941". . . . . **$65 (£35)**

PPSH DRUM MAGAZINE BELT POUCH

* Natural reinforced linen pouch for the PPSH drum magazine with brown leather closure strap and olive web belt loops. Interior of strap has 1942-dated maker stamps. . . . . **$150 (£75)**

AMMUNITION BANDOLEER

* Olive canvas six-pocket ammunition bandoleer with folding flap cover and tie straps, interior with issue stamps . . . . **$45 (£25)**

Polish bayonet frog designed to carry the Austrian M1895 bayonet, $50-$65 (£25-£35).

www.advanceguardmilitaria.com

STICK GRENADE CARRIER

- Olive cotton bag for carrying Model 1933 stick grenades. Pouch with interior divider and spare fuze pocket and leather strap and roller buckle closure. Reverse has olive web belt loops . . . . **$55 (£30)**

Weapon Slings and Accessories

MOISIN-NAGANT SLING

- Khaki web with brown leather and aluminum fittings . . . . **$30 (£15)**

PPSH SLING

- Olive web sling with brown leather fittings and attachment straps, adjustable brass buckle and Soviet issue stamp . . . . **$55 (£30)**

SPAIN

Belts, Buckles and Plates

FALANGE OFFICER BELT AND BUCKLE

- Gilded oval plate with yoke and arrows insignia, with white wool belt . . . . **$85 (£45)**

NATIONALIST INFANTRY BELT PLATE

- Model 1937 rectangular brass plate with "Catholic" crown over Infantry insignia . . . . **$50 (£25)**

REPUBLICAN GENERAL SERVICE BELT PLATE

- Iron clipped corner rectangular belt plate with five-pointed star embossed in bold relief. Reverse has Madrid manufacturer's stamp on catch. Retains original iron belt friction bar . . . . **$125 (£65)**

Combat Suspenders

INFANTRY COMBAT ACCOUTERMENTS "Y"-STRAP

- Model 1911 brown leather "Y"-straps with steel hooks and buckles, Civil War era production, standard issue for both sides . . . . **$55 (£30)**

Holsters

ASTRA AUTOMATIC PISTOL HOLSTER

- Scarce model with the extra magazine pouch mounted horizontally on the closure flap, of brown leather, approximately 10" long. Reverse with cleaning rod pouch, belt loop, and rings for attaching a cross strap . **$95 (£50)**

Leggings

LEGGINGS, MODEL 1926

- Pair, olive cotton with top strap and buckle, wooden buttons and white cotton lining with issue markings. . . . . **$35 (£20)**

Pouches, Ammunition

AMMUNITION POUCH, ARMY GARRISON

- 3" x 2-1/2" x 2" sewn brown leather pouch with belt loop and wire loop for 1911 equipment suspenders. Obverse of flap with billet and finial closure. Interior marked with Madrid manufacturer's stamp . . . . **$30 (£15)**

INFANTRY CARTRIDGE POUCH SET

- Comprised of three matching Model 1911 infantry pouches, manufactured of an unusual light gray leather. . . . . **$75 (£40)**

MOUNTED CARTRIDGE POUCH

- Model 1911 brown leather pouch, all riveted construction, reverse with belt loops only as configured for Cavalry and Mounted Artillery troops who wore just a single pouch . . . . **$35 (£20)**

SUB-MACHINE GUN MAGAZINE POUCH

- Brown leather, flap with billet attaches to brass closure stud, reverse with belt loop and support ring. Interior divided to hold three stick magazines for the Starr, Erma, or Bergmann pattern SMGs . . . . **$145 (£75)**

GRENADE POUCH

- 4" tall black leather cylinder with hinged cover and belt loop, brass stud, smaller version of the Laffet pouch possibly for the Republican Probellum grenade . . . **$65 (£35)**

UNITED KINGDOM

Accouterment Sets

INFANTRY ACCOUTERMENT SET, P37

- Khaki web lot includes belt, suspenders, two ammo pouches, bayonet frog and haversack . . . . **$55 (£30)**

INFANTRY ACCOUTERMENT SET, P39

- Matching set of russet grained leather Pattern 1939 equipment consisting of waist belt with P37 brass buckle, left and right two-pocket cartridge pouches, bayonet frog with hilt loop, canteen harness complete with blue enamel canteen with khaki wool cover and shoulder braces, complete with all brass fittings. P-39 equipment filled an important material shortage in the early days of the war and saw service not only with the Home Guard, but also in combat with exiled Polish and French forces . . . . **$245 (£125)**

INFANTRY ACCOUTERMENT SET, P40

- Partial set of the limited production Pattern 1940 equipment, use in limited number by the British Army in the early days of WWII, comprised of a matched pair of three pocket khaki web ammunition pouches marked "M.E.Co. 1940." Matching pair of braces marked "M.E.Co." and "M.S.and W.Ltd." and dated "1940". . . . . **$175 (£90)**

> *"When the ramps went down, the sea was so rough that they had to put us on our motorbikes on top of the tanks to get to the beach."-*
>
> JIMMY BRAMLEY, BRITISH MOTORCYCLE DISPATCH RIDER

OFFICER'S WEB EQUIPMENT SET WITH COMPASS AND BINOCULARS

- Includes khaki web waist belt and braces dated 1940, officer's haversack dated 1943, revolver holster with cleaning rod dated 1943, revolver ammunition pouch with 1943 date, water bottle and web carrier, blanco green compass pouch complete with 1944-dated military issue lensatic compass, and khaki web binoculars case dated 1941, complete with 1943-dated No. 2 Mk. 3 issue binoculars with khaki neck strap..........**$395 (£200)**

Bayonet Frogs

BAYONET FROG, P08

- Khaki web with strap for attaching the halve holder, pre-WWII dated .... **$35 (£20)**

Belts, Buckles and Plates

EQUIPMENT BELT, P08

- Olive khaki web, brass hardware, "Broad Arrow" marked, dated 1935................................. **$35 (£20)**

EQUIPMENT BELT, P37

- Khaki web with brass hardware, "Broad Arrow" marked and wartime dated........................ **$20 (£10)**

Canteen and Mess Equipment

CANTEEN AND CARRIER

- Blue enameled water bottle with cork stopper and khaki wool cover in web carrier dated "1941" ...... **$30 (£15)**

CANTEEN AND CARRIER, CANADIAN

- Blue enameled water bottle with cork stopper and olive drab wool cover in khaki web carrying harness **$35 (£20)**

Chemical Warfare Equipment

GAS MASK, GENERAL SERVICE, CANADIAN

- General Service Box Respirator with khaki fabric covered rubber face mask, hose and metal filter can, complete with olive khaki canvas carrier with khaki web shoulder sling. Mask is marked with "C" Broad Arrow proof and "6-42" date................................. **$85 (£45)**

GAS MASK AND POUCH, MK IV

- MK IV box respirator with khaki cloth covered facemask with size "LARGE" and February 1940 date. Light olive canvas carrier has "1941" maker's date stamp and is complete with the early style detachable web sling with brass hardware .... **$115 (£60)**

Commonwealth officer's set of web accouterments, including compass and binoculars, $375-$425 (£190-£215). www.advanceguardmilitaria.com

MK IV gas mask and pouch, $100-$125 (£50-£65).
www.advanceguardmilitaria.com

GAS MASK AND POUCH, MK V

- Mark V gas mask with black rubber face mask with all black head straps, khaki cloth covered rubber hose and black finished metal Type E filter, all dated "41." Complete with "42" dated khaki canvas and web Mark VII carrying bag with sling and tin of anti-dimming dubbing. .... **$60 (£30)**

GAS MASK, LIGHT SERVICE

- 1943 pattern black rubber mask with head straps and side mounted filter, complete with olive canvas carrying bag with khaki web sling. Mask dated "1944".. **$85 (£45)**

Combat Suspenders

SUSPENDERS, P08

- Matching pair of 2" wide khaki web straps with brass tips, marked with 1944 date................. **$25 (£15)**

Communications

HEADPHONES

- Basic double headphone headset with "PX / C-LR / 1940" designations cast into the sides of the earphones. Black metal head band has adjustable earphone brackets, and gray cloth-covered cord terminates into a single large plug attachment .... **$65 (£35)**

ARMORED VEHICLE HEADSET AND HAND MICROPHONE

- Black Bakelite "MICROPHONE HAND No 7" with rubber mouthpiece. Headset with black Bakelite earphones with rubber and olive felt pads, olive web retaining strap and cloth covered cords with British universal military plug..................................... **$75 (£40)**

TYPE C HEADSET WITH TYPE 21 MICROPHONE

- Marked with embossed crown Broad Arrow and Air Ministry "AM" throughout, the Type C "Headband" adjustable headset has white chamois and black rubber cushioned ear receivers, wiring loom complete with aircraft plug and Type 21 microphone assembly. .... **$225 (£115)**

RAF OXYGEN MASK MICROPHONE

- Black metal microphone assembly with rubber gasket, front-mounted switch and cloth-covered cord with plug receptacle. Example from an original carton stenciled with "A (crown) M" Air Ministry insignia and nomenclature "Microphone Assembly, Type 26"........ **$35 (£20)**

FIELD TELEPHONE, MK III

- 10" x 6" x 4-1/2" olive painted metal box with white stenciled inscription "TELEPHONE SET H MK III," side with generator crank handle, web carrying strap lacking. Lid lifts to reveal interior with printed instruction plate, and black hard plastic telephone receiver complete with cloth covered cord .... **$75 (£40)**

FIELD TELEPHONE, MK V

- 10" x 6" x 4-1/2" olive painted metal box with white stenciled inscription "TELEPHONE SET D MK V." Lid lifts to reveal interior with printed instruction plate, black hard plastic telephone receiver complete with cloth- covered cord, wire contact connectors, battery box, bell, and Morse Code key .... **$85 (£45)**

FIELD TELEPHONE SET L, CANADIAN

- Commonwealth set has metal case with olive painted finish. Interior complete with handset and phone jack, side with ringer handle. Lid is stenciled "Important: Stow Handle." The set is complete with khaki web shoulder strap .... **$55 (£30)**

Compasses

MARCHING COMPASS

- Black finished brass body with white direction indicators, floating compass dial reads in compass degrees and direction notations, flip-up lens with sighting device, lanyard ring, and base stamped with Broad Arrow proof, London maker's stamp, and 1938 date........ **$45 (£25)**

Entrenching Equipment

ENTRENCHING TOOL

- Pointed blade shovel finished black, Broad Arrow marked and dated "1939," complete with natural finish wooden "T" handle .... **$50 (£25)**

ENTRENCHING TOOL, LONG HANDLE

- Square blade shovel with dark khaki painted finish, Broad Arrow and maker marked, and dated "1942." Complete with wooden "T" handle. 36" total length .... **$55 (£30)**

ENTRENCHING TOOL AND COVER, P37

- P37 entrenching tool blade with black painted finish, Broad Arrow marked with maker's stamp and dated "1944." Wooden handle with bayonet mount finial and metal cap. Complete in khaki web cover, interior Broad Arrow marked and dated "1943"............. **$55 (£30)**

Eyewear

FLYING GOGGLES, MK VII

- Blue painted metal fittings with angular lenses, chamois-lined brown leather face pad, Air Ministry markings, brown leather headband.................. **$300 (£150)**

FLYING GOGGLES MK VIII

- Tinted angled lenses with blue/gray painted metal bezel frame on brown leather pad. Air Ministry stamped above the bridge, reverse lined with chamois leather, and complete with gray elastic head strap. Still in box with nomenclature stamp .... **$135 (£70)**

AIRCREW SPECTACLES, MK VIII

- Gray fabric covered metal glasses case has Broad Arrow proof and "SPECTACLES MARK VIII AIRCREW / ANTI-GLARE MEDIUM." Opens to reveal a rather heavy pair of silver spectacles .... **$90 (£45)**

Holsters

.38 WEBLEY HOLSTER, CANVAS

- Khaki canvas P37 holster for the .38 revolver, marked "M.E. Co. 1940" with Broad Arrow under flap. .... **$40 (£20)**

.38 WEBLEY HOLSTER, LEATHER

- Brown leather holster with characteristic British P14 style grained finish and pebble-grained dome snap closure, interior has British Broad Arrow proof stamp "Made in England" and maker's stamp. Interior has cleaning rod slot. Reverse has two belt loops . . **$45 (£25)**

REVOLVER HOLSTER, NO. 2 MK I

- Khaki web open-top holster with extended belt loop, bullet loops on the obverse, complete with metal cleaning rod. . . . . **$35 (£20)**

.455 WEBLEY HOLSTER, P37, CANADIAN

- Holster of mustard khaki canvas for the .455 automatic pistol. Faint date and manufacturer marks under flap with Canadian made Carr snap . . . . **$30 (£15)**

Leggings

LEGGINGS, P37

- Pair of khaki web Pattern 1937 "gaiters," marked with Broad Arrow and "M.E. Co. 1941 / 4" . . . . **$25 (£12)**

ATS LEATHER LEGGINGS

- Pair of brown pebble grain leather women's leggings. Short height, top worn between the meat of the calf and the ankle bone, Broad Arrow marked and dated 1942. . . . . **$35 (£20)**

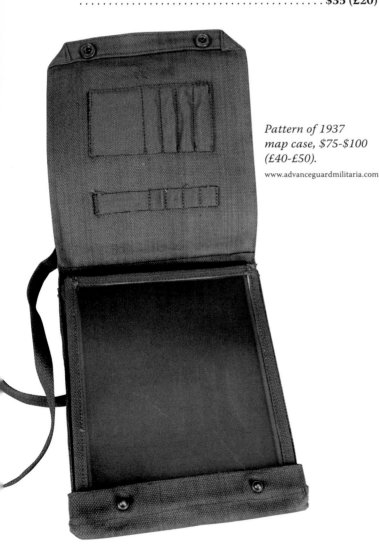

Pattern of 1937 map case, $75-$100 (£40-£50).

www.advanceguardmilitaria.com

Map Cases

MAP CASE, P37

- Khaki web cover protects brown Bakelite board with clear celluloid flap, which is held in place over maps by pivoting brass tabs, covers with light olive drab flap with implement pouches. Complete with strap. . . . . . **$75 (£40)**

Medical Equipment

WOUND DRESSING

- 1943-dated "First Field Dressing" unopened packet with printed instructions on the exterior cloth covering. . . . . **$15 (£7)**

MEDIC'S FIELD BAG

- Khaki canvas and web field bag with large Red Cross insignia on white disc painted on the front, adjustable web sling and leather closure straps. The bag is filled with twelve 1940-dated shell dressings, unopened khaki cotton outer shells printed with instructions and date. . . . . **$95 (£50)**

SHELL DRESSING BAG, P37

- Shell dressing bag marked "M and Co 1942." Front flap is stenciled "SHELL DRESSINGS" with large painted white circle with Red Cross in the center. Rear of bag has an adjustable shoulder strap attached . . . . **$45 (£25)**

Optics

BINOCULARS, MK II

- Blackened brass body with grained grip wraps, adjustable focus composition eyepieces and khaki web strap. Marked "Bino. Prism No. 2 Mk II / 1941" with maker stamp and Broad Arrow proof. . . . . **$260 (£130)**

7X BINOCULARS, MK V

- 9" overall length porro prism style British binoculars with black grained barrel wraps with yellow highlighted Broad Arrow proofs. Front of porro prism chamber has thumb switches that engage yellow filters. Adjustable focus eyepiece lenses. Reverse of prism chamber has British Broad Arrow proofs, 1940 patent date, "Barr and Stroud / London - Glasgow" maker stamp, and accountability number; complete with strap. . . . . **$245 (£125)**

10X ROSS BINOCULARS

- 17" x 10" x 6" wood case with brown leather closure strap has large Broad Arrow proof on lid with "BINOCULAR. PATT. 2112 / ROSS. LONDON." Case opens to reveal set of binoculars that measure 15" long with the sun shades retracted, and 8-1/2" across the objective lenses. Blackened brass metal has textured wraps, barrels have large yellow painted Broad Arrow proofs, eyepieces have rubber face shield, adjustable focus, and dial-in light filters operated by knobs forward of the porro prism chamber.

"The hardest part was the crossing because the sea was rough."

STANLEY BURROWS, 2ND BN ROYAL ULSTER RIFLES

White-filled markings include Broad Arrow proofs, "Power - 10 / Field 5-1/4°", "ROSS / LONDON / 1938".
....$725 (£365)

Parachutes and Flotation Devices

BOMBER CREWMAN PARACHUTE HARNESS
• Single point quick release Observer Type Harness 15A/137, webbing straps dated "1943" with large snap hooks for attaching chest pack parachute, khaki padded back cushion, and large round quick release mechanism
....$525 (£265)

INVASION LIFE BELT
• 36" x 6-1/2" khaki plaid rubberized fabric waist tube with rubber inflation hose and khaki web neck and waist straps, covered in numerous issue stamps, dated "1944"
....$65 (£35)

Pouches, Ammunition

RIFLE AMMUNITION BANDOLEER, LEATHER
• Pattern 1903 five-pocket black leather rifle ammunition bandoleer with London maker stamp on buckle side and 1916 date stamp on billet side $65 (£35)

P37 AMMUNITION POUCHES
• Pair of canvas P37 pouches both dated 1941. These were used to carry everything from standard ammo and grenades to Bren Gun clips $15 (£7)

STEN GUN BANDOLEER, FIRST PATTERN
• Khaki web bandoleer with large single flap divided from the reverse side for carrying seven 28-round Sten magazines. Carrying strap has Broad Arrow proof with maker's 1942 date. This pattern was made from 1941 to 42 when the design of the magazine dividers was changed to individual pockets............$255 (£130)

STEN GUN BANDOLEER, SECOND PATTERN
• Khaki web seven-pocket bandoleer for Sten Gun stick magazines. Strap well marked with maker, Broad Arrow proof, and wartime date $95 (£50)

Pouches and Packs, Personal Equipment

SMALL PACK, P08
• Khaki web, wartime date....................$35 (£20)

HAVERSACK, P37
• Pattern 37 khaki web haversack with pack straps that are dated 1942 and shoulder strap with 1943 date.
....$35 (£20)

HEAVY LOAD BEARING KNAPSACK
• Large khaki web pack with web slings and padded back support, interior divided into two equal compartments, flap marked "M.E. Co. 1941" and Broad Arrow proofed. Used to carry ammunition, signal equipment, rations, etc
....$45 (£25)

ATS ISSUE HANDBAG
• Tan canvas pocketbook as issued starting in 1943 to women of the Auxiliary Territorial Service. Single pouch with a zipper closure, leather trim and a leather shoulder strap. Broad Arrow marked and dated 1945 ... $45 (£25)

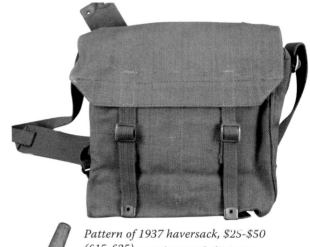

The tan pocketbook was issued to Auxiliary Territorial Service women beginning in 1943, $40-$65 (£20-£35). www.advanceguardmilitaria.com

Pattern of 1937 haversack, $25-$50 (£15-£25). www.advanceguardmilitaria.com

Every British airborne soldier was issued a toggle rope to aid in load bearing, $50-$75 (£25-£40). www.advanceguardmilitaria.com

TOGGLE ROPE, AIRBORNE TROOPS
• 1" thick hemp rope with 6" wood toggle at one end and eye splice at the other, issued to every British Airborne trooper with the idea that the men could combine their ropes for whatever purpose they needed, rather than carry large, full ropes......................$65 (£35)

U.S. officer's privately purchased belt, buckle and holster, $250-$350 (£125-£175). Rock Island Auction Company

M1923 riflemen's cartridge belt, $65-$95 (£35-£50). Charles D. Pautler

M1917 World War I-style riflemen's cartridge belt, $65-$85 (£35-£45). Author's collection

M1923 riflemen's cartridge belt in Olive Drab No. 7, typical of late war issue, $45-$65 (£25-£35). Charles D. Pautler

Weapon Slings, Scabbards and Accessories

RIFLE SLING, LEATHER
- Brown leather Enfield sling complete with sliding loops, dated "1941" $25 (£15)

RIFLE SLING, WEB
- Khaki web sling with brass tab ends for the British SMLE $15 (£7)

STEN GUN SLING
- Khaki web sling with blackened hook and ring attachments with brass adjustment buckle, marked "SLING 9MM MK II" with accountability number below. $15 (£7)

Wire Cutters

EXTENDED PATTERN FOLDING WIRE CUTTERS
- Dark metal folding wire cutters with locking handle extensions that, when deployed, bring their overall length to 15-1/2". Broad Arrow proof stamp and wartime date $35 (£20)

FOLDING WIRE CUTTERS AND CASE
- Black finished folding all metal cutters with good teeth, dated 1941, complete with khaki web cover with belt loop. $75 (£40)

UNITED STATES

Belts, Ammunition

M1910 MOUNTED CARTRIDGE BELT
- Khaki web Mills M1910 mounted pattern cartridge belt has gathered pocket bases, bronze hardware, and lift-the-dot fasteners, "Jan 1919" date stamp on all elements. Because of the space for the .45 clip pouch, these were extensively used by airborne troops $125 (£65)

MODEL 1923 RIFLEMEN'S CARTRIDGE BELT
- M1923 rifleman's cartridge belt of light olive web and blackened hardware has 1943-dated maker's stamp. $65 (£35)

MODEL 1923 RIFLEMEN'S CARTRIDGE BELT, BRITISH-MADE
- Khaki web ten-pocket rifle cartridge belt with lift-the-dot fasteners, gathered pocket bases, British style clasp closure, interior of pocket flap with Broad Arrow proof, and "BRITISH MADE 1943" date stamp $135 (£70)

USMC RIFLEMEN'S CARTRIDGE BELT
- Light olive drab ten pocket rifle cartridge belt with lift-the-dot fasteners. Interior marked with large "U.S.M.C." stencil and "Boyt 43" maker stamp $85 (£45)

MODEL 1937 BAR ASSISTANT GUNNER BELT
- "Boyt 41" dated khaki canvas and light olive drab web assistant gunner belt with blackened metal hardware and six BAR magazine pouches. Includes light olive drab web "Boyt 43" dated first-aid pouch $60 (£30)

British-made M1923 riflemen's cartridge belt, $125-$150 (£65-£75). www.advanceguardmilitaria.com

The Marine's cartridge belt was distinguished by a large USMC stamp on the interior, $75-$95 (£40-£50). www.advanceguardmilitaria.com

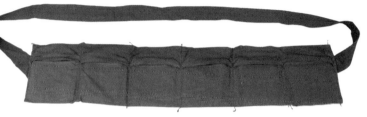

Expendable cotton bandoleer could be used for M1 rifle clips or carbine magazines, $10-$15 (£5-£7). Author's collection

M1937 Browning Automatic Rifle ("BAR") magazine belt, $55-$75 (£30-£40). Charles D. Pautler

Belts, Miscellaneous

TROUSERS WAIST BELT

- Olive drab web belt for trousers with black frame friction buckle . . . . **$15 (£7)**

ENLISTED GARRISON BELT

- Undyed brown leather belt with heavy brass frame buckle, unissued, maker marked and dated 1925. . . . . **$45 (£25)**

USMC GARRISON BELT

- Brown leather belt with heavy square brass buckle, underside marked "S. FROEHLICH CO. INC. N.Y.C." and dated "42" . . . . **$35 (£20)**

OFFICER'S SAM BROWNE BELT

- Dark brown leather Sam Browne belt with double cross strap arrangement as was worn by front line officers who actually needed the belts to be a functional part of their combat equipment. Includes a matching brown leather cartridge pouch or first-aid dressing pouch with pistol belt style hanger on the reverse . . . . **$75 (£40)**

Enlisted man's trouser belt with open-frame buckle, $5-$15 (£2-£7). Author's collection

This trouser belt was worn by a U.S. Navy sailor who adorned the buckle with commemorative artwork, $25-$50 (£15-£25). Author's collection

Enlisted man's leather garrison belt, $35-$65 (£20-£35). Author's collection

Model 1936 pistol belt, $25-$65 (£15-£35). Charles D. Pautler

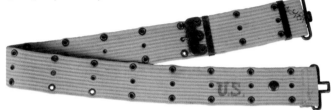

The Marine's M1936 pistol belt was the same as the Army's, except for a large "USMC" stamp on the inside, $85-$125 (£45-£65). www.advanceguardmilitaria.com

Model 1936 pistol belt set consisting of M1916 holster, .45 caliber clip pouch, first-aid pouch and compass carrier and compass, $200-$275 (£100-£140). Charles D. Pautler

Belts, Pistol

MODEL 1936 PISTOL BELT, KHAKI

- M1936 pistol belt with zinc buckle, "U.S." stencil. Interior has "K.E. CO / 1942"maker's stamp . . . . **$65 (£35)**

MODEL 1936 PISTOL BELT, OLIVE DRAB

- Light olive web pistol belt with adjustment keepers and gray metal 'T' buckle retaining 99% blackened finish. Obverse has "U.S." stencil. Interior has "S.F. Co. 1943" maker's stamp . . . . **$50 (£25)**

USMC PISTOL BELT

- M1936 light olive web pistol belt has "U.S.M.C." stencil with maker and 1942 date. . . . . **$95 (£50)**

NAVY PISTOL BELT

- Late war example of white web with 1936 pattern blacked gray metal "T" closure and fittings. . . . **$35 (£20)**

Blankets

ARMY BLANKET

- Olive drab wool issue blanket with 1941-dated contract tag . . . . **$45 (£25)**

ARMY MEDICAL DEPARTMENT BLANKET

- White wool blanket bound with a blanket stitch in maroon thread and "M.D. U.S. ARMY" and date "1944" stenciled in maroon . . . . **$40 (£20)**

USMC BLANKET

- 1942-dated contract tag on forest green wool blanket with dark woven end stripes and center "USMC". . . . . **$95 (£50)**

NAVY RACK BLANKET

- Off-white wool blanket with blue end stripes and embroidered "U.S. Navy" script on top and bottom. . . . . **$25 (£15)**

Camp Gear

COLLAPSIBLE BUCKET

- Olive drab canvas with canvas covered rope handle, maker marked . . . . **$25 (£15)**

FOLDING BASIN

- Olive drab canvas, maker marked and dated "1945". . . . . **$15 (£7)**

Canteens/Mess Kits

CANTEEN WITH BELT HANGER

- M1910 canteen in cover with a unit marked field artillery equipment tag, no cup. Comes with the sliding brown leather hanger as used on leather garrison belts or officer's Sam Browne belts . . . . **$45 (£25)**

CANTEEN COVER AND CANTEEN SET

- Near mint "SHANE MFG. CO. 1942" marked khaki canvas and web carrier and 1942-dated canteen with WWI style cap and 1941-dated cup. Excellent condition. . . . . **$45 (£25)**

1945 PATTERN CANTEEN COVER
WITH CANTEEN AND CUP

- Dark olive drab canvas and web carrier with 1945-dated maker's stamp and large 1945 equipment pattern rear belt hanger. Canteen and cup have 1945 date and are bright, bright metal . . . . **$25 (£15)**

BLACK ENAMEL CANTEEN

- Limited issue black enamel canteen has black plastic cap, unmarked base . . . . **$65 (£35)**

EXPERIMENTAL PLASTIC CANTEEN

- Golden yellow "Ethocel" molded plastic canteen with black plastic cap. Base marked "1943." Plastic has constricted a bit with age making the cap fit loosely. Complete with stained but solid 1942-dated cover and tinned iron, 1943-dated canteen cup. . . . . **$150 (£75)**

M1910 canteen, cup and cover, $35-$65 (£20-£35). Author's collection

Enameled canteen, cup and cover, $100-$165 (£50-£85). www.advanceguardmilitaria.com

Collapsible bucket, $25-$55 (£15-£25). Charles D. Pautler

Experimental "Ethocel" canteen, $125-$165 (£65-£85). www.advanceguardmilitaria.com

This three-piece cook set was designed for use by the mountain troops, $55-$85 (£30-£45). Author's collection

The mounted pattern canteen cover had a leather suspension strap. This style was purportedly popular with airborne troops as well, $40-$65 (£20-£35). www.advanceguardmilitaria.com

Marine Corps "crossover" style canteen cover and canteen, $65-$95 (£35-£50). Charles D. Pautler

MOUNTED CANTEEN SET

- Khaki web mounted pattern canteen cover marked "U.S." on the obverse and "J.Q.M.D. 1935" on the reverse. Complete with brown leather strap marked "J.Q.M.D. 1935" and "U.S." Strap has bronze snap attachment. Includes 1918-dated canteen and issue cup . . . . **$85 (£45)**

MOUNTED CANTEEN CARRIER, BRITISH MADE

- British-made khaki web canteen cover with suspension strap affixed to either side, with adjustment buckle and attachment snap fitting. Interior has Broad Arrow proof and 1944 date. Includes black plastic cap issue canteen. . . . . **$85 (£45)**

USMC CANTEEN AND COVER SET

- Marine crossover style, light olive drab cover with M1910 WWI style canteen . . . . **$65 (£35)**

DRINKING WATER KNAPSACK

- 17" x 21" olive drab canvas pack with interior rubberized water cell and separate opening to reveal the large olive drab plastic cap. Reverse has pack straps, obverse is stenciled "U.S. / Drinking Water Only" . . . . **$50 (£25)**

36-GALLON COMPANY WATER BAG

- 25" x 20" olive drab canvas drinking water bucket with four black plastic spigots. Complete with canvas cover and ropes to suspend the unit from a tree. Maker marked and dated "1945." . . . . **$75 (£40)**

MESS KIT WITH UTENSILS

- Aluminum mess kit and issue stainless fork, knife, and spoon . . . . **$35 (£20)**

Combat Suspenders

M1936 COMBAT SUSPENDERS

- Light khaki web M1936 combat suspenders have "U.S. VICTORY / 1943" maker's date, blackened metal fittings. . . . . **$65 (£40)**

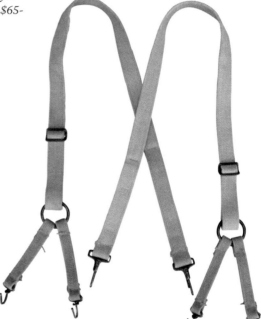

USMC Pattern of 1941 suspenders, $25-$45 (£15-£25). www.advanceguardmilitaria.com

M1936 combat suspenders, $35-$65 (£20-£35).

www.advanceguardmilitaria.com

MODEL 1936 COMBAT SUSPENDERS, BRITISH MADE

- Khaki web M1936 combat suspenders with bronze British style adjustment buckles, reverse with "U.S. M.E. CO. 1943 BRITISH MADE" stamp $85 (£45)

USMC PATTERN OF 1941 COMBAT SUSPENDERS

- USMC pattern combat suspenders of khaki web with bronze hardware. $35 (£20)

Chemical Warfare Equipment

M1A1 GAS MASK

- Light olive and khaki web carrier, khaki fabric covered rubber facemask with black elastic head straps, hose and flutter valve intact. Complete with filter and anti-dimming tin. Front of facemask has "US" and size "3" stencil. Includes 1932-dated packing slip $135 (£70)

M2A1 SERVICE GAS MASK

- Army M2A1 Diaphragm Gas Mask with olive drab rubber face mask, hose, and box respirator, complete in carrying bag with anti-dimming stick $65 (£35)

M3A1 DIAPHRAGM GAS MASK

- Issued in place of the normal service gas mask to officers and other troops who needed to speak and be heard to perform their duties. Gray rubber face with pasteboard form and all black elastic head straps, diaphragm speaker and gray rubber hose attached to the filter. Complete with khaki canvas carrying bag with all slings and original manufacturer's pasteboard box stenciled "GAS MASK DIAPHRAGM M3A1". $85 (£45)

M5-11-7 ASSAULT GAS MASK AND WATERPROOF BAG

- Black waterproofed fabric carrier with stenciled "US" and Chemical Corps insignias, "ARMY COMBAT SERVICE GAS MASK" stamp, Carr snap fasteners, and olive drab web straps. Interior is complete with black rubber mask with black elastic suspension $250 (£125)

ARMY SERVICE GAS MASK AND CARRIER

- Gray rubber face mask with matching hose and gray painted filter can, dated "4-42." Complete with olive drab canvas haversack marked with the Chemical Corps insignia and "ARMY SERVICE GAS MASK" $40 (£20)

M8 GAS MASK

- This mask was developed to replace the M5 Assault mask after it proved problematic. Mask consists of the standard M4A1 lightweight service mask face piece fitted with a cylindrical drum filter, reverse has black elastic head harness, complete with olive canvas and web carrier marked "ARMY SNOUT-TYPE SERVICE MASK". $85 (£45)

ARMY LIGHTWEIGHT SERVICE GAS MASK

- Gray rubberized face mask, dated "8-42," with elastic head straps, rubber hose and gray painted metal filter. Complete with olive drab canvas carrying bag $65 (£35)

M1 DUST RESPIRATOR IN ORIGINAL BOX

- M1 dust respirator with gray felt filter over gray rubber face mask and elastic retaining straps, dated "42," in original issue carton with instructions on the lid. Developed

M3A1 Diaphragm Gas Mask, $65-$95 (£35-£50).

www.advanceguardmilitaria.com

M6 Army Lightweight Service Mask carrier with M3 gas mask, $65-$95 (£35-£50). Author's collection

Anti-gas eye shields, $5-$10 (£2-£5). Author's collection

for personnel with extremely dusty jobs such as drivers of open vehicles .... **$20 (£10)**

NAVY MK I GAS MASK

- Navy Diaphragm Optical gas mask, earliest of the rear canister, double hose Navy gas masks. The Mk I version features small, round lenses that could be adjusted therefore allowing the wearer to use optics such as binoculars while still wearing the mask. This mask was carried in a gray canvas bag.......................... **$95 (£50)**

NAVY MK IV GASMASK AND CARRIER

- Mark IV Navy gas mask of black rubber with clear lenses and dual hoses leading to a filter. Complete with instructions, anti-dimming stick and gray canvas carrier with large "U.S.N." stencil and strap.............. **$55 (£30)**

M-4 HORSE GAS MASK

- M-4 model black rubber nose and mouth mask for the horse's muzzle, linked at the horse's chest through large flexible olive drab hoses to the two ribbed cylindrical filters that ride over the base of the neck and secure to the saddle rig or harness with adjustable brown leather straps. This set is complete with both carriers. .... **$775 (£390)**

INVASION GAS DETECTION ARM BRASSARD

- Khaki treated paper pentagonal brassard with twill tape loop for attaching to field jacket epaulette, reverse marked "1-43 / JLandS / 103"............. **$250 (£125)**

Communications Gear

"HANDIE-TALKIE" FIELD RADIO

- BC-611-D hand held radio transmitter and receiver with olive drab painted finish, 1943-dated Signal Corps nomenclature tag and khaki web carrying strap. The telescoping metal antenna has its protective metal cover intact and the rubber push-to-talk switch is still solid and flexible .... **$275 (£140)**

NAVY TALKER COMMUNICATIONS SET

- United States Instrument Corporation sound powered deck talker's headset receivers and chest mike Model A260 UA1614 .... **$95 (£50)**

FIELD SWITCHBOARD OPERATOR'S HEADSET

- "R-30-U" black composition earphones with black rubber ear inserts and blackened metal head strap, complete with clip for attaching to uniform and PL-540 plug .... **$15 (£7)**

SIGNAL CORPS HEADPHONE

- Issue "RECEIVER R-14" with russet leather-covered spring steel head brace and black Bakelite ear phones with dark olive drab rubber cushions. Complete with cord and plug. Signal Corps marked......... **$70 (£35)**

Troops went ashore at Normandy wearing paper gas detection brassards like the one shown here, $225-$275 (£115-£140).

www.advanceguardmilitaria.com

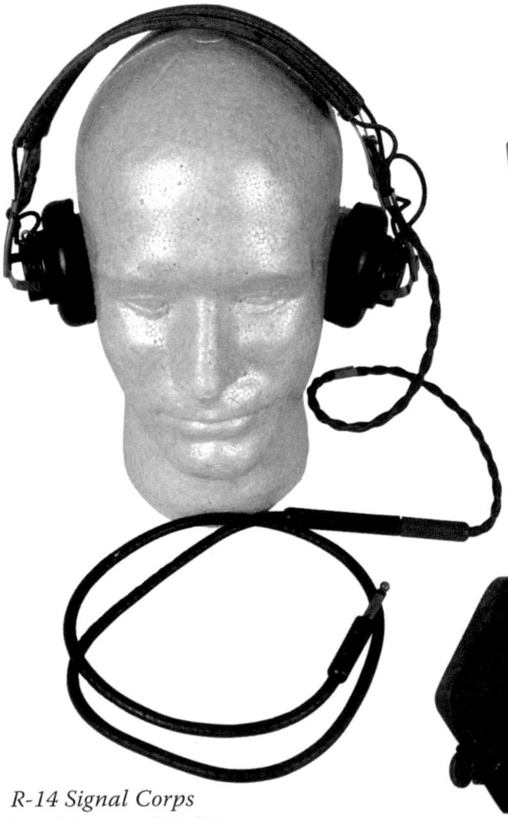

R-14 Signal Corps headphones, $50-$75 (£25-£40). Charles D. Pautler

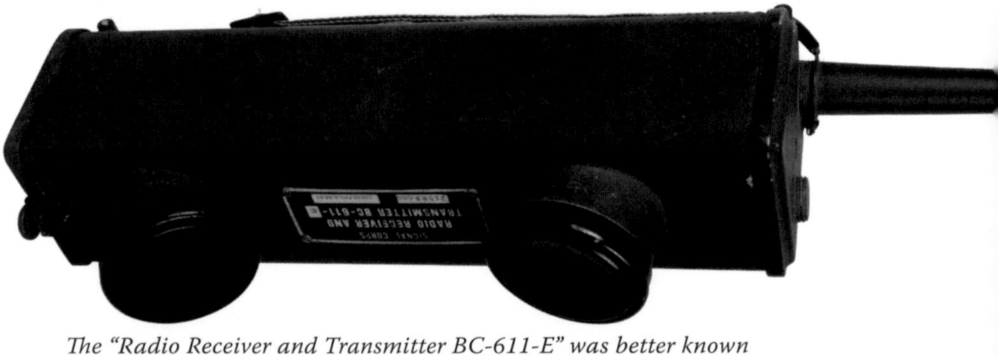

The "Radio Receiver and Transmitter BC-611-E" was better known as the "Handie-Talkie," $250-$325 (£125-£165). Charles D. Pautler

1930S ARMY FIELD TELEPHONE SET

* Brown leather rectangular case holds Western Electric field telephone set with silvered handset and wood mounted wire lead anchors with compartment holding the detachable crank handle. Complete set of two with shoulder straps and closure straps . . . .**$300 (£150)**

HS-33 HEADSET AND THROAT MICROPHONE LOT

* Set comprised of Army marked black plastic ANB-H-1 receivers with wires and HB-7 headband. Wiring loom intact with red "PL-354" standard plug. Receivers have black rubber ear cushions. Includes T-30 throat microphone with cord and elastic band . . . . **$70 (£35)**

TS-13-C AIRCRAFT INTERPHONE HANDSET

* Black plastic interphone handset with thumb switch for communications in crew-served aircraft, 1936 patent date, and complete with dual PL-55 and PL-86 plug attachments . . . . **$30 (£15)**

Entrenching Tools, Axes and Carriers

MODEL 1910 T-HANDLE SHOVEL

* M1910 T-Handle shovel has socket with "US" and "AMES 1942" maker's stamp. Retains 60% olive painted finish. Complete with light olive web cover also marked with 1942-dated contract stamp . . . .**$110 (£55)**

M1910 SHOVEL COVER

* Light olive drab web M1910 shovel cover has "SHANE MFG. CO. / 1941" maker's stamp on reverse . . **$30 (£15)**

MODEL 1910 SHOVEL COVER, BRITISH MADE

* Khaki web cover for the US M1910 T-Handle shovel has "U.S." stencil, British style hardware, and reverse with Broad Arrow proof and clear "BRITISH MADE" stamp . . . . **$90 (£45)**

MODEL 1943 ENTRENCHING SHOVEL

* Model 1943 shovel retains 95% olive drab painted finish and is stamped "U.S. / AMES / 1944" complete with second pattern adjustable olive drab web carrier dated "ATLAS AWNING / 1944" . . . . **$30 (£15)**

MODEL 1943 ENTRENCHING TOOL COVER, FIRST PATTERN

* Model 1943 shovel cover with the single, non-adjustable wire hanger on the reverse, dated 1943, but in dark olive drab canvas . . . . **$35 (£20)**

MODEL 1943 SHOVEL AND COVER, SECOND PATTERN

* Model 1943 folding shovel with "U.S. / AMES / 1945" maker's date stamp; includes second pattern olive drab 1944-dated cover . . . . **$35 (£20)**

> *"All five crew members wore leather helmets that contained earphones and throat mikes. The tank commander...used a larger, hand-held microphone."*
>
> LT. BOB GREEN, 763RD TANK BN.

Chest Set TD-1 with press-to-talk switch, $50-$75 (£25-£40). Charles D. Pautler

Two different field phones are seen here: early war and late war versions of the EE-8 A, $100-$200 (£50-£100) each. Charles D. Pautler

M1910 T-handle shovel and carrier, $100-$150 (£50-£75). Author's collection

M1943 folding shovel, $25-$45 (£15-£25). Author's collection

M1910 hand axe and carrier, $60-$85 (£30-£45). Charles D. Pautler

M1910 pick mattock and carrier, $50-$65 (£25-£35). Charles D. Pautler

A-11 leather flight helmet, type R-14 earphone receivers and A-14 demand oxygen mask, $650-$750 (£325-£375).

Rock Island Auction Company

M1910 PICK MATTOCK WITH CARRIER-KHAKI

• Khaki web M1910 pick mattock carrier includes olive drab painted pick mattock and helve assembly **$55 (£30)**

MODEL 1910 PICK MATTOCK WITH CARRIER-OD

• Dark OD web M1910 entrenching tool carrier with 1945 maker's date stamp, unmarked pick and helve . **$35 (£20)**

M1910 HAND AXE AND CARRIER

• M1910 hatchet entrenching tool marked "U.S." and "1944." Olive drab web carrier has "U.S." stencil and 1944-dated contract stamp . . . . **$80 (£40)**

Flight Masks

A-7A OXYGEN MASK

• Olive rubber oxygen mask that covers the nose only, leaving the mouth exposed. Complete with green rubber tube for attaching to the aircraft oxygen system but allowing the maximum freedom of movement. Rubber is imprinted with maker's information, patent stamp, and "42-5" stamp . . . .**$350 (£175)**

A-8-B OXYGEN MASK

• Complete A-8-B mask with hose attachment and good pliable rebreather bag, mask marked with AAF nomenclature, original band with leather attachment straps . . . .**$350 (£175)**

A-14 DEMAND OXYGEN MASK

• Olive drab rubber oxygen mask with embossed nomenclature "DEMAND / OXYGEN MASK / TYPE A-14 / MEDIUM" with AAF property stamp and "1-45" date. Complete with olive web suspension strap and hose. All rubber is pliable. Complete with its original green reinforced pasteboard carton labeled with nomenclature, Cleveland maker's "DEC. 1944" date stamp, and illustrations of AAF officer wearing the mask . . . . . .**$385 (£195)**

A-8-B oxygen mask with HS-33 headset and major's overseas cap displayed on an original Army Air Force plaster display head, $550-$650 (£275-£325). Rock Island Auction Company

Flotation Devices

TYPE AN6519-1 LIFE PRESERVER
- Type AN6519-1 yellow rubberized fabric life preserver with clear stamps and all straps and cords in fine condition . . . .**$245 (£125)**

B-3 PNEUMATIC LIFE PRESERVER VEST
- Type B-3, yellow material with brown leather center section and deflation hoses and catch intact. Retains original CO2 cartridges. Complete with life jacket dye marker . . . .**$245 (£125)**

B-4 FLYER'S LIFE PRESERVER
- Yellow rubberized flyer's life preserver is labeled with "OCT 1942" maker's date, nomenclature and AAF property stamp, last inspection date March 1945. Black rubber air outlet valve extensions are intact, vest is complete with all straps and snaps . . . .**$250 (£125)**

USMC FLOTATION BLADDER
- 11" x 15" rubberized canvas pouch with inflation tube and olive web attachment straps, stenciled "U.S.M.C. / FLOTATION BLADDER" with buoyancy specifications and contract "JUNE 29, 1944" . . . . **$60 (£30)**

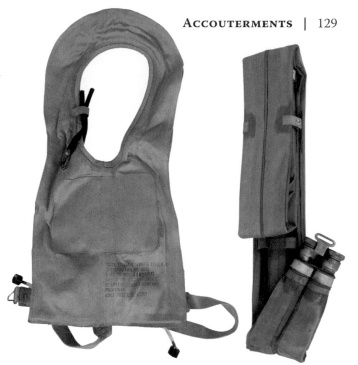

B-4 life preserver vest, $200-$275 (£100-£140). www.advanceguardmilitaria.com

Invasion life belt, $95-$150 (£50-£75). Charles D. Pautler

Goggles

A-1 RESISTAL FLYING GOGGLES
- Resistal aviator's goggles have blackened metal frames, clear lenses, black elastic headband, tan sidepieces and chenille cushions. Unused original example still has "RESISTAL / NON-SHATTERABLE" trademark label attached to one lens and includes the original pasteboard box. Both summer and winter versions were available under the same type designation, the summer version having chenille trimmed eye cups, the winter model being attached to a fur-lined leather face mask.
  . . . .**$125 (£65)**

AN6530 goggles, $250-$350 (£125-£175). www.advanceguardmilitaria.com

AN6530 GOGGLES
- Early production AN6530 goggles with tube vents, metal fittings with nickel finish, clear lenses, gray rubber eye cushion with chamois lining and black elastic band. Adjustable center bridge has "A-N 6530" designation
  . . . .**$275 (£140)**

ANTI-FLAK GOGGLES
- Goggle shaped eyeshield of thin armor plate with slitted eye openings. Interior has white corduroy padding on brow and bottom edge and black elastic retaining strap
  . . . .**$175 (£90)**

> *"I saw the plane in front of me blow up and I flew right through the pieces. I...recall seeing something yellow go by me and thinking it was the yellow 'Mae West' life vast we all wore."*
>
> LT. ROY BENSON, 9TH U.S. AIR FORCE

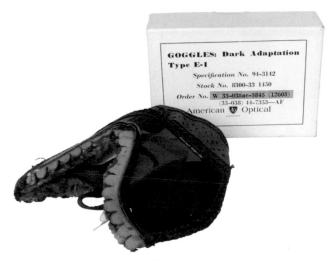

Type E-1 goggles were worn by both aviation and mountain troops, $25-$35 (£15-£20). Author's collection

M1943 goggles, $15-$25 (£7-£15). Author's collection

M1944 all-purpose goggles, $35-$65 (£20-£35). Author's collection

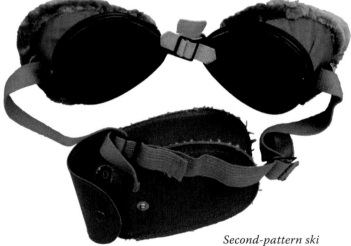

Second-pattern ski goggles, $35-$55 (£20-£30). Author's collection

Model 1916 .45 holster, $65-$100 (£35-£50). Charles D. Pautler

The Air Corps standardized the M3 pistol holster in 1942, $95-$165 (£50-£85). Charles D. Pautler

VARIABLE DENSITY AIR GUNNER'S GOGGLES

• Black rubber frames with red flip-down shield and polarization adjustment knob, reverse with olive elastic headband, complete with olive metal issue carton.
.... **$45 (£25)**

M1944 GOGGLES AND CASE

• Polaroid manufactured general purpose goggles, black rubber frame with clear lens and olive drab adjustable strap. Complete with olive drab issue pasteboard box with printed instructions on the cover and replacement green lens. .... **$30 (£15)**

MOUNTAIN TROOP'S SKI GOGGLES AND CASE

• Second pattern goggles with green tinted lenses, imitation fur trim and olive drab elastic head band. Complete with brown leatherette case .... **$35 (£20)**

Holsters

M2 REVOLVER HOLSTER

• Brown leather M2 pattern holster, WWII production for the 1917 Smith and Wesson and Colt .45 caliber double-action service revolvers and almost identical to the 1909/1917 pattern holster except that it is reversed. Has oval "US" cartouche. Reverse with maker's stamp and 1942 date. Base has a round boss with brass loop for attaching a leather thong .... **$95 (£50)**

MODEL 1916 .45 AUTOMATIC HOLSTER

• Brown leather holster for the .45 Automatic pistol in pliable condition with crisp "US" oval cartouche. Reverse has "BOYT 42" maker's date stamp .... **$75 (£40)**

WWII .45 AUTOMATIC SHOULDER HOLSTER

• Russet leather with embossed "US", bronze fittings. Reverse marked "U.S. ENGER-KRESS" .... **$65 (£35)**

USMC M7 SHOULDER HOLSTER

• Brown leather shoulder holster for the M1911 .45 Auto has a more elaborate suspension system than the M3 holster. Reverse marked "USMC / BOYT / 44"
.... **$155 (£80)**

NAVY/USMC .38 REVOLVER SHOULDER HOLSTER

- Brown leather shoulder holster for the .38 Caliber Victory Model revolver with a "US" oval cartouche and a shoulder strap with ten white elastic ammunition loops. Reverse has "U.S.N. / BOYT / 44" maker's stamp.
....$225 (£115)

Leggings

ARMY LEGGINGS

- Khaki canvas leggings marked with Philadelphia Q.M. Depot stamp, "3-15-35" date and size "4" $25 (£15)

WWII MOUNTAIN TROOP'S SKI LEGGINGS

- Khaki/light olive canvas and web short canvas gaiters with black leather arch straps. Contract marked "M / U.S. / HOOD RUBBER CO"................. $30 (£17)

USMC LEGGINGS

- Khaki canvas side lace leggings, contract tag marked "Depot of Supplies / U.S. Marine Corps," dated "1-4-40".
....$25 (£15)

WAC/ANC LEGGINGS

- Khaki canvas leggings stamped LEGGINGS, CANVAS, WOMEN'S SIZE 1 with contract data and date "11-6-44" $35 (£20)

Army khaki leggings, $15-$25 (£7-£15).
Charles D. Pautler

Mountain troops short ski leggings, $25-$35 (£15-£20).
Author's collection

Leggings for female troops, $25-$35 (£15-£20). www.advanceguardmilitaria.com

Shoulder holster for the .38 caliber Victory revolver, $200-$275 (£100-£140). www.advanceguardmilitaria.com

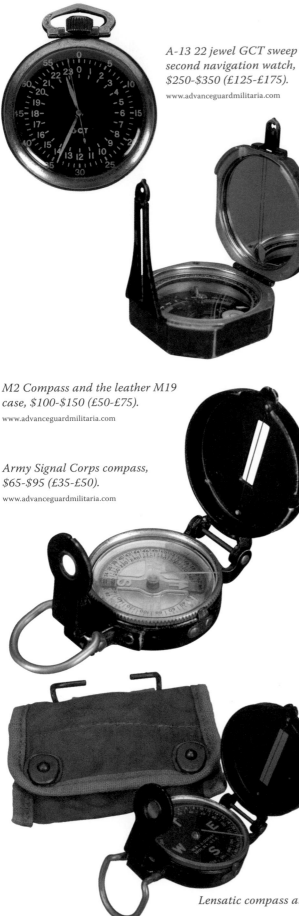

A-13 22 jewel GCT sweep second navigation watch, $250-$350 (£125-£175).

www.advanceguardmilitaria.com

M2 Compass and the leather M19 case, $100-$150 (£50-£75).

www.advanceguardmilitaria.com

Army Signal Corps compass, $65-$95 (£35-£50).

www.advanceguardmilitaria.com

Navigation, Compasses and Time Pieces

A-13 NAVIGATION (HACK) WATCH

- Elgin 581 grade B.W. Raymond, Type A-13 22 jewel GCT sweep second navigation watch with feature allowing the watch to be synchronized with a master time reference. Black face has luminous dial with 24-hour time interior and outer rim designated in seconds. Reverse has AN proof stamp and military nomenclature designation "TYPE A-13" with military spec. number, serial number, maker's part number, and maker "ELGIN." These were carried aboard bombers by the navigator in a circular metal spring-loaded "shock" case to protect them in flight . . . .**$295 (£150)**

A-12 NAVIGATOR'S CASED SEXTANT

- Type A-12 bubble sextant is housed in 12-1/2" x 9" x 4-1/4" olive grained paper covered wood case with leather handle and metal data plate. Sextant has black textured exterior finish, flip-down mirrors and filters, and is complete with rubber eyecup . . . . **$75 (£40)**

M2 MILITARY COMPASS

- Sometimes referred to as an "artillery compass" due to its extreme accuracy, metal body has olive drab finish marked "COMPASS, M2" with stock and serial numbers. Internal works has adjustable dial, several levels, mirror and sighting arm. Carried in a brown leather carrier marked "CASE, CARRYING, M19" . . . . **$125 (£65)**

WRIST COMPASS

- Khaki plastic compass, appears functional, reverse marked "CORPS OF ENGINEERS / US ARMY" and name of contractor. Complete with leather strap. . . . .**$75 (£40)**

ARMY COMPASS POUCH AND COMPASS

- Olive web compass carrying pouch contains a standard issue WWII compass. . . . .**$75 (£40)**

LENSATIC COMPASS AND WATERPROOFED CARRYING CASE

- Blackened metal lensatic compass has "W. and L.E. GURLEY / TROY, N.Y., U.S.A" maker's information on the dial. Case is made of waterproofed canvas and web and has lift-the-dot fasteners . . . .**$95 (£50)**

PARATROOPER ESCAPE AND EVASION COMPASS

- 1/4"-thick dime-size compass with luminescent dial, part of the issue Escape and Evasion Map Pouch that included this compass, a map of the Normandy coast, and a small saw blade . . . .**$125 (£65)**

Optics

ARMY 6 X 30 BINOCULARS

- Oive drab painted finish with adjustable focus eyepieces, white highlighted designation "BINOCULAR / M3 / 6X30" and maker "WESTINGHOUSE / 1942 H.M.R." Brown leather carrier marked, "CASE, CARRYING M17" complete with strap . . . .**$125 (£65)**

Lensatic compass and waterproof belt pouch, $75-$125 (£40-£65). www.advanceguardmilitaria.com

NAVY 6 X 30 BINOCULARS AND CASE

- 6x30 binoculars marked "U.S. NAVY BU. SHIPS MARK 33." Also has sticker advising that the optics are coated and require special care when cleaning. Black leather case is worn . . . . **$95 (£50)**

NAVY 7 X 50 BINOCULARS AND CASE

- Black Bausch and Lomb 7x50 porro prism binoculars with intact barrel wraps and marked "U.S. NAVY, BU. SHIPS / MARK 28, MOD 9 / NO. 72895. 1943." Complete with neck strap and carrying case . . . . . **$645 (£325)**

Parachutes and Flight/Airborne Gear

A-3 AVIATOR'S PARACHUTE

- Chest harness type parachute pack has olive drab canvas with "Type A-3 Parachute" AAF contractor label with 1943 date stamps, center marked with black numeral "25" on yellow painted stripe indicating that it is for use on Quick Attach Chest harness rigs also with yellow markings. Includes inspection log and "Emergency Uses of the Parachute" manual tucked into their proper pouch, rip cord, and all elastic opening cords. The parachute contained within is also dated 1943 . . . . **$225 (£115)**

B-8 BACKPACK PARACHUTE

- Flexible backpack parachute with light olive canvas body and heavy white web harness with metal snap fittings and shoulder-mounted release cord. Still contains the original packed parachute, parachute log record book indicating that this one was made in January 1944, and repacked for the last time in October 1945. The log pouch also contains a copy of "Emergency Uses of the Parachute". . . . . **$1,295 (£650)**

AVIATOR'S PARACHUTE HARNESS

- "Quick Attachable Chest" type parachute harness with ring and snap hook release mechanism, heavy white web harness with 1943 date stamps, and large attachment rings on the chest for attaching the QAC parachute. Shoulders are marked with red paint for quick reference when drawing flight gear. Complete with back pad. . . . . **$465 (£235)**

AVIATOR'S PARACHUTE HARNESS

- "Quick Attachable Chest" type parachute harness with the simplified spring twist-and-release mechanism, heavy olive web harness, and large seated attachment snap-hooks on the chest for attaching the QAC parachute. Shoulders have yellow fabric rectangles sewn to them for quick reference when drawing flight gear. Olive padded back pad present . . . . **$375 (£190)**

C-2 LIFE RAFT SEAT PACK

- Type C-2 life raft container of light olive drab canvas and web with snap hooks for attachment to the seat pack parachute harness, side with nomenclature panel stamped with 1945 "Air Cruisers" contract date. Lacks raft. . . . . **$55 (£30)**

M3 6 x 30 binoculars with M17 case, $100-$150 (£50-£75). Charles D. Pautler

A-3 aviator's parachute, $200-$300 (£100-£150). www.advanceguardmilitaria.com

Aviator's parachute harness and back pad, $400-$500 (£200-£250).

www.advanceguardmilitaria.com

"Quick attachable chest type" aviator's harness and back pad, $350-$450 (£175-£225).

www.advanceguardmilitaria.com

British-made .45 automatic pistol clip pouch, $30-$40 (£15-£20). www.advanceguardmilitaria.com

M1 Carbine ammo pouch and two 15-round clips, $30-$40 (£15-£20). Charles D. Pautler

Pouches and Carriers, Ammunition

.45 AUTOMATIC CLIP POUCH
* Light olive drab two pocket web pouch, marked "U.S." and maker's name and date .... **$15 (£7)**

.45 AUTOMATIC CLIP POUCH, BRITISH MADE
* Unissued khaki web .45 clip pouch with Broad Arrow, "BRITISH MADE," maker, and 1943 date stamps. Excellent condition .... **$35 (£20)**

M-1 CARBINE BUTTSTOCK CLIP POUCH
* Light olive drab canvas and web double magazine pouch for the M1 Carbine. This version has the open, pass-through back so that it could be either worn on the belt or slipped over the buttstock of the weapon. Reverse has contractor's name......................... **$30 (£15)**

USMC M-1 CARBINE MAGAZINE POUCH
* Light olive drab web two pocket magazine pouch, reverse with snap attachment, "U.S.M.C." and "BOYT-44" stamp. .... **$35 (£20)**

SHOTGUN AMMUNITION POUCH
* Khaki web pouch with light olive edge trim, flap lift-the-dot fasteners and "U.S." Stencil. Body stenciled "POUCH, AMMUNITION / SHOTGUN." Interior has "J.Q.M.D. 1943" maker's stamp, shell loops, reverse with belt loops and base with grommet hole .... **$265 (£135)**

THOMPSON SMG MAGAZINE POUCH AND PISTOL BELT SET
* Light olive web carrier for five 20-round Thompson SMG stick magazines with lift-the-dot fasteners. Includes khaki/light olive drab web M1936 pistol belt with "U.S." stencil............................. **$100 (£50)**

USMC THOMPSON SMG FIVE-POCKET MAGAZINE POUCH
* Khaki web magazine pouch for the Thompson submachine gun stick magazines with bronze lift-the-dot fasteners. Reverse with "USMC" stencil ....**$225 (£115)**

GRENADE CARRIER, TWO POCKET
* Two-pocket style commonly used by U.S. Marines. Made of olive drab canvas with light olive web edge binding and tape ties, obverse of each pocket has two lift-the-dot closures .... **$30 (£15)**

This group of 1945-dated M1 carbine pouches shows the range of the OD No. 7 shade, $15-$25 each (£7-£15 each). www.advanceguardmilitaria.com

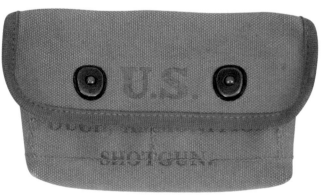

Shotgun ammo pouch for attaching to web belt, $250-$300 (£125-£150). www.advanceguardmilitaria.com

M1 AMMUNITION BAG

- Bag, Carrying, Ammunition, M1: light olive drab canvas and web bag has dark olive drab strap leads. Obverse has "U.S." stencil. Interior marked "ANCHOR CANVAS / 1944" . . . . **$45 (£25)**

M2 AMMUNITION BAG

- Khaki canvas double bag, vest style variant with front and rear pouches. Used by mortar and machine gun units, complete olive drab web straps and drawstring cords . . . . **$40 (£20)**

M2A1 AMMUNITION BAG

- Dark olive drab canvas double bag, vest style with front and rear pouches. Complete web straps, drawstring cords and quick release shoulder hook . . . . **$45 (£25)**

USMC T-7 LIGHT ANTI-TANK MINE BAG

- Late WWII production USMC carrying bag for the T-7 anti-tank mine. Marked "U.S.M.C. / Scranton Lace Co. 1945" maker's date stamp, tie straps, belt loop and snap attachment for carrying on the multi-snap web belt. . . . . **$35 (£20)**

BAZOOKA ROCKET BAG

- Olive drab canvas rocket bag has olive web sling, lift-the-dot closures, "U.S." stencil, and "VICTORY CANVAS CO. 1944" contract stamp . . . . **$35 (£20)**

Pouches, Medical and First-Aid

MODEL 1910 WOUND DRESSING POUCH

- M1910 wound dressing pouch of khaki web with domed snap fasteners would appear to be a WWI pouch, except for "J.Q.M.D. 1942" maker's stamp inside the flap. Includes Carlisle bandage . . . . **$45 (£25)**

1942 PATTERN WOUND DRESSING POUCH AND CARLISLE BANDAGE

- Light olive web first-aid pouch has "U.S." stencil and "The American Awning Company / 1943" maker's date stamp on reverse . . . . **$30 (£15)**

MODEL 1942 WOUND DRESSING POUCH, BRITISH MADE, WITH BANDAGE

- Khaki web wound dressing carrier with 1944 maker's date stamp and "BRITISH MADE" inside the flap. Exterior stenciled "U.S." and has a pebbled snap fitting. Olive drab Carlisle metal bandage packet present . . . **$30 (£15)**

USMC FIRST-AID DRESSING AND POUCH

- Khaki web single snap pouch, flap stenciled "U.S.M.C." Complete with belt hook and an unopened Carlisle model first-aid packet . . . . **$40 (£20)**

U.S. Army five-pocket pouch for Thompson submachine gun, $50-$95 (£25-45). A USMC marked example will sell for $200-$250 (£100-£125). www.advanceguardmilitaria.com

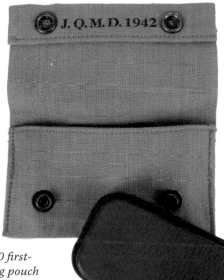

This M1910 first-aid dressing pouch is dated 1942, $35-$45 (£20-£25).

www.advanceguardmilitaria.com

1942 pattern first-aid pouch and Carlisle bandage in a sealed, tin packet, $25-$35 (£15-£20).

www.advanceguardmilitaria.com

> *"Joe [Walentowski] later told me I helped bandage his leg. I don't remember that. In that kind of chaos, you don't remember everything that happens."*
>
> PVT. HARRY HEINLEIN, 29TH U.S. INFANTRY DIVISION

Referred to as the "paratrooper's first-aid kit," this style of pouch could be tied to a helmet net, arm or leg, $300-$400 (£150-£200). www.advanceguardmilitaria.com

PARATROOPER FIRST-AID KIT

- This was tied to a helmet. This example was opened at one end, revealing the rubberized side of the fabric interior and exposing the contents for display, which include a tourniquet, sulfa wound tablets, and a Carlisle bandage. The morphine dose is no longer present . . . . **$325 (£165)**

JUNGLE FIRST-AID KIT

- Dark olive drab canvas pouch marked "U.S. / 1945." Contains first-aid dressing, insect repellent bottle, boric acid ointment tube, Mercuro Chrome bottle, Frazer's Solution bottle and band aids. . . . . **$60 (£30)**

FIELD MEDIC'S AID BAG

- Light olive canvas bag with flap and size adjusting rows of eyelets to shorten the bag's length. Bag is unlaced in the long position. . . . . **$75 (£40)**

MEDIC'S SHOULDER HARNESS, AID BAGS, AND CONTENTS

- Complete set includes light olive web medic's harness strap assembly, and aid bags. Both are complete with detachable connecting straps. One has the lace-in equipment panel with Medical Department tin, glass medical flask, and halzone tablets. Contents include issue tourniquet, Atribine tablets bottle (empty) for malaria, an assortment of gauze roller bandages in the maker's boxes, including four each of the small, medium, and large sizes, two camouflaged triangular compressed bandages, tin of adhesive plaster, six large Carlisle field dressings in 1942-dated boxes with cellophane wrappers, and six small-size Carlisle first-aid dressings in waxed paper boxes.
. . . .**$465 (£235)**

COMBAT MEDIC'S SHOULDER HARNESS

- Combat medic's shoulder harness of light olive web.
. . . .**$145 (£75)**

Jungle first-aid pouch and contents, $50-$75 (£25-£40).
Charles D. Pautler

In 1944, the Army introduced a three-pocket first-aid pouch, $35-$50 (£20-£25). Charles D. Pautler

Two pouches and a special harness completed a medic's specialized field gear. With contents, a set will sell for $400-$500 (£200-£250). www.advanceguardmilitaria.com

Medic's field aid bag, $50-$75 (£25-£40).
www.advanceguardmilitaria.com

NAVY CORPSMAN'S FIELD MEDICAL BAG

- Navy Corpsman's Unit-B field bag of khaki web and canvas marked with stenciled red cross and "U.S.N." Two front closure straps, two side ear closure snaps to prevent items from bouncing out in the field, and an adjustable khaki web shoulder strap. Reverse side has an extra white canvas duck external pouch . . . . **$265 (£135)**

FIELD SURGICAL OPERATING KIT

- Complete set of over 30 surgical tools and components, includes various scissors, forceps, probes, scalpels, syringe, needles, stitching silk and more. Tools outlined on a guide printed on the case interior. Complete with olive drab canvas roll up carrying case with straps, marked "SMALL OPERATING CASE" . . . . **$265 (£135)**

NAVY DOCTOR'S FIELD SURGICAL KIT

- 7" x 3" x 1" folded dimensions marked "POCKET CASE / M.D. - U.S.N." on the exterior. Interior has undated maker's stamp and compartments for surgical instruments, of which a four-scalpel set in a metal safety container and one probe remain . . . . **$95 (£50)**

AERONAUTIC FIRST-AID KIT

- Aeronautic First-Aid Kit comprised of zippered khaki pouch, 7" x 5" x 5", with almost all of the original contents (only the morphine was removed) including tourniquet, scissors, forceps boxed set, small first-aid dressing, eye dressing set, petrolatum, camouflaged first-aid set, scissors, tweezers, halazone water purification tablets, large field dressing, six iodine swabs, individual first-aid dressing, a burn injury set, boxed set of ammonia inhalants, and another eye dressing set. Includes the male portion of the lift-the-dots with screws on the back for installing in the aircraft. Exterior has nomenclature "KIT, FIRST AID AERONAUTIC U.S." . . . . **$125 (£65)**

Pouches, Packs and Bags, Personal Gear

MODEL 1938 MAP CASE

- Early war 1938 pattern khaki canvas and web map case has "American Leather Products Corp. / 1942" maker stamp, "U.S." stencil on obverse flap and interior implement pocket, and three interior sections. Complete with matching correct khaki web carrying strap with shoulder pad . . . . **$55 (£30)**

M1928 HAVERSACK AND PACK TAIL

- Light olive canvas and web M1928 haversack complete with meat can pouch, "RUBRO 1942" maker's stamp on reverse. Includes unissued "LANGDON TENT and AWNING 1942" maker's stamp . . . . **$70 (£35)**

MODEL 1928 HAVERSACK, BRITISH MADE

- Model 1928 haversack of light olive drab cotton canvas with khaki edge binding and straps with Commonwealth hardware, stamped "BRITISH MADE" and dated "1944". . . . . **$110 (£55)**

Navy Corpsman's Unit-B field medical bag and contents, $250-$300 (£125-£150). www.advanceguardmilitaria.com

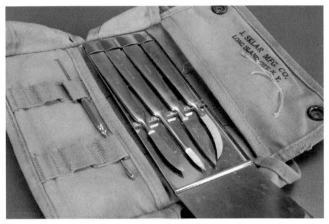

Navy doctor's surgical set, $95-$125 (£50-£65).
www.advanceguardmilitaria.com

"Kit, First-Aid, Aeronautic," $125-$150 (£65-£75).
www.advanceguardmilitaria.com

Model 1938 dispatch or "map" case, $50-$100 (£25-£50). Charles D. Pautler

A soldier stored his mess gear in the M1928 meat can pouch, $10-$25 (£5-£15). Author's collection

M1928 haversack and pack tail, $70-$95 (£35-£50). www.advanceguardmilitaria.com

MODEL 1928 MEAT CAN POUCH
- Light olive drab cotton canvas meat can pouch for the 1928 haversack . . . . **$15 (£8)**

MODEL 1928 MEAT CAN POUCH, BRITISH MADE
- Pouch for the M1928 haversack made of light olive drab canvas with khaki edge binding and Commonwealth hardware. Interior stamped "U.S. Jand A.H. Ltd. 1945 BRITISH MADE". . . . . **$25 (£15)**

MODEL 1928 PACK TAIL, BRITISH MADE
- Light OD canvas and web pack tail for the M1928 haversack . . . . **$35 (£20)**

MODEL 1936 MUSETTE BAG
- Light olive drab canvas and web M1936 field bag has "U.S." stencil on flap, and interior with 1943-dated maker's stamp. Complete with utility shoulder strap. . . . . **$55 (£30)**

MODEL 1936 MUSETTE BAG, BRITISH MADE
- Light olive drab cotton canvas with khaki tape binding and straps with Commonwealth style adjustment buckles, interior with 1944 date and "BRITISH MADE" stamp. . . . . **$85 (£45)**

USMC LIGHT FIELD PACK
- "Bag, Canvas, Field, Model 1936" made khaki canvas with light olive web trim, base with short retaining strap and lift-the-dot fastener used when configuring the bag as a knapsack, flap with double strap closure, interior with "U.S.M.C." stencil, exterior side pocket, and strap with two shoulder pads . . . . **$115 (£60)**

USMC M1941 KNAPSACK SET
- Includes both upper and lower components. Top portion has tab for suspending an e-tool, left side with tab for attaching bayonet . . . . **$95 (£50)**

Model 1936 "musette bag," $45-$85 (£25-£45). www.advanceguardmilitaria.com

The USMC light field pack resembled the Army's Model 1936 "musette bag," $75-$100 (£40-£50). www.advanceguardmilitaria.com

MODEL 1945 FIELD PACK SET

• Complete set includes both the Field Combat pack and the lower Field Cargo pack, both of olive drab #7 canvas and web with "U.S." stencils and 1945 maker date stamp. Each segment complete with original instruction sheet $125 (£65)

MOUNTAIN TROOPS RUCKSACK

• Light olive canvas rucksack is fitted to tubular steel pack frame with leather fittings and web straps, flap with "U.S." stencil. Interior with 1942 contract date stamp $75 (£40)

MODEL 1943 PACK

• Olive drab canvas with web straps, tall bag with draw-string top, complete with straps for contracting or expanding pack size, top flap with zippered pouch and tab for attaching bayonet for the side and entrenching tool on the back. Interior marked "T.E. SPEG CO. / 1942" $125 (£65)

JUNGLE PACK, CAMOUFLAGE

• Camouflage canvas with khaki web straps, tall bag with drawstring top, complete with straps for contracting or expanding pack size, top flap with zippered pouch and tab for attaching bayonet for the side and entrenching tool on the back. Interior marked "HINSON MFG. CO. / 1943". $250 (£125)

WAAC/WAC UTILITY BAG (PURSE)

• Brown leather bag with shallow, snap-down flap and removable brown leather shoulder strap. Interior lined in olive drab fabric and include the small separate accessory pouch with snap down flap $225 (£115)

NAVY WAVES ISSUE UTILITY BAG AND COVER

• Rectangular black leather purse with single center snap and black leather shoulder strap. Interior with three compartments. Includes the white cotton purse cover for use with the white summer uniform. $245 (£125)

USMC Pattern of 1941 pack system consisting of upper and lower components in Olive Drab No. 7, $75-$125 (£40-£65). Charles D. Pautler

Second pattern mountain rucksack, $65-$85 (£35-£45). Author's collection

Women's Army Corps purse was known as a "utility bag," $200-$250 (£100-£125). www.advanceguardmilitaria.com

The Model 1943 pack was intended to replace the M1928 haversack and was a variation of the Model 1942 jungle pack, $100-$150 (£50-£75). Author's collection

Model 1938 wire cutter carrier, $10-$15 (£5-£7). Charles D. Pautler

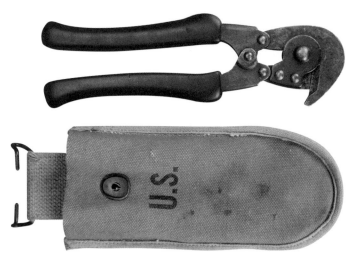

M1938 wire cutters with carrier, $95-$135 (£50-£70). www.advanceguardmilitaria.com

Lineman's pouch, wire cutters, knife and leather carrier, $35-$75 (£20-£40). Charles D. Pautler

Tents

SHELTER HALF-KHAKI

• Light olive khaki shelter half dated 1942 with clear US and manufacturer's marks, all buttons, buttonholes, peg loops, and grommets sound . . . . **$40 (£20)**

USMC CAMOUFLAGE SHELTER HALF

• 1943 pattern reversible Marine camouflage shelter half has two end closures and WWI style sunburst buttons. . . . . **$225 (£115)**

MOUNTAIN TROOPS TWO-MAN MOUNTAIN TENT

• Two-man mountain tent has one opening and a vent, reversible from olive drab to white, with screen protected closures and loops for attaching poles and ropes, poles are included, as are the required six angled sheet steel winter tent stakes . . . . **$225 (£115)**

Wire Cutters

MODEL 1938 WIRE CUTTER CARRIER, KHAKI

• Khaki web belt carrier for the M1938 wire cutter **$10 (£5)**

MODEL 1938 WIRE CUTTERS CARRIER, OLIVE DRAB

• Dark olive drab canvas wire cutters carrying case, dated "1945" . . . . **$10 (£5)**

MODEL 1938 WIRE CUTTER CARRIER, BRITISH MADE

• Olive drab web carrier for the issue wire cutters, interior with Broad Arrow and "BRITISH MADE" stamps and lift-the-dot fastener . . . . **$35 (£20)**

MODEL 1938 WIRE CUTTERS WITH CARRIER

• M1938 wire cutters with black rubber covered grips with "U.S." stamp and "1945" date. Complete with 1942-dated carrier . . . . **$115 (£60)**

LINEMAN'S TOOL

• Brown leather double pocket scabbard has belt loop and flap with bronze lift-the-dot snaps, complete with TL-29 lineman's folding knife made by Camillus and the TL-13-A pliers marked "U.S." . . . . **$85 (£45)**

CHAPTER 4

MEDALS

Medal collecting can become a hobby all within itself. Many medal collectors have never even considered branching out to other fields of militaria. To them, owning a fine German helmet is the same as owning a clay flower pot...of little interest and they certainly can't comprehend that it possesses any monetary value.

That said, medals are, by far, the most common military souvenir from World War II. All the participant nations minted and awarded medals in one form or another. After the war, medals came home with soldiers who received them as commendations or recognition, but also as war trophies. Three factors make medals a popular souvenir: medals are small, they are embodied with the mystique of "valor," "bravery," or "merit," and they exude the aura of monetary worth (perhaps because of the similarity to coinage or the perceived "precious metal" content). These three factors are still at the heart of the popularity of medal collecting.

Medals seem to be a fairly sound investment. Prices have steadily increased over the years and as supply of popular examples (like those of the Third Reich) decreases, the popularity of medals increases (like those of the Soviet Union). The end result is, even the most common medals have held their value over the years and few, if any, have dropped in value.

Because medals are an attractive collecting area, the field has attracted its share of unscrupulous dealers. It takes little effort to swap a ribbon, grind away or add a hallmark, or simply clean and embellish a medal. Reproductions of many medals and awards emerged on the market even during World War II! It is an old, tired saying, but your best defense, should you decide to collect medals, is to arm yourself with as many good books as possible. Study examples in a reputable collection. Remember: the real story of any medal is usually found on the back. Turn it over, consider how it was meant to be worn and examine the minting quality.

Collecting Hints

Pros:

- Medals are extremely personal. A collector can determine some of a soldier's history from a single piece.
- Supply is plentiful. It is easy for a collector to find a level of collecting that is both affordable and enjoyable.
- Display is not difficult. Hundreds of medals can be inexpensively and safely exhibited in a relatively small space.
- A wide variety of medals were produced, enabling collectors to choose an area in which to specialize.
- Medals are a sound investment.
- Items are small enough that shipping is not an obstacle, enabling a collector to buy from any source in the world.

Cons:

- A lot medals—especially those of the Germany's Third Reich—have been reproduced.
- Many medals contain metals that react to the environment and may require specialized storage and handling.
- It is easy to get carried away and acquire more than one can enjoy or even afford. Supply is high, so a collector needs to exercise discipline and purchase wisely rather than wildly.
- Advanced collections will cost thousands of dollars.
- It is easy to fake name and/or serial number engraving on a medal, so identified groupings must be regarded with a degree of skepticism.

Availability ★★★★

Price ★★★

Reproduction Alert ★★★

Notes on pricing:

- The following does not address medals authorized after 1946.
- Many medals have a "miniature" counterpart. The following prices do not cover any miniatures, though rarity of miniatures is roughly proportionate to the rarity of full-sized examples.
- The values of medals for which no recent report sales were reported are denoted with "n/a" for price "not available."

All of these can be signs of reproductions, forgery or simply spurious material.

Badge, Medal, Order or Decoration: Which is the Correct Term?

Go to any military show in the United States or Great Britain, and you will hear the terms "badge," "medal," "order," and "decoration" used interchangeably. The diehard dealer and collectors will know when to use which expression, but for the general militaria collector, all of these words will be used to describe the same object, depending on the speaker's mood. However, learning the terminology will give you an edge when interacting with a dealer. It could be the difference in being perceived as a "rube from the sticks" or as an informed customer. And you know how that difference is measured—in dollars (or pounds, of course)!

An Order dates back to the days of knighthood. Generally, an order is associated with nobility or religious belief. Today, orders are generally conferred on citizens for some act performed during peace or war. It is not uncommon, however, to find military medal groupings that contain an order.

A decoration refers to an award other than an order. Decorations are presented to soldiers for some act of distinction against an enemy in combat. An example of a decoration would be the U.S. Silver Star, German Iron Cross, I Class, or the United Kingdom's Victoria Cross.

A term you probably won't encounter in your collecting, but does come up in descriptions is Collar. A collar is the highest class of some orders. A collar may often be a chain from which the order is suspended.

The most common term in the field—and the most encompassing—is Medal. Properly, "medal" is used to describe any award that hangs from a ribbon. A medal will generally not be enamelled (a characteristic of an Order). A medal will commemorate a range of activities such as campaigns, long service, good conduct, or commemoration, or significant dates such as independence or a ruler's rise to power. Examples of medals include the United Kingdom's 1939-45 Star, Germany's Civil Service Honor Award, or the United States' Victory Medal. "Medal" is the term most commonly used to refer to the entire field of orders, decorations, and medals. If you are going to use just one word, this is the one to choose. A more experienced collector will not consider it a gaffe if you casually refer to a Medal of Honor as a "medal" (more correctly, it should be called a "decoration"). However, should you call a Romanian Anti-Communist Campaign Medal a "decoration," this will reveal your unfamiliarity (and, therefore, vulnerability) with the hobby. When in doubt, refer to orders, decorations and badges as "medals." For the purposes of this chapter, the term "medal" will be used interchangeably with "order" and "decoration."

A Badge is an outward symbol of a soldier having received a "passing grade" in a particular skill (and are not covered in this chapter). Badges include parachute or pilot wings and marksmanship awards. However, medal collectors reserve the word "badge" for an order that hangs from a ribbon. Yes, it is confusing. However, most diehard medal collectors are not going to be interacting regularly with general militaria collectors or dealers. So, for the purpose of this book, the term "badge" will generally imply that the item is a medal intended to be pinned directly to the wearer's uniform without an intervening ribbon.

There were 433 Medals of Honor awarded during WWII.

NAMED, NAMED, NAMED

In the real estate business, it is commonly said that the three most important factors contributing to value are location, location and location. Similarly, across the hobby of World War II collecting, and even more so in medal field, the three factors that determine the highest price for any medal are named, named, and named. The highest prices are being paid for medals that can be directly and conclusively linked to the names of the soldiers who originally received them. Many medals were inscribed with a soldier's name or number. This presents the collector with the opportunity to learn more about the circumstances surrounding the award of that actual medal! Collectors pay top price for that opportunity (some actually will do the research and learn the story of the award).

The next level of "value added" would be for medals that are accompanied with the original award certificate or documentation. This is a bit harder to sell. Consider for a moment a German Knight's Cross to the Iron Cross. Best estimates indicate that nearly 7,500 examples were awarded. However, none were engraved with the recipient's name or other identifying mark. Therefore, it is very hard to conclusively prove that a Knight's Cross belonged to a specific individual. All a dealer can use to determine pricing is condition and maker's marks. However, if the original award document (naming the recipient) accompanies the Knight's Cross, this is a clear advantage and will add hundreds, perhaps thousands, of dollars to the price. But unfortunately, nothing conclusively links the document to that particular example, so a collector will have to rely on his instincts and the perceived trustworthiness of the dealer. Remember, the lure of adding significantly to the value of a medal by placing it with an award document is very strong. An "assembled" medal/document combination should not command the same price as a set that has been together since the war.

COPIES, RESTRIKES, REPRODUCTIONS AND FAKES

German II Class Iron Crosses were produced and distributed in the hundreds of thousands during World War II. Common sense would suggest that a reproducer would not waste time on such a common medal—right? However, when it comes to evaluating the authenticity of a medal, resist the urge to use "common sense." In the case of the Iron Cross, some soldiers wanted something a bit more special, so they would visit a jeweler or other non-military associated business to purchase a finer example (perhaps made with real silver) than what the military had given them. These medals, though purchased and worn during the War, were not authorized examples provided by the military establishment. One of these would be best referred to as a copy.

After Germany's surrender, the market was hungry for souvenirs. The tooling that stamped the medals during the war still existed and was put right back into action to stamp out yet more Iron Crosses. These post-war Crosses that were made from the original dies are best referred to as restrikes.

Since the supply of originals, copies and restrikes didn't meet the demand for Iron Crosses, factories decided to make reproductions of the originals, either by creating new tooling or making a mold to produce castings that were then finished to look as close as possible to the original crosses. When sold as reproduction, some of the demand is adequately met.

And finally, there are those folks who just can't resist the lure of "easy money." They will do whatever it takes to inexpensively produce an item that they can sell to an unsuspecting customer as an original. Whether they alter and misrepresent an original, copy, restrike, or reproduction, they are producing a fake. It is illegal to do so but very difficult to prove intent. Therefore, a lot of people sell spurious medals, so use great caution!

BELGIUM

- Croix de Guerre, Type II (1940-45) $35 (£17.50)
- Armed Resistance Medal $20 (£10)
- Volunteers Medal. $20 (£10)
- Maritime Medal $25 (£12.50)
- War Commemorative Medal $25 (£12.50)
- Merit Cross for Military Chaplains. $300 (£150)
- Abyssinia Campaign Medal w/bar $25 (£12.50)
- Abyssinia Campaign w/o bar $20 (£10)
- Africa Service Medal w/o bar $20 (£10)
- Africa Service Medal with Nigerie bar. . . . $25 (£12.50)
- Africa Service Medal with Moyen
  Orient bar $25 (£12.50)
- Africa Service Medal with Madagascar bar $25 (£12.50)
- Africa Service Medal with Birmaniae bar . . $25 (£12.50)

BRAZIL

- Expeditionary Cross, First Class $75 (£38)
- Expeditionary Cross, Second Class. $50 (£25
- South Atlantic Anti-Submarine Patrol Medal. . $50 (£25)

BULGARIA

- Military Order of Bravery, III Class,
  Grade 1. . . . . $100 (£50)
- Military Order of Bravery, III Class,
  Grade 2. . . . . $95 (£48)
- Military Order of Bravery, IV Class,
  Grade 1. . . . . $70 (£35)
- Military Order of Bravery, IV Class,
  Grade 1 w/o swords. $80 (£40)
- Military Order of Bravery, IV Class,
  Grade 2. . . . . $40 (£20)
- Military Order of Bravery, IV Class ,
  Grade 2 w/o swords. $65 (£35
- Military Merit Order, Grand Cross. $575 (£290)
- Military Merit Order, Grand Cross
  w/war decoration $625 (£315)
- Military Merit Order, Grand Cross
  breast star $550 (£275)
- Military Merit Order, Grand Cross
  breast star w/war decoration $575 (£290)
- Military Merit Order, Grand Officer $400 (£200)
- Military Merit Order, Grand Officer
  w/war decoration $450 (£225)
- Military Merit Order, Grand Officer
  breast star $300 (£150)
- Military Merit Order, Grand Officer
  breast star w/war decoration $375 (£190)
- Military Merit Order, Commander. $425 (£215)

- Military Merit Order, Commander
  w/war decoration. $350 (£175)
- Military Merit Order, Officer. $325 (£165)
- Military Merit Order, Officer
  w/war decoration. $350 (£175)
- Military Merit Order, Knight. $250 (£125)
- Military Merit Order, Knight
  w/crown and war decoration. $150 (£75)
- Military Merit Order, Knight w/o crown. . . . $110 (£55)
- Military Merit Order, Knight
  w/war decoration. $95 (£50)
- Military Merit Order, Merit Cross w/crown. . . $50 (£25)
- Military Merit Order, Merit Cross
  w/o crown $35 (£20)
- Pilot's Badge $500 (£250)
- Observer's Badge $450 (£225)

CHINA

- Order of the Cloud and Banner, IV Class . . . $850 (£425)
- Order of the Cloud and Banner, V Class $750 (£375)
- Order of the Cloud and Banner, VI Class . . . $650 (£325)
- Order of the Cloud and Banner, VII Class. . . $475 (£240)
- Order of the Cloud and Banner, VIII Class. . $425 (£215)
- Order of the Cloud and Banner, IX Class . . . $350 (£175)
- Order of Victory. $600 (£300)
- Decoration for American Troops,
  Type I, numbered. $125 (£65)
- Decoration for American Troops,
  Type II, unnumbered. $65 (£35)
- Decoration for American Troops,
  Type III, U.S. made. $20 (£10)

Austrian Veteran's Medal. The medal was the same but the ribbon colors differed for various states, $25-$30 (£10-£15). Fred Borgmann

Czechoslovakian Order of the White Lion, Merit Medal, First Class, $400-$450 ($200-£2255) George S. Cuhaj

Germany lost 136 generals, which averaged one dead general every two weeks.

CROATIA (ALSO SEE YUGOSLAVIA)

- Order of the Iron Trefoil, I Class $600 (£300)
- Order of the Iron Trefoil, I Class
  w/oak leaves $650 (£325)
- Order of the Iron Trefoil, II Class $500 (£250)
- Order of the Iron Trefoil, II Class
  w/oak leaves $550 (£275)
- Order of the Iron Trefoil, III Class $325 (£165)
- Order of the Iron Trefoil, III Class
  w/oak leaves $375 (£190)
- Order of the Iron Trefoil, IV Class $225 (£115)
- Order of the Iron Trefoil, IV Class
  w/oak leaves $275 (£140)
- Croatia Order of Merit, Grand Cross,
  (Christian) $550 (£275)
- Croatia Order of Merit, Grand Cross,
  (Muslim) $1,000 (£500)
- Croatia Order of Merit, Grand Cross,
  breast star (Christian) $550 (£275)
- Croatia Order of Merit, Grand Cross,
  breast star (Muslim) $1,000 (£500)
- Croatia Order of Merit, I Class, w/star (
  Christian) $350 (£175)
- Croatia Order of Merit, I Class, w/star
  (Muslim) $750 (£375)
- Croatia Order of Merit, I Class, (Christian) . $325 (£165)
- Croatia Order of Merit, I Class, (Muslim) . . . $725 (£365)
- Croatia Order of Merit, I Class,
  breast star (Christian) $350 (£175)
- Croatia Order of Merit, I Class,
  breast star (Muslim) $750 (£375)
- Croatia Order of Merit, II Class (Christian) . $250 (£125)
- Croatia Order of Merit, II Class (Muslim) . . . $500 (£250)
- Croatia Order of Merit, III Class (Christian) $225 (£115)
- Croatia Order of Merit, III Class (Muslim) . . $400 (£200)
- Medal For Bravery, Gold $350 (£175)
- Medal For Bravery, Silver $225 (£115)
- Medal For Bravery, Silver, next-of-kin,
  officer $175 (£90)
- Medal For Bravery, Bronze $100 (£50)
- Wound Medal, Gold $150 (£75)
- Wound Medal, Iron $100 (£50)
- Independence Commemorative Medal $175 (£90)
- Incorporation of Dalmatia Medal . . . . **n/a**
- Labor Service Sports Badge $175 (£90)
- Army Legion Badge $325 (£165)
- Naval Legion Badge $375 (£190)
- Air Force Legion Badge $375 (£190)
- Pilot's Badge $400 (£200)
- Air Crew/Radio Operator Badge $375 (£190)
- Croat Legion Badge $400 (£200)

CZECHOSLOVAKIA (ALSO SEE SLOVAKIA)

- Military Order of the White Lion,
  I Class breast star w/gold swords $1,900 (£950)
- Military Order of the White Lion,
  II Class breast star w/silver swords $1,150 (£575)
- Military Order of the White Lion,
  III Class breast badge $400 (£200)

Czechoslovakian Bravery Medal, $100-$150 (£50-£75) George S. Cuhaj

Czechoslovakian War Cross, 1939, $15-$20 (£5-£10) George S. Cuhaj

Czechoslovakian Campaign Medal, 1939-45, with bar, $30-$40 (£15-£20) George S. Cuhaj

Czechoslovakian Medal for Merit, First Class, $40-$50 (£20-£25) George S. Cuhaj

Czechoslovakian Medal for Merit, Second Class, $20-$25 (£10-£15) George S. Cuhaj

- Military Order of the White Lion,
  Merit Medal, I Class $450 (£225)
- Military Order of the White Lion,
  Merit Medal, II Class.....................$375 (£190)
- Officer's Order of Jan Ziska, I Class $1,750 (£875)
- Officer's Order of Jan Ziska, II Class $950 (£475)
- Officer's Order of Jan Ziska, II Class $400 (£200)
- Military Order for Liberty, II Class........$400 (£200)
- Military Order for Liberty, II Class........$300 (£150)
- Bravery Medal...........................$150 (£75)
- Merit Medal, I Class $45 (£25)
- Merit Medal, II Class.....................$25 (£15)
- Slovak Commemorative Medal..............$50 (£25)
- War Cross, 1939.........................$20 (£10)
- Campaign Medal, 1939-45 ....$25 (£15)
- Campaign Medal, 1939-45 w/bar $35 (£20)
- Cross for Political Prisoners...............$75 (£40)

FINLAND

- Campaign Medal, 1939-40 ....$20 (£10)
- Campaign Medal, 1939-40 w/swords........$25 (£15)
- Campaign Medal for Foreign Volunteers......$35 (£20)
- Kainuu Cross, 1939-40 ....$50 (£25)
- Keski-Kannas Cross, 1939-40 ....$50 (£25)
- Kolvisto Cross, 1939-40 ....$50 (£25)
- Kollaa Cross, 1939-40 ....$65 (£35)
- Lappland Cross, 1939-40 ....$65 (£35)
- Ladoga Medal, 1939-40....................$65 (£35)
- Lansi-Kannas Cross, 1939-40 ....$50 (£25)
- Ladoga Medal, 1939-40....................$50 (£25)
- Mohia Cross, 1939-40.....................$50 (£25)
- Pitkaranta Cross, 1939-40.................$50 (£25)
- Summa Cross, 1939-40 ....$50 (£25)
- Taipale Cross, 1939-40 ....$50 (£25)

- Tolvajarvi Cross, 1939-40 ....$50 (£25)
- War Wound Badge, 1939-40 ....$75 (£40)
- War Wound Badge, 1939-40 & 1941-44 .....$150 (£75)
- War with USSR 1941-45 ....$15 (£7)

FRANCE

- Order of Military Merit, Commander $175 (£90)
- Order of Military Merit, Officer $50 (£25)
- Order of Military Merit, Knight $35 (£20)
- Croix de Guerre, undated...................$25 (£15)
- Croix de Guerre, 1939.....................$35 (£20)
- Croix de Guerre, 1939-45 ....$35 (£20)
- Combat Cross............................$15 (£7)
- Escaped Prisoners Medal $15 (£7)
- Combat Volunteers Cross..................$20 (£10)
- Resistance Medal, I Class $20 (£10)
- Resistance Medal, II Class $15 (£7)
- Wound Medal, combat $15 (£7)
- Wound Medal, non-combat..................$10 (£5)
- Deportees Medal $10 (£5)
- Medal for Internees $10 (£5)
- Reconnaissance Francaise, Type II, I Class $45 (£25)
- Reconnaissance Francaise, Type II, II Class ... $30 (£15)
- Reconnaissance Francaise, Type II, III Class... $20 (£10)
- Volunteers Medal..........................$10 (£5)
- Cross of Voluntary Military Service,
  Army/Navy $10 (£5)
- Cross of Voluntary Military Service, Air Force. . $15 (£7)
- Colonial Medal, large type $25 (£15)
- Colonial Medal, small type..................$15 (£7)
- Free French Cross..........................$15 (£7)
- Prisoner of War Medal $15 (£7)
- WWII Commemorative Medal...............$10 (£5)

*1939 French Croix de Guerre, $30-$35
(£15-£17).* www.advanceguardmilitaria.com

*Medals of the French "Vichy" government have gained
popularity in recent years. This simple award for railway
service sells for $50-$80 (£25-£40).* Colin R. Bruce II

- Medal of Liberated France $45 (£25)
- Italian Campaign 1943-44 .... $35 (£20)
- Military Chaplain's Cross $250 (£125)

FRANCE, VICHY

- Croix de Guerre $75 (£40)
- Combat Cross, 1939-40. .... $200 (£100)
- Black Africa Merit Medal $275 (£140)
- Levant Medal $50 (£25)
- Colonial Medal $50 (£25)

GERMANY

Civil Awards

- Order of the German Eagle, Grand Cross
  .... $6,000 (£3,000)
- Order of the German Eagle,
  Grand Cross w/swords $7,250 (£3,625)
- Order of the German Eagle,
  Grand Cross breast star $5,500 (£2,750)
- Order of the German Eagle,
  Grand Cross breast star w/swords $5,500 (£2,750)
- Order of the German Eagle, I Class $3,900 (£1,950)
- Order of the German Eagle,
  I Class w/swords. $3,750 (£1,675)
- Order of the German Eagle,
  I Class breast star $5,200 (£2,600)
- Order of the German Eagle,
  I Class breast star w/swords. $3,500 (£1,750)
- Order of the German Eagle, II Class..... $1,750 (£875)
- Order of the German Eagle, II Class
  w/swords $2,250 (£1,125)
- Order of the German Eagle, II Class
  breast star $2,250 (£1,125)
- Order of the German Eagle, II Class breast
  star w/swords $2,400 (£1,200)
- Order of the German Eagle, III Class..... $1,750 (£875)
- Order of the German Eagle,
  III Class w/swords $2,000 (£1,000)
- Order of the German Eagle, IV Class
  pinback............................ $1,500 (£750)
- Order of the German Eagle, IV Class
  pinback w/swords. $1,750 (£875)
- Order of the German Eagle,
  Silver Merit Medal, Gothic. $500 (£250)
- Order of the German Eagle, Silver Merit
  Medal, Gothic w/swords. $800 (£400)
- Order of the German Eagle, Silver Merit
  Medal, Roman. $800 (£400)
- Order of the German Eagle, Silver Merit
  Medal, Roman w/swords $900 (£450)
- Order of the German Eagle,
  Bronze Merit Medal. $450 (£225)
- Order of the German Eagle, Bronze Merit
  Medal w/swords $525 (£265)

- Honor Cross w/swords $10 (£5)
- Honor Cross w/o swords $15 (£7)
- Honor Cross for next-of-kin
  (blackened iron) $20 (£10)
- Lifesaving Medal $400 (£200)
- Mother's Cross, Type I, gold $3,250 (£1,625)
- Mother's Cross, Type I, silver......... $2,750 (£1,375)
- Mother's Cross, Type I, bronze $2,000 (£1,000)
- Mother's Cross, Type II, gold. $40 (£20)
- Mother's Cross, Type II, silver............. $30 (£15)
- Mother's Cross, Type II, bronze $25 (£12)
- Fire Service Cross, I Class pinback $1,200 (£600)
- Fire Service Cross, I Class on ribbon $550 (£275)
- Fire Service cross, II Class $125 (£65)
- Mine Rescue Service Badge, I Class $1,500 (£750)
- Mine Rescue Service Badge, II Class $375 (£190)
- Air Raid Service Decoration, I Class. $650 (£325)
- Air Raid Service Decoration, II Class........ $35 (£20)
- Civilian Faithful Service Cross, 50 years $250 (£125)
- Civilian Faithful Service Decoration,
  40 years $100 (£50)
- Civilian Faithful Service Decoration,
  40 years w/oak leaves. $500 (£250)
- Civilian Faithful Service Decoration,
  25 years $20 (£10)
- Police Long Service, I Class, 25 years....... $175 (£90)
- Police Long Service, II Class, 18 years $125 (£65)
- Police Long Service, III Class, 8 years $75 (£40)
- Customs Service Decoration $325 (£165)
- Labor Service, I Class $450 (£225)
- Labor Service, II Class. $225 (£115)
- Labor Service, III Class $175 (£90)
- Labor Service, IV Class................... $55 (£30)

Honor Badge of 9. November 1923 (also known as the "Blood Order"), Type II, $8,500-$9,500 (£4,250-£4,750). Hermann Historica OHG

- Labor Service, I Class female $500 (£250)
- Labor Service, II Class female $350 (£175)
- Labor Service, III Class female $275 (£140)
- Labor Service, IV Class female $200 (£100)
- Railroad Service Badge, I Class $650 (£325)
- Railroad Service Badge, II Class $500 (£250)
- Railroad Service Badge, III Class. $350 (£175)
- Olympic Decoration, I Class $2,750 (£1,375)
- Olympic Decoration, II Class. $1,150 (£575)
- Olympic Medal. $125 (£65)
- National Sports Badge, Type I, I Class $85 (£45)
- National Sports Badge, Type I, II Class $50 (£25)
- National Sports Badge, Type I, III Class $35 (£20)
- National Sports Badge, Type II, I Class $75 (£40)
- National Sports Badge, Type II, II Class $50 (£25)
- National Sports Badge, Type II, III Class. $30 (£15)
- National Sports Badge, Type III, I Class $85 (£45)
- National Sports Badge, Type III, II Class. $65 (£35)
- National Sports Badge, Type III, III Class $40 (£20)
- National Youth Sports Badge, Type I $65 (£35)
- National Youth Sports Badge, Type I, female . . $80 (£40)
- National Youth Sports Badge, Type II $75 (£40)
- National Youth Sports Badge, Type II,
  female. $80 (£40)
- German Rider's Badge, gold. $550 (£275)
- German Rider's Badge, silver $225 (£115)
- German Rider's Badge, bronze $95 (£50)
- German Youth Rider's Badge. $185 (£95)
- German Horse Driver's Badge, gold $300 (£150)
- German Horse Driver's Badge, silver $175 (£90)
- German Horse Driver's Badge, bronze. $125 (£65)
- German Rider & Driver Badge $500 (£250)
- German Master Rider Badge $2,300 (£1,150)
- Badge for Horse Care, gold. $300 (£150)
- Badge for Horse Care, silver. $250 (£125)

- Badge for Horse Care, bronze $195 (£100)
- Motor Sports Badge, gold. $1,850 (£925)
- Motor Sports Badge, silver $1,350 (£675)
- Motor Sports Badge, bronze $1,000 (£500)
- Heavy Athletics Badge. $275 (£140)
- SA Sports Badge, gold $300 (£150)
- SA Sports Badge, silver $150 (£75)
- SA Sports Badge, bronze. $35 (£20)
- Naval SA Sports Badge $750 (£375)
- SA Master Riding Badge $1,500 (£750)
- Germanic Proficiency Runes, silver $9,500 (£4,750)
- Germanic Proficiency Runes, bronze. . . $7,000 (£3,500)
- Gendarmerie High Alpine Award $2,500 (£1,250)
- Gendarmerie Alpine Award $2,300 (£1,150)
- Police Expert Skier Award $2,650 (£1,325)
- Police Expert Mountain Climber
  Award $2,650 (£1,325)
- DLV Pilot Badge $50 (£25)
- DLV Radioman's Badge $350 (£175)
- DLV Balloon Pilot, gold. $1,750 (£875)
- DLV Balloon Pilot, silver $1,500 (£750)
- DLV Balloon Pilot, bronze $1,300 (£650)
- NSFK Powered Flight Pilot's Badge,
  Type I $1,500 (£750)
- NSFK Powered Flight Pilot's Badge,
  Type II $1,650 (£825)
- NSFK Radioman's Badge. $150 (£75)
- NSFK Free Balloon Badge. $1,350 (£675)
- NSFK Large Glider Pilot's Badge. $1,300 (£650)
- NSFK Civil Gliding Proficiency Badge,
  Class A $45 (£25)
- NSFK Civil Gliding Proficiency Badge,
  Class B $65 (£35)
- NSFK Civil Gliding Proficiency Badge,
  Class C $75 (£40)

Honor Cross with swords for combatants in the World War, 1914-1918, $10-$15 (£5-£8).
www.advanceguardmilitaria.com

German Mother's Cross, Gold, Type II, $40-$60 (£20-£30). www.advanceguardmilitaria.com

German Mother's Cross, Silver, Type II, $30-50 (£15-£25).
www.advanceguardmilitaria.com

German Mother's Cross, Bronze, Type II, $25-$40 (£10-£20).
www.advanceguardmilitaria.com

Nuremburg Rally Day Badge, $275-$300 (£130-£150).
www.advanceguardmilitaria.com

- NSFK Areo-Modeling Proficiency Badge, Class A $950 (£475)
- NSFK Areo-Modeling Proficiency Badge, Class B $750 (£375)
- NSFK Areo-Modeling Proficiency Badge, Class C $425 (£215)
- Blood Order, Type I $12,000 (£6,000)
- Blood Order, Type II $8,500 (£4,250)
- Golden Party Badge, large (30mm).....$4,500 (£2,250)
- Golden Party Badge, small (24mm) $2,000 (£1,000)
- Party Badge $35 (£20)
- Party Badge for Foreigners $1,850 (£925)
- Frontbann Badge $850 (£425)
- Coburg Decoration $550 (£275)
- Nuremburg Party Day Badge $275 (£140)
- Brunswick SA Rally Badge, Type I $225 (£115)
- Brunswick SA Rally Badge, Type II........$325 (£165)
- NSDAP Long Service Cross, 25 years.....$1,750 (£875)
- NSDAP Long Service Cross, 15 years......$300 (£150)
- NSDAP Long Service Cross, 10 years......$125 (£115)
- Hitler Youth Badge, gold w/oak leaves .. $8,500 (£4,250)
- Hitler Youth Badge, gold.................$295 (£150)
- Hitler Youth Badge.......................$25 (£15)
- Hitler Youth Expert Skiing Badge $6,250 (£3,125)
- SS Long Service, 25 years $1,500 (£750)

- SS Long Service, 12 years $1,100 (£550)
- SS Long Service, 8 years $500 (£250)
- SS Long Service, 4 years $375 (£190)

Military Awards

- Spanish Cross, gold w/diamonds $39,000 (£19,500)
- Spanish Cross, gold w/swords $2,500 (£1,250)
- Spanish Cross, silver w/swords $1,000 (£500)
- Spanish Cross, silver w/o swords $1,300 (£650)
- Spanish Cross, bronze w/swords..........$800 (£400)

NSDAP Service Award for 15 years, $275-$300 (£135-£150).

www.advanceguardmilitaria.com

German Proficiency Badge of the SS in bronze, $6,500-$7,500 (£3,250-£3,800).

Hermann Historica OHG

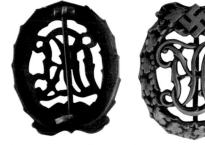

National Sport Badge, III Class, Type II, $25-$40 (£12-£20). www.advanceguardmilitaria.com

SA Sport Badge, III Class, bronze, $30-$50 (£15-£25).

www.advanceguardmilitaria.com

German Horse Rider's Badge, bronze, $75-$125 (£35-£65). www.advanceguardmilitaria.com

Civil Service Honor Award, I Class, $40-$50 (£20-£25).

www.advanceguardmilitaria.com

SA Rally at Brunswick Badge, Type II, $300-$375 (£150-£185). www.advanceguardmilitaria.com

NSDAP Party Badge, $25-$50 (£10-£25). www.advanceguardmilitaria.com

Hitler Youth Membership Pin, $25-$50 (£10-£25). www.advanceguardmilitaria.com

National Sport Badge, III Class, Type I, $30-$50 (£15-£25).

www.advanceguardmilitaria.com

- Spanish Cross, bronze w/o swords $600 (£300)
- Spanish Cross for next of kin $1,750 (£875)
- Condor Legion Tank Badge, silver $2,750 (£1,375)
- Annexation of Austria 13. März 1938 . . . .$45 (£25)
- Annexation of the Sudetenland
  1. Oktober 1938 . . . . $35 (£20)
- Memel Return Medal $150 (£75)
- West Wall Medal $20 (£10)
- Knight's Cross w/oak leaves
  & swords $35,000 (£17,500)
- Knight's Cross w/oak leaves $20,000 (£10,000)
- Knight's Cross $12,800 (£6,400)
- Iron Cross, I Class, pinback, flat $175 (£90)
- Iron Cross, I Class, pinback, vaulted $195 (£100)
- Iron Cross, I Class, screwback $275 (£140)
- Iron Cross, II Class. $45 (£25)
- 1939 Clasp to the Iron Cross, I Class $245 (£125)
- 1939 Clasp to the Iron Cross, II Class $95 (£50)
- War Merit Cross, Knight's Cross
  w/swords $12,500 (£6,250)
- War Merit Cross, Knight's Cross
  w/o swords $10,000 (£5,000)
- War Merit Cross, I Class w/swords,
  pinback. $125 (£65)
- War Merit Cross, I Class w/swords,
  screwback $150 (£75)
- War Merit Cross, I Class w/o swords,
  pinback. $100 (£50)
- War Merit Cross, I Class w/o swords,
  screwback $125 (£65)
- War Merit Cross, II Class w/swords. $30 (£15)
- War Merit Cross, II Class w/o swords $25 (£12)
- War Merit Medal $20 (£10)
- German Cross in Gold $2,200 (£1,100)
- German Cross in Silver $2,800 (£1,400)

- Honor Roll Clasp, Army $1,600 (£800)
- Honor Roll Clasp, Navy. $2,500 (£1,250)
- Honor Roll Clasp, Luftwaffe. $1,900 (£950)
- Winter Campaign in Russia Medal $25 (£15)
- Spanish Troops in Russia Commemorative
  Medal $125 (£65)
- 1936/39 Wound Badge, silver $450 (£225)
- 1936/39 Wound Badge, black. $225 (£115)
- 1939 Wound Badge, gold $85 (£45)
- 1939 Wound Badge, silver $65 (£35)
- 1939 Wound Badge, black $25 (£15)
- 20. Juli 1944 Wound Badge, gold. . . . . .n/a
- 20. Juli 1944 Wound Badge, silver $45,000 (£22,500)
- 20. Juli 1944 Wound Badge, black $38,000 (£19,000)
- Eastern People's Award, I Class, gold
  w/swords $300 (£150)
- Eastern People's Award, I Class, gold
  w/o swords $200 (£100)
- Eastern People's Award, I Class, silver
  w/swords $200 (£100)
- Eastern People's Award, I Class, silver
  w/o swords $175 (£90)
- Eastern People's Award, II Class, gold
  w/swords $150 (£75)
- Eastern People's Award, II Class, gold
  w/o swords $150 (£75)
- Eastern People's Award, II Class, silver
  w/swords $125 (£65)
- Eastern People's Award, II Class, silver
  w/o swords $100 (£50)
- Eastern People's Award, II Class, bronze
  w/swords $100 (£50)
- Eastern People's Award, II Class, bronze
  w/o swords $85 (£45)
- Army & Navy Long Service Award I Class
  w/oak leaves, 40 years $500 (£250)

Tank Badge for the Legion Condor, II Type, $2,500-$3,000 (£1,250-£1,500).
Hermann Historica OHG

Knight's Cross of the Iron Cross with oak leaves and swords, $30,000-$40,000 (£15,000-£20,000). Hermann Historica OHG

German Iron Cross, I Class, screwback, $275-$400 (£140-£200). www.advanceguardmilitaria.com

"I won my Iron Cross, First Class and the Knights Cross for my part in a single action on 2 April 1945."

OBERGEFREITER JOSEF ALLERBERGER, GEBIRGSJÄGER-REGIMENT 144

- Army & Navy Long Service Award I Class, 25 years $200 (£100)
- Army & Navy Long Service Award II Class, 18 years $150 (£75)
- Army & Navy Long Service Award III Class, 12 years $75 (£40)
- Army & Navy Long Service Award IV Class, 4 years..................................$50 (£25)
- Luftwaffe Long Service Award, I Class w/oak leaves, 40 years $625 (£315)
- Luftwaffe Long Service Award, I Class, 25 years $225 (£115)
- Luftwaffe Long Service Award, II Class, 18 years $175 (£90)
- Luftwaffe Long Service Award, III Class, 12 years $85 (£45)
- Luftwaffe Long Service Award, IV Class, 4 years..................................$55 (£30)
- Narvik Shield, silver................$500 (£250)
- Narvik Shield, gold...................$700 (£350)
- Cholm Shield......................$1,675 (£840)
- Crimea Shield......................$125 (£65)
- Demjansk Shield....................$250 (£125)
- Kuban Shield.......................$125 (£65)
- Lapland Shield $625 (£315)
- Lorient Shield $1,000 (£500)
- Kreta Cuff Title....................$375 (£190)
- Afrika Cuff Title $275 (£140)
- Kurland Cuff Title $650 (£325)
- Driver's Badge, gold....................$65 (£35)
- Driver's Badge, silver $35 (£20)
- Driver's Badge, bronze.................$25 (£15)
- Mountain Leader's Breast Badge.......$3,250 (£1,625)
- Close Combat Clasp, gold.............$975 (£490)
- Close Combat Clasp, silver...........$650 (£325)
- Close Combat Clasp, bronze $325 (£165)

- Infantry Assault Badge, silver $50 (£25)
- Infantry Assault Badge, bronze $75 (£40)
- General Assault Badge, 100 Engagements $5,500 (£2,750)
- General Assault Badge, 7 5 Engagements $4,000 (£2,000)
- General Assault Badge, 50 Engagements $2,500 (£1,250)
- General Assault Badge, 25 Engagements.. $1,100 (£550)
- General Assault Badge $55 (£30)
- Tank Battle Badge, Silver, 100 Engagements $8,500 (£4,250)
- Tank Battle Badge, Silver, 75 Engagements $5,200 (£2,600)
- Tank Battle Badge, Silver, 50 Engagements $3,500 (£1,750)
- Tank Battle Badge, Silver, 25 Engagements $1,050 (£525)
- Tank Battle Badge Silver $75 (£40)
- Tank Battle Badge, Bronze, 100 Engagements ....n/a
- Tank Battle Badge, Bronze, 75 Engagements $3,500 (£1,750)
- Tank Battle Badge, Bronze, 50 Engagements $1,750 (£875)
- Tank Battle Badge, Bronze, 25 Engagements $1,100 (£550)
- Tank Battle Badge, Bronze $85 (£45)
- Army Anti-Aircraft Badge $265 (£135)
- Single-Handed Destruction of a Tank Badge, gold.................................$1,500 (£750)
- Single-Handed Destruction of a Tank Badge, silver................................$400 (£200)
- Airplane Destruction Badge, gold..................n/a
- Airplane Destruction Badge, silver.................n/a
- Army Paratrooper Badge $2,250 (£1,125)
- Balloon Observer Badge, gold...................n/a

West Wall Medal, $20-$30 (£10-£15).
www.advanceguardmilitaria.com

German Iron Cross, II Class, $35-$75 (£20-£40).
Charles D. Pautler

1939 Clasp to the Iron Cross, II Class, $85-$125 (£40-£65).
www.advanceguardmilitaria.com

War Merit Cross, II Class, without swords, $20-$30 (£10-£15). Charles D. Pautler

War Merit Medal, $20-$30 (£10-£15).
www.advanceguardmilitaria.com

- Balloon Observer Badge, silver $5,500 (£2,750)
- Balloon Observer Badge, bronze $3,500 (£1,750)
- U-Boat Combat Clasp, silver $1,000 (£500)
- U-Boat Combat Clasp, bronze $750 (£375)
- U-Boat War Badge w/diamonds $20,500 (£10,250)
- U-Boat War Badge $525 (£265)
- Destroyer Badge $325 (£165)
- Minesweeper Badge $275 (£140)
- Auxiliary Cruiser War Badge w/diamonds . . . . n/a
- Auxiliary Cruiser War Badge $275 (£140)
- High Seas Fleet War Badge w/diamonds . . . . n/a
- High Seas Fleet War Badge $275 (£140)
- E-Boat War Badge, Type I $1,000 (£500)
- E-Boat War Badge, Type II w/diamonds . . . . n/a
- E-Boat War Badge, Type II $450 (£225)
- Coastal Artillery Badge $125 (£65)
- Blockade Runner Badge $275 (£140)
- Naval Combat Clasp $275 (£140)
- Naval Combat Badge for Small Battle Units, Grade I . n/a
- Naval Combat Badge for Small Battle Units, Grade II **n/a**
- Naval Combat Badge for Small Battle Units, Grade III . . . . n/a
- Naval Combat Badge for Small Battle Units, Grade IV . . . . n/a
- Naval Combat Badge for Small Battle Units, Grade V . . . . n/a
- Naval Combat Badge for Small Battle Units, Grade VI . . . . **n/a**

- Naval Combat Badge for Small Battle Units, Grade VII . . . . **n/a**
- Day Fighter Operational Flying Clasp, gold w/diamonds . . . . **n/a**
- Day Fighter Operational Flying Clasp, gold w/hanger & number . . . . **n/a**
- Day Fighter Operational Flying Clasp, gold w/hanger $1,300 (£650)
- Day Fighter Operational Flying Clasp, gold $950 (£475)
- Day Fighter Operational Flying Clasp, silver $700 (£350)
- Day Fighter Operational Flying Clasp, bronze $275 (£140)
- Night Fighter Operational Flying Clasp, gold w/hanger & number . . . . **n/a**
- Night Fighter Operational Flying Clasp, gold w/hanger $1,500 (£750)
- Night Fighter Operational Flying Clasp, gold $850 (£425)
- Night Fighter Operational Flying Clasp, silver $650 (£325)
- Night Fighter Operational Flying Clasp, bronze $500 (£250)
- Long Range Fighter & Night Intruder Operational Flying Clasp, gold w/hanger & number . . . . **n/a**
- Long Range Fighter & Night Intruder Operational Flying Clasp, gold w/hanger $1,350 (£675)

Close Combat Clasp in bronze (bronze coating worn away) $300-$350 (£150-£175). Charles D. Pautler

Knight's Cross of the War Merit Cross, $9,500-$11,000 (£4,800-£5,500).
Hermann Historica OHG

Twelve-year Faithful Service in the Armed Forces Medal on a parade mount, $50-$80 (£25-£40).
www.advanceguardmilitaria.com

War Merit Cross, I Class, with swords, $100-$150 (£50-£75).
www.advanceguardmilitaria.com

German General Assault Badge, 75 engagements, $3,000-$4,000 (£1,500-£2,000). Hermann Historica OHG

Infantry Assault Badge in Silver, $50-$80 (£25-£40). Charles D. Pautler

- Long Range Fighter & Night Intruder Operational Flying Clasp, gold $850 (£425)
- Long Range Fighter & Night Intruder Operational Flying Clasp, silver...........$700 (£350)
- Long Range Fighter & Night Intruder Operational Flying Clasp, bronze $550 (£275)
- Long Range Day Fighter Operational Flying Clasp, gold w/hanger & number ....n/a
- Long Range Day Fighter Operational Flying Clasp, gold w/hanger.......................n/a
- Long Range Day Fighter Operational Flying Clasp, gold......................$750 (£375)
- Long Range Day Fighter Operational Flying Clasp, silver......................$550 (£275)
- Long Range Day Fighter Operational Flying Clasp, bronze $500 (£250)
- Heavy & Medium Dive Bomber Operational Flying Clasp, gold w/hanger & number ....n/a
- Heavy & Medium Dive Bomber Operational Flying Clasp, gold w/hanger ...$975 (£490)
- Heavy & Medium Dive Bomber Operational Flying Clasp, gold $750 (£375)
- Heavy & Medium Dive Bomber Operational Flying Clasp, silver...........$400 (£200)
- Heavy & Medium Dive Bomber Operational Flying Clasp, bronze $225 (£115)
- Reconnaissance Operational Flying Clasp, gold w/hanger & number ....n/a
- Reconnaissance Operational Flying Clasp, gold w/hanger...........................$850 (£425)
- Reconnaissance Operational Flying Clasp, gold..............................$600 (£300)
- Reconnaissance Operational Flying Clasp, silver............................$400 (£200)

- Reconnaissance Operational Flying Clasp, bronze $325 (£165)
- Transport & Glider Squadron Operational Flying Clasp, gold w/hanger & number ....n/a
- Transport & Glider Squadron Operational Flying Clasp, gold w/hanger...............$800 (£400)
- Transport & Glider Squadron Operational Flying Clasp, gold.......................$600 (£300)
- Transport & Glider Squadron Operational Flying Clasp, silver.......................$500 (£250)
- Transport & Glider Squadron Operational Flying Clasp, bronze $225 (£115)
- Air to Ground Support Squadron Operational Flying Clasp, gold w/diamonds $1,400 (£700)
- Air to Ground Support Squadron Operational Flying Clasp, gold w/hanger & number ...$1,200 (£600)
- Air to Ground Support Squadron Operational Flying Clasp, gold $1,000 (£500)
- Air to Ground Support Squadron Operational Flying Clasp, silver............$550 (£275)
- Air to Ground Support Squadron Operational Flying Clasp, bronze $450 (£225)
- Luftwaffe Anti-Aircraft Badge.............$225 (£115)
- Luftwaffe Ground Assault Badge $325 (£165)
- Luftwaffe Close Combat Clasp, gold ....n/a
- Luftwaffe Close Combat Clasp, silver..............n/a

German Cross in silver, $1,600-$2,800 (£800-£1,500). Hermann Historica OHG

German Cross in gold, made by C.F. Zimmermann, $1,500-$2,500 (£740-£1,275). Hermann Historica OHG

Tank Battle (also known as "Panzer Assault") Badge in silver, $75-$150 (£40-£75).
www.advanceguardmilitaria.com

Luftwaffe Ground Assault Badge, $300-$350 (£150-£175). Minnesota Military Museum

Winter Campaign in Russia Medal, $25-$35 (£10-£17). Charles D. Pautler

- Luftwaffe Close Combat Clasp, bronze . . . .**n/a**
- Luftwaffe Tank Battle Badge, silver,
  100 Engagements . . . .**n/a**
- Luftwaffe Tank Battle Badge, silver,
  75 Engagements . . . .**n/a**
- Luftwaffe Tank Battle Badge, silver,
  50 Engagements . . . .**n/a**
- Luftwaffe Tank Battle Badge, silver,
  25 Engagements . . . .**n/a**
- Luftwaffe Tank Battle Badge, silver . . . . . . **$1,000 (£500)**
- Luftwaffe Tank Battle Badge, black,
  100 Engagements . . . .**n/a**
- Luftwaffe Tank Battle Badge, black,
  75 Engagements . . . .**n/a**
- Luftwaffe Tank Battle Badge, black,
  50 Engagements . . . .**n/a**
- Luftwaffe Tank Battle Badge, black,
  25 Engagements . . . .**n/a**
- Luftwaffe Tank Battle Badge, black . . . .**n/a**
- Luftwaffe Pilot's Badge . . . .**$400 (£200)**
- Luftwaffe Observer's Badge . . . .**$350 (£175)**
- Luftwaffe Pilot's and Observer's Badge,
  gold w/diamonds . . . .**$156,000 (£78,000)**
- Luftwaffe Pilot's and Observer's Badge . **$2,000 (£1,000)**
- Luftwaffe Radio Operator's/Air
  Gunner's Badge. . . . .**$550 (£275)**

- Luftwaffe Air Gunner's and Flight
  Engineer's Badge. . . . .**$300 (£150)**
- Luftwaffe Partrooper's Badge. . . . .**$495 (£250)**
- Luftwaffe Glider Pilot's Badge . . . .**$1,500 (£750)**
- Luftwaffe Former Flyer's
  Commemorative Badge. . . . .**$1,750 (£875)**
- Anti-Partisan War Badge, gold . . . .**$2,250 (£1,125)**
- Anti-Partisan War Badge, silver . . . .**$1,800 (£900)**
- Anti-Partisan War Badge, bronze . . . .**$750 (£375)**

GREECE

- Military Merit Cross, I Class . . . .**$75 (£40)**
- Military Merit Cross, II Class . . . .**$65 (£35)**
- Military Merit Cross, III Class. . . . .**$50 (£25)**
- Military Merit Cross, IV Class. . . . .**$35 (£20)**
- Merchant Marine Service Medal, I Class. . . . . .**$35 (£20)**
- Merchant Marine Service Medal, II Class. . . . .**$25 (£15)**
- Naval Good Shooting Medal . . . .**$75 (£40)**

Crimea Shield (backing cloth missing) $100-$150 (£50-£75). www.advanceguardmilitaria.com

Army Anti-Aircraft Badge, $200-$275 (£100-£140). www.advanceguardmilitaria.com

Service Award of the Armed Forces, 4th Class (4 years), $45-$65 (£22-£33). Charles D. Pautler

Narvik Shield in silver (without cloth backing) $450-$550 (£225-£275). Minnesota Military Museum

Balloon Observer Badge in silver, $5,000-$6,500 (£2,500-£3,250). Rock Island Auction Company

Luftwaffe Anti-Aircraft Badge, $200-$250 (£100-£125). Charles D. Pautler

Navy Coastal Artillery Badge, $100-$150 (£50-£75). www.advanceguardmilitaria.com

Black Wound Badge, stamped (paint rubbed from front) $15-$30 (£8-£15). www.advanceguardmilitaria.com

- Long Service & Good Conduct Medal,
  I Class, 20 years $45 (£25)
- Long Service & Good Conduct Medal,
  II Class, 15 years. $25 (£15)
- Long Service & Good Conduct Medal,
  III Class, 10 years $20 (£10)
- Medal for Outstanding Acts $55 (£30)
- Royal Navy Cross $85 (£45)
- Valor Cross in Flight $250 (£125)
- Distinguished Flying Cross. $275 (£140)
- Air Force Cross, non-combatant. $175 (£90)
- Air Force Cross, non-combatant, NCO. $180 (£90)
- Air Force Merit Medal. $150 (£75)
- Distinguished Service Medal, Air Force. . . . $200 (£100)
- Convoy Escort Medal $175 (£90)
- Commemorative Medal, 1940-41, Army $25 (£10)
- Commemorative Medal, 1940-41, Navy $25 (£10)
- Commemorative Medal, 1941-45, Army $25 (£16)
- Commemorative Medal, 1941-45, Navy $25 (£16)
- War Cross, I Class $45 (£20)
- War Cross, II Class. $35 (£16)
- War Cross, III Class. $20 (£11)

Hungary

- Merit Medal, Silver $75 (£40)
- Merit Medal, Bronze $50 (£25)
- National Defense Service Cross. $35 (£20)
- Medal for Bravery, gold. $300 (£150)
- Medal for Bravery, silver, large. $150 (£75)
- Medal for Bravery, silver, small $100 (£50)
- Medal for Bravery, bronze $75 (£40)
- Frontline Combat Cross, I Class $45 (£25)
- Frontline Combat Cross, I Class, 1941. . . . . . . $45 (£25)
- Frontline Combat Cross, I Class, 1942. . . . . . . $45 (£25)
- Frontline Combat Cross, I Class, 1943. . . . . . . $45 (£25)
- Frontline Combat Cross, I Class
  w/extra award bar. $75 (£40)
- Frontline Combat Cross, II Class $35 (£20)
- Frontline Combat Cross, II Class, 1941 . . . . . . $35 (£20)
- Frontline Combat Cross, II Class, 1942 . . . . . . $35 (£20)
- Frontline Combat Cross, II Class, 1943 . . . . . . $35 (£20)
- Frontline Combat Cross, II Class
  w/extra award bar. $45 (£25)
- Frontline Combat Cross, III Class. $25 (£15)
- Frontline Combat Cross, III Class, 1941 . . . . . $25 (£15)
- Frontline Combat Cross, III Class, 1942 . . . . . $25 (£15)
- Frontline Combat Cross, III Class, 1943 . . . . . $25 (£15)
- Civil Merit Cross, gold $95 (£50)
- Civil Merit Cross, silver $65 (£35)
- Civil Merit Cross, bronze $35 (£20)
- Officers' Long Service Decoration,
  I Class 35-40 years $75 (£40)
- Officers' Long Service Decoration,
  II Class 25-30 years $60 (£30)
- Officers' Long Service Decoration,
  III Class 15-20 years. $50 (£25)

- Enlisted Men's Long Service Award,
  I Class 20 years. $35 (£20)
- Enlisted Men's Long Service Award,
  II Class 10 years $25 (£15)
- Enlisted Men's Long Service Award,
  III Class 6 years. $15 (£7)
- Enlisted Men's Long Service Honor Medal,
  35 years $85 (£45)
- South Hungary Commemorative Medal $35 (£20)

Italy

- Military Order of Savoy, Grand Cross badge
  . . . . $3,000 (£1,500)
- Military Order of Savoy, Grand Cross
  breast star $2,000 (£1,000)
- Military Order of Savoy, Commander,
  I Class. $1,200 (£600)
- Military Order of Savoy, Commander,
  I Class breast star $1,200 (£600)
- Military Order of Savoy, Commander,
  II Class $1,000 (£500)

Silver Wound Badge, stamped (paint rubbed from front) $65-$75 (£33-£40).
www.advanceguardmilitaria.com

Wound Badge, "20. Juli 1944," in black, $30,000-$40,000 (£15,000-£20,000).
Hermann Historica OHG

U-Boat badge with diamonds, $20,000-$25,000 (£10,0000-£12,500). Hermann Historica OHG

Hungarian Occupation of North Transylvania Medal, $25-$35 (£10-£17).
www.advanceguardmilitaria.com

- Military Order of Savoy, Commander, Officer $800 (£400)
- Military Order of Savoy, Commander, Knight.................................. $650 (£325)
- Colonial Merit Order, Grand Cross $450 (£225)
- Colonial Merit Order, Grand Cross breast star $450 (£225)
- Colonial Merit Order, Grand Officer $300 (£150)
- Colonial Merit Order, Grand Officer breast star $300 (£150)
- Colonial Merit Order, Commander $200 (£100)
- Colonial Merit Order, Officer $150 (£75)
- Colonial Merit Order, Knight $125 (£65)
- Military Valor Medal, gold $50 (£25)
- Military Valor Medal, silver $25 (£15)
- Military Valor Medal, bronze............... $15 (£7)
- Military Valor Cross, 1941 .... $35 (£20)
- Military Valor Cross, 1942 .... $35 (£20)
- Civil Valor Medal, gold $20 (£10)
- Civil Valor Medal, silver $15 (£7)
- Civil Valor Medal, bronze.................. $10 (£5)
- Aeronautical Valor Medal, gold............. $50 (£25)
- Aeronautical Valor Medal, silver........... $40 (£20)
- Aeronautical Valor Medal, bronze $20 (£10)
- Campaign Medal, Albania $35 (£20)
- Campaign Medal, French Campaign .... n/a
- Campaign Medal, Occupation of Greece $75 (£40)
- Campaign Medal, North Africa Service....... $25 (£15)
- Long Service Cross, gold w/crown $50 (£25)
- Long Service Cross, gold w/o crown $35 (£20)
- Long Service Cross, silver w/crown $25 (£15)
- Long Service Cross, silver w/o crown $15 (£7)
- National Fire Service Medal................. $25 (£15)
- Fascist Militia Long Service Cross, 25 years .. $50 (£25)
- Fascist Militia Long Service Cross, 10 years ... $35 (£20)
- Colonial Police Long Serve Cross, gold w/crown 40 years.................... $45 (£25)
- Colonial Police Long Serve Cross, gold w/o crown 25 years.................... $30 (£15)
- Colonial Police Long Serve Cross, silver w/crown 25 years.................... $25 (£15)
- Colonial Police Long Serve Cross, silver w/o crown 16 years $20 (£10)
- Colonial Police Long Serve Cross, bronze w/crown 20 years $15 (£7)
- Colonial Police Long Serve Cross, bronze w/o crown 10 years.................. $10 (£5)
- Fire Serve Cross, 15 years................... $15 (£7)
- Navy Long Service Medal, gold 20 years $50 (£25)
- Navy Long Service Medal, silver 15 years $30 (£15)
- Navy Long Service Medal, bronze 10 years..... $15 (£7)
- Air Force Long Service Medal, gold 30 years .. $50 (£25)
- Air Force Long Service Medal, silver 15 years . $25 (£15)
- Air Force Long Service Medal, bronze 10 years $15 (£7)
- Army Long Service Medal, gold 30 years $40 (£20)
- Army Long Service Medal, silver 20 years..... $25 (£15)
- Army Long Service Medal, bronze 15 years $15 (£7)
- Customs Long Service Medal, gold 30 years... $35 (£20)
- Customs Long Service Medal, silver 20 years.. $20 (£10)
- Customs Long Service Medal, bronze 10 years . $10 (£5)
- Medal of the Italian Family.................. $15 (£7)
- Medal for Aeronautical Pioneer $25 (£15)
- National Balilla Merit Medal, gold $75 (£40)
- National Balilla Merit Medal, silver $50 (£25)
- National Balilla Merit Medal, bronze......... $25 (£15)
- Medal of Merit, Fascist Workers Recreation Service, gold $35 (£20)
- Medal of Merit, Fascist Workers Recreation Service, silver $20 (£10)
- Medal of Merit, Fascist Workers Recreation Service, bronze............................ $15 (£7)
- Fascist Youth Merit Medal, gold $40 (£20)
- Fascist Youth Merit Medal, silver $25 (£15)

Italian African Campaign Medal, $25-$35 (£10-£17). Fred Borgmann

Japanese China Incident Medal, $40-$60 (£20-£30). Colin R. Bruce II

Japanese Order of the Sacred Treasure, 7th Class, $80-$100 (£40-£50). Colin R. Bruce II

Japanese Order of the Rising Sun, 5th Class, $400-$450 (£200-£225). Colin R. Bruce II

Japanese Order of the Rising Sun, 7th Class, $70-$90 (£35-£45). Colin R. Bruce II

- Fascist Youth Merit Medal, bronze . . . . **$15 (£7)**
- Fascist Party Loyalty Medal . . . . **$35 (£20)**

Italy, Social Republic (1943-1945)

- Order of the Roman Eagle, Grand Cross . . . . **n/a**
- Order of the Roman Eagle, Grand Cross w/swords . . . . **n/a**
- Order of the Roman Eagle, Grand Cross gold breast star . . . . **n/a**
- Order of the Roman Eagle, Grand Cross gold breast star w/swords . . . . **n/a**
- Order of the Roman Eagle, Grand Cross silver breast star . . . . **n/a**
- Order of the Roman Eagle, Grand Cross silver breast star w/swords . . . . **n/a**
- Order of the Roman Eagle, Grand Officer . . . . **n/a**
- Order of the Roman Eagle, Grand Officer w/swords . **n/a**
- Order of the Roman Eagle, Grand Officer breast star . **n/a**
- Order of the Roman Eagle, Grand Officer breast star w/swords . . . . **n/a**
- Order of the Roman Eagle, Commander . . . . **n/a**
- Order of the Roman Eagle, Officer . . . . **$775 (£390)**
- Order of the Roman Eagle, Officer w/swords . . . . **$625 (£315)**
- Order of the Roman Eagle, Knight . . . . **$550 (£275)**
- Order of the Roman Eagle, Knight w/swords . . . . **$600 (£300)**
- Order of the Roman Eagle, Medal . . . . **$425 (£215)**
- Order of the Roman Eagle, Medal w/swords . . . . **$450 (£225)**

Japan (also see Manchuko)

- Supreme Order of the Chrysanthemum, collar . . . . **$13,500 (£6,750)**
- Supreme Order of the Chrysanthemum, sash badge . . . . **$13,500 (£6,750)**
- Supreme Order of the Chrysanthemum, breast star . . . . **$7,500 (£3,750)**
- Order of the Rising Sun, Grand Cordon, ... **$8,750 (£4,375)**
- Order of the Rising Sun, Grand Cordon, breast star . . . . **$5,750 (£2,875)**
- Order of the Rising Sun, I Class . . . . **$3,250 (£1,625)**
- Order of the Rising Sun, I Class breast star . . . . **$2,000 (£1,000)**
- Order of the Rising Sun, II Class . . . . **$900 (£450)**
- Order of the Rising Sun, II Class breast star . . . . **$2,000 (£1,000)**
- Order of the Rising Sun, III Class . . . . **$900 (£450)**
- Order of the Rising Sun, IV Class breast star . . . . **$500 (£250)**

- Order of the Rising Sun, V Class . . . . **$425 (£215)**
- Order of the Rising Sun, VI Class . . . . **$325 (£165)**
- Order of the Rising Sun, VII Class . . . . **$85 (£45)**
- Order of the Rising Sun, VIII Class . . . . **$50 (£25)**
- Order of the Golden Kite, I Class . . . . **n/a**
- Order of the Golden Kite, I Class breast star . . . . **n/a**
- Order of the Golden Kite, II Class . . . . . **$5,250 (£2,625)**
- Order of the Golden Kite, II Class, breast star . . . . **n/a**
- Order of the Golden Kite, III Class . . . . . **$5,250 (£2,625)**
- Order of the Golden Kite, IV Class . . . . . . **$1,500 (£750)**
- Order of the Golden Kite, V Class . . . . **$650 (£325)**
- Order of the Golden Kite, VI Class . . . . **$325 (£165)**
- Order of the Golden Kite, VII Class . . . . **$285 (£145)**
- Order of the Sacred Crown, I Class . . . . **n/a**
- Order of the Sacred Crown, II Class . . . . **n/a**
- Order of the Sacred Crown, III Class . . . . **n/a**
- Order of the Sacred Crown, IV Class . . . . **n/a**
- Order of the Sacred Crown, V Class . . . . **n/a**
- Order of the Sacred Crown, VI Class . . . . **n/a**
- Order of the Sacred Crown, VII Class . . **$2,250 (£1,125)**
- Order of the Sacred Crown, VIII Class . . . **$1,950 (£975)**
- Order of the Sacred Treasure, I Class . . . . . **$1,750 (£875)**
- Order of the Sacred Treasure, I Class breast star . . . . **$1,250 (£625)**
- Order of the Sacred Treasure, II Class breast star . . . . **$1,000 (£500)**
- Order of the Sacred Treasure, III Class . . . . . **$600 (£300)**
- Order of the Sacred Treasure, IV Class breast badge . . . . **$450 (£225)**
- Order of the Sacred Treasure, V Class . . . . . **$325 (£165)**
- Order of the Sacred Treasure, VI Class . . . . . **$225 (£115)**
- Order of the Sacred Treasure, VII Class . . . . . . **$95 (£50)**
- Order of the Sacred Treasure, VIII Class . . . . . . **$65 (£35)**
- Manchurian Incident Medal . . . . **$65 (£35)**
- China Incident Medal . . . . **$50 (£25)**
- Great East Asia War Medal . . . . **$150 (£75)**
- Medal of Merit, red ribbon . . . . **$400 (£200)**
- Medal of Merit, blue ribbon . . . . **$400 (£200)**
- Medal of Merit, green ribbon . . . . **$400 (£200)**
- Medal of Merit, gold, yellow ribbon . . . . **n/a**
- Medal of Merit, silver, yellow ribbon . . . . . . **$400 (£200)**
- Field Marshal's badge . . . . **n/a**
- Wound Badge, combatant . . . . **$265 (£135)**
- Wound Badge, non-combatant . . . . **$200 (£100)**
- Graduate of Staff Academy . . . . **$225 (£115)**
- Army Officer Pilot's Badge . . . . **$850 (£425)**
- Army Enlisted Man Pilot's Badge . . . . **$650 (£325)**
- Time Expired Soldier's Badge . . . . **$35 (£20)**

Lithuania

- Order of Vytautus the Great, collar . . . . **n/a**
- Order of Vytautus the Great, breast star . . . . **n/a**
- Order of Vytautus the Great, I Class . . . **$3,250 (£1,625)**
- Order of Vytautus the Great, I Class breast star . . . . **$2,500 (£1,250)**
- Order of Vytautus the Great, II Class . . . **$2,250 (£1,125)**

- Order of Vytautus the Great, II Class
  breast star $2,000 (£1,000)
- Order of Vytautus the Great, III Class . . $2,100 (£1,050)
- Order of Vytautus the Great, Officer $1,200 (£600)
- Order of Vytautus the Great, Knight $1,000 (£500)
- Order of Vytautus the Great Medal, gold . . . $375 (£190)
- Order of Vytautus the Great Medal, silver . . $325 (£165)
- Order of Vytautus the Great Medal, bronze . $275 (£140)
- Order of the Cross of Vytis, I Class. $1,500 (£750)
- Order of the Cross of Vytis, I Class
  breast star $1,500 (£750)
- Order of the Cross of Vytis, II Class $1,000 (£500)
- Order of the Cross of Vytis, II Class
  breast star $1,000 (£500)
- Order of the Cross of Vytis, III Class $900 (£450)
- Order of the Cross of Vytis, IV Class $700 (£350)
- Order of the Cross of Vytis, V Class. $650 (£325)
- Vytis Cross, I Class. $550 (£275)
- Vytis Cross, II Class. $475 (£240)
- Vytis Cross, III Class $400 (£200)
- Order of Gedeminas, Grand Cross. $650 (£325)
- Order of Gedeminas, Grand Cross
  breast star $600 (£300)
- Order of Gedeminas, Grand Officer. $575 (£290)
- Order of Gedeminas, Grand Officer
  breast star $550 (£275)
- Order of Gedeminas, Commander. $500 (£250)
- Order of Gedeminas, Officer. $300 (£150)
- Order of Gedeminas, Knight $225 (£115)
- Order of Gedeminas, Merit Medal, gold $175 (£90)
- Order of Gedeminas, Merit Medal, silver $150 (£75)
- Order of Gedeminas, Merit Medal, bronze. . . $125 (£65)
- Volunteer Combatants Medal $200 (£100)
- Lifesaving Cross $400 (£200)
- Star for Partisan Service $425 (£215)
- National Guard Merit Cross $250 (£125)

MANCHUKO (ALSO SEE JAPAN)

- Order of the Illustrious Dragon, Badge
  of the Order. $5,500 (£2,750)
- Order of the Illustrious Dragon,
  breast star $4,250 (£2,125)
- Order of the Auspicious Clouds, I Class $3,000 (£1,500)
- Order of the Auspicious Clouds, I Class
  breast star $2,650 (£1,325)
- Order of the Auspicious Clouds, II Class
  breast star $2,500 (£1,250)
- Order of the Auspicious Clouds, II Class. . $1,500 (£750)
- Order of the Auspicious Clouds, III Class. $1,250 (£625)
- Order of the Auspicious Clouds, IV Class. . . $800 (£400)
- Order of the Auspicious Clouds, V Class . . . $650 (£325)
- Order of the Auspicious Clouds, VI Class. . . $500 (£250)
- Order of the Auspicious Clouds, VII Class . . $300 (£150)
- Order of the Auspicious Clouds, VIII Class . $225 (£115)
- Orders of the Pillars of State, I Class badge. . . . . n/a
- Orders of the Pillars of State, I Class,
  breast star $2,500 (£1,250)
- Orders of the Pillars of State, II Class. . . $2,250 (£1,125)
- Orders of the Pillars of State, III Class . . $2,000 (£1,000)
- Orders of the Pillars of State, IV Class $1,350 (£675)
- Orders of the Pillars of State, V Class. $775 (£390)
- Orders of the Pillars of State, VI Class $650 (£325)
- Orders of the Pillars of State, VII Class $575 (£290)
- Orders of the Pillars of State, VIII Class . . . $450 (£225)
- National Foundation Merit Medal $200 (£100)
- Enthronement Commemorative Medal. $500 (£250)
- Imperial Visit to Japan. $125 (£65)
- Border Incident War Medal. $550 (£275)
- National Shrine Foundation Medal $300 (£150)
- National Census Commemorative Medal . . . $250 (£125)

Manchuko National Census Commemorative Medal, $225-$250 (£112-£125). Colin R. Bruce II

Norway's War Participant's Medal, $75-$85 (£35-£42). Fred Borgmann

NETHERLANDS

- Bronze Lion Decoration $150 (£75)
- Cross for Merit $100 (£50)
- Bronze Cross for Gallantry. $125 (£65)
- Flying Cross. $300 (£150)
- Resistance Cross, Europe $150 (£75)
- East Asia Resistance Star $100 (£50)
- Air Raid Service Medal $35 (£20)
- Commemorative Cross. $25 (£15)
- War Commemorative Cross. $25 (£15)
- Officer's Long Service Cross, 40 years $125 (£115)
- Officer's Long Service Cross, 35 years $100 (£50)
- Officer's Long Service Cross, 30 years $75 (£40)
- Officer's Long Service Cross, 25 years $65 (£35)
- Officer's Long Service Cross, 20 years $45 (£25)
- Officer's Long Service Cross, 15 years $30 (£15)
- Officer's Long Service Cross, 5 years $15 (£7)
- Long Service Medal, Army, gold, large,
  50 years $700 (£350)
- Long Service Medal, Army, gold, small,
  35 years $450 (£225)
- Long Service Medal, Army, silver, 24 years $50 (£25)
- Long Service Medal, Army, bronze. $40 (£20)
- Long Service Medal, Navy $50 (£25)
- Long Service Medal, Coast Guard,
  military issue. $60 (£30)
- Long Service Medal, Coast Guard, naval issue . $75 (£40)

NORWAY

- War Cross w/swords $75 (£40)
- War Cross w/o swords $60 (£30)
- War Medal. $50 (£25)
- King Haakon VII's Liberty Cross. $400 (£200)
- King Haakon VII's Liberty Medal $250 (£125)
- War Participation Medal $85 (£45)
- King Haakon VII's 70th Anniversary
  Medal, 1942. . . . .$75 (£40)

PHILIPPINES

- Medal of Valor . . . . .n/a
- Distinguished Conduct Star. $575 (£290)
- Bravery Cross for the Air Force. $250 (£125)
- Distinguished Aviation Cross $150 (£75)
- Gold Cross for Valor $85 (£45)
- Distinguished Service Star $275 (£140)
- Military Merit Medal. $65 (£35)
- Silver Wing Medal $45 (£25)
- Cross for Wounded $50 (£25)
- Exemplary Efficiency & Devotion in Duty $35 (£20)
- Long Service Cross $45 (£25)
- Defense Medal $75 (£40)
- Liberation Medal $75 (£40)
- Independence Medal $75 (£40)

POLAND

- Order of Virtuti Militari, Grand Cross. . . . . .n/a
- Order of Virtuti Militari, Grand Cross breast star . . . .n/a
- Order of Virtuti Militari, Commander. . $3,500 (£1,750)
- Order of Virtuti Militari, Knight $1,750 (£875)
- Order of Virtuti Militari, Merit Cross, gold . .$900 (£450)
- Order of Virtuti Militari, Merit
  Cross, silver $400 (£200)
- Order of the White Eagle, ... $3,250 (£1,625)
- Order of the White Eagle, breast star . . . $3,500 (£1,750)
- Order of Polonia Restituta,
  Grand Cross (London-made). $450 (£225)
- Order of Polonia Restituta, Grand
  Cross breast star (London-made) $425 (£215)
- Order of Polonia Restituta, II Class
  (London-made). $325 (£165)
- Order of Polonia Restituta, II Class
  breast star (London-made). $400 (£200)
- Order of Polonia Restituta, Commander
  (London-made). $325 (£165)
- Order of Polonia Restituta, Officer
  (London-made). $150 (£75)
- Order of Polonia Restituta, Knight
  (London-made). $100 (£50)
- Cross of Merit, I Class $200 (£100)
- Cross of Merit, I Class w/swords. $300 (£150)
- Cross of Merit, II Class $150 (£75)
- Cross of Merit, II Class w/swords. $200 (£100)
- Cross of Merit, III Class $75 (£40)
- Cross of Merit, III Class w/swords $100 (£50)
- Valor Cross, 1939. . . . .$100 (£50)
- Valor Cross, 1940. . . . .$100 (£50)
- Valor Cross, WWII-issue made in
  England, Italy or Middle East. $75 (£40)
- Long Service Medal, 20 years. $85 (£45)
- Long Service Medal, 10 years. $50 (£25)
- Volunteers at War Cross. $150 (£75)
- Volunteers at War Medal $125 (£65)
- Army Active Service Medal $50 (£25)
- Navy Active Service Medal. $300 (£150)
- Air Force Active Service Medal. $175 (£90)
- Merchant Navy Service Medal. $300 (£150)
- Monte Cassino Cross. $150 (£75)
- Red Cross Medal $150 (£75)
- Home Army Cross $150 (£75)
- Resistance Medal, France $50 (£25)
- Polish Army in France. $65 (£35)
- Oder-Neisse-Baltic Campaign Medal $45 (£25)
- Liberation of Warsaw $45 (£25)
- Conquest of Berlin. $55 (£30)
- Victory over Germany. $35 (£20)

ROMANIA

- Order of Merit, Grand Cross $700 (£350)
- Order of Merit, Grand Cross w/swords. $800 (£400)

- Order of Merit, Commander $550 (£275)
- Order of Merit, Commander w/swords $600 (£300)
- Order of Merit, Officer $400 (£200)
- Order of Merit, Officer w/swords $450 (£225)
- Order of Merit, Knight $350 (£175)
- Order of Merit, Knight w/swords $375 (£190)
- Order of Merit, Merit Cross $250 (£125)
- Order of Merit, Merit Cross w/swords $275 (£140)
- Honor Cross for Merit, I Class $350 (£175)
- Honor Cross for Merit, I Class w/swords . . .$400 (£200)
- Honor Cross for Merit, I Class for females . .$350 (£175)
- Honor Cross for Merit, II Class $200 (£100)
- Honor Cross for Merit, II Class w/swords . . .$250 (£125)
- Faithful Service Order, Collar . . . . .n/a
- Faithful Service Order, Grand Cross $450 (£225)
- Faithful Service Order, Grand Cross
  w/swords $500 (£250)
- Faithful Service Order, Grand Cross
  breast star, Type II $450 (£225)
- Faithful Service Order, Grand Cross
  breast star w/swords $500 (£250)
- Faithful Service Order, Grand Officer $350 (£175)
- Faithful Service Order, Grand Officer
  w/swords $400 (£200)
- Faithful Service Order, Grand Officer
  breast star, Type II $350 (£175)
- Faithful Service Order, Grand Officer
  breast star w/swords $425 (£215)
- Faithful Service Order, Commander $350 (£175)
- Faithful Service Order, Commander
  w/swords $400 (£200)
- Faithful Service Order, Officer $250 (£125)
- Faithful Service Order, Officer w/swords . . .$300 (£150)
- Order of the Star of Rumania, Type II,
  Grand Cross $300 (£150)
- Order of the Star of Rumania, Type II,
  Grand Cross w/swords $350 (£175)
- Order of the Star of Rumania, Type II,
  Grand Cross w/swords on ring $350 (£175)
- Order of the Star of Rumania, Type II,
  Grand Cross w/swords & swords on ring . . .$400 (£200)
- Order of the Star of Rumania, Type II,
  Grand Cross breast star $250 (£125)
- Order of the Star of Rumania, Type II,
  Grand Cross breast star w/swords $300 (£150)
- Order of the Star of Rumania, Type II,
  I Class badge $250 (£125)
- Order of the Star of Rumania, Type II,
  I Class badge w/swords $250 (£125)
- Order of the Star of Rumania, Type II,
  I Class badge w/swords on ring $300 (£150)
- Order of the Star of Rumania, Type II, I Class
  badge with swords & swords on ring $350 (£175)
- Order of the Star of Rumania, Type II,
  I Class breast star $250 (£125)
- Order of the Star of Rumania, Type II,
  I Class breast star w/swords $300 (£150)

- Order of the Star of Rumania, Type II,
  Grand Officer badge $200 (£100)
- Order of the Star of Rumania, Type II,
  Grand Officer w/swords $250 (£125)
- Order of the Star of Rumania, Type II,
  Grand Officer w/swords on ring $300 (£150)
- Order of the Star of Rumania, Type II,
  Grand Officer w/swords & swords on ring . .$350 (£175)
- Order of the Star of Rumania, Type II,
  Grand Officer breast star $200 (£100)
- Order of the Star of Rumania, Type II,
  Grand Officer breast star w/swords $250 (£125)
- Order of the Star of Rumania, Type II,
  Commander $200 (£100)
- Order of the Star of Rumania, Type II,
  Commander w/swords $225 (£115)
- Order of the Star of Rumania, Type II,
  Commander w/swords on ring $275 (£140)
- Order of the Star of Rumania, Type II,
  Commander w/swords & swords on ring . . .$300 (£150)
- Order of the Star of Rumania, Type II,
  Officer $100 (£50)
- Order of the Star of Rumania, Type II,
  Officer w/swords $150 (£75)
- Order of the Star of Rumania, Type II,
  Officer w/swords on ring $200 (£100)
- Order of the Star of Rumania, Type II,
  Officer w/swords & swords on ring $250 (£125)
- Order of the Star of Rumania, Type II,
  Knight $85 (£45)
- Order of the Star of Rumania, Type II,
  Knight w/swords $125 (£65)
- Order of the Star of Rumania, Type II,
  Knight w/swords on ring $150 (£75)
- Order of the Star of Rumania, Type II,
  Knight w/swords & swords on ring $175 (£90)
- Order of the Crown, Type II,
  Grand Cross badge $350 (£175)
- Order of the Crown, Type II,
  Grand Cross badge w/swords $400 (£200)
- Order of the Crown, Type II, Grand
  Cross breast star $300 (£150)
- Order of the Crown, Type II, Grand
  Cross breast star w/swords $340 (£170)
- Order of the Crown, Type II, Grand Officer . .$250 (£125)
- Order of the Crown, Type II,
  Grand Officer w/swords $300 (£150)

*Rumanian Anti-Communist
Campaign Medal, $20-$30
(£10-£15).*

www.advanceguardmilitaria.com

- Order of the Crown, Type II,
  Grand Officer breast star $250 (£125)
- Order of the Crown, Type II,
  Grand Officer breast star w/swords $300 (£150)
- Order of the Crown, Type II,
  Commander $250 (£125)
- Order of the Crown, Type II,
  Commander w/swords $300 (£150)
- Order of the Crown, Type II, Knight $100 (£50)
- Order of the Crown, Type II, Knight
  w/swords $125 (£65)
- Order of the Crown, Type II, Ladies'
  Cross of the Order $200 (£100)
- Air Force Bravery Medal, Commander $325 (£165)
- Air Force Bravery Medal, Commander
  w/swords $350 (£175)
- Air Force Bravery Medal, Officer $275 (£140)
- Air Force Bravery Medal, Officer
  w/swords $300 (£150)
- Air Force Bravery Medal, Knight $175 (£90)
- Air Force Bravery Medal, Knight
  w/swords $200 (£100)
- Air Force Bravery Medal, Merit Cross $100 (£50)
- Air Force Bravery Medal, Merit Cross
  w/swords $125 (£65)
- Honor Decoration of the Rumanian Eagle,
  Grand Officer $300 (£150)
- Honor Decoration of the Rumanian Eagle,
  Grand Officer breast star $500 (£250)
- Honor Decoration of the Rumanian Eagle,
  Commander, I Class. $300 (£150)
- Honor Decoration of the Rumanian Eagle,
  Commander, II Class $275 (£140)
- Honor Decoration of the Rumanian Eagle,
  Officer $225 (£115)
- Honor Decoration of the Rumanian Eagle,
  Knight. $100 (£50)
- Military Bravery (Army), I Class, Type I $300 (£150)
- Military Bravery (Army), I Class, Type II $175 (£90)
- Military Bravery (Army), II Class, Type I $100 (£50)
- Military Bravery (Army), II Class, Type II. $75 (£40)
- Air Force Bravery, I Class $250 (£125)
- Air Force Bravery, I Class w/swords $275 (£140)
- Air Force Bravery, II Class $185 (£95)
- Air Force Bravery, II Class w/swords $200 (£100)
- Air Force Bravery, III Class. $160 (£80)
- Air Force Bravery, III Class w/swords $175 (£90)
- Naval Bravery, I Class $200 (£100)
- Naval Bravery, I Class w/crown. $225 (£115)
- Naval Bravery, I Class, w/crown & swords . .$230 (£115)
- Naval Bravery, II Class. $175 (£90)
- Naval Bravery, II Class w/crown $185 (£95)
- Naval Bravery, II Class, w/crown & swords. .$200 (£100)
- Naval Bravery, III Class. $125 (£65)
- Naval Bravery, III Class w/crown $85 (£45)
- Naval Bravery, III Class w/crown & swords . . .$60 (£30)
- Civil Guard Order, I Class $200 (£100)

- Civil Guard Order, II Class. $150 (£75)
- Civil Guard Order, III Class $100 (£50)
- Civil Guard Order, IV Class $75 (£40)
- Civil Guard Merit Decoration, I Class $150 (£75)
- Civil Guard Merit Decoration, II Class $95 (£50)
- Civil Guard Merit Decoration, III Class. $50 (£25)
- Pro Virtute Cross of the Civil Guard $75 (£40)
- Civil Guard Merit Medal, I Class $50 (£25)
- Civil Guard Merit Medal, II Class. $35 (£20)
- Civil Guard Merit Medal, III Class $20 (£10)
- Faithful Service Cross, Type II, I Class. $50 (£25)
- Faithful Service Cross, Type II,
  I Class w/swords. $45 (£25)
- Faithful Service Cross, Type II, II Class $40 (£20)
- Faithful Service Cross, Type II,
  II Class w/swords. $35 (£20)
- Faithful Service Cross, Type II, III Class $25 (£15)
- Faithful Service Cross, Type II,
  III Class w/swords $20 (£10)
- Faithful Service Medal, Type II, I Class $30 (£15)
- Faithful Service Medal, Type II,
  I Class w/swords. $30 (£15)
- Faithful Service Medal, Type II, II Class $25 (£14)
- Faithful Service Medal, Type II,
  II Class w/swords. $25 (£15)
- Faithful Service Medal, Type II, III Class. $20 (£10)
- Faithful Service Medal, Type II,
  III Class w/swords $15 (£14)
- Medal For Steadfastness & Loyalty, I Class. . . .$40 (£20)
- Medal For Steadfastness & Loyalty,
  I Class w/swords. $45 (£25)
- Medal For Steadfastness & Loyalty, II Class . . .$30 (£15)
- Medal For Steadfastness & Loyalty,
  II Class w/swords $35 (£20)
- Medal For Steadfastness & Loyalty, III Class . .$20 (£10)
- Medal For Steadfastness & Loyalty,
  III Class w/swords. $35 (£20)
- National Recognition Medal for Rumania, I Class. . . .n/a
- National Recognition Medal for Rumania, II Class. . .n/a
- National Recognition Medal for Rumania, III Class . .n/a
- Anti-Communist Campaign Medal $25 (£15)
- Anti-Communist Campaign Medal, one bar . .$45 (£25)
- Anti-Communist Campaign Medal, two bars. .$65 (£35)
- Anti-Communist Campaign Medal, three bars. $90 (£45)
- Anti-Communist Campaign Medal, four bars. $125 (£65)

SLOVAKIA (ALSO SEE CZECHOSLOVAKIA)

- Order of Prince Pribina, Grand Cross $1,200 (£600)
- Order of Prince Pribina, Grand Cross
  w/swords $1,450 (£725)
- Order of Prince Pribina, Grand Cross
  breast star $1,100 (£550)
- Order of Prince Pribina, Grand Cross
  breast star w/swords $1,275 (£640)

- Order of Prince Pribina, Grand Officer Cross $850 (£425)
- Order of Prince Pribina, Grand Officer Cross w/swords. $975 (£490)
- Order of Prince Pribina, Grand Officer breast star. $800 (£400)
- Order of Prince Pribina, Grand Officer breast star w/swords $1,150 (£575)
- Order of Prince Pribina, Commander $850 (£425)
- Order of Prince Pribina, Commander w/swords $950 (£475)
- Order of Prince Pribina, Officer $675 (£340)
- Order of Prince Pribina, Officer w/swords . .$750 (£375)
- Order of Prince Pribina, Knight $550 (£275)
- Order of Prince Pribina, Knight w/swords . .$625 (£315)
- Order of the Slovak Cross, Grand Cross . . $1,850 (£925)
- Order of the Slovak Cross, Grand Cross w/swords. $2,000 (£1,000)
- Order of the Slovak Cross, Grand Cross breast star. $1,700 (£850)
- Order of the Slovak Cross, Grand Cross breast star w/swords. $1,500 (£750)
- Order of the Slovak Cross, Commander . . $1,250 (£635)
- Order of the Slovak Cross, Commander w/swords $1,500 (£750)
- Order of the Slovak Cross, Officer $900 (£450)
- Order of the Slovak Cross, Officer w/swords $1,000 (£500)
- Order of the Slovak Cross, Knight $750 (£375)
- Order of the Slovak Cross, Knight w/swords $800 (£400)
- Order of the War Victory Cross, Type I. . .$1,500 (£750)
- Order of the War Victory Cross, Type I, I Class $1,500 (£750)
- Order of the War Victory Cross, Type I, I Class breast star $800 (£400)
- Order of the War Victory Cross, Type I, II Class $750 (£375)
- Order of the War Victory Cross, Type I, III Class. $650 (£325)
- Order of the War Victory Cross, Type II, Grand Cross. $1,250 (£625)
- Order of the War Victory Cross, Type II, Grand Cross w/swords. $1,500 (£750)
- Order of the War Victory Cross, Type II, Grand Cross breast star $1,300 (£650)
- Order of the War Victory Cross, Type II, Grand Cross breast star w/swords $1,300 (£650)

Slovakian Eastern Front Service Badge of Honor in silver, $250-$300 (£125-£150). www.advanceguardmilitaria.com

- Order of the War Victory Cross, Type II, I Class neck. $900 (£450)
- Order of the War Victory Cross, Type II, I Class breast star $1,200 (£600)
- Order of the War Victory Cross, Type II, II Class neck. $800 (£400)
- Order of the War Victory Cross, Type II, III Class. $600 (£300)
- Order of the War Victory Cross, Type II, IV Class. $550 (£275)
- Order of the War Victory Cross, Type II, IV Class w/swords. $650 (£325)
- Order of the War Victory Cross, Type II, V Class. $200 (£100)
- Order of the War Victory Cross, Type II, V Class w/swords $225 (£115)
- Order of the War Victory Cross, Type II, VI Class. $150 (£75)
- Order of the War Victory Cross, Type II, VI Class w/swords. $200 (£100)
- Order of the War Victory Cross, Type II, VII Class $125 (£65)
- Order of the War Victory Cross, Type II, VII Class w/swords $175 (£90)
- Bravery Medal, I Class. $225 (£115)
- Bravery Medal, II Class. $150 (£75)
- Bravery Medal, III Class $100 (£50)
- Defense of Slovakia, Type I. $175 (£90)
- Defense of Slovakia, Type II. $150 (£75)
- Suppression of the National Uprising, Large gold $550 (£275)
- Suppression of the National Uprising, Large silver $350 (£175)
- Suppression of the National Uprising, Large bronze $225 (£115)
- Suppression of the National Uprising, Small silver $175 (£90)
- Suppression of the National Uprising, Small, bronze. $100 (£50)
- Eastern Front Honor Badge, silver $350 (£175)
- Eastern Front Honor Badge, bronze. $200 (£100)
- Crimean Service Badge. $350 (£175)
- Tank Service Badge $275 (£140)
- Military Sport Badge. $250 (£125)
- Pilot/Observer Badge $650 (£325)
- Flight Engineer Badge $375 (£190)

SOVIET UNION

- Hero of The Soviet Union (Gold Star Medal) $1,200 (£600)
- Hero of Socialist Labor $850 (£425)
- Order of Lenin, Type I . . . . .n/a
- Order of Lenin, Type II. $800 (£400)
- Order of Lenin, Type III $600 (£300)
- Order of the Red Banner, Type I $350 (£175)
- Order of the Red Banner, Type II $50 (£25)

- Order of the Red Banner, Type II w/ no. 2. . .$200 (£100)
- Order of the Red Banner, Type II w/ no. 3. . .$300 (£150)
- Order of the Red Banner, Type II w/ no. 4. . .$650 (£325)
- Order of the Red Banner, Type II w/ no. 5. . . . . .n/a
- Order of Suvorov, I Class $8,500 (£4,250)
- Order of Suvorov, II Class. $2,750 (£1,375)
- Order of Suvorov, III Class. $1,200 (£600)
- Order of Ushakov, I Class $8,250 (£4,125)
- Order of Ushakov, II Class $3,400 (£1,700)
- Order of Kutuzov, I Class $6,500 (£3,250)
- Order of Kutuzov, II Class $1,800 (£900)
- Order of Kutuzov, III Class. $550 (£275)
- Order of Nakhimov, I Class $5,000 (£2,500)
- Order of Nakhimov, II Class $3,750 (£1,875)
- Order of Bohdan Khmelnitsky, I Class. . $4,600 (£2,300)
- Order of Bohdan Khmelnitsky, II Class . . .$1,450 (£725)
- Order of Bohdan Khmelnitsky, III Class $500 (£250)
- Order of Alexander Nevsky, Type I. $900 (£450)
- Order of Alexander Nevsky, Type II. $650 (£325)
- Order of the Patriotic War, I Class $250 (£125)
- Order of the Patriotic War, I Class,
  ribbon mounted $425 (£215)
- Order of the Patriotic War, II Class $100 (£50)
- Order of the Patriotic War, II Class,
  ribbon mounted $200 (£100)
- Order of the Red Star, first type. $14,000 (£7,000)
- Order of the Red Star, second type $3,000 (£1,500)
- Order of the Red Star, third type. $800 (£400)
- Order of the Red Star, fourth type. $80 (£40)
- Order of Glory, I Class $1,200 (£600)
- Order of Glory, II Classs. $175 (£90)
- Order of Glory, III Class $45 (£25)
- Order of Honor, Type I $100 (£50)
- Order of Honor, Type II $35 (£20)
- Order of the Red Banner of Labor, Type I. . .$500 (£250)
- Order of the Red Banner of Labor, Type II $50 (£25)
- Order of Service to the Motherland
  in the Armed Forces, I Class . . . . .n/a
- Order of Service to the Motherland
  in the Armed Forces, II Class. .n/a
- Order of Service to the Motherland
  in the Armed Forces, III Class $875 (£440)
- Order of Mother Heroine. $200 (£100)
- Order of Motherhood Glory, I Class $50 (£25)
- Order of Motherhood Glory, II Class. $30 (£15)
- Order of Motherhood Glory, III Class $20 (£10)
- Motherhood Medal, I Class $20 (£10)
- Motherhood Medal, II Class $10 (£5)
- Marshal's Star . . . . .n/a
- Medal for Valor, first issue $225 (£115)
- Medal of Valor, Type I, numbered. $65 (£35)
- Medal of Valor, Type I, unnumbered $35 (£20)
- Meritorious Service in Battle, first issue $165 (£85)
- Meritorious Service in Battle, Type I,
  numbered $50 (£25)
- Meritorious Service in Battle, Type I,
  unnumbered $35 (£20)
- Ushakov Medal. $150 (£75)
- Nakhimvo Medal $75 (£40)
- Partisan Warfare Medal, I Class $150 (£75)
- Partisan Warfare Medal, II Class. $100 (£50)
- Valiant Labor During WWII $20 (£10)
- Defense of Soviet Arctic $25 (£12)
- Defense of Leningrad. $25 (£12)
- Defense of Moscow $25 (£12)
- Defense of Odessa $125 (£65)
- Defense of Sevastopol $150 (£75)
- Defense of Stalingrad. $50 (£25)
- Defense of Caucasus $40 (£20)
- Defense of Kiev. $150 (£75)
- Victory over Germany. $20 (£10)
- Victory over Japan $30 (£15)
- Capture of Budapest $35 (£20)
- Capture of Koenigsberg $35 (£20)
- Capture of Vienna $50 (£25)

Order of the Red Banner, Type I, $300-$400 (£150-£200). Colin R. Bruce II

Gold Medal of the Hero of Socialist Labor, $1,000-$1,200 (£500-£600).

Order of the Red Banner, Type II, $100-$150 (£50-£75). Colin R. Bruce II

Ushakow-Medal, $275-$325 (£140-£165). Colin R. Bruce II

Nachimow Medal, $175-$225 (£85-£115). Colin R. Bruce II

The repatriation of Italian POWs from Russia took place between September 1945 and March 1946. A total of 10,087 were released from the Soviet camps.

- Capture of Berlin $25 (£12)
- Liberation of Prague $50 (£25)
- Liberation of Belgrade. $100 (£50)
- Liberation of Warsaw $25 (£12)
- Valiant Labor. $15 (£7)
- Distinguished Labor Service $25 (£15)
- Good Conduct Medal, I Class $25 (£15)
- Good Conduct Medal, II Class $20 (£10)
- Good Conduct Medal, III Class. $15 (£7)

SPAIN, FRANCO DICTATORSHIP

- Military Merit Order, War Merit, IV Class, Grand Cross $275 (£140)
- Military Merit Order, War Merit, IV Class, breast star $275 (£140)
- Military Merit Order, War Merit, III Class $75 (£40)
- Military Merit Order, War Merit, II Class. $50 (£25)
- Military Merit Order, War Merit, I Class $35 (£20)
- Military Merit Order, War Merit, Silver Merit Cross $25 (£15)
- Naval Merit Order, War Merit, IV Class, Grand Cross $200 (£100)

Order of the Red Banner of Labor, II Type, $35-$50 (£17-£25). Colin R. Bruce II

Order of the Patriotic War, I Class, Type II, $200-$250 (£100-£125). Colin R. Bruce II

Order of Nakhimov, II Class, $3,500-$3,800 (£1,750-£1,900). Colin R. Bruce II

Order of Glory, II Class, $150-$175 (£75-£90). Colin R. Bruce II

Order of Suvorov, II Class, Type II, $2,400-$2,800 (£1,200-£1,400). Colin R. Bruce II

Order of the Red Star, fourth type, $50-$80 (£10-£17). Colin R. Bruce II

Medal for Distinguished Labor, II Type, $20-$35 (£10-£17). Colin R. Bruce II

Order of the Patriotic War, II Class Type III, $125-$175 (£60-£90). Colin R. Bruce II

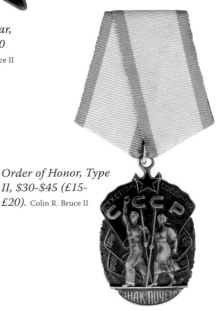

Order of Honor, Type II, $30-$45 (£15-£20). Colin R. Bruce II

- Naval Merit Order, War Merit, IV Class, breast star $200 (£100)
- Naval Merit Order, War Merit, III Class $75 (£40)
- Naval Merit Order, War Merit, II Class....... $50 (£25)
- Naval Merit Order, War Merit, I Class........ $35 (£20)
- Naval Merit Order, War Merit, Silver Merit Cross $25 (£15)
- Air Force Merit Order, War Merit, III Class, Grand Cross......................$150 (£75)
- Air Force Merit Order, War Merit, III Class, breast star $150 (£75)
- Air Force Merit Order, War Merit, II Class.... $75 (£40)
- Air Force Merit Order, War Merit, I Class $35 (£20)
- Air Force Merit Order, War Merit, Silver Merit Cross $25 (£15)
- Order of Maria Christina, Military Division, III Class, Grand Cross $150 (£75)
- Order of Maria Christina, Military Division, III Class breast star...............$150 (£75)

- Order of Maria Christina, Military Division, II Class...........................$100 (£50)
- Order of Maria Christina, Military Division, I Class $75 (£40)
- Order of Maria Christina, Military Division, Knight $50 (£25)
- Order of Maria Christina, Naval Division, III Class, Grand Cross...................$225 (£115)
- Order of Maria Christina, Naval Division, III Class breast star $225 (£115)
- Order of Maria Christina, Naval Division, II Class.................................$175 (£90)
- Order of Maria Christina, Naval Division, I Class.................................$150 (£75)
- Order of Maria Christina, Naval Division, Knight.................................$100 (£50)
- Order of Africa, Grand Cross $250 (£125)
- Order of Africa, Grand Cross breast star....$250 (£125)
- Order of Africa, Grand Officer $125 (£65)

Medal for Valor, Type I, unnumbered, first issue on small ribbon, $225-$250 (£112-£125). Colin R. Bruce II

Meritorious Service in Battle, Type I, numbered, $50-$75 (£25-£40). Colin R. Bruce II

Medal for Bravery, Type II (1943) numbered, on standard ribbon, $50-$75 (£25-£40). Colin R. Bruce II

Defense of the Soviet Polar Regions $30-$40 (£15-£20).
www.advanceguardmilitaria.com

Honorable Railroad Worker, Type II, $75-$100 (£38-£50). Colin R. Bruce II

Honorable Railroad Worker, Type III, $65-$85 (£30-£45). Colin R. Bruce II

Outstanding Cook, $100-$135 (£50-£70). Colin R. Bruce II

"I lay there unscrewing the insignia from my collar tabs so that if I did get taken prisoner, they would take me for a private and torture me less."

ALEKSANDR VASILIEVICH BODNAR, 20TH SOVIET TANK BRIGADE

- South Africa Permanent Force Long
  Service and Good Conduct Medal . . . . **$250 (£145)**
- Efficiency Medal (South Africa) . . . . **$100 (£65)**
- Voluntary Medical Service Medal, silver . . . . . . **$30 (£20)**
- Voluntary Medical Service Medal,
  cupro-nickel . . . . **$20 (£15)**
- Service Medal of the Order of St. John, silver . . **$30 (£20)**
- Service Medal of the Order of St. John,
  base metal . . . . **$15 (£12)**
- Royal Air Force Long Service and Good
  Conduct Medal. . . . . **$80 (£50)**
- Air Efficiency Award . . . . **$150 (£100)**
- Special Constabulary Long Service Medal . . . . **$15 (£10)**
- Colonial Police Long Service Medal . . . . **$100 (£65)**
- Hong Kong Royal Naval Dockyard Police
  Long Service Medal . . . . **$400 (£200)**
- Colonial Fire Brigade Long Service Medal . . **$500 (£250)**
- Ceylon Fire Brigade Long Service and
  Good Conduct Medal . . . . **$600 (£400)**
- South African Prison Service Faithful
  Service Medal . . . . **$60 (£40)**
- King's Messenger Badge . . . . **$1,400 (£700)**
- Order of the League of Mercy . . . . **$100 (£60)**

- Badge of Honour (African countries) . . . . **n/a**
- Badge of Honour (Non-African countries) . . . . **n/a**
- Indian Recruiting Badge . . . . **$80 (£60)**
- Army Best Shot Medal . . . . **$1,500 (£600)**
- Shanghai Volunteer Corps Long Service
  Medal . . . . **$500 (£300)**
- Royal Canadian Mounted Police Long
  Service Medal . . . . **$1,800 (£1,000)**

UNITED STATES

- Medal of Honor
  **Note: Under current U.S. law, it is illegal to sell, buy
  or transfer a Medal of Honor. Therefore, no pricing
  information is provided here.**
- Distinguished Service Cross, numbered . . . . **$325 (£165)**
- Distinguished Service Cross, unnumbered . . . **$175 (£90)**
- Navy Cross. . . . . **$400 (£200)**
- Distinguished Service Medal, Army,
  numbered . . . . **$300 (£150)**
- Distinguished Service Medal, Army,
  unnumbered . . . . **$150 (£75)**
- Distinguished Service Medal, Navy . . . . **$400 (£200)**

*U.S. Distinguished
Service Cross, numbered,
$300-$350 (£150-£175).*
Minnesota Military Museum

*Distinguished Service
Medal, U.S. Navy,
$350-$400 (£175-
£200).* Colin R. Bruce II

*Legion of Merit, Chief
Commander breast star,
unnumbered, $700-$1,000
(£350-£500).* Fred Borch

*Legion of Merit, Legionnaire,
unnumbered, $100-$150
(£50-£75).* Fred Borch

*Navy Good Conduct
Medal, Type II, unnamed,
$15-$25 (£7-£12).*

www.advanceguardmilitaria.com

*U.S. Army Distinguished
Flying Cross, slot brooch,
unnumbered, $100-$150 (£50-
£75).* www.advanceguardmilitaria.com

- Silver Star, Army, numbered, wrap brooch . . .**$125 (£65)**
- Silver Star, Army, numbered, slot brooch . . . .**$100 (£50)**
- Silver Star, Army, unnumbered, slot brooch . . .**$75 (£40)**
- Silver Star, Navy, unnumbered. . . . .**$250 (£125)**
- Legion of Merit, Chief Commander breast star, numbered . . . . **$2,500 (£1,250)**
- Legion of Merit, Chief Commander breast star, unnumbered . . . .**$1,000 (£500)**
- Legion of Merit, Commander, numbered . . .**$950 (£475)**
- Legion of Merit, Commander, unnumbered.**$450 (£225)**
- Legion of Merit, Officer, numbered . . . .**$375 (£190)**
- Legion of Merit, Officer, unnumbered. . . . . .**$150 (£75)**
- Legion of Merit, Legionnaire, numbered. . . .**$200 (£100)**
- Legion of Merit, Legionnaire, unnumbered . .**$150 (£75)**
- Meritorious Service Medal. . . . . **$15 (£7)**
- Distinguished Flying Cross, Army, numbered . . . .**$200 (£100)**
- Distinguished Flying Cross, Army, unnumbered . . . .**$100 (£50)**
- Distinguished Flying Cross, Army, frosted . . .**$115 (£60)**
- Distinguished Flying Cross, Navy . . . .**$175 (£90)**
- Soldier's Medal, numbered. . . . .**$150 (£75)**
- Soldier's Medal, unnumbered . . . . **$65 (£35)**
- Navy & Marine Corps Medal. . . . .**$225 (£115)**
- Bronze Star, Army . . . . **$35 (£20)**
- Bronze Star, Navy. . . . .**$150 (£75)**
- Air Medal, Army, wrap brooch, numbered. . . .**$85 (£45)**
- Air Medal, Army, wrap brooch, unnumbered . **$55 (£30)**
- Air Medal, Army, slot brooch . . . .**$40 (£20)**
- Air Medal, Navy . . . .**$125 (£65)**
- Purple Heart, Army, Type I . . . .**$125 (£65)**
- Purple Heart, Army, Type II. . . . . **$85 (£45)**
- Purple Heart, Army, Type II. . . . . **$45 (£25)**
- Purple Heart, Navy, Type I . . . .**$125 (£65)**
- Purple Heart, Navy, Type II . . . . **$85 (£45)**
- Good Conduct Medal, Army, ring suspension, numbered . . . .**n/a**
- Good Conduct Medal, Army, knob suspension, numbered . . . . **$75 (£40)**
- Good Conduct Medal, Army, knob suspension, unnumbered . . . . **$15 (£8)**
- Good Conduct Medal, Navy, Type II, engraved. . . . . **$50 (£25)**
- Good Conduct Medal, Navy, Type II, impressed. . . . . **$40 (£20)**
- Good Conduct Medal, Navy, Type II unnamed . . . . **$20 (£10)**
- Good Conduct Medal, Marine, impressed . . . . **$65 (£35)**
- Good Conduct Medal, Marine, unnamed. . . . . **$25 (£15)**
- Good Conduct Medal, Coast Guard, Type I, named. . . . .**$185 (£95)**
- Good Conduct Medal, Coast Guard, Type I, unnamed . . . .**$100 (£50)**
- Good Conduct Medal, Coast Guard, Type II . .**$20 (£10)**
- Naval Reserve Medal, Type I . . . . **$75 (£40)**
- Naval Reserve Medal, Type II . . . . **$20 (£10)**
- Fleet Marine Corps Reserve. . . . .**$950 (£475)**

- Selected Marine Corps Reserve Medal . . . . . .**$165 (£85)**
- American Defense Service Medal, Type I . . . . .**$35 (£20)**
- American Defense Service Medal, Type II . . . . .**$15 (£7)**
- American Defense Service Medal, bar, Foreign Service . . . .**$25 (£15)**
- American Defense Service Medal, bar, Fleet. . .**$20 (£10)**
- American Defense Service Medal, bar, Base . . .**$30 (£15)**
- American Defense Service Medal, bar, Sea . . . .**$75 (£40)**
- American Campaign Medal. . . . .**$15 (£7)**
- European-African-Middle Eastern Campaign Medal . . . .**$15 (£7)**
- Asiatic Pacific Campaign Medal . . . .**$15 (£7)**
- World War II Victory Medal . . . .**$10 (£5)**
- Women's Army Corps Medal, 1st issue . . . .**$65 (£35)**
- Women's Army Corps Medal, 2nd issue . . . . . .**$35 (£20)**
- Army of Occupation . . . .**$15 (£7)**
- Army of Occupation, bar, Germany . . . .**$20 (£10)**
- Army of Occupation, bar, Japan . . . .**$20 (£10)**
- Navy Occupation . . . .**$20 (£10)**

U.S. Army Good Conduct Medal, knob suspension, named, $25-$50 (£10-£25). Author's collection

U.S. Victory Medal, $10-$15 (£5-£7). Charles D. Pautler

European-African-Middle Eastern Campaign Medal, $10-$15 (£5-£7). Charles D. Pautler

- Navy Occupation, bar, Asia $25 (£12)
- Navy Occupation, bar Europe $30 (£15)
- USMC Occupation $25 (£12)
- USMC Occupation, bar, Asia. $30 (£15)
- USMC Occupation, bar, Europe $40 (£20)
- China Service, USN $40 (£20)
- China Service, USMC $40 (£20)
- Merchant Marine, Distinguished
  Service Medal $1,750 (£875)
- Merchant Marine, Meritorious Service,
  numbered $300 (£150)
- Merchant Marine, Meritorious Service,
  named & numbered. $400 (£200)
- Merchant Marine, Mariner's Medal $200 (£100)
- Merchant Marine, Defense Medal $25 (£12)
- Merchant Marine, Atlantic War Zone Medal. . $30 (£15)
- Merchant Marine, Mediterranean
  Middle East War Zone Medal $25 (£12)
- Merchant Marine, Pacific War Zone Medal . . . $25 (£12)
- Merchant Marine, World War II Victory. $95 (£50)

YUGOSLAVIA (ALSO SEE CROATIA)

- Order of the Crown, Grand Cross. $450 (£225)
- Order of the Crown, Grand Cross
  breast star $450 (£225)
- Order of the Crown, Commander, I Class. . .$325 (£165)
- Order of the Crown, Commander, I Class
  breast star $350 (£175)
- Order of the Crown, Commander, II Class . .$325 (£165)
- Order of the Crown, Officer. $200 (£100)
- Order of the Crown, Knight. $175 (£90)
- Commemorative Medal of the Liberation
  of the Northern Territories $50 (£25)
- Commemorative Medal of the Liberation
  of Southern Serbia $50 (£25)
- World War II Commemorative Cross $150 (£75)

U.S. Army Purple Heart with Oak Leaf cluster signifying an additional receipt of the award, $75-$100 (£40-£50). www.advanceguardmilitaria.com

Women's Army Corps Service Medal, second issue, $20-$50 (£10-£25). Charles D. Pautler

This Victory Medal was made in the Philippines, $25-$35 (£12-£18). Colin R. Bruce II

New Mexico "Bataan" Medal, $200-$250 (£100-£125). Minnesota Military Museum

U.S. Army Bronze Star, $30-$50 (£15-£25). Minnesota Military Museum

Weapons have long been considered to be the "perfect" trophy for someone who served in combat. Soldiers returning from the war selected examples of captured weapons or even one of their own favorites to remind them of their days in service. Apart from the occasional presentation piece or rare sniper weapon that might have returned as a trophy, the bulk of the weapons available to collectors entered the market through surplus sources.

The millions of rifles, handguns, and submachine guns that were collected after the war could not be absorbed by the current military structure. Furthermore, many of the weapons were simply out of date and no longer of interest to a nation rearming itself. Therefore, stacks of weapons became available to the secondary, civilian market.

Like all areas of World War II collecting, if you intend to collect long arms, decide how you are going to collect before making your initial purchase. For example: Do you simply desire a representative weapon from both sides? If so, an M1 Garand or a British SMLE and a German 98k or Japanese Arisaka Type 99 might suffice. But, perhaps you want to collect weapons used by a particular nation. For example, if you decide to assemble a collection of rifles used by the United States, you would be able to limit yourself to about a dozen weapons (albeit, a few will cost you several thousand dollars!). This sort of approach will provide for a limited variety and also help develop a feel for the arming of one nation.

Collecting long arms can be addictive. Perhaps you will begin by buying a Inland M1 Carbine at a show. Pretty soon, you might think, "Hmm, it might be fun to collect one of each of the M1 carbine manufacturers." After spending several thousand dollars, your habit might blossom to the point that you think, "Now that I have those, I need to have a rep-

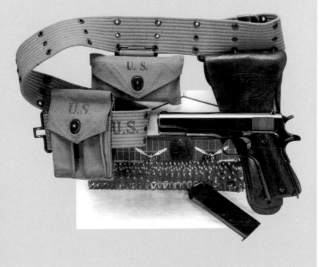

Collecting Hints

Pros:

- Firearm are great visual aids for learning or teaching about World War II. A soldier's existence depended on the weapon he carried. Collecting weapons places your hands on the very tools that made history.
- Firearms tend to hold their value, making them a tangible hedge against inflation.
- World War II firearms are plentiful, so it is fairly easy to enter the hobby and find a niche that will provide variety and collecting satisfaction.

Cons:

- It is easy for those who don't understand your hobby to label you as a "gun nut."
- Many laws govern private firearm ownership. It is your responsibility to know what they are.
- Guns draw attention, both welcome and unwelcome. They are a prime target for thieves.
- Long arms are cumbersome to display. As your collection grows, it will quickly fill wall space.
- You must determine whether you will restore a weapon to the way it appeared when issued, or keep it in the condition in which you found it.
- Because of the quantity and variety of weapons available, you will be faced with a limited collection unless you are independently wealthy.

Availability ★★★★

Price ★★★

Reproduction Alert ★

resentative M1 rifle." Before you know it, you have branched out into full-auto machine guns and you are mortgaging your house to buy an M2 Browning! As pointed out earlier, you should formulate a plan before you begin to buy. There are too many weapons available, and you simply can't buy them all. You will have to make choices to form a meaningful and valuable collection.

Know the Law

Before you buy, become familiar with local and national laws laws that regulate the private ownership of firearms. In the United States, these vary from state to state. In many locations in the United States and Europe, one may not own a weapon capable of firing. For these people and for those who simply do not want the liability of owning live weapons, a market of "demilitarized" weapons has emerged. These weapons, though usually built with original parts, are totally non-firing and cannot be made to fire. Values of these weapons are proportional to their live-firing counterparts.

Who hasn't fantasized about owning their own Sherman tank? It is possible, but it will cost more than $100,000 (£50,000)!

This brief guide will give you an idea of the prices of some of the most popular vehicles:

WILLYS OR FORD JEEP
$10,000-$18,000 (£5,000-£9,000)

WC 3/4 TON WEAPONS CARRIER
$7,000-$12000 (£3,5000-£6,000)

CCKW 2-1/2 TON TRUCK
$9,000-$15,000 (£4,5000-£7,500)

M3/M3A1 HALF-TRACK
$20,000-$30,000 (£10,0000-£15,000)

M29 WEASEL
$7,000-$12,000 (£3,5000-£6,000)

US 37MM ANTI-TANK GUN (NON-FIRING)
$12,000-$15,000 (£6,0000-£7,500)

M4A3 SHERMAN MEDIUM TANK
$90,000-$140,000 (£45,0000-£70,000)

M5A1 STUART LIGHT TANK
$70,000-$90,000 (£35,0000-£45,000)

GERMAN KÜBELWAGEN
$17,000-$25,000 (£8,500-£12,500)

GERMAN SCHWIMMWAGEN
$40,000-$70,000 (£20,000-£35,000)

GERMAN "HETZER" TANK DESTROYER
$150,000-$190,000 (£75,000-£95,000)

SOVIET T34 TANK
$65,000-$85,000 (£32,500-£42,500)

BRITISH BREN CARRIER
$25,000-$35,000 (£12,5000-£17,500)

HOW MUCH FOR THAT TANK?

There is hardly a World War II buff alive who hasn't at one time thought, "Gee, I would like to own a tank…I wonder how much one would cost?" It isn't as crazy as what one's neighbors might think!

In the United States, nearly 30,000 people call themselves "MV (military vehicle) enthusiasts." The most common World War II vehicle to be restored is the most widely produced during the war—the Jeep. But, many also like to restore and drive larger vehicles ranging from 2-1/2-ton GMC trucks to Sherman tanks.

The largest club for MV enthusiasts is the Military Vehicle Preservation Association (www.mvpa.org). With 9,000 members worldwide, it serves as a connecting point for people who yearn for drving something in olive drab. The most popular magazine for folks in the hobby is *Military Vehicles Magazine*. Filled with technical and historical articles about military jeeps, trucks and tracked vehicles, it is also the place to find dealers in vehicles and parts. Check it out online at www.militaryvehiclesmagazine.com

A fully restored, running British Mk I "Bren" carrier costs $25,000-$35,000 (£12,5000-£17,500).

Jeeps, parts and folks who know about them are plentiful. For about $10,000-$18,000 (£5,000-£9,000), one can own one of these famous war horses.

Austrian Steyr Model 29/40 (600) rifle, $300-$750 (£150-£375). Rock Island Auction Company

Mk. 1* John Inglis & Company pistol, Chinese contract model, $950-$2,250 (£475-£1,250). Rock Island Auction Company

Fabrique Nationale ("FN") Model 1935 High Power pistol with Nazi Waffenamt stamp, $750-$1,500 (£375-£750). Rock Island Auction Company

Belgian De L'Etat-produced Model 1935 short rifle, $250-$550 (£125-£275). Rock Island Auction Company

Canadian Long Branch Number 4 Mark I rifle, $400-$600 (£200-£300). Rock Island Auction Company

Austria

Submachine Guns

- Steyr-Solothurn MP 30
  ....**$8,000-$10,000 (£4,000-£5,000)**
- Steyr-Solothurn S1-100 (MP34(o))
  ....**$7,500-$10,000 (£3,750-£5,000)**

Rifles

- Steyr Model 1888/1890 Mannlicher rifle
  ....**$150-$500 (£75-£250)**
- Steyr Model 1890 Mannlicher carbine
  ....**$200-$750 (£100-£375)**
- Steyr Model 1895 Mannlicher rifle
  ....**$75-$300 (£40-£150)**
- Model 35 Fegyvergyar..........**$150-$500 (£75-£250)**

Machine Guns

- Model 07/12 Schwarzlose
  ....**$25,000-$35,000 (£12,500-£17,500)**

Belgium

Handguns

- Armand Gavage 7.65mm pistol..**$150-$550 (£75-£275)**
- Model 1903 FN pistol ....**$275-$650 (£140-£325)**
- Model 1922 FN pistol ....**$150-$500 (£74-£250)**
- Model 1935 FN pistol ....**$600-$1,200 (£300-£600)**
- German Military Pistole Model 640(b) pistol
  ....**$300-$650 (£150-£325)**
- Captured Pre War Commercial Model 1935 pistol
  ....**$750-$1,500 (£375-£750)**

Rifles

- M1935 Mauser Short rifle .....**$250-$525 (£125-£280)**
- M1889/36 Mauser Short rifle ....**$90-$300 (£45-£150)**
- M24/30 Mauser Training rifle, Army
  ....**$200-$450 (£100-£225)**
- M24/30 Mauser Training rifle, Navy
  ....**$200-$450 (£100-£225)**
- FN BAR Model D
  ....**$27,500-$40,000 (£13,750-£20,000)**

Canada

Handguns

- Mk. 1, No. 1 John Inglis & Company pistol, Chinese marked . . . . **$950-$2,250 (£475-£1,125)**
- Mk. 1, No. 1 John Inglis & Company pistol . . . . **$850-$1,500 (£425-£750)**
- Mk. 1, No. 2 John Inglis & Company pistol . . . . **$775-$1,200 (£390-£600)**

Submachine Guns

- Canadian Sten Mk II . . . **$4,500-$7,000 (£2,250-£3,500)**

Rifles

- Lee Enfield Rifle No. 4, Mark I (T) . . . . **$500-$1,200 (£250-£600)**

Machine Guns

- Canadian Bren Mk I . . . . **$35,000-$45,000 (£17,500-£22,500)**
- Canadian Bren Mk II . . . . **$35,000-$45,000 (£17,500-£22,500)**
- Canadian Chinese Bren Mk II . . . . **$35,000-$45,000 (£17,500-£22,500)**

China

Handguns

- Chinese marked handmade Mauser 96 pistol . . . . **$250-$450 (£125-£225)**
- Taku-Naval Dockyard Mauser 96 pistol . . . . **$500-$2,750 (£250-£1,375)**
- Shansei Arsenal Mauser 96 pistol . . . . **$1,500-$4,500 (£750-£2,250)**

Rifles

- M98/22 Mauser rifle . . . . **$100-$350 (£150-£175)**
- FN M24 Mauser short rifle. . . . . . **$60-$200 (£30-£150)**
- FN M30 Mauser short rifle. . . . . . **$90-$250 (£45-£125)**
- Chiang Kai-shek Mauser short rifle . . . . **$90-$250 (£45-£125)**
- VZ24 Mauser short rifle . . . . **$65-$200 (£35-£100)**
- VZ24 Mauser short rifle w/Japanese folding bayonet . . . . **$150-$300 (£75-£150)**
- M1933 Standard Model Mauser short rifle . . . . **$150-$250 (£75-£125)**

Machine Guns

- Type 24. . . . . **$18,500-$25,000 (£9,250-£12,500)**
- Type 26. . . . . **$25,000-$30,000 (£12,500-£15,000)**

Czechoslovakia

Handguns

- Army Pistole 1922 . . . .**$200-$675 (£100-£340)**
- CZ 1927 pistol. . . . .**$200-$400 (£100-£200)**
- CZ 1927 pistol, Nazi-proofed . . . . **$600-$1,000 (£300-£500)**
- CZ 1938 . . . .**$250-$500 (£125-£250)**

Submachine Guns

- CZ 23/25 . . . . **$12,000-$15,000 (£6,000-£7,500)**
- ZK 383 . . . . **$13,000-$17,500 (£6,500-£8,750)**

Chinese Shansei Arsenal Type 18 .45 caliber "broom handle" pistol, $1,500-$4,500 (£750-£2,250).
Rock Island Auction Company

CZ Model 27 semi-automatic pistol with Nazi Waffenamt mark, $750-$1,000 (£375-£500). Rock Island Auction Company

This CZ Model 27 is marked with typical German Waffenamt markings, but has an additional letter "K" stamped on the trigger guard. This denotes that it was intended for police use, $1,000-$1,600 (£500-£800). Rock Island Auction Company

Rifles

- M1898/22 Mauser rifle . . . . **$75-$265 (£40-£135)**
- VZ23 Mauser rifle . . . . **$50-$250 (£25-£125)**
- VZ16/33 Mauser carbine . . . . . **$200-$500 (£100-£250)**
- M1895 Mannlicher rifle . . . . **$150-$375 (£75-£190)**
- Model 24 (VZ24) rifle . . . . **$250-$500 (£125-£250)**
- Model G24(t), Nazi-proofed
  . . . . **$2,000-$3,000 (£1,000-£1,500)**
- Model ZH29 . . . . **$5,000-$15,500 (£2,500-£7,750)**

Machine Guns

- ZB VZ26. . . . . **$37,000-$42,500 (£18,500-£21,250)**
- ZB VZ30. . . . . **$20,000-$25,000 (£10,000-£12,500)**
- ZGB VZ30 . . . . **$18,000-$20,000 (£9,000-£10,000)**
- ZB VZ37. . . . . **$25,000-$32,000 (£12,500-£16,000)**

FINLAND

Handguns

- M35 Lahti pistol . . . . **$600-$1,500 (£300-£750)**

Submachine Guns

- Suomi Model 1931 . . **$15,000-$18,000 (£7,500-£9,000)**
- Suomi Model 1944 . . **$15,000-$18,000 (£7,500-£9,000)**

Rifles

- Model 91/24 Civil Guard infantry rifle
  . . . . **$75-$350 (£40-£175)**
- Model 1927 Army short rifle . . . . **$100-$375 (£50-£190)**
- Model 1927 Cavalry carbine . . . **$250-$775 (£125-£390)**
- Model 1928.30 Civil Guard short rifle
  . . . . **$100-$350 (£50-£175)**
- Finnish Model 91/30 rifle . . . . **$50-$200 (£25-£100)**
- Model 1939 short rifle . . . . **$75-$200 (£40-£100)**
- Swedish Model 1896 rifle . . . . **$75-$250 (£40-£125)**
- Italian Carcano . . . . **$50-$200 (£25-£100)**

FRANCE

Handguns

- Le Francais Model 28 Type Armee pistol
  . . . . **$500-$1,500 (£250-£750)**
- Model 1935A pistol . . . . **$100-$300 (£50-£150)**
- Model 1935A pistol, Nazi-proofed
  . . . . **$150-$600 (£75-£300)**
- Model 1935S . . . . **$100-$325 (£50-£165)**
- MAB Model D pistol . . . . **$325-$600 (£165-£300)**
- Unique Model 16 pistol, Nazi-proofed
  . . . . **$150-$350 (£75-£175)**

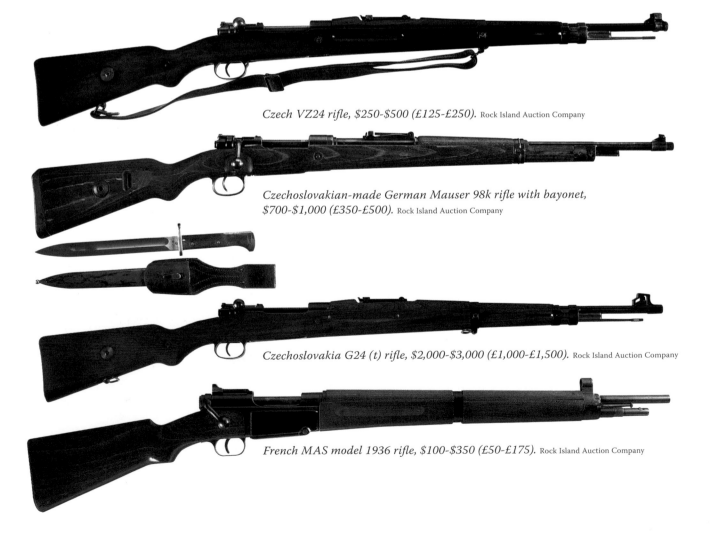

Czech VZ24 rifle, $250-$500 (£125-£250). Rock Island Auction Company

Czechoslovakian-made German Mauser 98k rifle with bayonet, $700-$1,000 (£350-£500). Rock Island Auction Company

Czechoslovakia G24 (t) rifle, $2,000-$3,000 (£1,000-£1,500). Rock Island Auction Company

French MAS model 1936 rifle, $100-$350 (£50-£175). Rock Island Auction Company

- Unique Model 17 pistol, Nazi-proofed
  . . . .**$200-$375 (£100-£190)**
- Unique Kriegsmodell pistol, Nazi-proofed
  . . . .**$250-$650 (£125-£325)**

Submachine Guns

- MAS 35 SE . . . .**$6,000-$8,000 (£3,000-£4,000)**
- MAS 38 . . . .**$6,000-$7,500 (£3,000-£3,750)**

Rifles

- Lebel Model 1886/M93/R35 rifle
  . . . .**$150-$550 (£75-£275)**
- Lebel Model 1886/M93/R35 rifle, Nazi-proofed
  . . . .**$250-$800 (£125-£400)**
- Berthier-Mannlicher Model 1907/15-M34
  . . . .**$250-$650 (£125-£325)**
- MAS 36 rifle . . . .**$100-$350 (£50-£175)**
- MAS 44 rifle . . . .**$250-$650 (£125-£325)**
- MAS 45 rifle . . . .**$200-$500 (£100-£250)**

Machine Guns

- Hotchkiss Model 1914
  . . . . **$12,500-$17,000 (£6,250-£8,500)**
- Chatellerault M1924/M29
  . . . . **$17,500-$20,000 (£8,750-£10,000)**

GERMANY

Handguns

- Steyr Hahn Model 1911 (WWII issue marked "P.08")
  . . . .**$250-$850 (£125-£425)**
- Mauser Snellfeuer Model 712 (also know as "Model 32")
  . . . .**$8,000-$10,000 (£4,000-£5,000)**
- Luger, Death's Head Rework
  . . . . **$650-$2,600 (£325-£1,300)**
- Luger, Kadetten Institute Rework
  . . . . **$800-$3,300 (£400-£1,650)**
- Luger, Mauser unmarked rework
  . . . . **$650-$1,500 (£325-£750)**
- Luger, Mauser Oberndorf
  . . . .**$1,500-$5,000 (£750-£2,500)**
- Luger, 1935/06 Portuguese "GNR"
  . . . . **$950-$3,800 (£475-£1,900)**
- Luger S/42 K Date . . . .**$1,350-$6,200 (£675-£3,100)**
- Luger S/42 G Date . . . . **$650-$2,800 (£325-£1,400)**
- Luger, dated chamber S/42 . . . **$500-$1,600 (£250-£800)**
- Luger, code 42 dated chamber
  . . . . **$450-$1,600 (£225-£800)**
- Luger, 41/42 code . . . .**$750-$1,700 (£375-£850)**
- Luger, byf code . . . .**$700-$1,900 (£350-£950)**
- Luger, 1934 Mauser Dutch contract
  . . . .**$1,200-$3,500 (£600-£1,750)**
- Luger, 1934 Mauser Swedish contract
  . . . .**$1,500-$4,300 (£750-£2,150)**
- Luger, 1934 Mauser German contract
  . . . . **$750-$3,000 (£375-£1,500)**

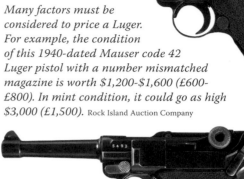

Many factors must be considered to price a Luger. For example, the condition of this 1940-dated Mauser code 42 Luger pistol with a number mismatched magazine is worth $1,200-$1,600 (£600-£800). In mint condition, it could go as high $3,000 (£1,500). Rock Island Auction Company

Krieghoff 1936 Luger pistol, $1,500-$5,000 (£750-£2,500).
Rock Island Auction Company

Because this Mauser-produced "byf" code 41 Luger had two magazines with matching numbers, it fetched $2,300 (~£1,150) at auction—nearly $400 more than if it had just a single clip. Rock Island Auction Company

This factory cased and engraved Walther Model PP pistol was presented as an award at a Nazi party pistol shoot in 1937. It sold for $57,500 (~£28,750). Rock Island Auction Company

German Walther "ac 43" code P.38 pistol, $700-$900 (£350-£450). Rock Island Auction Company

This engraved Sauer & Sohn Model 38H pistol was presented to SS General Friedrich Kruger, $40,000-$50,000 (£20,000-£25,000). Rock Island Auction Company

Sauer Model 38-H, Type IV police pistol, $350-$800 (£175-£400). Rock Island Auction Company

Walther Model PPK semi-automatic pistol, RZM-marked, $500-$1,300 (£250-£650). Rock Island Auction Company

Engraved presentation Walther PPK Pistol with case, $15,000-$20,000 (£7,500-£10,000). Rock Island Auction Company

Walther PP with an NSKK badge on the slide, $8,500-$9,500 (£4,250-£4,750). Rock Island Auction Company

- Luger, Mauser 2-digit date . $900-$3,000 (£450-£1,500)
- Luger, S code Krieghoff . . .$1,000-$5,500 (£500-£2,750)
- Luger, 36 date Krieghoff . .$1,500-$5,000 (£750-£2,500)
- Luger, 4-digit date Krieghoff
  . . . .$1,000-$4,500 (£500-£2,250)
- P.38, Model HP, early w/high gloss bluing
  . . . . $600-$3,000 (£300-£1,500)
- P.38, Model HP, late w/military blue finish
  . . . . $550-$2,000 (£275-£1,000)
- P.38, First issue zero series
  . . . .$2,500-$8,500 (£1,250-£4,250)
- P.38, Second issue zero series
  . . . .$2,000-$7,000 (£1,000-£3,500)
- P.38, 480 code . . . .$1,750-$8,500 (£875-£4,250)
- P.38, ac code . . . .$2,800-$9,500 (£1,400-£4,750)
- P.38, ac40 code ("40" added)
  . . . .$1,000-$3,800 (£500-£1,900)
- P.38, ac40 code . . . . $700-$2,500 (£350-£1,250)
- P.38, ac41 code . . . . $400-$2,200 (£200-£1,100)
- P.38, ac42 code . . . . $300-$1,300 (£150-£650)
- P.38, ac43 code . . . . $350-$1,200 (£175-£600)
- P.38, ac44 code . . . .$350-$900 (£175-£450)
- P.38, ac45 code . . . .$350-$950 (£175-£475)
- P.38, byf42 code . . . . $500-$2,300 (£250-£1,150)
- P.38, byf43 code . . . .$350-$950 (£175-£475)
- P.38, byf44 code . . . .$350-$950 (£175-£475)
- P.38, cyq code (first variation) $600-$1,500 (£300-£750)
- P.38, cyq code (standard variation)
  . . . .$300-$900 (£150-£450)
- P.38, cyq zero series . . . . $350-$1,300 (£175-£650)
- P.38, AC43/44-FN slide . . . . $600-$2,200 (£300-£1,100)
- Mauser Model 1934 pistol . . . . .$350-$650 (£175-£325)
- Mauser Model HSC early Army model
  . . . . $550-$1,600 (£275-£800)
- Mauser Model HSC late Army model
  . . . . $400-$1,400 (£200-£700)
- Mauser Model HSC Navy model
  . . . . $400-$1,600 (£200-£800)
- Mauser Model HSC early police model
  . . . . $300-$1,250 (£150-£625)
- Mauser Model HSC wartime police model
  . . . . $250-$1,200 (£125-£600)
- Mauser Model HSC wartime commercial model
  . . . . $200-$1,150 (£100-£575)
- Sauer Model 1913, second series, paramilitary marked
  . . . .$450-$600 (£225-£300)
- Sauer Model 38, one-line legend
  . . . . $650-$1,700 (£325-£850)
- Sauer Model 38, two-line legend
  . . . . $600-$1,800 (£300-£900)
- Sauer Model 38 paramilitary marked
  . . . . $550-$2,200 (£275-£1,100)
- Sauer Model 38-H . . . .$300-$700 (£150-£350)
- Sauer Model 38-H paramilitary marked
  . . . . $450-$2,000 (£225-£1,000)
- Sauer Model 38-H L.M. Model
  . . . .$1,500-$4,000 (£750-£2,000)

- Sauer Model 38-H Type II, military variation
  ....$300-$1,200 (£150-£600)
- Sauer Model 38-H Type III, military accepted
  ....$300-$850 (£150-£425)
- Sauer Model 38-H Type III, commercial
  ....$375-$800 (£190-£400)
- Sauer Model 38-H Type III, police
  ....$375-$850 (£190-£425)
- Sauer Model 38-H Type IV, military accepted
  ....$375-$850 (£190-£425)
- Sauer Model 38-H Type IV, SA marked
  .... $500-$3,000 (£250-£1,500)
- Sauer Model 38 Type IV, military accepted
  ....$300-$500 (£150-£250)
- Sauer Model 38-H Type V .....$250-$800 (£125-£400)
- Walther Model PP, .22 caliber ..$300-$850 (£150-£425)
- Walther Model PP, .25 caliber
  ....$1,650-$6,000 (£825-£3,000)
- Walther Model PP, .32 caliber, high polished finish
  ....$250-$700 (£125-£350)
- Walther Model PP, .32 caliber, milled finish
  ....$200-$600 (£100-£300)
- Walther Model PP, .380 caliber
  .... $500-$1,000 (£250-£500)
- Walther Model PP, .32 caliber, Duraluminum frame
  ....$450-$800 (£225-£400)
- Walther Model PP, .32 w/bottom magazine
  .... $450-$1,200 (£225-£600)
- Walther Model PP, .32 caliber with Verchromt finish
  .... $750-$2,250 (£375-£1,125)
- Walther Model PP, .32 caliber, blue, silver or gold finish
  and full engraving ....$1,200-$7,000 (£600-£3,500)
- Walther Model PP, .32 cal., w/Waffenamt stamp, high
  finish.................... $300-$1,300 (£150-£650)
- Walther Model PP, .32 cal., w/Waffenamt stamp, milled
  finish.........................$275-$500 (£140-£250)
- Walther Model PP, .32 cal., police, high polished finish
  .... $300-$1,300 (£150-£650)
- Walther Model PP, .32 cal., police, milled finish
  ....$300-$950 (£150-£475)
- Walther Model PP, .32 cal., NSKK marked
  .... $600-$3,000 (£300-£1,500)
- Walther Model PP, .32 cal., NSDAP group marked
  .... $550-$2,500 (£275-£1,250)
- Walther Model PP, .32 cal., PDM marked
  ....$500-$900 (£250-£450)
- Walther Model PP, .32 cal., RJ marked
  ....$450-$800 (£225-£400)
- Walther Model PP, .32 cal., RFV mark, high polished
  finish.........................$500-$800 (£250-£400)
- Walther Model PP, .32 cal., RBD marked
  .... $675-$2,200 (£340-£1,100)
- Walther Model PP, .32 cal., RpLt Marked
  ....$400-$1,000 (£200-£500)
- Walther Model PP, .32 cal., RZM marked
  .... $750-$3,000 (£375-£1,500)

SA inscribed, engraved and cased Walther PPK pistol,
$20,000-$25,000 (£10,000-£12,500). Rock Island Auction Company

Senior Nazi Party official's cased, engraved Walther
Model PP pistol with monogrammed ivory grips, $40,000-
$45,000 (£20,000-£22,500). Rock Island Auction Company

Gold-plated and engraved Walther PP pistol, $13,000-
$15,500 (£6,500-£7,750). Rock Island Auction Company

S/42 "K" date P.08 Luger pistol with original capture papers, $14,000-$15,000 (£7,000-£7,500). Rock Island Auction Company

Navy marked "K" date Luger, $3,000-$3,500 (£1,500-£1,750). Rock Island Auction Company

Walther Model PP semi-automatic pistol, milled finish, $200-$600 (£100-£300). Rock Island Auction Company

Late-war Army Mauser HSC pistol, $400-$1,400 (£200-£700). Rock Island Auction Company

The World War I Hebel-pattern flare pistols were used by the German troops in World War II as well, $200-$300. www.advanceguardmilitaria.com

Kriegsmarine Walther double-barrel Model SLD flare pistol, $800-$1,400.

www.advanceguardmilitaria.com

- Walther Model PP, .32 cal., Statens Vattenfallsverk marked . . . . **$375-$1,000 (£190-£500)**
- Walther Model PP, .32 cal., AC marked . . . . **$275-$500 (£140-£250)**
- Walther Model PP, .32 cal., Duraluminum frame . . . . **$500-$800 (£250-£400)**
- Walther Model PP, .380 cal., bottom release, Waffenamt marked . . . . **$550-$2,200 (£275-£1,100)**
- Walther Model PPK, .22 caliber . . . . **$350-$1,300 (£175-£650)**
- Walther Model PPK, .25 caliber . . . . **$1,000-$6,000 (£500-£3,000)**
- Walther Model PPK, .32 caliber, high polished finish . . . . **$300-$600 (£150-£300)**
- Walther Model PPK, .32 caliber milled finish . . . . **$250-$550 (£125-£275)**
- Walther Model PPK, .380 caliber . . . . **$750-$2,300 (£375-£1,150)**
- Walther Model PPK, .32 caliber, Duraluminum frame . . . . **$400-$1,000 (£200-£500)**
- Walther Model PPK, .32 caliber, Verchromt finish . . . . **$700-$2,500 (£350-£12,500)**
- Walther Model PPK, .32 cal., blue, silver or gold finish and full engraving . . . . . . **$1,500-$7,000 (£750-£3,500)**
- Walther Model PPK, .32 cal., marked "Mod. PP" . . . . **$1,500-$5,500 (£750-£2,750)**
- Walther Model PPK, .32 cal., panagraphed slided . . . . **$300-$700 (£150-£350)**
- Walther Model PPK, .32 cal., Czechoslovakia contract . . . . **$600-$1,600 (£300-£800)**
- Walther Model PPK, .32 cal., Allemagne marked . . . . **$500-$900 (£250-£450)**
- Walther Model PPK, .32 cal., Waffenamt proofed, high polished finish. . . . . **$500-$1,400 (£250-£700)**
- Walther Model PPK, .32 cal., Waffenamt proofed, milled finish. . . . . **$300-$900 (£150-£450)**
- Walther Model PPK, .32 cal., police, high polished finish. . . . . **$350-$750 (£175-£375)**
- Walther Model PPK, .32 cal., police, milled finish . . . . **$300-$700 (£150-£350)**
- Walther Model PPK, .32 cal., police, Duraluminum frame. . . . . **$400-$800 (£200-£400)**
- Walther Model PPK, .22 cal., late war, black grips . . . . **$500-$1,300 (£250-£650)**
- Walther Model PPK, .32 cal., party leader grips, brown . . . . **$2,500-$3,500 (£1,250-£1,750)**
- Walther Model PPK, .32 cal., party leader grips, black . . . . **$2,500-$5,000 (£1,250-£2,500)**
- Walther Model PPK, .32 cal., RZM marked . . . . **$500-$1.300 (£250-£650)**
- Walther Model PPK, .32 cal., PDM marked, Duraluminum frame . . . . . . **$800-$2,700 (£400-£1,350)**
- Walther Model PPK, .32 cal., RFV marked . . . . **$700-$2,200 (£350-£1,100)**
- Walther Model PPK, .32 cal., DRP marked . . . . **$500-$900 (£250-£450)**

- Walther Model PPK, .32 cal., Statens Vattenfallsverk ....$500-$1,500 (£250-£750)

Flare Pistols

- Fliegerleuchtpistole Model L double barrel flare pistol ....$350-$700 (£175-£350)
- Hebel flare pistol ....$200-$300 (£100-£150)
- LP 42 flare pistol.............$350-$450 (£175-£225)
- Walther Model 1934 flare pistol . $100-$200 (£50-£100)
- Walther-type, aluminum flare pistol ....$300-$350 (£150-£175)
- Walther-type, steel flare pistol. .$375-$450 (£190-£225)
- Walther-type, zinc flare pistol . .$500-$550 (£250-£275)
- Walther Model SLD double barrel flare pistol ....$800-$1,400 (£400-£700)

Submachine Guns

- Bergman MP28.......$9,000-$14,000 (£4,500-£7,000)
- Erma EMP..........$7,000-$12,000 (£3,500-£6,000)
- MP34/I.............$8,000-$11,000 (£4,000-£5,500)
- MP35/I.............$9,000-$12,000 (£4,500-£6,000)
- MP38 ....$18,000-$25,000 (£9,000-£12,500)
- MP40 ....$13,000-$18,000 (£6,500-£9,000)
- MP41 ....$12,000-$17,500 (£6,000-£8,750)

Rifles

- Model 98 transitional rifle .....$350-$875 (£175-£440)
- Model 98 rifle ....$350-$850 (£175-£425)
- Model 98k Carbine ....$250-$800 (£125-£400)

- Model 98k Carbine w/extended magazine ....$1,500-$4,500 (£750-£2,250)
- Model 98 training rifle .... $800-$5,000 (£400-£2,500)
- Model 98k sniper rifle (high turret) ....$4,000-$15,000 (£2,000-£7,500)
- Model 98k sniper rifle (low turret) ....$4,000-$13,000 (£2,000-£6,500)
- Model KAR 98k sniper rifle (short rail) ....$4,000-$10,000 (£2,000-£5,000)
- Model KAR 98k sniper rifle (long rail) ....$4,000-$14,000 (£2,000-£7,000)
- Model KAR 98k sniper rifle (claw mount) ....$4,000-$14,000 (£2,000-£7,000)
- Model KAR 98k sniper rifle (zf41 scope) ....$3,000-$7,500 (£1,500-£3,750)
- Model 1933 standard model short rifle ....$300-$800 (£150-£400)
- Model 1933 standard model carbine ....$500-$1,500 (£250-£750)
- Model 33/40 carbine . . .$2,000-$2,500 (£1,000-£1,250)
- Model 29/40 rifle (G29o) .... $350-$1,200 (£175-£600)
- Model 24 (t) rifle ....$200-$675 (£100-£340)
- Model VG-98 ....$1,500-$4,000 (£750-£2,000)
- Model VG-1 ....$3,500-$7,000 (£1,750-£3,500)
- Model VG-5 ....$5,500-$13,500 (£2,800-£6,750)
- Model G41 (M) rifle. .$8,500-$16,500 (£4,250-£8,250)
- Model G41 (W) rifle .....$1,500-$7,000 (£750-£3,500)
- Model G43(W) (K43) ....$1,250-$8,000 (£625-£4,000)
- Model FG42......$30,000-$50,000 (£15,000-£25,000)

This early German Gewehr 98 was converted to KAR 98K for SS use. It sold for $4,887.50 (~£2,440). Rock Island Auction Company

German G98/40 bolt action rifle, $750-$900 (£375-£450). Rock Island Auction Company

Standard German 98K carbine, $250-$800 (£125-£400). Charles D. Pautler

Early German G-41(M) semi-automatic rifle, $12,000-$16,500 (£6,000-£8,250). Rock Island Auction Company

Late-war German K43 semi-automatic rifle, $2,250-
$5,000 (£1,125-£2,500). Rock Island Auction Company

German 98K long side rail sniper rifle with Hensold-Wetzlar
scope, $9,000-$13,000 (£4,500-£6,500). Rock Island Auction Company

Early Walther G43 semi-automatic rifle, $1,300-
$1,900 (£650-£950). Rock Island Auction Company

The German G33/40 bolt action mountain rifle
was a version of the Czech VZ33 carbine, $2,000-
$2,500 (£1,000-£1,250). Rock Island Auction Company

German 98k high turret sniper rifle, $10,000-
$13,000 (£5,000-£6,500). Rock Island Auction Company

German K-43 sniper rifle with matching sniper scope mount,
$9,000-$13,000 (£4,500-£6,500). Rock Island Auction Company

- MKb42(W) ...... **$17,500-$20,000 (£8,750-£10,000)**
- MKb42(H) .... **$10,000-$16,000 (£5,000-£8,000)**
- MP43 .... **$9,000-$12,000 (£4,500-£6,000)**
- MP44 .... **$14,000-$17,500 (£7,000-£8,750)**
- StG44 .... **$12,000-$15,000 (£6,000-£7,500)**

Machine Guns

- MG13 .... **$17,500-$25,000 (£8,750-£12,500)**
- MG15 .... **$17,000-$22,000 (£8,500-£11,000)**
- MG15 water-cooled, ground gun
  .... **$15,000-$20,000 (£7,500-£10,000)**
- MG15 air-cooled, ground gun
  .... **$23,000-$28,000 (£11,500-£14,000)**
- MG34 .... **$30,000-$40,000 (£15,000-£20,000)**
- MG42 .... **$35,000-$45,000 (£17,500-£22,500)**

GREAT BRITAIN

Handguns

- Webley & Scott Mark IV, .380 caliber revolver
  .... **$200-$550 (£100-£225)**
- Enfield No. 2, Mark I revolver . . **$200-$400 (£100-£200)**
- Enfield No. 2, Mark I* revolver . **$200-$450 (£100-£225)**
- Model 1935 FN pistol .... **$600-$1,200 (£300-£600)**
- Smith & Wesson Model 10 M&P revolver
  .... **$650-$1,000 (£325-£500)**

Flare Pistols

- No.1 Mk I flare pistol .... **$300-$350 (£150-£175)**
- No. 2 Mk I flare pistol .... **$250-$350 (£125-£175)**
- No. 4 Mk I flare pistol .... **$300-$350 (£150-£175)**
- No. 3 Mk II flare pistol .... **$250-$300 (£125-£150)**
- No. 1 Mk III flare pistol .... **$300-$350 (£150-£175)**
- No. I Mk V flare pistol .... **$150-$250 (£75-£125)**
- No. 2 Mk V flare pistol .... **$150-$250 (£75-£125)**
- Webley Mk III* .... **$400-$500 (£200-£250)**
- Webley & Scott flare pistol ..... **$250-$300 (£125-£150)**
- Model M Royal Air Force flare pistol
  .... **$200-$250 (£100-£125)**

Submachine Guns

- Austen Mark I ...... **$12,000-$16,500 (£6,000-£8,250)**
- Lancaster Mk1 .... **$7,000-$9,500 (£3,500-£4,750)**
- Sten Mark II .... **$5,500-$6,500 (£2,750-£3,250)**
- Sten Mark III .... **$5,500-$6,500 (£2,750-£3,250)**
- Sten Mark V .... **$5,750-$7,500 (£2,875-£3,750)**

Rifles

- No. 1 SMLE Mark III .... **$75-$300 (£40-£150)**
- No. 1 SMLE Mark III Drill rifle . . . **$50-$150 (£25-£175)**
- Mo. 1 Mark III single shot rifle . . . **$65-$200 (£35-£100)**
- No. 1 Mark III grenade launching rifle
  .... **$100-$300 (£50-£150)**
- Lee-Enfield .410 musket (shotgun)
  .... **$55-$200 (£30-£100)**
- No. 1 SMLE Mark IV .... **$75-$250 (£40-£125)**
- No. 1 SMLE Mark III* .... **$100-$250 (£50-£125)**
- No. 1 SMLE Mark III* H ...... **$200-$500 (£100-£250)**
- No. 1 SMLE Mark V .... **$300-$750 (£150-£375)**
- No. 1 SMLE Mark VI .... **$1,000-$4,250 (£500-£2,125)**

Smith & Wesson Model 10 M&P revolver, British RAF issue, $650-$1,000 (£325-£500). Rock Island Auction Company

Mk V flare pistol manufactured by I.L. Berridge, $250-$350 (£125-£175). www.advanceguardmilitaria.com

Signal Pistol No. 1 Mk I, $300-$350. www.advanceguardmilitaria.com

---

"German machine gunners also felt like tough guys when they were shooting at us. Their MGs chattered at a faster and fiercer tempo than ours."

PFC. JOHN BABCOCK, 78TH U.S. INFANTRY DIVISION

- Rifle No. 4, Mark I trials model
  ....**$1,000-$2,800 (£500-£1,400)**
- Rifle No. 4, Mark 1.............**$150-$375 (£75-£190)**
- Rifle No. 4, Mark 1*...........**$100-$350 (£50-£175)**
- Rifle No. 4, Mark 1/2...........**$100-$300 (£50-£150)**
- Rifle No. 6, Mark 1........**$850-$3,000 (£425-£1,500)**
- Rifle No. 5, Mark 1............**$200-$600 (£100-£300)**
- SMLE Sniper rifle (optical sights)
  ....**$2,000-$4,000 (£1,000-£2,000)**
- SMLE Sniper rifle (telescopic sights)
  ....**$2,000-$4,000 (£1,000-£2,000)**
- No. Mark III* H.T. Sniper rifle
  ....**$1,500-$3,500 (£750-£1,750)**
- Rifle No. 4, Mark I (T) Sniper rifle
  ....**$500-$1,750 (£250-£875)**
- De Lisle Carbine......**$7,000-$10,000 (£3,500-£5,000)**
- Boys Anti-Tank Rifle ...**$3,000-$6,000 (£1,500-£3,000)**

Machine Guns

- Australian Bren... **$20,000-$35,000 (£10,000-£17,500)**
- Bren Mk1........**$30,000-$40,000 (£15,000-£20,000)**
- Bren Mk2........**$40,000-$47,000 (£20,000-£23,500)**
- Vickers Mark I.... **$30,000-$38,000 (£15,000-£19,000)**
- Hotchkiss Mark I ... **$10,000-$12,000 (£5,000-£6,000)**

HUNGARY

Handguns

- Steyr Model 1929 pistol ....**$200-$550 (£100-£275)**
- Steyr Model 37 pistol, Nazi proofed
  .... **$800-$1,550 (£400-£7,525)**

Submachine Guns

- Model 39 ....**$7,500-$15,000 (£3,750-£7,500)**
- Model 43 .... **$10,000-$15,000 (£5,000-£7,500)**

Rifles

- Mannlicher Model 1935 ....**$150-$375 (£75-£190)**
- Fegyvergyar Model Gewehr 98/40
  ....**$2,000-$2,600 (£1,000-£1,300)**
- Fegyvergyar Model 43 ....**$150-$700 (£75-£350)**
- Fegyvergyar 44.M...............**$75-$200 (£40-£100)**
- Steyr Model 95 ....**$40-$200 (£20-£100)**

ITALY

Handguns

- Modello 1874 revolver.........**$200-$900 (£100-£450)**
- System Bodeo Modello 1889 revolver (enlisted)
  ....**$100-$850 (£50-£425)**
- System Bodeo Modello 1889 revolver (officer)
  ....**$100-$850 (£50-£425)**

Generally, an Enfield No. 4 Mk I would sell for $150-$400, but when fitted as a sniper rifle with original No. 15 Mk I wooden storage case like this example, the price jumps to $4,000-$6,000 (£2,000-£3,000). Rock Island Auction Company

Enfield No. 4 Mk I with a later No. 32 Mk II scope and bayonet, $2,500-$3,500 (£1,250-£1,750). Rock Island Auction Company

Hungarian 98/40 rifle, $2,000-$2,600 (£1,000-£1,800). Rock Island Auction Company

Hungarian Femaru M1937 semi-automatic pistol with Nazi proofs, $800-$1,550 (£400-£775). Rock Island Auction Company

- Glisenti Model 1910 pistol . . . . .$250-$750 (£125-£375)
- Beretta Model 1915 pistol. . . . . .$200-$425 (£100-£215)
- Beretta Model 1915 pistol, 2nd variation
  . . . .$200-$450 (£100-£225)
- Beretta Model 1915/1919 pistol
  . . . .$150-$450 (£75-£225)
- Beretta Model 1923 pistol. . . . . .$250-$650 (£125-£325)
- Beretta Model 1931 pistol. . . . . .$200-$800 (£100-£400)
- Beretta Model 1934 pistol. . . . . . .$150-$500 (£75-£250)
- Beretta Model 1934 pistol, Air Force, RA marked
  . . . .$250-$700 (£175-£350)
- Beretta Model 1934 pistol, Navy, RM marked
  . . . .$275-$800 (£140-£400)
- Beretta Model 1935 pistol. . . . . .$200-$500 (£100-£250)

Submachine Guns

- Villar Perosa Model 1918
  . . . .$8,500-$10,000 (£4,250-£5,000)
- Beretta Model 1938A
  . . . . $10,000-$12,000 (£5,000-£6,000)
- Beretta Model 38/42 . .$8,500-$11,500 (£4,250-£5,750)
- F.N.A.-B Model 1943
  . . . . $10,000-$13,000 (£5,000-£6,500)

Rifles

- Carcano Fucile Modello 1891 rifle $75-$350 (£40-£175)
- Carcano Model 1891 carbine. . . . .$75-$350 (£40-£175)
- Carcano Model 1891 Truppe Speciali
  . . . .$100-$400 (£50-£200)
- Carcano Model 1891/24 carbine. . $75-$350 (£40-£175)
- Carcano Model 1891/28 carbine
  . . . .$1,000-$5,500 (£5,000-£2,750)
- Carcano Model 1938 short rifle. . . $75-$300 (£40-£150)
- Carcano Model 1938 T.S. carbine . $50-$250 (£25-£125)
- Carcano Model 1938/43 cavalry & T.S. carbine
  . . . .$100-$400 (£50-£200)
- Carcano Model 1941 . . . . $75-$300 (£40-£150)
- Carcano Italian Youth rifle . . . . .$200-$500 (£100-£250)
- Breda Model PG. . . . .$250-$800 (£125-£400)

Machine Guns

- Revelli Model 1914. . . . .$7,000-$9,500 (£3,500-£4,750)
- Revelli/Fiat Model 35. . .$6,500-$8,000 (£3,250-£4,000)
- Breda Model 30 . . . . . .$8,500-$10,500 (£4,250-£5,250)
- Breda Model 37 . .$25,000-$30,000 (£12,500-£15,000)

JAPAN

Handguns

- Type 26 revolver. . . . .$300-$850 (£150-£425)
- 4th Year Nambu pistol "Grandpa" pistol
  . . . .$1,500-$6,000 (£750-£3,000)
- 4th Year Nambu pistol "Papa" pistol
  . . . .$1,500-$2,700 (£750-£1,350)

- 4th Year Nambu pistol "Baby" pistol
  . . . .$1,200-$5,500 (£600-£2,750)
- 14th Year Nambu pistol "Type 14" pistol
  . . . .$850-$1,600 (£425-£800)
- Type 94 pistol . . . .$200-$650 (£100-£325)
- Hamada Skiki Type 2. . .$2,000-$5,000 (£1,000-£2,500)

Flare Pistols

- Type 10 flare pistol 37mm . . . . .$550-$600 (£275-£300)

Submachine Guns

- Type 100/40. . . . .$12,500-$15,000 (£6,250-£7,500)
- Type 100/44. . . . .$13,000-$16,500 (£6,500-£8,250)

Rifles

- Arisaka Type 30 rifle (M.1897) .$250-$800 (£125-£400)
- Arisaka Type 30 carbine . . . .$200-$700 (£100-£350)
- Arisaka Type 35 Navy rifle (M.1902)
  . . . .$200-$500 (£100-£250)
- Arisaka Type 38 rifle (M.1905) . .$150-$300 (£75-£150)
- Arisaka Type 38 carbine . . . .$250-$700 (£125-£350)
- Manchurian Mauser Rifle. . . . . .$300-$800 (£150-£400)
- Arisaka Type 44 carbine . . . . .$650-$1,500 (£325-£750)
- Arisaka Type 97 sniper rifle
  . . . . $650-$4,500 (£325-£2,250)
- Arisaka Type 99 short rifle. . . . . .$100-$300 (£50-£150)

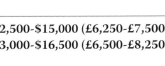

Kokura Arsenal Type 14 Nambu pistol, $850-$1,600 (£425-£800). Rock Island Auction Company

Japanese "Baby Nambu" pistol, $3,000-$5,500 (£1,500-£2,750). Rock Island Auction Company

Japanese Papa Nambu pistol, $1,500-$2,700 (£750-£1,350).

Rock Island Auction Company

- Arisaka Type 99 "last ditch" rifle
  ....**$150-$350 (£75-£175)**
- Type 100 paratroop rifle
  ....**$3,5000-$5,500 (£1,750-£2,750)**
- Type 2 paratroop rifle ..... **$750-$3,500 (£375-£1,750)**
- Type 99 sniper rifle .... **$850-$3,000 (£425-£1,500)**
- Type 5 rifle........ **$14,000-$28,000 (£7,000-£14,000)**

Machine Guns

- Type 1............ **$12,000-$17,500 (£6,000-£8,750)**
- Type 3............ **$10,000-$13,500 (£5,000-£6,750)**
- Type 11.............**$9,000-$12,000 (£4,500-£6,000)**
- Type 89.......... **$15,000-$20,000 (£7,500-£10,000)**
- Type 92.......... **$15,000-$20,000 (£7,500-£10,000)**
- Type 92 Lewis...... **$11,000-$15,000 (£5,500-£7,500)**
- Type 96.............**$7,500-$10,000 (£3,750-£5,000)**

- Type 97.............**$7,500-$10,000 (£3,750-£5,000)**
- Type 98........... **$10,000-$12,000 (£5,000-£6,000)**
- Type 99.............**$9,500-$13,500 (£4,750-£6,750)**
- Machine gun trainer ...**$2,000-$3,500 (£1,000-£1,750)**

Norway

Handguns

- Model 1883 revolver .... **$300-$1,250 (£150-£625)**
- Model 1887/93 revolver ..... **$300-$1,250 (£150-£625)**
- Kongsberg Vappenfabrikk M1914 pistol
  .... **$600-$3,000 (£300-£1,500)**
- Kongsberg Vappenfabrikk M1914 pistol w/Nazi proofs
  ....**$3,000-$5,000 (£1,500-£2,500)**

Japanese prewar Type 30 rifle, $600-$700 (£300-£350). Rock Island Auction Company

Arisaka Type 38 carbine, $250-$700 (£125-£350). Rock Island Auction Company

Early Jinsen Arsenal Type 38, $450-$800 (£225-£400). Rock Island Auction Company

Japanese Type 44 cavalry carbine, $650-$1,500 (£325-£750). Rock Island Auction Company

Izawa-produced fourth series Japanese Type 99 short rifle, $100-$300 (£50-£150). Rock Island Auction Company

Late war 40th series Type 99 short rifle, $100-$300 (£50-£150). Rock Island Auction Company

Condition is what pushes the value of the 24th series Type 99 rifle to $350-$480 (£175-£240). Rock Island Auction Company

Rifles

- Krag Jorgenson Model 1894 rifle
  . . . .**$450-$1,250 (£225-£625)**
- Krag Jorgenson Model 1895 carbine
  . . . .**$500-$1,500 (£250-£750)**
- Krag Jorgenson Model 1904 carbine
  . . . .**$450-$1,500 (£225-£750)**
- Krag Jorgenson Model 1907 carbine
  . . . .**$450-$1,500 (£225-£750)**
- Krag Jorgenson Model 1912 carbine
  . . . .**$350-$1,250 (£175-£625)**
- Krag Jorgenson Model 1923 sniper rifle
  . . . . **$650-$4,000 (£325-£2,000)**
- Krag Jorgenson Model 1925 sniper rifle
  . . . . **$650-$3,750 (£325-£1,875)**
- Krag Jorgenson Model 1930 sniper rilfe
  . . . . **$650-$3,750 (£325-£1,875)**

POLAND

Handguns

- Radom Ng 30 revolver. . . . . . .**$550-$1,800 (£275-£900)**
- Radom VIS-35 pistol . . . .**$400-$1,800 (£200-£900)**
- Radom VIS-35 pistol, Nazi captured, Waffenamt
  marked . . . . **$650-$2,000 (£325-£1,000)**
- Radom VIS-35, Nazi produced (Model 35[p])
  . . . .**$250-$850 (£125-£425)**
- Radom VIS-35, Nazi produce, bnz code
  . . . . **$650-$2,500 (£325-£1,250)**

Rifles

- Mauser M98 rifle . . . .**$100-$400 (£50-£200)**
- Mauser M98AZ rifle . . . .**$300-$800 (£150-£400)**
- Wz 29 short rifle. . . . .**$400-$1,000 (£200-£500)**
- Wz 98a rifle . . . .**$300-$900 (£150-£450)**
- Wz 29 .22 caliber training rifle
  . . . . **$900-$2,200 (£450-£1,100)**
- Kbk 8 Wz 31 .22 caliber training rifle
  . . . . **$900-$2,200 (£450-£1,100)**
- Model 1891 Nagant . . . .**$150-$300 (£75-£150)**
- Model 1891/30 sniper rifle . . . **$650-$1,350 (£325-£675)**

- Model 1891/98/25 Nagant . . . . .**$300-$550 (£150-£275)**
- Model 1944 Nagant . . . .**$400-$2,000 (£200-£1,000)**

Machine Guns

- Wz 28 BAR . . . . . . **$25,000-$35,000 (£12,500-£17,500)**

ROMANIA

Handguns

- Steyr Hahn Model 1911 pistol . .**$250-$500 (£125-£250)**
- Beretta Model 1934 Rumanian contract
  . . . .**$250-$550 (£125-£275)**

Rifles

- Mauser VZ24 short rifle . . . .**$300-$700 (£150-£350)**
- Rumanian Mosin-Nagant . . . .**$100-$300 (£50-£150)**

> "Besides having the standard issue infantry weapons, each [Japanese] rifle company also contained nine Nambu light machine guns and nine 50mm knee mortars."
>
> LT. BOB GREEN, 763RD TANK BN.

Norwegian M1914 .45 caliber pistol with Nazi proof marks, $3,000-$5,000 (£1,500-£2,500). Rock Island Auction Company

Polish Radom VIS Model 35 semi-automatic pistol with Nazi proof marks, $650-$1,200 (£325-£600). Rock Island Auction Company

Japanese Type 2 paratrooper rifle, $3,000-$3,500 (£1,500-£1,750). Rock Island Auction Company

Polish Model WZ29 rifle with bayonet, $400-$1,000 (£200-£500). Rock Island Auction Company

SOVIET UNION

Handguns

- Nagant Model 1895 "gas seal" revolver . . . . **$75-$250 (£40-£125)**
- Nagant Model 1895 .22 caliber revolver . . . . . **$350-$900 (£175-£450)**
- Nagant Model 1895 KGB revolver . . . . **$900-$2,000 (£450-£1,000)**
- FN 1900 Russian contract pistol . . . . **$350-$1,000 (£175-£500)**
- Tokarev TT-30 pistol. . . . . **$150-$550 (£75-£275)**
- Tokarev TT-33 pistol. . . . . **$150-$550 (£75-£275)**
- Tokarev TT-30 or TT-33 pistol, Nazi captured . . . . **$250-$850 (£125-£425)**
- Tokarev Model R-3 pistol . . . . . **$300-$700 (£150-£350)**
- Tokarev Model R-4 pistol . . . . . **$300-$700 (£150-£350)**
- TK TOZ pistol . . . . **$250-$500 (£125-£250)**

Submachine Guns

- PPD-1934/38 . . . . . . **$15,000-$20,000 (£7,500-£10,000)**
- PPD-1940 . . . . **$15,000-$20,000 (£7,500-£10,000)**
- PPsh-41 . . . . **$15,000-$18,000 (£7,500-£9,000)**
- PPS 1943 . . . . **$14,000-$18,000 (£7,000-£9,000)**

Rifles

- Mosin-Nagant Model 1891/30. . . **$100-$250 (£50-£125)**
- Mosin-Nagant Model 1891/30 sniper rifle w/3.5x scope . . . . **$500-$1,500 (£250-£750)**
- Mosin-Nagant Model 1891/30 sniper rifle w/4x scope . . . . **$1,000-$2,500 (£500-£1,250)**
- Model 1907/1910 carbine . . . . . . **$100-$200 (£50-£100)**
- Model 1938 carbine . . . . **$150-$400 (£75-£200)**
- Model 1944 carbine . . . . **$100-$300 (£50-£150)**
- Tokarev M1938 rifle (SVT) . . **$250-$1,400 (£125-£700)**
- Tokarev M1940 rifle (SVT) . . . . **$250-$750 (£125-£375)**
- Simonov AVS-36 rifle . . . . **$8,000-$12,000 (£4,000-£6,000)**

Machine Guns

- Model 1905 Maxim . . . . **$18,000-$25,000 (£9,000-£12,500)**
- Model 1910 Maxim (SPM) . . . . **$16,500-$25,000 (£8,250-£12,500)**
- Model DP 28 . . . . . . **$15,000-$20,000 (£7,500-£10,000)**
- Model DPM . . . . **$13,000-$18,500 (£6,500-£9,250)**
- Model DShK M38 . . . . **$42,500-$47,000 (£21,250-£23,500)**
- Goryunov SG43 . . **$23,000-$27,000 (£11,500-£23,500)**

SPAIN

Handguns

- Astra 400 (Model 1921) pistol . . . **$100-$500 (£50-£250)**
- Astra 400 pistol (Republican copy) . . . . **$150-$550 (£75-£275)**
- Astra 300 pistol. . . . . **$150-$500 (£75-£250)**
- Astra 300 pistol Nazi-proofed . . **$400-$850 (£200-£425)**

Russian Tokarev M1940 semi-automatic rifle, $500-$750 (£250-£375). Rock Island Auction Company

Russian M1940 SVT rifle with commercial mount and Russian PU sniper scope, $650-$1,000 (£325-£500). Rock Island Auction Company

Tokarev M1940 rifle fitted as a sniper rifle with short M1941 PU scope, $1,500-$1,800 (£750-£900). Rock Island Auction Company

Russian Mosin-Nagant sniper rifle fitted with an Ishevsk-made PU scope, $1,000-$1,500 (£500-£750). Rock Island Auction Company

- Astra 600 pistol. . . . .$150-$450 (£75-£225)
- Astra 600 pistol Nazi-proofed . .$500-$850 (£250-£425)
- Astra 900 pistol. . . . . $650-$2,500 (£325-£1,250)
- Astra 900 pistol German used (sn 32788-33774)
  . . . . $950-$3,750 (£475-£1,875)
- Astra 901 machine pistol
  . . . .$7,500-$10,000 (£3,750-£5,000)
- Astra 902 machine pistol
  . . . .$7,500-$10,000 (£3,750-£5,000)
- Astra 903 machine pistol
  . . . .$8,500-$10,000 (£2,250-£5,000)
- Astra 904 machine pistol (Model F)
  . . . . $10,000-$14,000 (£5,000-£7,000)
- Royal MM31 machine pistol (1st model)
  . . . . $20,000-$25,000 (£10,000-£12,500)
- Royal MM31 machine pistol (2nd model)
  . . . .$8,500-$10,000 (£4,250-£5,000)
- Super Azul machine pistol
  . . . .$9,000-$10,500 (£4,500-£5,250)
- Royal MM34 machine pistol
  . . . .$9,000-$10,500 (£4,500-£5,250)
- Llama Model IX pistol. . . . .$150-$400 (£75-£200)
- Llama Model IX-A pistol . . . .$150-$350 (£75-£175)
- Star Model 1914 pistol . . . .$150-$350 (£75-£175)
- Star Model CO pistol. . . . .$300-$650 (£300-£325)
- Star Model A pistol . . . .$200-$400 (£100-£200)
- Star Model A Super pistol . . . . .$200-$450 (£200-£225)
- Star Model M (MD) machine pistol
  . . . .$7,000-$8,000 (£3,500-£4,000)
- Star Model B pistol . . . .$200-$500 (£100-£250)

Submachine Guns

- Star Z-45 . . . . $15,000-$18,500 (£7,500-£9,250)

Rifles

- Mauser GM/G 98 modified rifle . $150-$350 (£75-£175)
- Mauser M1916 short rifle. . . . . . .$100-$300 (£50-£150)
- Mauser M1916 carbine. . . . .$100-$300 (£50-£150)
- Mauser M1933 standard model short rifle
  . . . .$200-$500 (£100-£250)
- Mauser M1943 short rifle. . . . . . .$100-$350 (£50-£175)

UNITED STATES

Handguns

- Colt U.S. Army Model 1917 revolver
  . . . . $350-$1,500 (£175-£7,500)
- Colt Official Police revolver (U.S. Army marked)
  . . . .$350-$800 (£175-£400)
- Colt Commando revolver (U.S. Army marked)
  . . . .$500-$900 (£250-£450)
- Colt Detective Special revolver (U.S. Army marked)
  . . . .$500-$700 (£250-£350)
- Colt Air Crewman Special (U.S. Army marked)
  . . . . $800-$4,500 (£400-£2,250)
- Colt Model 1911 pistol, serial number below 101
  . . . . $10,000-$40,000 (£5,000-£20,000)
- Colt Model 1911 pistol, serial number 100-500
  . . . .$4,500-$18,000 (£2,250-£9,000)
- Colt Model 1911 pistol, serial number 501-1000
  . . . . $6,500-$22,000 (£3,250-£11,000)
- Colt Model 1911 pistol, four digit number, w/fire blue
  parts . . . .$3,000-$14,500 (£1,500-£7,250)
- Colt Model 1911 pistol, four-digit number w/o fire blue
  parts . . . .$2,500-$7,000 (£1,250-£3,500)
- Colt Model 1911 pistol, four digit number, Navy, w/fire
  blue parts. . . . . $5,000-$22,000 (£2,500-£11,000)

Colt .380 caliber Model M pistol that belonged to General Curtis LeMay, $35,000-$40,000 (£17,500-£20,000). Rock Island Auction Company

Spanish Mauser M1933 standard short rifle, $200-$500 (£100-£250). Rock Island Auction Company

Spanish Astra Model 600 semi-automatic pistol with Nazi proof marks, $500-$850 (£250-£425). Rock Island Auction Company

Colt U.S. Army Colt Commando Model revolver, $500-$900 (£250-£450).
Rock Island Auction Company

Smith & Wesson Victory Model revolver, $250-$650 (£125-£325). Rock Island Auction Company

Smith & Wesson 1899 Navy Model revolver, $800-$1,200 (£400-£600). Rock Island Auction Company

Union Switch & Signal Company M1911A1 pistol, $2,000-$3,000 (£1,900-£1,500). Rock Island Auction Company

Liberator .45 caliber pistol with original box and ammunition, though estimated at $3,000-$4,000 (£1,500-£2,000), sold for $9,000 (£4,500)! Rock Island Auction Company

- Colt Model 1911 pistol, four digit number, Navy, w/o fire blue parts............**$2,500-$12,000 (£1,250-£6,000)**
- Colt Model 1911 pistol, serial number 3501-3800, USMC................**$3,500-$14,000 (£1,750-£7,000)**
- Colt Model 1911 pistol, serial number 36401-37650, USMC................**$2,500-$6,500 (£1,250-£3,250)**
- Colt Model 1911 pistol, five digit number, Navy ....**$2,500-$7,500 (£1,250-£3,750)**
- Colt Model 1911 pistol, five digit number, Army ....**$2,750-$8,000 (£1,375-£4,000)**
- Remington UMC Model 1911 pistol ....**$2,300-$6,500 (£1,150-£3,250)**
- Colt Model 1911 pistol, six digit number, Army ....**$1,500-$4,500 (£750-£2,250)**
- North American Arms Model 1911 .... **$10,000-$26,000 (£5,000-£13,000)**
- Colt Service Model Ace .22 caliber pistol ....**$1,200-$3,500 (£600-£1,750)**
- Colt Model 1911A1 pistol, transition model, 1924 ....**$2,200-$6,500 (£1,100-£3,250)**
- Colt Model 1911A1 pistol, transition model, 1937 ....**$4,000-$8,500 (£2,000-£4,250)**
- Colt Model 1911A1 pistol, 1938 production .... **$6,500-$20,000 (£3,250-£10,000)**
- Colt Model 1911A1 pistol, 1939 production ....**$2,000-$5,500 (£1,000-£2,750)**
- Colt Model 1911A1 pistol, 1940 production ....**$2,000-$5,500 (£1,000-£2,750)**
- Colt Model 1911A1 pistol, 1941 production ....**$1,500-$4,500 (£750-£2,250)**
- Colt Model 1911A1 pistol, 1942 production ....**$1,200-$3,000 (£600-£1,500)**
- Colt Model 1911A1 pistol, 1942 Navy ....**$1,500-$3,500 (£750-£1,750)**
- Colt Model 1911A1 pistol, 1943 production .... **$900-$2,500 (£450-£1,250)**
- Colt Model 1911A1 pistol, 1943 production w/commercial slide ......**$1,500-$3,200 (£750-£1,600)**
- Colt Model 1911A1 pistol, 1943 production, Canadian marked................**$1,500-$3,000 (£750-£1,500)**
- Colt Model 1911A1 pistol, 1944 production ....**$1,000-$2,300 (£500-£1,150)**
- Colt Model 1911A1 pistol, 1945 production, GHD marked................**$1,000-$2,100 (£500-£1,050)**
- Colt Model 1911A1 pistol, 1945 production, JSB marked ....**$2,500-$6,000 (£1,250-£3,000)**
- Colt Model 1911A1 pistol, 1945 production, no mark ....**$650-$1,800 (£325-£900)**
- Ithaca Model 1911A1 pistol **$800-$2,000 (£400-£1,000)**
- Remington Rand M1911A1 pistol, 1942-43 production..............**$1,200-$3,500 (£600-£1,750)**
- Remington Rand M1911A1 pistol, 1943 production..............**$1,000-$2,400 (£500-£1,200)**
- Remington Rand M1911A1 pistol, 1943-45 production..............**$850-$2,200 (£425-£1,100)**
- Singer Model 1911A1 pistol, educational order, 1941 ....**$14,000-$36,000 (£7,000-£18,000)**

- Union Switch M1911A1 pistol, 1943 production
  ....$2,000-$3,500 (£1,000-£1,750)
- Colt Military Woodsman Match pistol
  .... $500-$3,000 (£250-£1,500)
- Smith & Wesson Model 1899 Navy revolver
  .... $800-$1,200 (£400-£600)
- Smith & Wesson Victory Model revolver
  .... $250-$650 (£125-£325)
- Smith & Wesson Model 11......$150-$450 (£75-£225)
- High Standard Model B-U.S pistol
  .... $200-$775 (£100-£390)
- High Standard Model USA/Model HD
  .... $275-$800 (£140-£400)
- High Standard Model USA/Model HD-MS
  .... $4,500-$6,500 (£2,250-£3,250)
- GuideLamp Liberator .45 caliber pistol
  .... $350-$4,500 (£175-£2,250)

International Flare Signal Co. pistol, $300-$350 (£150-£175). www.advanceguardmilitaria.com

Flare Pistols

- Remington Mk III flare pistol .... $100-$150 (£50-£75)
- Sedgley Mk IV Navy flare pistol ... $75-$150 (£40-£75)
- Sedgley Mk V Navy flare pistol .. $150-$200 (£75-£100)
- Harrington & Richardson MK VI flare pistol
  .... $200-$350 (£100-£175)
- International brass frame flare pistol
  .... $200-$300 (£100-£150)
- International Model 52 .... $300-$350 (£150-£175)
- Sklar flare pistol .... $75-$150 (£40-£75)
- M8 Army Air Force flare pistol
  .... $100-$200 (£50-£100)

U.S. Navy Mk IV flare pistol, $75-$150 (£40- £75). www.advanceguardmilitaria.com

U.S. Navy Mk V flare pistol, $150-$175 (£75-£90). www.advanceguardmilitaria.com

Submachine Guns

- Reising 50............$4,000-$6,500 (£2,000-£3,250)
- Thompson Model 1921AC/21A, 1921/28 Navy
  .... $25,000-$35,000 (£12,500-£17,500)
- Thompson Model 1928A1
  .... $20,000-$35,000 (£10,000-£17,500)
- Thompson M1/M1A1
  .... $15,000-$20,000 (£7,500-£10,000)
- United Defense M42
  .... $12,500-$17,500 (£6,250-£8,750)
- M3............. $15,000-$20,000 (£7,500-£10,000)
- M3A1 .... $14,000-$19,000 (£7,000-£9,500)

U.S. Sklar flare pistol, $75-$150 (£40-£75).

www.advanceguardmilitaria.com

Rifles

- Pedersen rifle ....$6,500-$13,500 (£3,250-£6,750)
- Pedersen carbine .....$7,500-$16,500 (£3,750-£8,250)
- Model 1903 rifle.............$450-$900 (£225-£450)
- Model 1903 rifle, modified.....$400-$750 (£200-£375)
- Model 1903A3 rifle ....$400-$750 (£200-£375)
- Model 1903A4 sniper rifle
  ....$3,500-$5,000 (£1,750-£2,500)
- Model 1917 rifle.............$350-$800 (£175-£400)
- IBM M1 carbine.......... $450-$2,000 (£225-£1,000)
- Inland M1 carbine .... $450-$1,750 (£225-£875)
- Irwin Pedersen M1 carbine
  .... $700-$4,200 (£350-£2,100)

U.S. Army Air Force M8 flare pistol, $75-$150 (£40-£75).

www.advanceguardmilitaria.com

- National Postal Meter M1 carbine
  .... **$450-$2,000 (£225-£1,000)**
- Rockola M1 carbine....... **$500-$2,200 (£250-£1,100)**
- Saginaw (Grand Rapids) M1 carbine
  .... **$500-$2,200 (£250-£1,100)**
- Standard Products M1 carbine
  .... **$450-$2,100 (£225-£1,050)**
- Winchester M1 carbine.... **$500-$2,200 (£250-£1,100)**
- M1A1 paratrooper carbine
  .... **$2,500-$5,000 (£1,250-£2,500)**
- M2 carbine .... **$5,500-$7,000 (£2,750-£3,500)**
- Springfield M1 rifle, gas trap, serial number 81-52000
  .... **$25,000-$40,000 (£12,500-£20,000)**
- Springfield M1 rifle, gas port, serial number
  ca. 500000-410000 .... **$800-$4,500 (£400-£2,250)**
- Springfield M1 rifle, serial number 410000-3880000
  .... **$750-$3,500 (£375-£1,750)**
- Winchester M1 rifle, serial number 10000-100500
  .... **$3,000-$11,000 (£1,500-£5,500)**
- Winchester M1 rifle, serial number 100501-165000
  .... **$1,500-$7,000 (£750-£3,500)**
- Winchester M1 rifle, serial number 1200000-1380000
  .... **$1,000-$4,500 (£500-£2,250)**

- Winchester M1 rifle, serial number 2305850-2536493
  .... **$900-$3,000 (£450-£1,500)**
- Winchester M1 rifle, serial number 1601150-1640000
  .... **$850-$3,500 (£425-£1,750)**
- Harrington & Richardson M1 rifle
  .... **$550-$2,000 (£275-£1,000)**
- International Harvester M1 rifle
  .... **$450-$2,200 (£225-£1,100)**
- Lend-Lease M1 rifle......**$1,200-$2,500 (£600-£1,250)**
- Johnson Model 1941 rifle
  .... **$2,250-$6,500 (£1,250-£3,250)**
- Harrington & Richardson Reising Model 60 rifle
  .... **$500-$2,000 (£250-£1,000)**
- Harrington & Richardson Model 65 .22 caliber rifle
  .... **$150-$500 (£75-£250)**

Shotguns

- Ithaca Model 37 trench gun
  .... **$2,500-$12,000 (£1,250-£6,000)**
- Remington Model 10 trench gun
  .... **$7,500-$15,500 (£3,750-£7,750)**
- Remington Model 11 military riot gun
  .... **$1,000-$2,500 (£500-£1,250)**

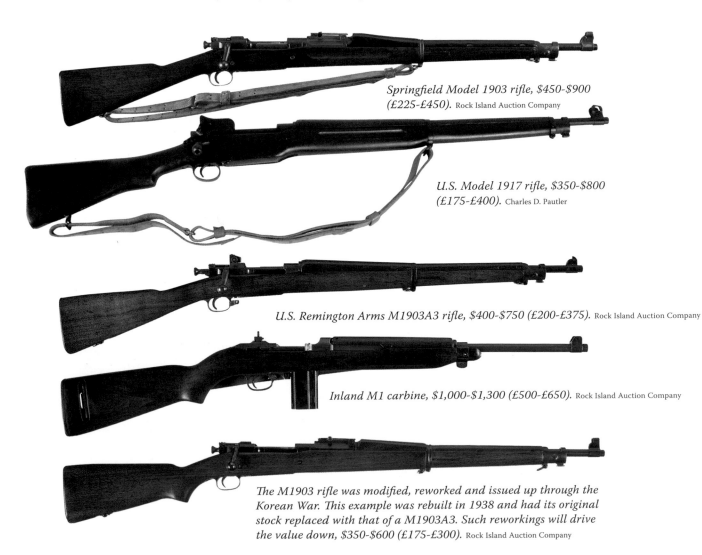

Springfield Model 1903 rifle, $450-$900 (£225-£450). Rock Island Auction Company

U.S. Model 1917 rifle, $350-$800 (£175-£400). Charles D. Pautler

U.S. Remington Arms M1903A3 rifle, $400-$750 (£200-£375). Rock Island Auction Company

Inland M1 carbine, $1,000-$1,300 (£500-£650). Rock Island Auction Company

The M1903 rifle was modified, reworked and issued up through the Korean War. This example was rebuilt in 1938 and had its original stock replaced with that of a M1903A3. Such reworkings will drive the value down, $350-$600 (£175-£300). Rock Island Auction Company

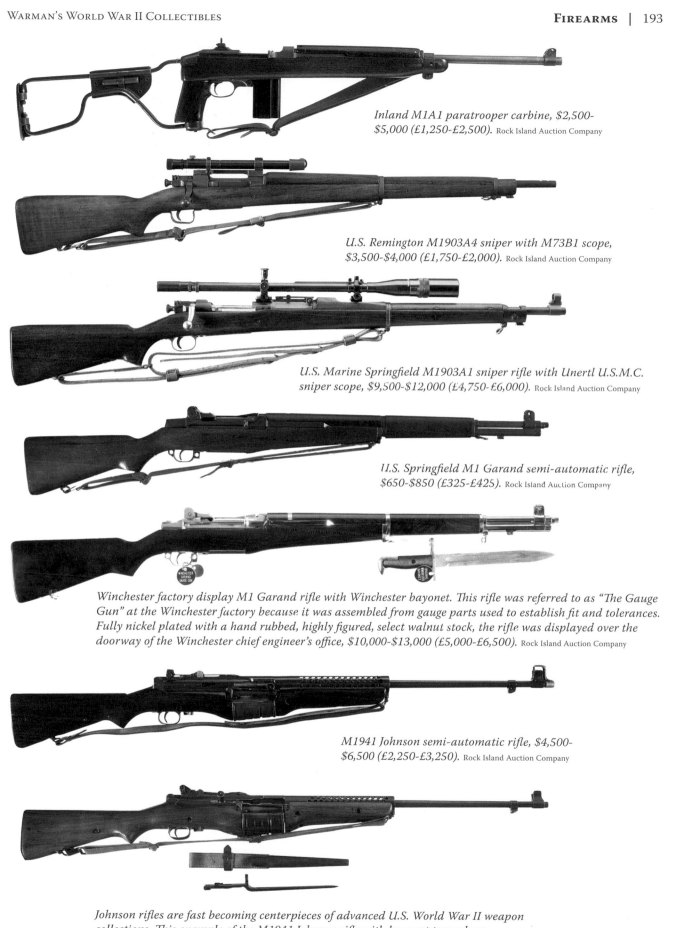

Inland M1A1 paratrooper carbine, $2,500-$5,000 (£1,250-£2,500). Rock Island Auction Company

U.S. Remington M1903A4 sniper with M73B1 scope, $3,500-$4,000 (£1,750-£2,000). Rock Island Auction Company

U.S. Marine Springfield M1903A1 sniper rifle with Unertl U.S.M.C. sniper scope, $9,500-$12,000 (£4,750-£6,000). Rock Island Auction Company

U.S. Springfield M1 Garand semi-automatic rifle, $650-$850 (£325-£425). Rock Island Auction Company

Winchester factory display M1 Garand rifle with Winchester bayonet. This rifle was referred to as "The Gauge Gun" at the Winchester factory because it was assembled from gauge parts used to establish fit and tolerances. Fully nickel plated with a hand rubbed, highly figured, select walnut stock, the rifle was displayed over the doorway of the Winchester chief engineer's office, $10,000-$13,000 (£5,000-£6,500). Rock Island Auction Company

M1941 Johnson semi-automatic rifle, $4,500-$6,500 (£2,250-£3,250). Rock Island Auction Company

Johnson rifles are fast becoming centerpieces of advanced U.S. World War II weapon collections. This example of the M1941 Johnson rifle with bayonet topped pre-auction estimates, selling for $7,475 (£3,740). Rock Island Auction Company

- Remington Model 31 military riot gun
  .... **$500-$1,600 (£250-£800)**
- Savage Model 720 riot gun
  .... **$900-$2,750 (£450-£1,275)**
- Stevens Model 520-30 trench gun
  .... **$550-$2,500 (£275-£1,250)**
- Stevens Model 620A trench gun
  ....**$1,250-$2,750 (£625-£1,375)**
- Winchester Model 97 take-down
  .... **$1,250-$3,250 (£625--£1,625)**
- Winchester Model 12 trench gun
  ....**$1,200-$5,500 (£600-£2,750)**

Machine Guns

- Browning M1917/M1917A1 water-cooled machine gun
  .... **$30,000-$38,000 (£15,000-£19,000)**
- Browning M1919A1/A2/A4/A6 air-cooled machine
  gun .... **$25,000-$30,000 (£12,500-£15,000)**
- Browning M2/M2HB .50 machine gun
  .... **$30,000-$35,000 (£15,000-£17,500)**
- Browning automatic rifle ("BAR")
  .... **$26,000-$32,000 (£13,000-£16,000)**
- Johnson M1941/M1944 automatic rifle
  .... **$25,000-$30,000 (£12,500-£15,000)**

U.S. Army Remington Model 11 shotgun with Cutts compensator, $1,000-$2,500 (£500-£1,250). Rock Island Auction Company

Winchester Model 1897 trench shotgun, $1,250-$3,250 (£625-£1,625). Rock Island Auction Company

Browning M2 .50 caliber machine gun, $26,000-$32,000 (£13,000-£16,000). Private collection

CHAPTER 6

BAYONETS, KNIVES, DAGGERS & SWORDS

Blades of one variety or another hold the fascination of many World War II collectors. The idea of soldiers marching into battle with bayonets affixed or brandishing large fighting knives or samurai swords in bloody hand-to-hand combat is a hard notion to dislodge from the spirited collector's mind. Even though blade-related wounds of any variety (including sword or saber-inflicted) were minimal during the war, the weapons that *could* have delivered such a wound are at the top of many collectors' "premium pieces" list. In fact, many collectors focus only on blades and forgo any other paraphernalia related to the war.

Bayonets are a rather straightforward item to collect. Rarely reproduced, plentiful, and with an endless variety, bayonets present a collector with the opportunity to assemble a diverse and meaningful collection for a minimum amount of cash.

Knives, on the other hand, present a bit cloudier picture. The knife was often regarded as a personal sidearm. As a result, many knives were personalized by the soldiers. These "field alterations" can either increase or decrease the value. Unfortunately, outside of collecting types of specific-issue examples, knife collecting can become quite subjective, making it hard to determine consistent values.

Collecting Hints

Pros:

- Swords, knives, bayonets and daggers are impressive. More so than other relics, blades capture the attention of young, old, male, and female. There is a lot of "wow" factor for the dollar when you own and display a sword, dagger or knife.
- Swords, knives, bayonets and daggers are relatively stable. As long as you don't handle the blades and you store the relics in a low humidity environment, deterioration will be minimal.
- Research has been intense in this area. Good references are available to assist a collector in determining origin, use and scarcity.
- Due to the materials involved, bayonets, knives, daggers and swords are plentiful.

Cons:

- Because iron is the primary material, these items are prone to rust if not stored in a very dry environment.
- Japanese samurai swords and German daggers sell for very large sums. The high values have lured some into creating swords and daggers by assembling pieces or by outright manufacturing forgeries.
- This is an area of the hobby where repairs and replacement of missing parts seems to be an accepted norm. It can be difficult to ascertain if the grip on a sword or all of the parts of it were always there, or if they had been expertly replaced in the last twenty years. This sort of alteration does not seem to be regarded as inappropriate within the hobby, so it is up to collectors (and not dealers) to know exactly what they are examining.

Availability ★★★★

Price ★★★★

Reproduction Alert ★★★

In the collecting world, the term "dagger," refers to a personal, ceremonial sidearm of the Third Reich. Other nations presented its soldiers with daggers, but German daggers captured the fancy of collectors from the very beginning of the hobby. German dagger and sword collecting is one of the most thoroughly researched areas in the hobby. Plenty of books are available to new collectors to guide them into the hobby with a degree of certainty. Before buying or selling a German dagger, take the time to do some research—a slight difference in a marking can mean the difference between hundreds or even thousands of dollars.

Japanese swords (referred to generically as "samurai swords") present another minefield in the hobby. Thankfully, there are a number of books and web sites dedicated to explaining the nuances of the Japanese blade collecting. Again, the difference of a few markings or components can mean the difference between a $300 blade and a $3,000 blade.

Though often used interchangeably, the terms "sword" and "saber" denote two very different weapons. A sword is a long, straight-bladed weapon with the primary function to denote rank or status. A saber, on the other hand, is a weapon with a curved blade with the sole function being that of enabling the user to strike a blow. Sabers were usually intended for mounted personnel.

BELGIUM

MODEL 1916/24 BAYONET AND FROG

- 17-1/2" double-edged blade in excellent polish retains dark factory finish, crossguard with 1924 size muzzle ring, side stamped with accountability number, walnut two-piece scale grips, and pommel with functional press stud. Scabbard retains blued finish and is complete with black leather frog . . . . **$95 (£50)**

M1924 GENDARMERIE BAYONET

- 17-1/2" blade with the distinctive Gendarmerie "T" back spine, crossguard with 1924 pattern bushed muzzle ring, walnut wood grips, and pommel with functional press stud attachment . . . . **$65 (£35)**

MODEL 1930 B.A.R. MOUNT RIFLE BAYONET

- 17-5/8" cruciform blade with dark finish, ricasso with stepped muzzle ring stamped with accountability number "978", cylindrical steel grip, and notched pommel with locking stud. This rare bayonet fits the standard Belgian Mauser rifle, but was also designed to be used with a very unusual scabbard that would convert the rifle, bayonet, and scabbard into an anti-aircraft mount for the Belgian FN Browning Automatic Rifle. . . . .**$550 (£275)**

FINLAND

TYPE 30 JAPANESE BAYONET, FINNISH WINTER WAR REISSUED

- Japanese Type 30 bayonet with fullered blade in good finish, ricasso with Tokyo arsenal mark as well as a possible secondary Finnish mark, hilt with hooked quillion crossguard, forward face with stud attached above blade which locks into a slot on the scabbard throat; this appears to be a Finnish alteration. Wooden grips now crosshatched and all hilt metal Finnish arsenal reblued. Early metal scabbard with altered throat slotted for stud and blued to match hilt. Complete with brown leather double loop Japanese frog with aluminum buckle. The Finns acquired a number of Japanese rifles and bayonets from the Red Army during the Independence War of 1918 . . . .**$275 (£140)**

M1928 BAYONET

- Model 1928 bayonet for the Nagant rifle, 11-3/4" fullered blade in fair polish with a few age spots and light pitting near the tip, ricasso with "HACKMAN & CO." maker's stamp, crossguard with forward swept quillion and muzzle ring, dark wood two-piece grips, and pommel with press stud attachment mechanism. Ribbed steel scabbard has blued finish . . . .**$265 (£135)**

M1939 BAYONET/FIGHTING KNIFE

- Bayonet for the Finnish modified Mosin-Nagant rifle has 7-1/8" clipped point blade, ricasso marked "O.Y.VELJEKSET KULMALAA.B" and "Sk.Y", indicating use by the elite White Guard. One-piece wooden grips and pommel with oil hole, complete with olive green leather scabbard with integral frog and retaining strap with broad metal reinforcement on the edge and back of the scabbard tip retaining 80% olive green painted finish, stamped "Sk.Y" near throat. This limited production bayonet was used by the Finns as a fighting knife. . . . .**$425 (£215)**

1922 PATTERN TRENCH KNIFE

- 1922 pattern Finnish issue trench knife, 5-5/8" clipped point fullered blade has "HACKMAN & Co." maker stamp at the ricasso, short oval cross guard with hooked quillion, and nickeled backstrap and pommel cap combination encloses black two-piece checkered wood grips. Complete with black finished metal scabbard with the traditional hooked point at the end, top with thin brown leather belt loop with sliding retaining strap. . . . .**$350 (£175)**

MODEL 1938 TOKAREV BAYONET AND SCABBARD

- Model 1938 SVT bayonet with 14" bright finished blade, with deep, overall pitting, ricasso with accountability marking, crossguard with traces of blued finish, pommel with unusual shaped button stud and walnut grips. Complete with tubular steel scabbard . . . . . .**$400 (£200)**

FRANCE

LEBEL BAYONET AND FROG

- M1886/91/16/35 short pattern Lebel bayonet with 12-3/4" cruciform blade and white metal hilt. Scabbard is complete with brown WWI pattern sewn leather belt frog with retaining strap . . . . **$85 (£45)**

LEBEL BAYONET AND SCABBARD

- Model 1886/35 with quadrilateral blade shortened to 13-1/2". Curved quillion and white alloy handle complete in appropriate blued metal scabbard. . . . . **$75 (£40)**

MAS 1936 BAYONET

- 17" overall length, cruciform blade with dark even finish, cross hatched finger grip and two digit number stamped on the reverse cap . . . . **$45 (£25)**

The French Model 1886 Lebel bayonet was shortened and issued in the 1930s. With scabbard and frog, it sells for $65-$95 (£35-£50). www.advanceguardmilitaria.com

GERMANY

Knives

SOLDIER'S FIGHTING KNIFE

* German "boot" knife has 5-1/2" unfullered blade and unmarked ricasso, short oval steel guard, wood two-piece scale contoured grips. Knife is complete with black painted steel scabbard fitted with spring steel belt attachment clip . . . . **$145 (£75)**

CLOSE COMBAT KNIFE

* German close combat knife with steel scabbard in black finish. Reverse of scabbard has spring steel attachment clips. Knife has wood two-piece grips . . . . **$150 (£75)**

CLOSE COMBAT KNIFE

* 5-5/8" blade, ricasso stamped in script "42 CVL." Short crossguard, and two-piece contoured wood scale grips. Complete with scabbard retaining black painted finish and spring clip belt attachment . . . . **$200 (£100)**

LUFTWAFFE FALLSCHIRMJÄGER GRAVITY KNIFE, SECOND PATTERN

* 4" blade. Ricasso marked "PAUL WEYERSBERG & CO. SOLINGEN" in an oval cartouche. Spike attachment has Luftwaffe proof stamp. Walnut two-piece grips show light wear, release switch functions smoothly. Base has lanyard ring . . . . **$450 (£225)**

FALLSCHIRMJÄGER GRAVITY KNIFE, EARLY "TAKE-DOWN" PATTERN

* Gravity knife has 4" blade exhibiting repeated sharpening. Bolster has arrow stamp. Spike attachment has Luftwaffe proof stamp and walnut two-piece grips show only normal light wear . . . . **$575 (£290)**

Bayonets

CZECH VZ-24 GERMAN-MODIFIED BAYONET

* 12" fullered blade in factory subdued finish. Cutting edge faces toward the muzzle ring. Ricasso marked "CSZ / N." Double riveted crossguard with "high ears" muzzle ring ground down to leave about one quarter of the bottom of the ring, hilt with wooden grips; steel scabbard with black painted finish . . . . **$55 (£30)**

98K MAUSER BAYONET, "BERG & CO.," MATCHING NUMBERS

* Issue pattern Mauser bayonet marked "Berg&Co." with an accountability number. Scabbard has matching accountability number and maker's stamp "Berg&Co. 1940." Unusual to find bayonets with matching numbers. . . . . **$145 (£75)**

LUFTWAFFE RLM MARKED 98/05 N/A. BAYONET

* Fullered blade with "Weyersberg & Co. / Solingen" maker stamp, and spine with Prussian proof and "17" date. Hilt has age-toned finish, ricasso with "RLM" stamp on left side, "1920" on the right, and walnut ribbed grips with flashguard. Bayonet is complete with metal scabbard retaining several layers of painted finish. "RLM" or Reichsluftfahrtministerium marked bayonets were part of Germany's effort to avoid the restrictions of the Versailles treaty, marking equipment to the "National Air Transport Ministry" (under Göring) was less obvious than "Luftwaffe" . . . . **$325 (£180)**

German soldier's fighting knife, $150-$250 (£75-£125). www.advanceguardmilitaria.com

German combat knife, $200-$250 (£100-£125). www.advanceguardmilitaria.com

Luftwaffe Fallschirmjäger gravity knife, $350-$650 (£175-£325). Charles D. Pautler

84/98 MAUSER RIFLE BAYONET, "HÖRSTER"

- 84/98 issue pattern Mauser bayonet retains 85% blued finish. Ricasso has "E.u.F. Hörster" maker stamp on obverse and accountability number "1958" on reverse.
....$85 (£45)

MAUSER RIFLE BAYONET, "HÖRSTER," WITH MATCHING NUMBERS

- 84/98 issue pattern Mauser bayonet retains 95% blued finish, ricasso has "E.u.F. Hörster" maker stamp on obverse and accountability number "1607" on reverse. Scabbard is service worn with traces of black finish blending with light oxidation and patina, throat has "1607" on obverse; "E.u.F. Hörster" on reverse with "1940" date.............................$165 (£85)

MAUSER SAWBACK K98 BAYONET WITH MATCHING NUMBERS

- Early war example 84/98 pattern bayonet with a fullered sawback blade, ricasso marked with "J Sch" maker stamp, reverse with "3833 / C" accountability number, pommel has Waffenamt proofs, scabbard throat stamped "3833 / C" on frog stud side, reverse with "J. Sch / 1937".
....$425 (£215)

OFFICER'S KURZES 98 DRESS BAYONET

- KS 98 has 9-7/8" fullered blade, ricasso marked with "ALCOSO / SOLINGEN" maker's trademark, hilt has checkered black composition grips, KS 98 profile pommel, functional press-stud, and attachment mortise with original red thick felt filler. Includes black lacquered private purchase scabbard and brown leather frog.
....$125 (£65)

98/05 N/A WEIMAR REISSUED BAYONET, SAXON POLICE "1920" AND UNIT MARKED

- Fullered blade retains 80% blued finish, ricasso with very faint WKC maker stamp, and spine with Prussian proof and "17" date stamp, hilt has ribbed walnut grips, crossguard, pommel with Weimar modified press-stud, and flashguard with traces of blued finish; crossguard stamped "1920" with "184" individual number matching the scabbard, opposite side with large "S.P.L. 443" Saxon Police markings. Includes blued steel scabbard.
....$325 (£165)

The price of this Mauser bayonet by Hörster escalates because the bayonet and scabbard numbers match, $150-$180 (£75-£90). www.advanceguardmilitaria.com

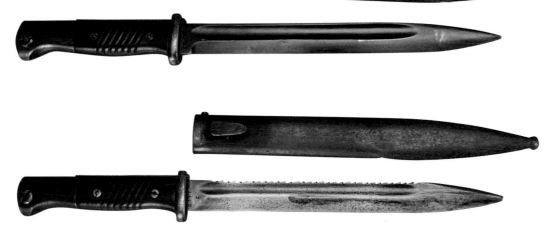

84/98 Mauser rifle bayonet by "Hörster" with scabbard, $65-$85 (£35-£45). www.advanceguardmilitaria.com

Very early Mauser sawback K98 bayonet with matching numbers, $400-$475 (£200-£240). www.advanceguardmilitaria.com

CARBINE PATTERN DRESS BAYONET, "SEILHEIMER"

- 7-3/4" fullered blade with false edge forward of fuller, ricasso with "PS" (Paul Seilheimer, Solingen) trademark. Crossguard has rearward swept quillion, cross-hatched black composition scales retained by two rivets, and eagle head pommel with functional press stud. Scabbard retains 75% black painted finish . . . .**$125 (£65)**

POLICE BAYONET WITH STAG GRIPS AND BELT FROG

- 13" fullered blade with bright finish, ricasso mark with "Paul Weyersberg & Co. / Solingen" maker's stamp. Hilt has nickeled finish on metal surfaces, crossguard cast with oak leaf motifs and has unit stamp "S.W.II.198," stag two-piece grips, and non-functional eagle's head pommel. Black leather scabbard has nickeled throat and drag, complete with brown leather belt frog. . . . . . **$525 (£265)**

POLICE CLAMSHELL DRESS BAYONET

- 11" fullered blade with "Anton Wingen Jr / Solingen" maker's stamp with armored knight logo and retains original brown leather scabbard washer. Hilt has nickel fittings, clamshell with eagle, stag grips with Police eagle grip ornament, and crossguard with stamped accountability number "12." Scabbard of black leather with nickel fittings remains in matching excellent condition. . . . .**$950 (£475)**

84/98 BAYONET, KRIEGSMARINE UNIT MARKED WITH WAR ART

- Ricasso has "W.K.C." maker's stamp, "38" date on the spine, and accountability number on reverse. Hilt has walnut grips, flashguard with service dents, pommel and crossguard with 80% blackened finish. Guard has Nordsee unit stamp "N 4531." Scabbard retains 90% blued finish, with early secret rearmament period "S-code" maker's stamp "S / 241" and date "1936." Below that is a gray painted eagle and swastika insignia flanked by "M / IV" and "Ruby" below . . . .**$295 (£150)**

REGIMENT 11 ENGRAVED PRESENTATION BAYONET

- Model 1940 dress "carbine" bayonet with 8" blade with fuller and false edge in excellent polish, obverse with leaf motifs and inscription on frosted ground "Fur Erinnerung an meine Dienstzeit beim Inf. Rgt. 11." Unmarked ricasso with leather scabbard washer, short crossguard with swept quillion, black checkered composition grips secured by two low-mounted rives, and bird's head pommel with functional press stud. Complete with scabbard retaining 95% black finish and black leather belt frog, outstanding example . . . .**$375 (£190)**

84/98 BAYONET, KRIEGSMARINE UNIT MARKED

- Bayonet has "S/239.K" accountability stamp and "500" on reverse. Hilt has blued finish and walnut grips, cross-

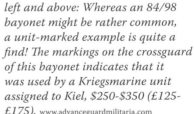

left and above: Whereas an 84/98 bayonet might be rather common, a unit-marked example is quite a find! The markings on the crossguard of this bayonet indicates that it was used by a Kriegsmarine unit assigned to Kiel, $250-$350 (£125-£175). www.advanceguardmilitaria.com

The crossguard on this early wood-handled 84/98 bayonet is stamped "O.5472P." This is a Marine property stamp indicating Ostsee (Baltic) fleet $250-$350 (£125-£175). www.advanceguardmilitaria.com

below and right: These two photos show the details of the mounted style bayonet frog used on many German 84/98 pattern bayonets. www.advanceguardmilitaria.com

guard with "O.1615.K" Marine property stamp indicating Ostsee (Baltic) and port - Kiel. Scabbard has mismatched accountability number and 1940 maker code. Mounted pattern black leather frog has Marine "Eagle-M" proof stamp . . . . **$275 (£140)**

84/98 BAYONET, KRIEGSMARINE UNIT MARKED

- Bayonet with "CARL EICKHORN" maker's stamp, "38" date on the spine and "3303" accountability number on reverse. Crossguard stamped "O.5472P." This is a Marine property stamp indicating Ostsee (Baltic) fleet. Scabbard has mismatched accountability number and "cof / 44" (also Eickhorn) maker's stamp . . . . **$200 (£100)**

84/98 MAUSER RIFLE BAYONET
WITH SCABBARD AND FROG

- Fullered blade with "43 cvl" maker's date and "1597" accountability number. Hilt has brown oxidized age patina on the pommel, two-piece wood grips, and flashguard. Scabbard has mismatched accountability number and brown oxidized patina. Black leather mounted pattern scabbard has "KVZ / 1942" maker's date stamp on the reverse . . . . **$95 (£50)**

84/98 MAUSER RIFLE BAYONET WITH
SCABBARD AND FROG: MATCHING NUMBERS

- Fullered blade in excellent polish retains 90% blued finish, ricasso has "44 fnj" maker's date and "1186" accountability number. Hilt has blued finish, red-brown Bakelite grips, and flashguard. Scabbard has matching accountability number, retains blackened finish, and is fitted with black leather mounted pattern scabbard marked with accountability number on the reverse . . . . . **$195 (£100)**

98/05 N/A WEIMAR REISSUED
BAYONET, BAVARIAN POLICE

- Fullered blade with faint "Fichtel & Sachs / Schweinfurt" maker stamp, and spine with Bavarian proof and "17" date stamp. Hilt has ribbed walnut grips, crossguard, pommel with unmodified press-stud. Crossguard stamped "1920," opposite side with large "Pw.B." Bavarian "Polizeiwehr Bayern" stamp. Includes blued steel scabbard with matching "Pw.B" stamp . . . . **$375 (£190)**

98K DRESS BAYONET, "HÖRSTER"

- Fullered blade in excellent polish has "E.u.F. Hörster / Solingen" maker's stamp and leather scabbard guard. . . . . **$125 (£80)**

98K DRESS BAYONET, "ALEX COPPEL"

- 7-3/4" "carbine blade" in very bright polish, ricasso marked with balance scales and initials "A / C / S" logo of Alex Coppel. Retains leather scabbard washer, metal scabbard has black finish, black lacquered leather frog present . . . . **$120 (£60)**

84/98 DRESS BAYONET, "PAUL SEILHEIMER"

- 9-3/4" fullered blade finished bright, ricasso marked with "Paul Seilheimer / Solingen" stamp . . . . **$110 (£55)**

98K DRESS BAYONET, "C.D. SCHAAFF"

- Dress bayonet has 9-7/8" fullered blade with "C.D. Schaaff / Solingen" on obverse ricasso, reverse with pipe-smoking mariner maker's logo. Hilt has black plastic grips secured by two rivets, and bird's head pommel with functional press stud, red felt filler in the mortise. Bayonet is complete with black lacquered steel scabbard fitted with brown leather . . . . **$145 (£75)**

Later 84/98 bayonets were fitted with Bakelite grips. This does not generally affect the value of a bayonet. This particular example, because of matching blade and scabbard numbers in addition to an original, very good condition frog, is worth $175-$200 (£90-£100). www.advanceguardmilitaria.com

The finish of the scabbard of this dress bayonet by "Hörster" would be considered at about 70%. www.advanceguardmilitaria.com

This particular 84/98 bayonet features a "W.K.C." maker's stamp, "38" date on the spine, and accountability number on reverse. Hilt has walnut grips. Guard has Nordsee unit stamp "N 4531." The scabbard has the early rearmament period "S-code" maker's stamp "S / 241" and date "1936." Below that is a gray painted eagle and swastika, unit mark and name, $300-$400 (£150-£200). www.advanceguardmilitaria.com

98K DRESS BAYONET, "E. PACK & SOHNE"

- Dress bayonet with 9-1/2" fullered blade in good polish finished bright with "E. Pack & Sohne / Solingen" and trademark maker's logo on the ricasso. Hilt has black plastic grips secured by two rivets. Bayonet is complete with steel scabbard fitted with brown leather frog. $125 (£65)

98K DRESS BAYONET, "EICKHORN"

- Dress bayonet in excellent polish finished bright with "Original / Eickhorn / Solingen" and trademark maker's logo on the ricasso. Bayonet is complete with steel scabbard retaining 70% black finish, frog stud a bit loose. $145 (£75)

LUFTWAFFE 98/05 REISSUE BAYONET

- 98/05 sawback-removed bayonet with fullered blade. Hilt retains blued finish on metal with "55" stamped in the crossguard. Bayonet has Reichswehr alteration style press stud. Black leather frog has Luftwaffe eagle issue stamp. $255 (£130)

FIRE POLICE DRESS BAYONET

- 9-5/8" fullered blade, unmarked ricasso, recurved crossguard, black checkered composition two-piece scale grips secured by two domed rivets and bird's head pommel. Complete with black painted metal scabbard retaining its original black leather belt frog ... $85 (£45)

DRESS BAYONET, ARMY NCO

- 7-7/8" "carbine" blade has fuller and false edge, in excellent polish finished bright, ricasso has scarce "Anton Wingen / Solingen" maker's stamp and armored knight logo, complete with original leather scabbard washer. Hilt has short crossguard, checkered black composition grips, and bird's head pommel with functional press stud. Black metal scabbard has black leather frog. Frog also has Army green and silver aluminum bullion NCO's bayonet troddel $135 (£70)

ARMY ENGRAVED DRESS BAYONET, "TIGER"

- Dress bayonet with 7-7/8" fullered blade in excellent polish featuring an acid-etched center panel on one side with inscription "Fur Erinnerung / an meine Dienstzeit" (for memory of my service), flanked by a double-decal helmet on one side and Army eagle and swastika national emblem on the other. Ricasso has prowling tiger maker's logo, opposite side with "TIGER / Solingen." Complete with scabbard $345 (£175)

Dress bayonets derive their value from condition of the blade and the scarcity of the maker mark found on the ricasso, $100-$250 (£50-£125). www.advanceguardmilitaria.com

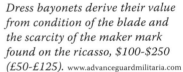

Mauser dress bayonet by one of the best blade makers, "Eickhorn," $120-$200 (£60-£100). www.advanceguardmilitaria.com

Fire police dress bayonet. Black leather frog marked "Carl Hepting & Co. / Stgt. Feuerbach / 1941," $60-100 (£30-£50). www.advanceguardmilitaria.com

Landsjaegerei ("rural police") dress bayonet with scabbard, frog and portapee, $650-$1,000 (£325-£500). Rock Island Auction Company

Daggers

HITLER YOUTH KNIFE

- Unfullered blade dark with gray age patina, engraved with motto "Blut und Ehre!," ricasso with RZM stamp and 1938 date, reverse ricasso with R. Klaas crane maker's logo, nickeled crossguard and pommel.
....**$265 (£135)**

ARMY OFFICER'S DAGGER, WKC

- Double-edge blade well preserved under old protective lacquered finish, would easily be removed, ricasso with Knight's helmet logo and "WKC SOLINGEN" maker's stamp, crossguard with Army eagle, and spiral-ribbed orange composition grip. Scabbard with dull gray age patina ....**$385 (£190)**

ARMY OFFICER'S DAGGER, SPITZER

- Double edge blade in good finish, tip slightly bent, ricasso with "Lion" logo and "C. GUSTAV SPITZER / SOLINGEN" maker's mark. Dagger retains aluminum bullion portepee.........................**$525 (£265)**

ARMY OFFICER'S DAGGER, ALCOSO

- Double-edged blade in very good polish has "ALCOSO / SOLINGEN" maker's logo at the ricasso, early silver fittings throughout, and brown composition twist grip. Scabbard has pebbled finish and is mounted with two suspension loops ....**$495 (£250)**

RED CROSS LEADER'S DAGGER

- Deutsches Rotes Kreuz leader's dagger with 9-3/4" unmarked double-edged blade in excellent polish and leather scabbard washer. Hilt has straight oval crossguard with oval langlet and DRK eagle insignia, light orange composition grip, and heavy tapered flat oval pommel. Scabbard has square hanger rings differentiating this from the DRK Social Welfare leader's dagger.
....**$950 (£475)**

RED CROSS ENLISTED HEWER

- 10-1/2" sawtooth blade with sharpening marks along the edge, sawtooth spine, squared tip, ricasso marked "GES. GESCHUTZ." Hilt has nickel crossguard with Red Cross eagle and swastika insignia, flat head pommel and black composition grips, checkered on the obverse according to pattern. Hewer is complete with metal scabbard retaining 70% black painted finish, nickel throat and tip, and complete with its original black leather frog.
....**$725 (£365)**

KRIEGSMARINE OFFICER'S DAGGER

- 9-7/8" double-fullered blade with attractive etching of scrollwork, fouled anchor, and sea creatures on both sides. Ricasso has Eickhorn maker's logo. Hilt retains gilt finish with wire wrapped white composition grip and national eagle and swastika pommel cap. Scabbard has gilt finish with oak leave bands terminating in hanger rings and lightning bolt design near the tip.......**$895 (£450)**

Hitler Youth knives are quite common, so condition makes all the difference. These with rust and flaking paint are worth about $125-$250-$70 (£65-£125). In very good condition, $250-$350 (£125-£175). Charles D. Pautler

This example of an HJ knife has been polished so many times the lightly etched inscription on the blade has disappeared, $150-$250 (£75-£125). www.advanceguardmilitaria.com

Depending on condition and maker, German Army officer daggers will run from $285-$600 (£145-£300). www.advanceguardmilitaria.com

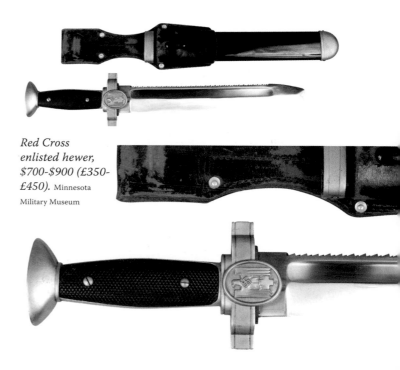

Red Cross enlisted hewer, $700-$900 (£350-£450). Minnesota Military Museum

KRIEGSMARINE OFFICER'S DAGGER, F.W. HÖLLER BLADE WITH TALL SHIP MOTIFS

- 9-7/8" double-edged and double-fullered blade with etching of scrollwork and fouled anchors and tall sailing ships. Ricasso marked with oval "F.W. Höller / Solingen" maker's logo. Dagger hilt is correctly wrapped with aluminum bullion portepee . . . . **$1,100 (£550)**

LUFTWAFFE OFFICER'S DAGGER, FIRST PATTERN

- First pattern Luftwaffe officer's dagger with double-edged blade in good polish with a light coat of preservative oil. Ricasso has Puma maker's logo, three-tiered wing crossguard with mobile swastika emblem, twisted silver wire wrap is intact. Dagger is complete with blue leather scabbard with silvered metal fittings . . . . **$665 (£335)**

LUFTWAFFE OFFICER'S DAGGER, FIRST PATTERN "EMIL VOOS"

- "Emil Voos / Solingen" maker's logo, leather scabbard washer, and hilt with nickel silver fittings on the crossguard and pommel, grip retains its blue leather wrap. . . . . **$695 (£350)**

LUFTWAFFE OFFICER'S DAGGER, SECOND PATTERN

- Double-edged blade, light surface pitting throughout. Luftwaffe eagle gray metal crossguard and white composition wire wrapped grip . . . . **$525 (£265)**

LUFTWAFFE OFFICER'S DAGGER, SECOND PATTERN, "CARL JULIUS KREBS"

- Ricasso marked with "Carl Julius Krebs / Solingen" oval maker's logo, crossguard with aluminum Luftwaffe eagle and swastika, yellow composition handle retains aluminum bullion wire wrap. Scabbard has mellow dark age patina . . . . **$585 (£290)**

NSKK CHAINED DRESS DAGGER, 1936 PATTERN

- Double-edged blade in fair polish has normal scabbard scratches and a slightly blunted tip, strong "Alles Für Deutschland" inscription, and reverse ricasso with "RZM / M7/33" hallmark. Hilt has metal fittings and good wood grips with Nazi eagle "SA" emblem. Scabbard retains black painted finish and nickeled fittings, chain suspension of alternating eagles and mobile swastika links terminating in attachment clip with oak leaf design; reverse of chain with "MUSTERSCHUTZ / NSKK / KORPSFUHRUNG" marking on first top link and "RZM" proof on another link. . . . . **$3,500 (£1,750)**

Luftwaffe Officer's Dagger, first pattern made by Emil Voos, $550-$650 (£225-£325). Charles D. Pautler

Luftwaffe Officer's Dagger, second pattern, $400-$500 (£200-£250). www.advanceguardmilitaria.com

The orange color of the handle of the second pattern Luftwaffe officer's dagger is very typical of how the plastic ages. This color does not adversely affect the value of a dagger. Charles D. Pautler

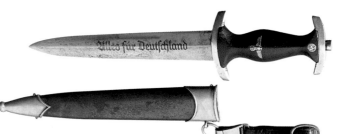

SA Honor Dagger with Ernst Roehm inscription, $2,500-$3,500 (£1,250-£1,750). Hermann Historica OHG

RLB SUBORDINATE'S DAGGER

- Second pattern 1938 RLB subordinate's dagger with double-edged blade with mild scabbard wear. Ricasso has "Ernst Erichwitte / Solingen" maker's trademark. Hilt has nickel plated fittings, crossguard with RLB eagle langlet, black wood grip with silver starburst grip insignia presenting swastika retaining 80% black enameled finish, and ridged dome pommel. Black finished scabbard has nickel-plated tip and integral single strap hanger $950 (£475)

SA DAGGER, "ROBERT KLAAS"

- Double-edged blade has normal scabbard wear, strong "Alles Für Deutschland" inscription, and reverse ricasso with "Robert Klaas / Solingen" maker's trademark with "RZM - M7/37" accountability number.....$625 (£315)

SA DAGGER, "CARL KLOOS"

- 1933 pattern SA dagger marked "CARL KLOOS / SOLINGEN / LANDWEHR." Hilt nickel crossguard is unit marked. Complete with its RZM marked leather hanger.................................$675 (£340)

SS DAGGER, "GOTTLIEB HAMMESFAHR"

- Early Pattern 1933 SS dagger with double-edged blade with "Meine Ehre heist Treue" motto. Ricasso marked with "Gottlieb Hammesfahr / Solingen - Foche" maker's logo, normal light scabbard and finger wear. Hilt has nickel silver fittings and black ebony grip with eagle and "SS" insignia inset, light age patina throughout. Reverse crossguard has accountability number "1/26" matching one on the throat of the scabbard. Scabbard has silver fittings $1,750 (£875)

TENO LEADER'S DAGGER

- Technical Emergency Corps leader's dagger has double-edged blade with bright finish. Ricasso has accountability number "0361." Reverse has acid-etched TeNo party eagle, "GES. / GESCH" (patent applied for), c.1935-41 Eickhorn maker's logo, and original thin leather scabbard washer. Hilt has silver fittings, TeNo cogged wheel pommel, orange composition grip, and crossguard with TeNo eagle insignia. Scabbard has matching accountability number............................ $3,800 (£1,900)

TENO SUBORDINATE HEWER

- Technical Emergency Corps subordinate hewer has Bowie blade with bright finish. Fuller terminates 1" from the crossguard. Ricasso has acid-etched TeNo party eagle, "GES. / GESCH" (patent applied for), and c.1935-41 Eickhorn maker's logo, reverse with accountability number "2291." Blackened steel scabbard has silver fittings and throat with number "2291" matching the hewer.............................. $2,500 (£1,250)

Once quite common, SA daggers are eagerly collected today and will regularly fetch prices from $350-$700 (£175-£350). www.advanceguardmilitaria.com

SA Dagger with hangers by "Ed. Wusthof, Solingen," $575-$750 (£290-£375). Rock Island Auction Company

Reichsarbeitsdienst ("RAD") hewer, $1,500-$2,500 (£750-£1,250). Rock Island Auction Company

By late 1944, the Waffen SS accounted for 10% of the German military personnel and possessed 25% of all German armored vehicles.

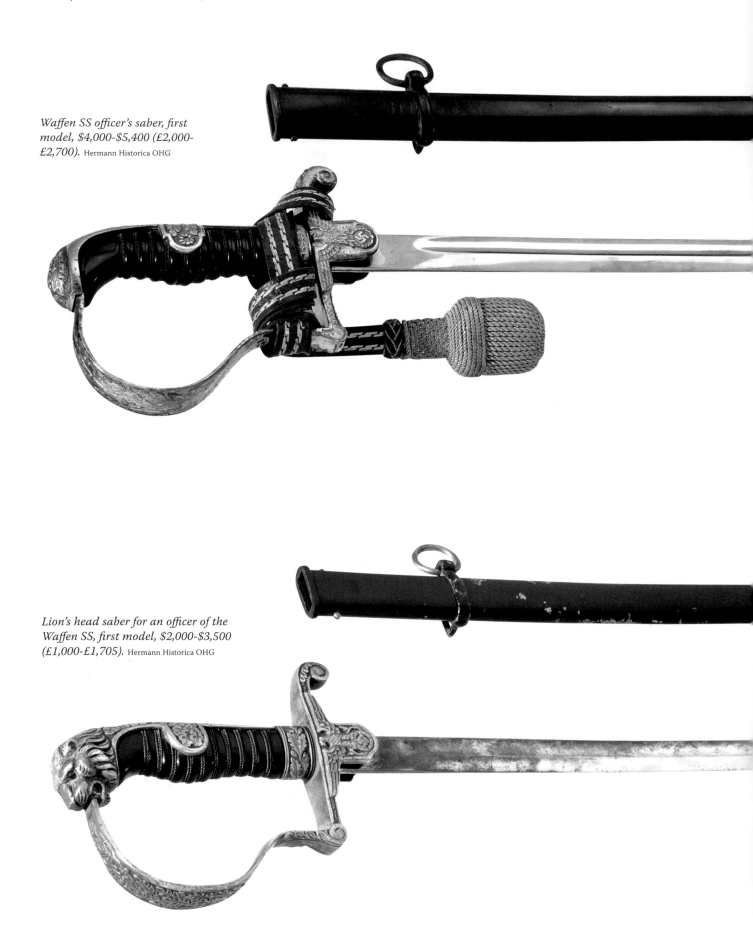

Waffen SS officer's saber, first model, $4,000-$5,400 (£2,000-£2,700). Hermann Historica OHG

Lion's head saber for an officer of the Waffen SS, first model, $2,000-$3,500 (£1,000-£1,705). Hermann Historica OHG

THIRD REICH GOVERNMENT OFFICIAL'S DAGGER

- Silver dagger has double-edged blade. Reverse has "Alcosa / Solingen" maker's stamp and logo, and retains the original thin brown leather scabbard washer. Hilt has silver fittings with eagle's head pommel, mother-of-pearl grips, and crossguard with right-facing eagle clutching wreathed swastika insignia. Dagger is complete with scabbard. . . . . **$3,700 (£1,850)**

Swords and Sabers

ARMY NCO SABER AND KNOT, MATCHING NUMBERS

- Mildly curved fullered blade in excellent polish has "Alex Coppel / Solingen" hiding under unadorned hilt langlet, with original leather scabbard washer. Hilt has brass single branch "P" guard with dove's head pommel, black composition grip with bullion wire wrap, and brown leather finger guide. Reverse of guard has accountability number "6297." Hilt is fitted with standard Army NCO saber knot of gray leather with gray leather plaited slide, silver flecked dark green crown and silver knot. Blued steel scabbard has matching accountability number. . . . .**$495 (£250)**

ARMY SABER BY EICKHORN

- Pattern No. 1714 "Freiherr von Stein" 32-1/2" mildly curved fullered blade. Ricasso has Eickhorn squirrel maker's stamp, hilt has gilt finish with bold relief Wehrmacht pattern national emblem on langlet, and wire-wrapped ribbed composition grip. Complete with black metal scabbard . . . .**$400 (£200)**

ARMY OFFICER'S SABER, EICKHORN

- Hilt retains fire gilt finish, featuring lion head pommel with ruby paste gem eyes, backstrap and guard with running oakleaf and acorn motif, black composition grip with aluminum bullion wire wrap intact, and obverse langlet with Army eagle and swastika motif. Ricasso has Eickhorn maker's logo visible. . . . .**$685 (£340)**

ARMY OFFICER'S SABER, EICKHORN, "PRINZ EUGEN" PATTERN

- Eickhorn pattern number 1765 "Prinz Eugen" officer's saber with 34-1/4" mildly curved blade in good polish with Eickhorn maker's logo at ricasso, Army eagle on obverse langlet, unadorned reverse langlet, wire-wrapped black composition grip, and Army eagle in bold relief on pommel cap . . . .**$700 (£350)**

ARMY OFFICER'S LION HEAD POMMEL SWORD, LÜNESCHLOSS

- Model unique to Lüneschloss, which has gilt finish, obverse langlet with small "Political" style national eagle emblem, oakleaf embossed scrollwork, and lion head pommel with red paste gem eyes. Black composition grip has brass wire wrap. Lüneschloss maker logo on ricasso under the langlet. Complete with black painted metal scabbard. . . . .**$795 (£400)**

ARMY OFFICER'S SABER

- Dove pommel saber has unadorned 32" fullered blade in excellent polish. Though unattributed, likely a Puma sword judging by the pattern of hilt decoration. Late style gray metal hilt with bronze tone finish, obverse langlet has detailed national eagle decoration with wings extending across the crossguard, backstrap is decorated with oak leaf motif, scabbard retains blackened finish. . . . .**$535 (£270)**

ARMY OFFICER'S SABER, F.W. HOLLER

- F.W. Holler Model Nr. 2, fullered blade maker stamp and thermometer hallmark. Hilt has dove head pommel, "P" guard, bolster, and unadorned langlets with a nickeled finish, black composition grips . . . .**$525 (£265)**

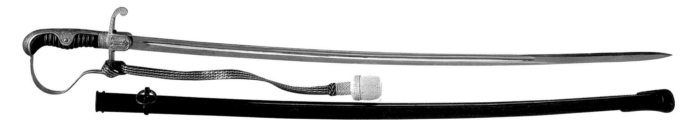

*Late war German officer's sword marked "Robert Klass * Solingen," $350-$600 (£175-£300).* Rock Island Auction Company

Sword for an SS Unterfuehrer, $1,500-$2,500 (£750-£1,250). Hermann Historica OHG

LUFTWAFFE OFFICER'S SWORD

• 1934 pattern "Fliegerschwert'" with fullered double-edged blade in excellent polish, ricasso with "EMF / Solingen" maker's hallmark; hilt has post-1940 regulation aluminum fittings, down-turned feathered quillion, wire-wrapped blue leather grip, and disc pommel with brass-toned mobile swastika. Aluminum ferrule beneath grip is stamped with unit marking "L.P.P. 20.".
. . . .**$975 (£490)**

POLICE OFFICER'S SWORD, "PETER KREBBS"

• Police officer's "Degen" with fullered blade in good polish with Peter Krebbs / Solingen maker's logo with crab insignia inside a shield. Hilt retains 70% nickel finish, wire-wrapped ebony grip with bronze Police wreathed eagle and swastika insignia, base with oakleaf and acorn motif ferrule with dark age patina, scabbard retains 85% black finish with nickel silver throat and drag.
. . . .**$795 (£400)**

ITALY

M91 CARCANO BAYONET

• 12" fullered blade with smooth aged finish, crossguard has "TERNI" arsenal mark, good wooden grips. Complete with ribbed metal scabbard . . . . **$60 (£30)**

M91 CARCANO BAYONET

• Model 1891, 11-3/4" fullered blade retains blued finish, straight crossguard terminating in ball finial, closed muzzle ring, two-piece riveted wood grips, and complete with brass mounted black leather scabbard dated "1935".
. . . . **$55 (£28)**

> *"I saw a whole gaggle of little, uniformed, bandy-legged men carrying rifles with long gleaming bayonets, led by two sword-waving officers."*
>
> LT. BOB GREEN, 763RD TANK BN.

Luftwaffe 1934-pattern officer's sword, $750-$850 (£375-£425). Minnesota Military Museum

Model 1938 sword for a general of the Luftwaffe, $10,000-$13,500 (£5,000-£6,750). Hermann Historica OHG

JAPAN

Bayonets

TYPE 18 BAYONET
- Leather scabbard, 18" blade . . . . **$625 (£315)**

TYPE 30 BAYONET, TRAINING
- 14-1/2" polished steel blade, OD-painted wood scabbard. . . . . **$150 (£75)**

TYPE 30 BAYONET, DENKI
- 15-3/4" fullered blade with blued finish, ricasso with maker's hallmark for National Denki under Kokura Supervision, crossguard with forward swept quillion, two-piece wood grips, and bird's head pommel; complete with steel scabbard. **$95 (£50)**

TYPE 30 BAYONET, TOYADA AUTOMATIC LOOM
- Fullered blade in excellent polish is finished bright, ricasso has Toyada Automatic Loom under Nagoya arsenal supervision maker's stamp. Hilt retains traces of blued finish, crossguard with hooked quillon, two-piece contoured wood grips, and rounded sided bird's head pommel. Complete with blued steel scabbard. . **$85 (£45)**

TYPE 30 BAYONET WITH RUBBER TROPICAL SCABBARD
- Scarce Type 30 has unfullered blade in fair polish, retains 65% blued finish, ricasso with National Denki (Kokura Supervision) maker's stamp, straight guard, two-piece wraparound contoured wood grips, and flat-sided bird's head pommel. Blade tip has minor pitting, dark oxidized patina and pitting on the pommel. Includes the very scarce rubberized fabric scabbard and frog (one piece unit) . . . . **$225 (£115)**

TYPE 30 BAYONET, JINSEN ARSENAL
- Jinsen Arsenal stamp on fullered blade. Crossguard with forward-swept quillion, contoured one-piece wood grips and bird's head pommel . . . . **$95 (£50)**

TYPE 30 BAYONET WITH SCABBARD AND FROG, KOKURA ARSENAL
- Type 30 Arisaka bayonet with Tokyo/Kokura Arsenal stamp, mid-war production steel scabbard retains blued finish, brown leather frog has attachment strap and brass buckle . . . . **$135 (£70)**

Japanese Type 30 bayonet with a National Denki hallmark, $85-$135 (£45-£70). www.advanceguardmilitaria.com

30th Year production Type 30 bayonet, $85-$135 (£45-£70). Minnesota Military Museum

Type 30 Bayonet, Toyada Automatic Loom, $85-$135 (£45-£70). www.advanceguardmilitaria.com

TYPE 30 BAYONET WITH SCABBARD AND FROG, NAGOYA ARSENAL

- Ricasso with Nagoya Arsenal stamp, hilt has brown patina finish, guard with hooked quillion, contoured two-piece wood grips, and bird's head pommel with accountability number, mid-war production steel scabbard. .... **$35 (£20)**

TYPE 30 BAYONET WITH SCABBARD AND FROG, TOYADA AUTOMATIC LOOM

- Ricasso has Toyada Automatic Loom (Nagoya supervision) maker's stamps. Hilt has blued finish, straight crossguard, contoured two-piece wood grips, and bird's head pommel with accountability number, mid-war production steel scabbard. .... **$135 (£70)**

TYPE 30 BAYONET WITH WOOD SCABBARD

- Type 30 bayonet with National Denki maker's stamp, straight crossguard, two-piece wood scale grips, and bird's head profile pommel, wood scabbard has olive painted finish with metal throat and tip, and wrapped-cord reinforcement bands. .... **$225 (£115)**

TYPE 30 ARISAKA BAYONET, EARLY PATTERN

- Fullered blade with unknown company under Kokura (arsenal) supervision hallmarks, scabbard has extruded tubular tip rather than the end button .... **$145 (£75)**

Swords and Sabers

BROADSWORD, ARTILLERY

- 21" bayonet-shaped blade .... **$200 (£100)**

GENDAITO

- 25-3/4" shinogi-zukuri blade with Itame hada and Suguha hamon, signed "Kanesige" on nakago, 39" mounted length .... **$2,500 (£1,250)**

KATANA, ARMY OFFICER

- 25-1/2" blade .... **$400 (£200)**

KATANA, LATE WAR

- 25-1/4" shinogi-zukuri machine-made katana, blade not signed but ca. 1944. .... **$285 (£145)**

KATANA, SHINTO

- 27-1/4" shinogi-zukuri katana with two-hole tang, single copper habaki, stored in black lacquered saya with horn kurikata and kojiri .... **$4,300 (£2,150)**

KATANA, SHINTO

- 25-1/4" shinogi-zukuri blade showing a suguha hamon, dark brown wrapped handle with matching brass "bird in a bush" motif, 38" mounted length ..... **$3,350 (£1,675)**

KATANA, SHOWA

- 23-1/4" shinogi-zukuri blade with Gunome hamon signed "Munehiro," ca. 1940, mounted in black lacquered wood scabbard covered in leather, 39" mounted length. .... **$975 (£490)**

Type 30 Bayonet with scabbard, frog and belt, $130-$150 (£65-£75). Minnesota Military Museum

Type 30 bayonet with wood scabbard, $175-$250 (£90-£125). Minnesota Military Museum

KATANA, SHOWA

- 23" shinogi-zukuri blade with Itame hada and hunome hamon, mounted in OD metal army officer scabbard with single hanger . . . .**$950 (£475)**

KATANA, SUKESADA

- 26-1/4" shinogi-zukuri blade showing notare/sugua hamon and Itame hada, ubu two-hole tang signed "Busho Osafune Sukesada saku" and dated "Eiroku" (1569), 40" mounted length . . . . **$3,500 (£1,750)**

SABER, ARMY OFFICER, DRESS

- Dress/parade, 29" blade. . . . .**$225 (£115)**

SABER, CAVALRY

- Type 32 (1899) cavalry saber with "86223" accountability number on the ricasso. Hilt has checkered steel and wood grip, spring steel latch, leather thumb finger loop is unusually pliable and intact, and knuckle bow slotted for a saber knot. Complete with steel scabbard fitted with single suspension ring. Metal scabbard and hilt retain olive painted finish. . . . .**$355 (£180)**

SABER, NAVAL OFFICER, DRESS

- 24-1/4" machine-made blade with etched hamon, mounted in a polished Same skin saya with matching brass fittings and double hanger . . . .**$650 (£325)**

SAMURAI SWORD, OKINAWA SOUVENIR

- Hand-made souvenir "Samurai sword" that has a 10-3/4" blade, aluminum tsuba with trench art engraving "OKINAWA 1946," cord wrapped handle, and metal scabbard covered in red and black electrical wire wrap. . **$65 (£35)**

SAMURAI SWORD, PILOT

- Has 19-1/2" long shinogi-zukuri blade. . . . .**$3,675 (£1,840)**

SWORD, CIVIL OFFICIAL

- Police sword measures 28-1/2" overall with bright finished fullered blade. Hilt has pierced floral openwork French style guard with single branch knuckle bow slotted for knot, Phrygian helmet pommel, brown wood grip with wire-wrap accent, and backstrap with Japanese chrysanthemum motif. Edge was manufactured dul. . . . .**$100 (£50)**

SWORD, NCO

- Late war production Shin-gunto, Army NCO sword, 27-1/2" machine-made serial numbered steel blade with copper habaki, plain blackened iron tsuba, and cross-hatched solid wood grip with iron mountings. Complete with metal scabbard retaining khaki painted finish. . . . .**$485 (£245)**

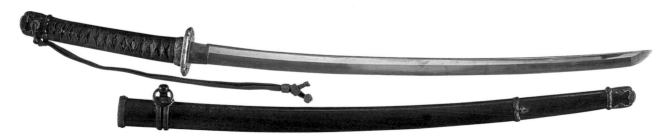

Noncommissioned officer's Shin-gunto were first produced in 1935, $500-$750 (£250-£375). Minnesota Military Museum

Unsigned 23-1/8" blade with unnumbered military mounts, $400-$600 (£200-£300). Rock Island Auction Company

Tachi 24-3/4" blade in military mounts but no signature, $600-$800 (£300-£400). Rock Island Auction Company

SWORD, OFFICER

• 21-3/4" machine-made shinogi-zukuri blade showing a Notare hamon, single-hole nakago signed "Masaharu," 36" overall mounted length ....**$675 (£340)**

SHIN-GUNTO, ARMY OFFICER, IRON SCABBARD

• Classic late-war production Army sword with 27-1/4" with brass habaki and simple unadorned black iron tsuba, hilt has ferrule with scabbard release button, white rayskin covered almost entirely with brown cord wrap, simple iron Army style chrysanthemum sakuras, and simple one-piece pebbled pommel cap with open hole for the tassel. Iron scabbard has simple fittings with throat guard and solid ishizuke with chrysanthemum on either side. Scabbard retains khaki painted finish.
....**$825 (£415)**

SHIN-GUNTO, ARMY OFFICER, LATE WAR, ALUMINUM SCABBARD

• 27-1/2" blade, hilt has cast brass tsuba with brown painted pebbled background and bold relief chrysanthemums, three mixed metal seppa and dia-seppa on the blade side of the tsuba, two seppa and one dia-seppa on the hilt side, ferrule with press stud for scabbard catch, handle with Army pattern sakuras, cord wrap and rayskin grip. Pommel has knot loop with company-grade officer tassel. Aluminum scabbard has brown tinted brass or bronze fittings including throat, decorative shibabiki, and ishizuke (drag)..........................**$625 (£315)**

SWORD, ARMY OFFICER, LATE WAR

• 26" shinogi-zukuri machine-made blade with buffed suguha hamon..........................**$795 (£400)**

SWORD, ARMY OFFICER, PARADE

• Chinese-made for Japanese Army officer ...**$225 (£115)**

SWORD, NAVAL OFFICER

• Kai-gunto, Naval officer's sword. Stainless steel blade, tang stamped with Toyokawa Naval Arsenal's anchor and circle stamp, serial numbered "174," and etched, cosmetic temper line--all indicators of a machine-made sword. Matching serial number "174" is also stamped into the plain iron tsuba as well as the four rayed "seppa" (spacers). Wooden handle has green cloth "ito" wrapped over dark rayskin covering and is held in place by one wooden "mekugi" (peg). Scabbard is black lacquered wood with

Japanese Tachi with 27-1/4" inch blade with two mekugeana but no signature, $600-$800 (£300-£400). Rock Island Auction Company

Japanese NCO sword with 32-1/2" blade, $300-$400 (£150-£200). Rock Island Auction Company

Miniature Japanese Katana in Tashe mounting, 15-1/2" blade, $750-$1,200 (£375-£600). Rock Island Auction Company

Japanese police sword with wood scabbard with a rayskin cover, $300-$400 (£150-£200). Rock Island Auction Company

two hangers, which, along with the other metal mounts, are gilded brass with a heavy patina . . . .**$795 (£400)**

SWORD, POLICE

- 17-1/4" machine-made shinogi-zukuri blade with silver habaki. Flared brass handle and backstrap with police crest . . . .**$425 (£215)**

SWORD WITH LEATHER-COVERED SCABBARD

- Late war kai-gunto, or one of the many swords made in Asia during and just after the war for the sole purpose of satisfying the souvenir market among allied troops, 25-3/8" blade and crudely made brass habaki, simple unadorned brass tsuba. Handle has simple brass pommel and ferrule, and olive cord wrapped rayskin grip devoid of further ornamentation. Brown leather covered saya has brass suspension mount and ring and brass throat guard. . . . .**$175 (£90)**

TANTO, KIMONO

- 6" handmade hira-zukuri tanto from early Showa period. . . . .**$285 (£145)**

TANTO, KOTO

- Lato Hira-zukuri tanto, Notare hamon with Masame hada, signed lightly with false name of "Masamune," 19-1/2" overall. . . . .**$1,200 (£600)**

TANTO

- Late Shinto Hira-zukuri 10" tanto . . . .**$850 (£425)**

WAKIZASHI, KOTO

- 19-3/4" shinogi-zukuri blade with full-length grooves to both sides, black silk-wrapped handle with matching shakudo and gold menuki with design of old man. . . . .**$3,200 (£1,600)**

WAKIZASHI, LATE SHINTO KIRA-SUKURI

- 14-1/2", stored in black lacquered saya with shakudo kuikata with gold and silver leaf and vine design. . . . .**$4,200 (£2,100)**

WAKIZASHI, MOUNTED

- 20-1/2" showing Midare hamon and vivid Itame hada. . . . .**$450 (£225)**

WAKIZASHI, SHINTO

- 23-1/4" shinogi-zukuri blade with two-hole nakago signed by Katsutoshi, 38" mounted length . . . .**$1,100 (£550)**

WAKIZASHI, TADATSUGU

- 13-1/4" shinogi-zukuri wakizashi with single-hole hakago crudely signed "Tadatsugu" . . . .**$450 (£225)**

WAKIZASHI

- 16-3/4" shinogi-zukuri blade signed "Bishu Sukemitsu," 28 mounted length. . . . .**$950 (£475)**

Late war Shin-gunto, or one of the many swords made in Asia during and just after the war for the souvenir market. Features of such a sword include a blade in poor polish, crudely made brass habaki, simple unadorned brass tsuba and a handle with simple brass pommel and ferrule with a rayskin grip devoid of ornamentation, $175-$300 (£85-£150). Minnesota Military Museum

Japanese Tanto with 9-1/8" blade, $750-$1,200 (£375-£600). Rock Island Auction Company

Wakizashi with 20-3/4" blade identified as the work of Satsuma Kuni Masafuso, 3rd, $4,000-$6,000 (£2,000-£3,000). Rock Island Auction Company

YARI, MOUNTED
* 10-1/2" three-sided yari with suguha hamon, 19" mounted length $625 (£315)

DAGGER, NAVY
* 8" machine-made plated hira-zukuri blade and wire-wrapped same skin handle with brass cherry blossom fittings $525 (£265)

DAGGER, POLICE
* 12" hira-zukuri machine-made blade with etched hamon mounted with solid brass crossguard $300 (£150)

POLAND

M1924 (WZ24) BAYONET
* Mauser rifle bayonet with fullered blade, well-marked ricasso has proof stamps, accountability number, and "WP" stamp, truncated oval crossguard with short muzzle "ears," wood two- piece grips, flashguard, and heavy steel pommel stamped with accountability number, complete with steel scabbard $120 (£60)

M1924 (WZ24) BAYONET WITH SCABBARD AND FROG
* Mauser bayonet with fullered blade with "W.P." and Polish eagle hallmark on ricasso, hilt has wood two-piece grips and pommel with "WZ 24" stamp, Mauser scabbard has brown leather sewn and riveted belt frog. $145 (£75)

ROMANIA

CLOSE COMBAT KNIFE
* Germanic style trench knife, 5-3/4" nickel-plated unfullered spear point blade, crossguard with reverse quillion

and tear-drop finial, black wood grips carved in a basket weave pattern, stylized bird's head pommel with loop for bayonet knot. Complete with nickeled metal scabbard. $235 (£120)

CLOSE COMBAT KNIFE
* Austrian influenced trench knife, 6-1/4" nickel-plated unfullered spear point blade, hilt has crossguard with hooked quillon, black composition grips and flat knob pommel with loop for bayonet knot. Complete with nickel finished metal scabbard. $255 (£130)

OFFICER AND NCO DRESS DAGGER
* Bayonet configuration Model 1930 dress dagger 5-3/4" blade in good polish, forward swept crossguard and bird's head pommel cast with textured designs and paste gem eyes in the pommel, black crosshatched two-piece grips have brass Royal cypher of King Carol II on obverse. Dagger is complete with nickeled scabbard and brown leather frog with nickeled spring clip hanger. $475 (£240)

SOVIET UNION

M91/30 BAYONET
* Quadrilateral socket bayonet for the Moisin-Nagant rifle. $40 (£20)

UNITED KINGDOM

Pocket Knives

POCKET KNIFE
* Variant made without the marlin spike, complete with folding knife and can opener blades, short screwdriver

British machete and 1943-dated leather scabbard, $100-$150 (£50-£75).

www.advanceguardmilitaria.com

British machete and early scabbard, marked "KITCHIN / SHEFFIELD / ENGLAND 'SNAKE' BRAND" with snake logo, "Made in England" and Broad Arrow proof, $100-$150 (£50-£75).

www.advanceguardmilitaria.com

blade on the end, black checked composition grips and lanyard loop. Broad Arrow and maker marked, dated "1944" . . . . **$75 (£40)**

POCKET KNIFE, WILKINSON

* 3-3/4" length closed, black checkered composition grips with short marlin spike, prow point blade, and can opener blade marked with "WILKINSON 1944" date. . . . .**$55 (£30)**

Machetes

MACHETE, COLLINS, U.S.-MADE

* 17-1/2" steel blade with U.S. contract Collins "LEGITIMUS" maker's logo with 1943 date, two-piece black composition grips with white leather lanyard. Complete with brown grained leather sheath trimmed with white buff throat guard . . . . **$95 (£50)**

MACHETE

* 20" overall with blackened finish, Broad Arrow proof, and black two-piece composition scale grips complete with 1944-dated grained brown leather sheath. . . . .**$125 (£65)**

MACHETE, KITCHIN

* 20" overall gray blade marked "KITCHIN / SHEFFIELD / ENGLAND 'SNAKE' BRAND" maker's stamp with snake logo, "Made in England," and Broad Arrow proof, riveted black two-piece composition scale grips. Complete with early 1938-dated brown leather sheath . . . . . .**$125 (£65)**

Bayonets

P07 BAYONET

* Fullered blade, Broad Arrow proof and "1-43" date. Hilt has smooth wood two-piece grips marked "SALZ 42." Brown leather scabbard marked with Australian maker and date stamps . . . . **$75 (£40)**

PARACHUTIST MACHETE BAYONET MK I

* A rare bayonet, of which only 3,411 were produced, 16" bolo profile unsharpened machete blade with blued finish, Broad Arrow proof stamp at ricasso and an oval crossguard with closed muzzle ring. Two-piece walnut wood grips stamped "SLAZ" indicating manufacture by Slazengers firm in Sidney. Pommel has press stud rifle attachment mechanism and stamped accountability number. Has issue pattern olive and khaki canvas and web sheath with metal throat, sewn and riveted construction, with retaining strap and belt loop. Reverse with 1944-dated maker stamp and Broad Arrow proof. . . . . **$1,525 (£765)**

NO. 1 MK II BAYONET, INDIAN MADE

* Unfullered blade with false edge and blued finish. Ricasso marked "42" with a crown proof and "R.F.I" arsenal mark. Wood two-piece grips and bird's head pommel, complete with black leather scabbard with metal fittings. . . . . **$65 (£35)**

NO. 1 MK III BAYONET, INDIAN MADE

* Unfullered blade with a false edge near the tip. Marked "Rifle Factory Ishapore" and dated "6-45." Square pommel, spine is stamped "England" . . . . **$55 (£30)**

Combat Knives

FAIRBAIRN-SYKES COMMANDO KNIFE, THIRD PATTERN

* Late-war or early post-war production J. Nowill & Sons F/S commando knife with double-edged blade. Unmarked crossguard, and ribbed hilt with Nowill maker's trademark crossed keys and asterisk over "D" in bold relief, pommel cap with hexagonal pommel nut likewise characteristic to this maker. Complete with scabbard of brown leather with blued metal tip and tabs for attaching to uniform . . . .**$325 (£165)**

UNITED STATES

Pocket Knives

TL-29 LINEMAN'S KNIFE

* Camillus TL-29 folding knife with wood grips, faintly stamped TL-29, blades marked "CAMILLUS NEW YORK" . . . . **$40 (£20)**

M2 POCKET KNIFE

* 7-1/4" overall with black composition faux bone handle fitted with snap release stud and sliding safety and clip point blade. Ricasso marked "PRESTO / PAT. JAN.30-40" and "GEO. SCHRADE / KNIFE CO. INC" . .**$475 (£240)**

The Army TL-29 folding knife was part of the Lineman's tool set and was one of the best military pocket knives ever made, a pattern which remained in use long after. Alone, it sells for $30-$50 (£15-£25). As part of the entire belt-carried leather set, it will run $80-$100 (£40-£50). Charles D. Pautler

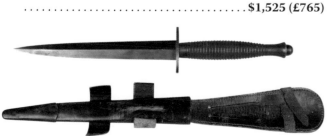

Fairbairn-Sykes commando knife, third pattern, $250-$600 (£125-£300). Minnesota Military Museum

M2 POCKET KNIFE WITH LANYARD

- 7-1/4" overall with black composition faux bone handle fitted with snap release stud and sliding safety, clip point blade. Marked "SCHRADE / WALDEN." One of the versions of this knife manufactured with a lanyard loop. This knife has its olive drab synthetic cord lanyard, which passed from the knife in the hidden zipper pocket to the epaulette of the paratrooper's jump jacket. . . . . **$475 (£240)**

NAVY SURVIVAL KIT FOLDING KNIFE, "COLONIAL"

- 6" closed, folding survival knife with checkered bolster grips. Blade marked "COLONIAL / PROV. R.I." Knife has folding knife and saw blades . . . . **$130 (£65)**

NAVY SURVIVAL KIT FOLDING KNIFE, "UNITED"

- 6" closed length folding survival kit knife with textured black hard rubber grips, primary blade marked "UNITED G.R. MICH." . . . . **$120 (£60)**

USMC POCKET KNIFE

- Manufactured knife marked "U.S. MARINE CORPS" on the side. One blade marked "Can Opener Pat. Pend." Knife is steel and brass construction typical of wartime manufactured knives. Postwar knives are marked "U.S.M.C." and are all steel construction . . . . . . **$95 (£50)**

Belt Knives

V-44 FIGHTING KNIFE, "COLLINS"

- 9-3/8" clipped point Bowie blade with "COLLINS & Co. / LEGITIMUS" maker stamp, tip is very slightly blunted, ricasso has straight brass crossguard with ball finials.

M2 "paratrooper" pocket knife made by Shrade Knife Co., $450-$550 (£225-£250). www.advanceguardmilitaria.com

Navy survival kit folding knife marked "Colonial / Prov. R.I.," $100-$150 (£50-£60). www.advanceguardmilitaria.com

V-44 fighting knife made by Collins, no scabbard, $300-$350 (£150-£175). www.advanceguardmilitaria.com

This example has the correct tooled matching Collins scabbard with sewn modification on the bottom, and reverse has belt loop riveted near the base to retain a wire belt hanger to facilitate easier use with the issue web gear.. . . . . **$425 (£215)**

V-44 FIGHTING KNIFE, "CASE"

- 9-3/8" Bowie blade with two shallow parallel grooves near the spine, "CASE XX" maker stamp, ricasso has straight brass crossguard with ball finials, grip and pommel of heavy black composition material, knife is complete with brown leather scabbard fitted with belt loop. These were made by Case, Collins, Western, and Kinfolks . . . . **$400 (£200)**

MARK I FIGHTING KNIFE, "SHRADE"

- Has clipped point blade in gray Parkerized finish with factory edge, ricasso marked "SCHRADE - WALDEN / N.Y. U.S.A." on obverse, unmarked on the reverse, Parkerized oval crossguard and contoured stacked brown leather washer grip with red-brown composition top and bottom spacers and flat oval metal pommel cap. . . . . **$95 (£50)**

MK I FIGHTING KNIFE, "PAL"

- U.S.N. MK. I fighting knife with 5-3/16" clipped point blade with gray Parkerized finish, ricasso with marked "U.S.N. / MK I" and "PAL RH-35," short crossguard leads to stacked leather washer grip and gray metal oval pommel cap. Complete with gray composition and web Navy MK I scabbard. . . . . **$175 (£90)**

MARK II FIGHTING KNIFE, "ROBESON SHUREDGE"

- Mark II fighting knife marked "U.S.N. / MARK 2" on obverse of ricasso. On the reverse is the scarce maker's

Stainless steel general purpose knives appeared late in the war, $35-$55 (£16-£30). Minnesota Military Museum

The V-44 fighting knives were made by Case, Collins, Western, and Kinfolks. This example has the correct tooled matching Collins scabbard, $400-$500 (£200-£250). www.advanceguardmilitaria.com

mark, "ROBESON SHUREDGE." Hilt has crossguard bent backwards on either side, stacked leather washer grip, and round pommel cap. Complete with gray composition and web scabbard, throat stamped "USN / MK 2". . . . .**$195 (£100)**

MK II FIGHTING KNIFE, "CAMILLUS," COMPOSITION SCABBARD

• Camillus MK II stamped "USN / MK II / CAMILLUS NY" on the crossguard. Stacked leather washer grip and disc pommel. Navy gray composition and web scabbard stamped "USN MK 2" on the throat. . . . .**$150 (£75)**

MK II FIGHTING KNIFE, "KA-BAR," COMPOSITION SCABBARD

• MK II fighting knife with clipped point and fullered blade. Crossguard is marked "KA / BAR" on one side and "USN / MK II" on the other. Hilt has stacked leather washer grip and flat iron disc pommel. Complete with the standard Navy gray composition and web MK II scabbard. . . . .**$145 (£75)**

MK II FIGHTING KNIFE, UNMARKED, LEATHER SCABBARD

• Clipped point, fullered blade finished bright from use. Unmarked straight crossguard, stacked leather washer grip, and iron disc pommel. Complete with brown leather sheath marked with maker's date "BOYT - 43". . . . .**$125 (£65)**

M3 FIGHTING KNIFE, "IMPERIAL"

• 6-3/4" blade stamped "U.S. M3 IMPERIAL," flat oval pommel marked with Ordnance bomb. Complete with a US M8 scabbard. . . . .**$225 (£115)**

M3 FIGHTING KNIFE, "U.C."

• 6-3/8" blade stamped "M3-U.C.-1943," stacked leather

MK I fighting knife marked "PAL RH-35 with Navy Mk I scabbard, $150-$200 (£75-£100). www.advanceguardmilitaria.com

MK III fighting knife with M8 scabbard (which replaced the earlier leather M6 scabbard), $200-$300 (£100-£150). Minnesota Military Museum

washer grip and flat oval pommel. Complete with US M8 scabbard. . . . .**$245 (£125)**

M3 FIGHTING KNIFE, "CAMILLUS"

• 6-3/8" blade stamped "U.S. M3 CAMILLUS," stacked leather washer grip, and flat oval pommel. Complete with US M8A1 scabbard retaining leather leg lace. . . . .**$275 (£140)**

M3 FIGHTING KNIFE, "CASE"

• 6-3/8" blade stamped "U.S. M3 CASE," crossguard top edge properly bent slightly forward as thumb rest, stacked leather washer grip and flat oval pommel. Complete with US M8A1 scabbard. . . . .**$295 (£150)**

M3 FIGHTING KNIFE, "PAL"

• Very scarce, 6-3/8" blade stamped "U.S. M3 PAL," stacked leather washer grip. Complete with proper "US M8" scabbard. "PAL" is one of the more scarce M3 contractors. . . . .**$325 (£165)**

M3 FIGHTING KNIFE, "UTICA"

• Blade stamped "U.S. M3-UTICA" on one side of the blade. Hilt has crossguard with forward swept thumb rest, oval pommel cap stamped with Ordnance bomb. Includes M8 scabbard. . . . .**$295 (£150)**

M3 FIGHTING KNIFE, "UTICA" WITH M6 LEATHER SCABBARD

• M3 trench with "U.S. M3-UTICA" on the blade, hilt has short guard, stacked leather washer grip, and oval disc pommel with Ordnance bomb insignia. Complete with field-modified M6 leather scabbard that has had the long suspension segment shortened into something more manageable and retained in place by rawhide laces, throat has metal staple guard and "U.S. M6" / MOOSE CO. / 1943," base has metal edge guard and leather tie lace. . . . .**$325 (£165)**

MARINE BOLO KNIFE

• 11-3/8" thick bolo blade with "U.S.M.C. / CHATILLON, N.Y." maker's stamp and two-piece wood scale grips, brown leather scabbard with brass throat that has "U.S. Boyt 42" maker's stamp. . . . .**$225 (£115)**

O.S.S. KNUCKLE FIGHTING KNIFE

• 9" blued three-sided blade face and back flutes, steel knuckle bow and ribbed black rubber grip. Complete with blued steel scabbard fitted with leather chape frog and retaining strap with snap closure. These knives were manufactured from surplus M1873 socket bayonets and

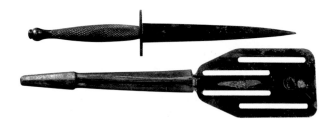

American-made Fairbairn-Sykes type fighting knife with "spatula" scabbard, $750-$900 (£375-£450). Rock Island Auction Company

dropped by the O.S.S. to irregular units fighting in the Philippines..............................$425 (£215)

O.S.S. "PANCAKE FLIPPER" STILETTO

- Fairbairn-Sykes style double-edged stiletto with black finish, straight oval crossguard, and knurled contoured grip. Includes the classic L.F.&C. "pancake flipper" scabbard of olive painted metal and brown leather. $2,250 (£1,125)

FIGHTING KNIFE, "WESTERN"

- 8" fullered clip point blade in excellent polish retains 70% blued finish, ricasso with "WESTERN" maker stamp. Hilt has tight stacked leather washer grip and iron disc pommel. Knife is complete with brown leather sheath. $265 (£135)

FIGHTING KNIFE, UNMARKED

- Knife measures 12" overall, with 7" double-edged blade dark with traces of blued finish, heavy nickeled hilt has crossguard with "LT. M. SULLIVAN" stamped on one edge, ribbed and contoured grip, and flat spheroid pommel, lacks scabbard $125 (£65)

BRASS KNUCKLE BOWIE-STYLE FIGHTING KNIFE

- Collectors call this style the "1st Ranger Battalion Special Knife." Most likely, it was an Australian-made fighting knife. It is a substantial fighting knife with a 9-3/8" unful-

Developed during World War I, "knuckle" trench knives were a popular item with frontline troops, if not for their lethality, for their perceived lethality! $300-$600 (£150-£300) www.advanceguardmilitaria.com

M1918 pattern trench knife, $450-$600 (£225-£300). www.advanceguardmilitaria.com

lered Bowie blade. Has roughly finished brass solder fill along the edge of the ricasso. The cast brass, one-piece contoured grip and fighting knuckle guard has no visible markings. Includes the correct original brown sewn leather sheath with belt loop $625 (£315)

Machetes

TRUE TEMPER MACHETE

- Manufactured by TRUE TEMPER with two-piece olive drab composite grip, no scabbard, dated 1944. ....$85 (£45)

TRUE TEMPER MACHETE AND SCABBARD

- Army issue machete with "U.S." stamp and "TrueTemper / 1945" maker's stamp. Handle has two-piece olive plastic grips. Machete is complete with "Boyt 42" dated khaki. $95 (£50)

USN MACHETE

- Collins No. 105, 26" blade with traces of blackened finish and black plastic handle. Blade stamped "COLLINS" and dated "1944" also retains a good portion of the black and gold Collins paper label on the ricasso. Complete in khaki scabbard $105 (£55)

SURVIVAL KNIFE LC-14-B

- "Woodsman's Pal" manufactured by the Victor Tool Co., Reading, PA with long, machete edge, square entrenching edge and curved brush hook edge, curved guard and leather washer grip. Complete with olive drab canvas sheath with zipper closure $150 (£75)

USMC COLLINS MACHETE

- Slightly curved 20" blade with traces of Collins paper label, and Collins crown and hammer logo on the ricasso. Hilt comprised of two-piece black composition grips. Includes matching scabbard of brown leather with "US / BOYT / 42" stamped on the reverse below the M1910-style belt hanger $150 (£75)

USMC MK II MACHETE

- Machete with 18" blade, ricasso marked "USMC / MK 2 / 1944 / SWI." Has riveted two-piece black plastic grips. Includes light olive canvas and web scabbard with reinforced tip and bronze throat guard with light green patina. Reverse with "U.S.M.C." and date stamp "1943". $185 (£95)

TYPE A-1 AAF SURVIVAL FOLDING MACHETE AND CARRIER

- Type A-1 by Imperial, 10" bolo blade retains 95% blackened non-reflective finish, unmarked ricasso, heavy black grip with metal blade guard extension, and complete with gray leather carrier stamped with nomenclature, base with gray leather leg thong, and lift-the-dot closure. Interior complete with original sharpening stone. $155 (£80)

Seven American volunteer pilots fought alongside the RAF pilots during the Battle of Britain. Only one survived the war.

Collectors call this style the "1st Ranger Battalion Special Knife" though it was, most likely, an Australian-made fighting knife. Nevertheless, it is an impressive fighting knife and will sell for $600-$700 (£300-£350). www.advanceguardmilitaria.com

Collins Model 1005 was also known as the "Army Engineers Machete." Widely used in World War I, many of these saw service again in World War II, $100-$200 (£50-£100). www.advanceguardmilitaria.com

"Woodsman's Pal" manufactured by the Victor Tool Co., Reading, Pennsylvania, $90-$200 (£45-£100). Minnesota Military Museum

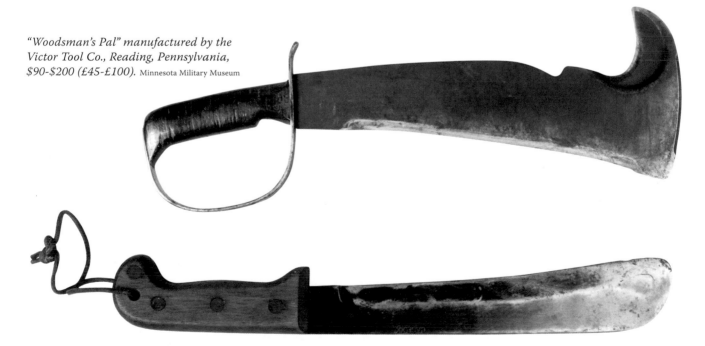

This non-folding machete, marked "Case XX," was included in an USN survival kit, $75-$150 (£40-£75). Minnesota Military Museum

Bayonets

MODEL 1917 BAYONET

- Fullered blade retains 95% parkerized finish, ricasso with encircled "W" Winchester maker's stamp and "1917" date. Bayonet has walnut two-piece grips. Complete with production olive drab composition fiber scabbard with metal throat marked with Ordnance bomb and "M-1917." Used with the trench shotgun as well as the P17 rifle
. . . .**$235 (£120)**

MODEL 1905 DRESS BAYONET

- Pre-WWI manufactured M1905 bayonet with nickel-plate finish to all metal parts, blade in very good polish, ricasso marked with ordnance bomb, "S A" and dated "1907." Reverse with "US" and serial number, hilt with polished walnut grips. Complete with brown leather-covered scabbard retaining M1910 belt hanger, marked "R. I. A. / 1907," hand inscribed on obverse "Dr G / Dress / Bayonet / Hawaii / 1930 / 1937 / 27th. / Inf.".
. . . .**$295 (£150)**

M1905 BAYONET, CHROME FINISH

- M1905 bayonet with walnut grips, mirror-bright chrome finish and matching finish on the metal portions of the hilt, ricasso marked "S.A. / (ordnance bomb) / 1911" and "U.S. / 478681." Complete with ordnance bomb-marked metal and fiber scabbard retaining white-painted finish on the scabbard and black-painted finish on the throat.
. . . .**$185 (£95)**

M1905 BAYONET, ARSENAL RECONDITIONED

- Early 1909 production M1905 bayonet refitted with brown plastic grips and OD composite scabbard. Fullered blade marked with "R.I.A. / (Ordnance bomb) /

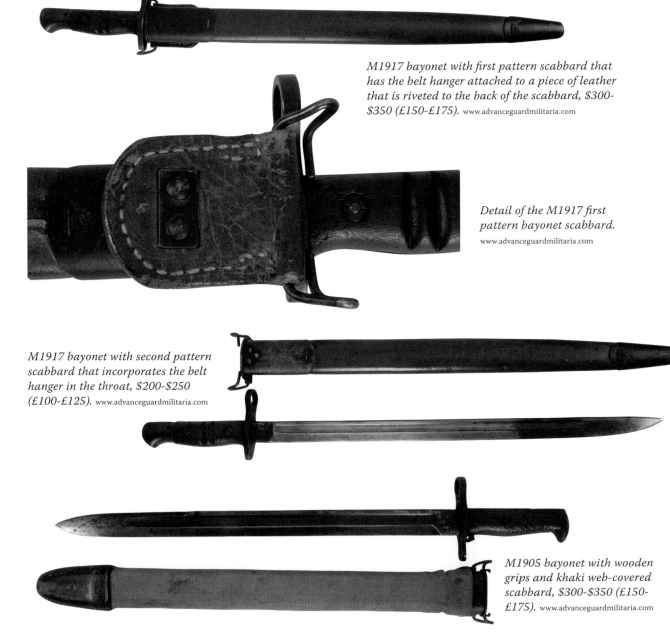

M1917 bayonet with first pattern scabbard that has the belt hanger attached to a piece of leather that is riveted to the back of the scabbard, $300-$350 (£150-£175). www.advanceguardmilitaria.com

Detail of the M1917 first pattern bayonet scabbard.
www.advanceguardmilitaria.com

M1917 bayonet with second pattern scabbard that incorporates the belt hanger in the throat, $200-$250 (£100-£125). www.advanceguardmilitaria.com

M1905 bayonet with wooden grips and khaki web-covered scabbard, $300-$350 (£150-£175). www.advanceguardmilitaria.com

M1905 bayonet with original wooden grips, no scabbard,
$180-$200 (£90-£100). www.advanceguardmilitaria.com

M1905 bayonet with fullered blade and two-piece black ribbed plastic grips. Housed
in an olive drab composition scabbard, $270-$320 (£135-£165), Author's collection

M1905 bayonet with USN MK 1 scabbard,
$250-$300 (£125-£150). www.advanceguardmilitaria.com

M1905 "AFH 1942" bayonet with USN MK 1
scabbard, $250-$300 (£125-£150). Charles D. Pautler

1909" and "US / 153278" on ricasso. Hilt has gray finish on the metal and brown ribbed plastic grips, composition scabbard has OD finish and "US" with Ordnance Bomb on the gray metal throat . . . .**$285 (£145)**

M1905 BAYONET, USN SCABBARD

* M1905 bayonet with fullered blade finished bright and rounded tip. Ricasso has "S.A. / (bomb) / 1910" on obverse and "US" with "467751" accountability number on reverse. Hilt has metal fittings and walnut grips. "U.S.N. / MK1" scabbard has olive painted finish. . . . .**$265 (£135)**

M1 GARAND RIFLE BAYONET, WARTIME SHORT PATTERN, AFH

* Short pattern bayonet with "AFH / (Bomb) / U.S." maker's stamp, black ribbed plastic grips, and issue M7 scabbard. . . . .**$135 (£70)**

M1 GARAND RIFLE BAYONET, WARTIME SHORT PATTERN, UFH

* M1905 E1 shortened M1942 bayonet with fullered blade marked "U.F.H. / U.S. / 1943." Has black plastic ribbed two-piece grips and M7 scabbard. . . . .**$125 (£65)**

M1 GARAND RIFLE BAYONET, WARTIME SHORT PATTERN UC

* Ricasso marked "U.C. / U.S. / 1942." Black plastic ribbed two-piece grips and M7 scabbard. . . . .**$155 (£80)**

M1 GARAND RIFLE BAYONET, WARTIME SHORT PATTERN, PAL

* M1905 E1 bayonet with spear point and Parkerized finish. Ricasso marked with "U.S." and an Ordnance Department bomb. "PAL" maker and "1943". . . . .**$125 (£65)**

M1 GARAND RIFLE BAYONET, WARTIME SHORT PATTERN, SA

* Arsenal shortened M1905 bayonet, 10" blade with prow style point. Ricasso stamped "SA / (ordnance bomb) / 1908." Reverse has "US" and accountability number "246610.". . . . .**$135 (£70)**

M1 GARAND RIFLE BAYONET, WARTIME SHORT PATTERN

* Arsenal shortened M1942 bayonet, 10" with spear style point. Ricasso stamped "U.P.H. / U.S. (ordnance bomb) / 1942". . . . .**$125 (£65)**

JOHNSON RIFLE BAYONET

* 13" overall, with 8-1/2" fluted trilateral blade, muzzle ring, and flat metal hilt with spring attachment system. Bayonet is complete with brown leather scabbard with retaining strap and belt loop . . . .**$300 (£150)**

NAVY MK I TRAINING BAYONET 1

* Mark I bayonet with black plastic 16" unfullered blade. Ricasso marked "U.S.N. / MARK I" with an accountabil-

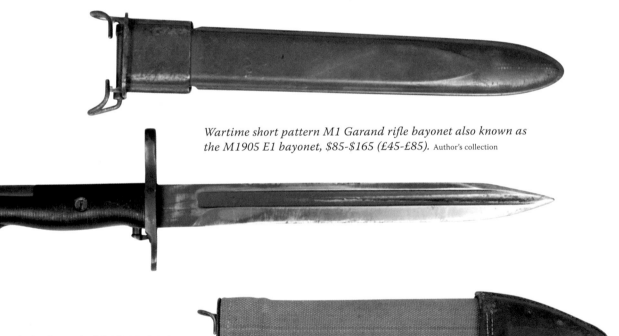

Wartime short pattern M1 Garand rifle bayonet also known as the M1905 E1 bayonet, $85-$165 (£45-£85). Author's collection

M1917 Bolo knife marked "U.S. Mod /1917 CT" and "Plumb / St. Louis," $150-$200 (£75-£100). www.advanceguardmilitaria.com

ity number on the reverse. Black plastic crossguard, grip and pommel encasing metal spring mechanisms for attachment to rifle and retaining stud of scabbard. Includes olive drab composition scabbard with U.S. ordnance bomb stamp on the throat . . . .**$155 (£80)**

NAVY MK I BAYONET SCABBARD

- 17" olive drab composition fiber scabbard with metal throat marked "USN / MK I." Fits both the plastic blade Mk I Navy bayonet as well as any of the Model 1905 Springfield bayonet variations . . . .**$75 (£40)**

Miscellaneous Blades

M1917 BOLO

- Made at Springfield Armory marked "U.S. Mod /1917 CT" and "Plumb / St. Louis." Housed in khaki web-covered rawhide scabbard with brown leather tip. . . . .**$175 (£90)**

USMC HOSPITAL CORPSMAN KNIFE, "CHATILLON"

- Heavy steel blade has "USMC / CHATILLON, N.Y." stamp. Hilt has two-piece riveted wood handle scales. Complete with "USMC / BOYT / 45" marked brown leather scabbard with wire belt hanger and metal throat guard. . . . .**$175 (£90)**

USMC HOSPITAL CORPSMAN KNIFE, "BRIDDELL"

- Heavy steel blade marked "USMC / BRIDDELL." Hilt has two-piece riveted wood handle scales, lacks scabbard. Briddell is one of the less commonly encountered makers.. . . . .**$125 (£65)**

USMC HOSPITAL CORPSMAN'S KNIFE, "BRIDDELL"

- "USMC / BRIDDELL" stamped blade. Complete with "USMC / BOYT / 44" marked brown leather scabbard with wire belt hanger and metal throat guard. . . . .**$195 (£100)**

M1902 OFFICER'S SABER

- Pre-era M1902 officer's saber with mildly curved blade and frosted field on obverse, reverse, and spine presenting U.S. eagle, martial panoplies, and "U.S." intertwined monogram. Unmarked ricasso. Spine has "GERMANY" import stamp. Hilt has black composition grip and three-branch knuckle bow complete with brown leather knot. Scabbard has nickeled finish . . . .**$185 (£95)**

M1910 HATCHET AND COVER

- M1910 hand axe as carried in each squad on a distribution relative to the number of T-handle shovels, bolo knives, and pick-mattock sets. Head has "US / 1944" stamped on the poll, head pitted from poor storage but still quite usable and certainly fine for display. Wood handle retains olive painted finish. Complete with khaki web carrier stamped with 1918 maker's date stamp. . . . . **$60 (£30)**

OSS SPRING COSH

- Referred as an "asp" or "expandable baton," this OSS example measures 11" long when compacted, 16-1/4" long when extended, with an an iron grip and striking tip. . . . .**$175 (£90)**

M1902 officer's saber marked "GERMANY" on the spine import stamp, $180-$250 (£90-£125). www.advanceguardmilitaria.com

Model 1913 officer's "Patton" cavalry saber, marked "L.F.&C. / 1919," $400-$500 (£200-£250).
www.advanceguardmilitaria.com

CHAPTER 7

PERSONAL ITEMS

Looking at a military dealer's list or perusing the Internet often leaves one with the impression that personal items carried or used during the World War II abound and are available for minimal investment. That is only partially true.

This is a frustrating area to collect and, even more so, to describe. Many items were made or used from 1939 to 1945. That does not mean a soldier used the item or carried it in his knapsack. Many of the items that can be loosely placed in this category rely on imagination and very little on documentation. Selling personal items, or "smalls," is a profitable business. Simple utilitarian antiques can often be found for a few dollars at antiques shows or flea markets. With some wishful thinking and some clever writing, an average mid-20th century item can immediately become a soldier's item. Unfortunately, this wishful thinking is infectious, and soon, plenty of customers believe the romantic yarns spun by a dealer.

Toothpaste in vintage containers, sweetheart jewelry, personal toiletry items, or vintage canned goods—a lot of antiques are currently being imported that look "period appropriate" and sold as "World War II" items. Again, it cannot be emphasized enough: Buyer Beware! If you are in the market for items that are typical of the period (or simply "look good"), then you will have no shortage of available artifacts to purchase. On the other hand, if you stick with items that have a *known* provenance linking them to a soldier, or the period 1939 to 1945, be prepared to pay! Personal items that were actually carried or used by a soldier are harder to find and document—for the simple reason that they were *used*. The items were, by their very intent, expendable. Survival after 60 years was not the goal when these items were manufactured.

Collecting Hints

Pros:
- Genuine articles identified to a soldier are a very immediate link to the soldier's life.
- Items with strong, proven provenance are good investments. The prices of these items keep going up.
- Collecting personal items allows World War II enthusiasts to inject a bit of their own personality into the hobby by collecting items that appeal directly to themselves.

Cons:
- Few items with solid provenance have survived. Personal items that are identified as having belonged to a soldier are uncommon. Those that do exist are often part of a larger grouping of items associated with the soldier, further driving the price beyond a beginner's reach.
- This area is inundated with items represented as "World War II" when, in fact, there is no provenance to support the claims.
- World War II experts are usually not experts in decorative arts. Therefore, a lot of items that look time appropriate are represented as typical of items from the World War II era.
- Provenance for items is often "created" by a dealer looking to increase the value of relatively common World War II-era items. Many items that never had any association suddenly become part of a group, or in the worst case, sprout markings that identify them to a soldier.
- Personal items do not follow any set of regulation designs or patterns, so it is very difficult to clearly identify an item as having been made or used before or during the war.

Availability ★★★★★

Price ★★

Reproduction Alert ★★★

The best defense against the wishfully ordained, but woefully lacking in documentation "World War II" personal items is patience and study. Limit yourself to known entities—items with a strong provenance or documented period use.

Closely examine the items in this chapter. You will notice that the items that have a known association with a World War II soldier sold for strong prices. The rest of the items are low-level collectibles. Resist the temptation to say or believe, "a soldier *could* have used it." Just saying it doesn't make it so. Visit museums, study books and period magazines to determine a sense of construction and use of items from the World War II era.

Personal items might seem—at first—the easiest area in which to begin collecting. It is, in fact, the most difficult. Because civilian-produced and used items followed no "regulation" pattern or order, the variety is endless. For example, notice the number of "toiletry kits" listed below. It's easy to say, "Sure! A soldier would have needed this to shave and keep clean in the field!" Yet very few have solid provenance linking them to a soldier.

To successfully collect in this area, you must first become familiar with the material culture of the mid-20th century. A lot of time and effort can be spent on studying decorative arts to hone the skill of recognizing a period-appropriate civilian ware. It is a lot easier to recognize a M1923 riflemen's cartridge belt or an M1 carbine, than it is to determine whether a can of body powder or a toothbrush dates to World War II.

GERMANY

Entertainment

SOLDIER'S FIELD RADIO

- 14" x 9-1/2" x 6" stout metal radio retains textured field gray finish. All switches and dials have German metal labels. Top has leather carrying handle, and side has sliding port that opens to reveal attachment points for external power . . . .**$295 (£150)**

SOLDIER'S SONG BOOK

- Softbound, pocket sized volume of "Das Neue Soldaten Liederbuch," 80 pages of German songs . . . . . . **$25 (£15)**

Identification

WEHRPASS

- Soldier's ID book . . . . **$65 (£30)**

SOLDBUCH

- The Soldbuch kept track of payment, clothing and equipment records. . . . . **$60 (£30)**

German soldier's field-made wallet, $50-$75 (£25-£40). Minnesota Military Museum

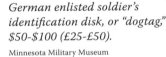

German enlisted soldier's identification disk, or "dogtag," $50-$100 (£25-£50).
Minnesota Military Museum

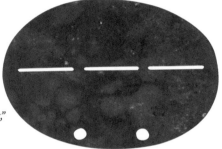

The value of German Soldbuchs and Wehrpasses is determined by the unit in which the particular soldier served and what types of citations he may have received. An SS Soldbuch will command top prices from $150-$300 (£75-£150). Charles D. Pautler

Regular Army Wehrpass, $60-$100 (£30-£50). Charles D. Pautler

German Army Soldbuch, $50-$100 (£25-£50). Charles D. Pautler

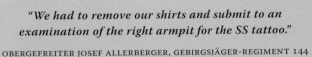

"We had to remove our shirts and submit to an examination of the right armpit for the SS tattoo."

OBERGEFREITER JOSEF ALLERBERGER, GEBIRGSJÄGER-REGIMENT 144

Lighting

ARMY FIELD LANTERN
- 9-1/2" tall metal carbide lantern with vented top, wood grip on wire-top handle, sides with removable covers, base with carbide chamber, interior white enameled reflector, and "ago" stamps on side and front.
....**$125 (£65)**

BAKELITE CARBIDE LANTERN
- 9" x 5" x 5" brown Bakelite lantern with bail handle, threaded base for carbide mechanism, side panels with shutters, and front with gray metal light discipline filter plate lifts to reveal carbide mechanism and reflector dish, Bakelite embossed with proof and maker's initials.
....**$65 (£35)**

LUFTWAFFE ISSUE CANDLE LANTERN
- 5" x 5" x 11" metal candle lantern with silver aluminum finish and crossed wire guards protecting two opaque and two clear glass lights, interior with candle holder, top with vented crown, bail handle, and hook. Base marked with Luftwaffe eagle and "1941" maker's date stamp. Shows normal light wear...................**$125 (£65)**

BAKELITE CARBIDE LANTERN
- 9" x 5" x 5" brown Bakelite lantern with bail handle, threaded base with carbide mechanism, and side panels with shutters. Interior has carbide system and reflector dish, Waffenamt marked on the reverse belt hook.
....**$75 (£40)**

Mess and Ration Related

JUWEL 33 BUNKER HEATER/
SMALL COOKING STOVE
- 6" tall "JUWEL 33" gas stove has olive painted finish. Interior is complete with maintenance and operation tools.
....**$110 (£55)**

SOLDIER'S POCKET FIELD STOVE
- Stamped metal folding field stove embossed with "Esbit" maker name...............................**$35 (£20)**

SOLDIER'S "SCHO-KA-KOLA" TIN
- 3-3/8" diameter red-orange and white printed tin with oak leaves and gothic inscription "Scho-ka-kola," and "DIE STÄRKENDE SCHOKOLADE," date "1939" surrounded by ray burst in center; reverse listing the ingredients, maker's name and "WEHRMACHT-PACKUNG".
....**$90 (£45)**

SOLDIER'S FOLDING FORK AND SPOON
- Aluminum fork and spoon set marked "LGK & F / 40".
....**$30 (£15)**

SS MARKED RATION SACK
- 26" x 13" natural burlap ration sack has black Third Reich eagle and swastika with "SS" and "1943" stamps.
....**$125 (£65)**

ARMY LARD RATION CONTAINER
- Orange composition lid with knurled edge on brown composition dish, base with maker stamp.....**$35 (£20)**

German enlisted soldier's fork and spoon combination, $30-$50 (£15-£25). Charles D. Pautler

Luftwaffe issue candle lantern, $100-$150 (£50-£75). www.advanceguardmilitaria.com

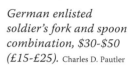

Bakelite carbide lantern with Waffenamt marked on the belt hook, $75-$100 (£40-£50).
www.advanceguardmilitaria.com

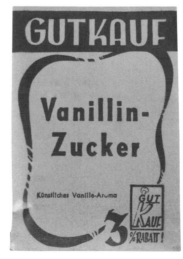

Wartime sugar packet, $5-$10 (£2-£5). Charles D. Pautler

RAD Mess Hall Plate, $30-$50 (£15-£25). www.advanceguardmilitaria.com

German issued service glasses and case, $50-$75 (£25-£40). Charles D. Pautler

Private-purchase razor in original box, $30-$50 (£15-£25). Charles D. Pautler

German issue sewing kit, $50-$75 (£25-£40). Minnesota Military Museum

ARMY MESS HALL BOWL
- 6-1/2" white porcelain bowl has Army eagle on base with "Bohemia 1940" maker logo $30 (£15)

ARMY MESS HALL GRAVY BOAT
- KPM porcelain gravy boat with green Army eagle and KPM logo on base $65 (£35)

ARMY MESS HALL SOUP BOWL
- 9" diameter white porcelain soup bowl has Army eagle, maker proof, and date $30 (£15)

LUFTWAFFE MESS BOWL
- 15-1/2" diameter deep-dish aluminum serving bowl, base marked with the Luftwaffe flying eagle, maker marked and dated "AW 40" $35 (£20)

LUFTWAFFE MESS HALL 10-INCH SERVING BOWL
- 10-3/4" square serving bowl, base has nice Bavarian Haviland Co. maker's stamp with early droop tail style Luftwaffe eagle. $65 (£35)

LUFTWAFFE MESS HALL SMALL BOWL
- 6-1/2" white porcelain bowl has Luftwaffe eagle, maker, and wartime date on reverse $20 (£10)

LUFTWAFFE MESS FLATWARE LOT
- Includes aluminum knife, fork, and spoon, each with Luftwaffe eagle, maker's stamp and 1940 date.
. . . . $55 (£30)

RAD MESS HALL PLATE
- Heavy white stoneware mess plate segregated into three portion areas. Reverse has "FELDA / RHÖN" glider trademark stamp and swastika within a cogged wheel insignia $35 (£20)

WAFFEN-SS MESS HALL PLATTER
- 16" x 10-3/4" white stoneware serving platter, reverse marked with crown over "VICTORIA" maker's log, and gothic lettered "WAFFEN-SS" $150 (£75)

Personal Hygiene and Uniform Care

SOLDIER'S RAZOR KIT
- Black Bakelite box has lid with maker's name; interior with complete razor assembly and extra blades in matching original package $40 (£20)

LUFTWAFFE SOLDIER'S ISSUE TOOTHBRUSH
- White and amber composite toothbrush with Luftwaffe eagle issue stamp $35 (£20)

ISSUE EYEGLASSES AND CASE
- Gray painted metal case with black stencil "Masken-Brille." Contains the pair of round metal frame eyeglasses with lenses and twill tape ear loops for use with the gas mask $55 (£30)

LUFTWAFFE "CHANNEL SUIT"
CASED SUNGLASSES
- Luftwaffe blue-painted aluminum case opens to reveal brown tortoiseshell green-tinted sunglasses with brown leather side pieces and elastic strap. $85 (£45)

SOLDIER'S NEEDLE KIT
- Folded paper packet filled with assorted sizes of needles. Packet is printed "Nadelsortiment fur den deutchen Soldaten" $10 (£5)

CLOTHING BAG
* Olive canvas bag with black leather straps, welting, and carrying handle, not for use in the field, but was used in rear areas or left on the unit's train $35 (£20)

Tobacco and Smoking Accessories

CIGARETTE ROLLING PAPERS
* Packet of 50 EFKA rolling papers with a Waffenamt tax seal and inspector's stamp inside $5 (£2)

PACKAGE OF TOBACCO
* Paper wrapped package of loose tobacco with an Austrian tax sticker that is embossed with a Nazi eagle and swastika $50 (£25)

SOLDIER'S CIGARETTE CUTTER
* Aluminum guillotine for cigarettes has maker's script trademark and "D.R.G.M." stamp, complete with original blade $10 (£5)

TROPICAL PACKED TOBACCO TIN
* 3-1/2" tall oval tin with a rubber gasket to help seal the friction fit lid. Lid is embossed with the German brand name "OVERSTOLZ" and HAUS NEUERBURG / TROPEN PACKUNG" $25 (£12)

SOLDIER'S ISSUE LIGHTER
* 2-1/4" tall aluminum cylinder with a domed friction lid and knurled base with Waffenamt $15 (£7)

German privately purchased body powder, $10-$15 (£5-£7). Charles D. Pautler

"Translanta" German tobacco, $35-$65 (£20-£35).
Charles D. Pautler

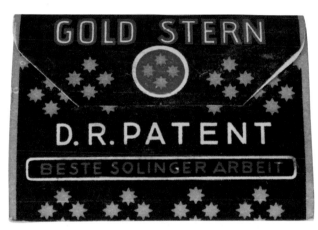

German privately purchased razor blade, $15-$25 (£7-£15). Charles D. Pautler

German commercial stick matches, $10-$20 (£5-£10). Minnesota Military Museum

Silver matchsafe with SS runes, $75-$100 (£40-£50).
Colin R. Bruce II

Soldier's personal items
bag, $30-$50 (£15-£25).
www.advanceguardmilitaria.com

Pasteboard pack of 10 Japanese cigarettes,
$50-$100 (£25-£50). www.advanceguardmilitaria.com

*Japanese soldier's personal items bag and identity
book, $75-$100 (£35-£50).* www.advanceguardmilitaria.com

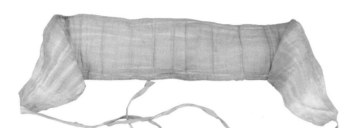

*Japanese soldier's "Thousand Stitch" belt,
$225-$300 (£115-£150).* www.advanceguardmilitaria.com

*Japanese military bugle, $250-$300
(£125-£150).* www.advanceguardmilitaria.com

*Japanese wounded soldier's hospital
robe, $150-$175 (£75-£90).*

www.advanceguardmilitaria.com

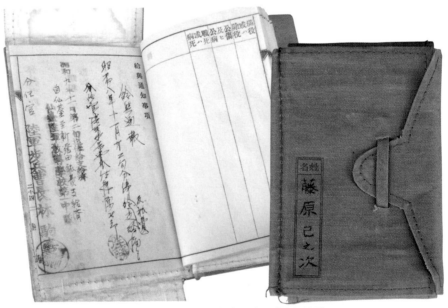

Japanese soldier's identification book, $40-$50 (£20-£25). www.advanceguardmilitaria.com

JAPAN

Individual Items

JAPANESE WOUNDED SOLDIER'S HOSPITAL ROBE

- White domet flannel robe with hand felled interior seams and reinforced shoulder yoke, right sleeve has Red Cross insignia, and the front closes with a single white cotton tape tie. Interior is well-marked with 1942 date. $165 (£85)

JAPANESE SOLDIER'S "THOUSAND STITCH" BELT

- Thousand Stitch belt with its original white cotton outer covering intact (normally removed by collectors so that the stitch design is more visible) with center interior pocket, stitches visible through the thin white cotton exterior, edges with white cotton fabric attachment ties. $225 (£115)

SOLDIER'S ID BOOK

- Hand book with printed cloth cover.........$45 (£25)

JAPANESE MILITARY BUGLE

- Japanese military issue pattern bugle, unmarked, and is complete with original worsted orange-red wool tassels. $275 (£140)

JAPANESE CIGARETTES

- Pasteboard pack of 10 cigarettes with sliding cover opens like a match book........................$75 (£40)

SOLDIER'S PERSONAL ITEMS BAG

- Olive cotton issue "ditty" bag has black printed Japanese inscriptions, top with drawstring closure $45 (£25)

SOLDIER'S PERSONAL ITEMS BAG AND ID BOOK

- Olive cotton issue "ditty" bag has black printed Japanese inscriptions, top with drawstring closure. Inside is a Japanese soldier's hand book with printed cloth cover. $75 (£40)

SOLDIER'S TROPICAL WALLET

- Olive rubberized fabric wallet with Japanese character printed inscription and olive tape ties $50 (£25)

JAPANESE FEMALE DEFENSE ORGANIZATION RELIGIOUS SHRINE SET

- Wooden box has lid with Japanese inscription that indicates this shrine set was purchased by individual donations in Tanomura village for a Defense Branch Women's Association. Contents include printed fringed banner with wreathed military rayed disc insignia in the center. The rest of the box is full of wooden and paper prayer papers intended for different results that would be achieved when the prayers are made and papers ceremonially burned............................$175 (£90)

Japanese female defense organization religious shrine set, $150-$200 (£75-£100).
www.advanceguardmilitaria.com

"You ought to be getting the box of souvenirs I sent from Okinawa pretty soon...I sent two sabers and a rifle. I hope they didn't rust. Those Samurai blades are beautiful."

LT. BOB GREEN, 763RD TANK BN. TO HIS MOTHER, OCT. 15, 1945

Saki Cups, Bottles and Trays

SAKE CUP, MANCHURIA DEFENSE

- 3" white porcelain sake cup has gilt vaulted star over crossed Japanese national and war flags with Japanese inscription that translates "Infantry 50th Regiment / Manchuria Defense" . . . . **$35 (£20)**

SAKE CUP, NAVY CONSTRUCTION UNIT CUP

- 2" diameter black porcelain sake cup has inscription around the outside edge, gilded interior has orange-red star and insignia with anchor, chrysanthemum and crossed construction implements . . . . **$45 (£25)**

SAKE CUP, CHRYSANTHEMUM AND ANCHOR BOWL INSERT

- Light violet porcelain sake cup has silver rim, center with white Chrysanthemum & Anchor bowl insert flanked by rayed war flag and chrysanthemum color motifs, interior rim with Japanese inscription "Memory of Release".
. . . . **$30 (£15)**

SAKE CUP, TRADITIONAL FIGURA

- 2" white porcelain sake cup has center bowl with color glaze depiction of a figure in traditional costume. Exterior has attractive blue-green glazed finish with embossed scallop decorations and maker's hallmark on base.
. . . . **$20 (£10)**

SAKE CUP, 33RD INFANTRY, MACHINE GUN MOTIF

- 2-1/8" olive green porcelain sake cup has chrysanthemum and machine gun with bipod in gilt. Japanese inscription "33rd Infantry Memory of Release".
. . . . **$45 (£25)**

SAKE CUP, CHINA INCIDENT VICTORY

- 2" cup with blue glazed basket weave exterior, gilt rim and inscription. Interior has color image of a soldier with a Japanese flag hanging from his bayonet in front of a map of China. . . . . **$35 (£20)**

SAKE CUP, HELMET AND FLAG

- 2" white porcelain sake cup has light blue rim with gilt edge, center of the bowl has Japanese war flag and

The value of any sake cup is determined by the type of picture and inscription that is on it. Unit-specific cups command the highest value. This cup commemorates the 50th Infantry Regiment's participation in the Manchurian Defense, $30-$50 (£15-£25). www.advanceguardmilitaria.com

Sake cup, chrysanthemum and anchor motif commemorating "release from service," $25-$35 (£12-£20). www.advanceguardmilitaria.com

Sake cup, 33rd Infantry with a machine gun motif, $40-$50 (£20-£25). www.advanceguardmilitaria.com

Sake cup, helmet and flag design, $25-$35 (£12-£20). www.advanceguardmilitaria.com

Sake cup, Imperial Guard 4th Regiment, $30-$50 (£15-£25).

www.advanceguardmilitaria.com

Sake cup, Imperial Guard 4th Regiment, $30-$50 (£15-£25).

www.advanceguardmilitaria.com

helmet with five-pointed vaulted Army star insignia and Japanese inscription "Triumph Memory" . . . . . **$25 (£15)**

SAKE CUP, IMPERIAL GUARD 4TH REGIMENT

- 2-1/4" white porcelain sake cup has red glazed bowl with gilt wreathed star and inscription "Imperial Guard 4th Regiment" and name "Kasugahara," exterior with decorative color floral motif. . . . . **$35 (£20)**

SAKE CUP, IMPERIAL GUARD 4TH REGIMENT

- 3-1/8" white porcelain sake cup has gilt wreathed star over crossed flags and inscription "Imperial Guard 4th Regiment" and name "Ota". . . . . **$35 (£20)**

SAKE BOTTLE, KAMIKAZI
SPECIAL ATTACK FORCE

- 5-1/2" white porcelain sake bottle has red Navy anchor, large fighter aircraft, star and crossed flags motif, and Japanese inscriptions that translate "Navy / Divine Wind Special Attack Force / Type 0 Fighter Airplane" with well-known maker "Kutani" and date 1944. .**$255 (£130)**

COMMUNICATION TROOPS SAKE
BOTTLE AND TRAY SET

- 6" light blue sake bottle embossed with decorative floral motifs throughout, center has chrysanthemum field featuring radio flag and Manchuko flags with signal lines, 9" square lacquered sake tray features signal lines and radio flag. Inscriptions translate "In Memory of the Triumph / Communication Troop / 1st Regiment / Manchuria". . . . .**$155 (£80)**

SAKE TRAY, SOLDIER'S MEMORIAL

- 9-1/4" square black lacquered wood sake tray with 3/4" lip with gilt edge, interior with Japanese flags and globe turned to highlight Japan and China, Army star insignia, helmet, and Japanese inscription that translates "He gave his life into the Emperor's hand, and he survived. Memory of his service" . . . . **$65 (£35)**

SAKE TRAY, FLAG AND CHRYSANTHEMUM

- 11-1/2" diameter circular tray has 1-1/4" edge, black lacquered wood with full color Japanese war flag surmounted by a large chrysanthemum, with star and floral motif. . . . .**$70 (£35)**

SAKE TRAY, EARLY ARMY HELMET AND FLAG

- 8-1/2" x 8-1/2" x 7/8" tall brown lacquered wood sake tray with gilt highlights, depicts early style Army helmet over war flag, with star insignia and inscriptions. . . . .**$75 (£40)**

This sake bottle is particularly prized because it commemorates Japan's special Kamikazi attack forces, $200-$300 (£100-£150).
www.advanceguardmilitaria.com

Communication troops sake bottle and tray set, $150-$175 (£75-£90). www.advanceguardmilitaria.com

Sake tray featuring a Japanese flag and a chrysanthemum, $50-$80 (£25-£40). www.advanceguardmilitaria.com

Sake tray decorated with an early style Army helmet and flag, $75-$100 (£35-£50). www.advanceguardmilitaria.com

UNITED KINGDOM AND UNITED STATES

Entertainment

AAF FILM PROJECTOR

- 17" x 13" x 9" black hinge-front carrying case is stenciled with "A/F STOCK NO." and "PROJECTOR, TYPE D-1B, SILENT." Opens to reveal a film projector with heavily textured brown finish, top with Army Air Forces metal data plate listing maker "Bell & Howell" and 1944-dated serial number code. . . . . **$175 (£90)**

ARMED SERVICES EDITION NOVEL LOT

- Includes serviceman's editions of five novels including *Wheels in his Head, Tomorrow's Another Day, The White Tower, Trelawny,* and *Earth and High Heaven*. These small, lightweight but unabbreviated books were treasured by soldiers in the field. . . . . **$35 (£20)**

ARMED SERVICES EDITION BOOK LOT

- Pocket size editions of *The Private Life of Helen of Troy* and *The Travels of Marco Polo*. . . . . **$25 (£15)**

CBI POINTIE TALKIE PHRASE BOOK

- *C.B.I. Pointie Talkie Number 4* phrase book for flyers downed in enemy territory with Chinese, Burmese, French, Thai, and other Southeast Asian language translations. 190 pages, bound in heavy cream paper. . . . . **$45 (£25)**

ARMY ISSUE PHONOGRAPH

- 17" x 15" x 7-1/2" olive drab metal case has leather handle and socket for crank handle on obverse, and top lid has "U.S." stencil. Interior has large metal instruction and data plate "MECHANICAL FIELD PHONOGRAPH." Interior of lid with operation and care instruction plate from a Hollywood, California, maker. . . . . . .**$275 (£140)**

NAVY FIELD PHONOGRAPH

- 17" x 15" x 8" case retains 95% Navy battleship gray finish with "MECHANICAL FIELD PHONOGRAPH" label and instructions on the inside of the lid. Exterior has circular "USN" and anchor insignia. Interior has 78 rpm crank record player complete with stowed crank handle, olive drab finished tone arm, and well with extra needles. Side has gray painted leather carrying handle. Interior of lid with operation and care instruction plate from Hollywood, California, maker. . . . .**$225 (£115)**

ARMY GERMAN LANGUAGE LESSON RECORDS

- U.S. Armed Forces Institute set includes six 78 rpm records . . . .**$25 (£15)**

RED CROSS PLAYING CARDS

- Complete deck of 52 standard playing cards complete in a pasteboard box printed with the Red Cross emblem and inscribed "Gift of the American Red Cross / NOT TO BE SOLD". Reverse imprinted "FOR USE OF U.S. GOVERNMENT" and dated "OCT 10 1944". . . . .**$35 (£20)**

SOLDIER'S COMMERCIAL ENTERTAINMENT KIT

- Much like the shaving and personal kits sold to soldiers, this kit has a brown leatherette folding case that opens to reveal dice and checkers, center section has complete set of patriotic playing cards with tax stamp, instructions and scorebook for Gin Rummy, instructions for playing chess and checkers, a pencil, and a folding chess / checkers game board . . . . **$65 (£35)**

SOLDIER'S PORTABLE CHECKERS GAME

- 5" x 5" x 1" original mailing carton with Jan. 1944 date opens to reveal a folding checkers game with wood playing board and internal drawer that contains black and white peg game pieces. . . . . **$40 (£20)**

Women's Army Corps playing cards, $50-$75 (£25-£40). Charles D. Pautler

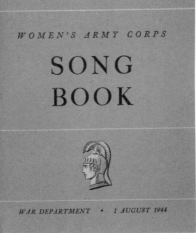

Women's Army Corps songbook, dated 1944, $15-$25 (£7-£12). Charles D. Pautler

Model 9-C portable phonograph, $200-$275 (£100-£140). Charles D. Pautler

Music-Related

ARMY SNARE DRUM

- Military parade drum by WFL Drum Co., Chicago, ca. 1937-1942, 15" tall x 16" diameter, obverse with brass keystone badge "W.F.L. / DRUM CO. / Wm F Ludwig / President / 1728 N DAMEN AVE / CHICAGO." Wood shell, natural finish, with "U.S." painted on side in blue. Rope tension with wood rims, metal screw strainer in wood brace, and side with harness attachment ring. $425 (£215)

ARMY BAND CLARINET AND CASE

- Silvered metal "E flat" clarinet complete with mouthpiece, mouthpiece cover, and red velvet fabric lined case with gilt "U.S." embossed on grained lid. Clarinet bell has maker's mark, "U.S." stamp, and 1945 date by hand inscription $395 (£200)

ARMY OLIVE PLASTIC BUGLE WITH CARRIER

- 18" long olive composition bugle with matching original mouthpiece, 4-1/2" bell stamped with eagle and shield "AMAN OFFICIAL BUGLE," complete with olive canvas carrier. $125 (£65)

BRITISH OFFICER/NCO WHISTLE & LANYARD

- German silver cylindrical whistle with Broad Arrow proof, Birmingham maker stamp and 1943 date, complete with braided khaki cord lanyard $40 (£20)

Rations/Foodstuffs

K RATION, BREAKFAST

- Boxed breakfast ration in the 1941 style brown pasteboard carton $135 (£70)

K RATION, BREAKFAST

- Boxed breakfast ration in the 1943 style brown and tan camouflaged carton......................$145 (£75)

K RATION, SUPPER

- Boxed ration in the 1941 style natural pasteboard carton, inscribed "U.S. ARMY FIELD RATION K / SUPPER UNIT," maker marked $135 (£70)

K RATION, DINNER

- Boxed dinner ration in the 1943 style blue and tan camouflaged carton $165 (£85)

Army snare drum made by WFL Drum Co., Chicago, ca. 1937-1942, $400-$500 (£200-£250).
www.advanceguardmilitaria.com

British officer/NCO whistle and lanyard, $35-$50 (£15-£25). www.advanceguardmilitaria.com

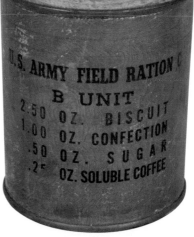

B-unit of the Army C-Rations, $85-$125 (£45-£60).
Author's collection

Boxed breakfast K-Ration in the 1941-style brown pasteboard carton, $135-$150 (£70-£75). Author's collection

The D-Bar was popular with troops because of its high-energy chocolate content, $65-$125 (£35-£60). Author's collection

Breakfast K-Ration in the 1943-style box, $135-$150 (£70-£75). Author's collection

K-Rations were a component of 10-in-1 ration boxes. The packaging, however, was different from individually issued K-Ration boxes. As such, a K-Ration from a 10-in-1 pack is much rarer but probably not as sought-after by collectors, $75-$150 (£35-£75). Author's collection

Boxed dinner K-Ration in the 1943-style blue and tan camouflaged carton, $135-$175 (£70-£90). Author's collection

> *"We ate with our army mess kits and rinsed them out in a barrel of hot water."*
>
> LT. ROY BENSON, 9TH U.S. AIR FORCE

SQUARE BISCUITS, TYPE "C"

- Box of Square Biscuits Type "C" . . . . **$65 (£35)**

COAST GUARD LIFE RAFT RATION

- "Life Boat Ration...packed to meet requirements of the Coast Guard", 7-1/2" x 4-1/2" sealed tin containing pemmican, "ration c," chocolate, and malted milk, New London Conn. maker. . . . . **$85 (£45)**

MALTED MILK DEXTROSE TABLET RATION

- Unopened individual issue box of 15 tablets marked "MALTED MILK-DEXTROSE AND DEXTROSE TAB-LETS / U.S. ARMY FIELD RATION K" with contractor information. . . . . **$25 (£15)**

ARMY "C" RATION WOODEN CRATE

- 19" x 12-1/2" x 7" wood transport case marked with the Commissary half moon, "U.S. ARMY FIELD RATION C" and a list of contents. Maker marked and inspection dated "NOV. 1942." Retains express shipping labels. . . . . **$150 (£75)**

10-IN-1 RATION CARTON

- 10-1/2" x 6-1/2" x 6-1/2" pasteboard carton with label "MENU #2 / SECOND HALF OF / 5 RATIONS," "For 5 Complete Rations / Use This Box and One Marked 'First Half of 5 Rations'". . . . . **$75 (£40)**

Box of "Square Biscuits Type C," $50-$75 (£25-£40). Author's collection

Cans of Spanish peanuts were included in the special "jungle rations" that were sent to the Pacific theater, $100-$150 (£50-£75). Author's collection

BRITISH EMERGENCY RATION BOX

- Most likely from a ground vehicle or aircraft, 9" x 6" x 5" olive drab painted metal box has khaki web hinge and closure strap, top is stenciled "RATIONS" on one side of the strap and "No. 1 / 2 MEN 1 DAY" on the other.
.... $50 (£25)

MOUNTAIN RATION SHIPPING BOX

- 23" x 9" x 12" heavy dark pasteboard outer box has faint Quartermaster Depot stencil, opens to reveal the brown pasteboard inner carton. This inner box has side stenciled with Commissary Corps crescent moon insignia and "3 MOUNTAIN RATION UNITS / (4 RATIONS PER UNIT)" with contract number and packing information, base with box specifications and 1942 date.
.... $395 (£200)

SHIPPING CRATE FOR CHARMS CANDY

- 15" x 13" x 8-1/2" nailed construction wooden crate has green and black painted corners "STOCK NO. / 35-C-1735 / CELLO CANDY SQUARES / 48 12 OZ PKGS / PACKED MAR. 45 / WT. 47 CU. .9" with maker's name on side "SCHIKOROWSKY / ER WINONA MINN".
.... $75 (£40)

Charms candies were included in a variety of ration packets, $15-$25 (£7-£12). Author's collection

Malted milk-dextrose tablets, $15-$25 (£7-£12). Author's collection

Individual packets of "soluable" (instant) coffee were included in both K- and C-Rations, $5-$10 (£2-£5).
Author's collection

The U.S. military shipped most of its canned goods in wooden crates made to the Quartermaster Department's specifications. Crates for foodstuffs, such as this example for Vienna sausages, command the most collector attention, $100-$200 (£50-£100). Author's collection

10-in-1 cardboard ration container, $65-$100 (£35-£50).
Author's collection

Wooden C-Ration crate, without lid, $150-$200 (£75-£100). Author's collection

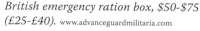

British emergency ration box, $50-$75 (£25-£40). www.advanceguardmilitaria.com

Mountain Ration shipping box, $350-$450 (£175-£225). Author's collection

Military shipping crate for Charms candy, $75-$100 (£35-£50). www.advanceguardmilitaria.com

Religious Items

CATHOLIC SOLDIER'S FIELD PRAYER KIT

- Pocket-size folding grained black leather wallet has rosary, crucifix, and 1941-dated "Devotions Under The Flag: A Prayer Book for Catholic Men in Every Branch of the Service" . . . . **$40 (£20)**

JEWISH SOLDIER'S PRAYER BOOK

- Published by the Jewish Welfare Board, pocket-sized "Abridged Prayer Book / For Jews in the Armed Forces of the United States, in English and Hebrew . . . . . **$45 (£25)**

LUTHERAN SOLDIER'S FAITH ID TOKEN

- 30mm silver coin has hole on the top for wear with the ID tags or on a cord of its own, with eagle and cross emblem and "LOYALTY TO CHRIST AND COUNTRY," reverse "IN CASE OF NEED NOTIFY LUTHERAN CHAPLAIN." Issued by the Army and Navy Commission of the Lutheran Church . . . . **$40 (£20)**

POCKET BIBLE WITH METAL COVER

- Small issue New Testament with statement with metal slipcover on the front inscribed MAY THIS COMFORT AND PROTECT YOU . . . . **$30 (£15)**

CHAPLAIN'S CATHOLIC COMMUNION SET

- 11" x 7" x 2" black grained box with gilt cross emblem opens to reveal violet lined interior with two candle stands, slot for the crucifix, and contents including two wrapped original candles, two metal plates, spoon, bottle with molded designation "HOLY WATER" and crown seal stopper, wood crucifix in its carrying envelope, and 1942-dated "My Military Missal" Catholic mass book with advice to Catholic soldiers . . . . **$165 (£85)**

Catholic priest's field altar set, $250-$400 (£125-£200).

www.advanceguardmilitaria.com

Catholic soldier's bible, rosary and case, $20-$30 (£10-£15).

www.advanceguardmilitaria.com

"There were four of us in each tent sleeping on army cots with a stove in the middle for heat. On warm days we could roll up the sides of the tent for ventilation."

LT. ROY BENSON, 9TH U.S. AIR FORCE

Sewing Kits

SOLDIER'S "ARMY SERVICE KIT"

+ Olive drab rectangular stiffened sewing kit has Army enlisted eagle printed in gold on the flap. Interior has complete original contents including needles, a large selection of thread, and a purple plastic thimble.
.... **$45 (£25)**

SOLDIER'S "HOUSEWIFE" SEWING KIT

+ Trifold olive drab cotton sewing kit has U.S. eagle printed on the exterior. Interior is well-supplied with thread, buttons, needles, etc. .... **$35 (£18)**

ARMY THREAD SET

+ Pasteboard threadwinder has six skeins of "heavy duty 3 ply sewing thread" in "regulation colors," 10 yards each skein. Varying shades of olive drab .... **$15 (£7)**

Sporting Goods

USMC MARKED CATCHER'S MITT

+ Brown leather catcher's mitt is dark from long service but remains good and pliable, with "USMC" property stamp and accountability numbers on one side.
.... **$175 (£90)**

USMC BASEBALL GLOVE

+ Brown leather baseball glove, palm is stamped with large "USMC" designation and contract numbers. . **$165 (£85)**

ARMY SPECIAL SERVICES BASEBALL GLOVE

+ Soft brown leather "Wilson" ball glove marked "PROFESSIONAL MODEL / SPECIAL SERVICES / U.S. ARMY" stamp .... **$125 (£65)**

Service man's bible in presentation box, $25-$35 (£12-£14). Charles D. Pautler

Sewing kit in a leather-covered hard case, $15-$25 (£7-£15). Author's collection

The variety of soldier's sewing kits (known as "housewives") is seemingly endless. Most will range in value from $10-$25 (£5-£15). Author's collection

Lutheran soldier's faith identification token, $35-$50 (£15-£20). www.advanceguardmilitaria.com

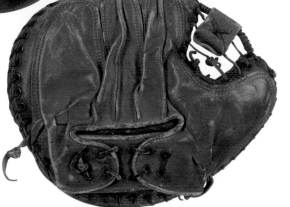

USMC marked catcher's mitt with "USMC" property stamp and accountability numbers, $150-$175 (£75-£90).

www.advanceguardmilitaria.com

U.S. marked and 1945-dated first baseman's glove, $150-$175 (£75-£90). Charles D. Pautler

Survival map in the form of a bowtie, $35-$65 (£20-£35). www.advanceguardmilitaria.com

British Vaporite hand lantern, $75-$100 (£40-£50).

www.advanceguardmilitaria.com

SKI WAX, BLUE

- "Blue" ski wax, 3" tall, 1-1/2" diameter cardboard tube with olive drab metal friction lid, blue label indicating "FOR DRY SNOW" and instructions for application.
.... **$5 (£2)**

Survival Accessories

AAF CBI SILK ESCAPE MAP, MANCHURIA

- Two-sided AAF silk escape map features Shen-Yang and Jehol. Sheet numbers are NK 50 and NK 51, 1944 date.
.... **$45 (£25)**

AAF CBI SILK ESCAPE MAP, CHINA

- 1944-dated silk full-color escape map of the Harbin China area .... **$45 (£25)**

AAF SILK ESCAPE MAP, CENTRAL EUROPE

- Obverse is sheet "43/C" covering Holland, Belgium, France, and Germany. Reverse is sheet "43/E" covering Northern Germany, Protectorate (Bohemia & Moravia), Slovakia, Poland, and Hungary .... **$75 (£40)**

ARMY COT MOSQUITO BAR

- 1942-dated light olive canvas and mesh mosquito bar has tape ties, cot must be fitted with a wood stick frame to make this work .... **$35 (£20)**

ARMY JUNGLE HAMMOCK

- Light olive drab canvas, rubberized fabric, mosquito netting, ropes, cords and zippers .... **$75 (£40)**

MILITARY ISSUE INSECT REPELLENT

- 2-ounce glass bottle has black screw-on cap and paper label "REPELLENT, INSECT / For Mosquitoes, Biting Flies, Gnats, and Fleas" .... **$12 (£6)**

AAF PENLIGHT AND BOX

- Type A-6B "Justrite Penlight" pocket flashlight, 5-1/4" long olive drab plastic body with aluminum cap with red filter and pocket clip, marked with nomenclature and "PROPERTY - AF. U.S. ARMY." Complete with opened issue pasteboard box printed with contractor information .... **$30 (£15)**

ARMY FLASHLIGHT

- TL-122-D green plastic flashlight with angled head and spring metal belt clip, made by "NIAGARA" . . **$35 (£20)**

BRITISH VAPORITE HAND LANTERN

- 13" tall including the handle, tinned iron lantern retains black painted finish, with vented crown, hinged door with circular lens opening to reveal a small oil lamp with adjustable wick and rear reflector. Side has stamped metal oval maker's data plate "C. EASTGATE & SON, Ltd. / 1944 / (Broad Arrow) / BIRMINGHAM".
.... **$75 (£40)**

AAF AIRCREW INSULATED THERMOS

- Olive drab painted metal aircrew thermos has threaded cap, push-button spout, bail handle with black wood grip, and base with "Container, Insulated, Liquid / Type F-1" AAF metal nomenclature label and "Stanley" trademark stamped in the base................... **$65 (£35)**

Military issue insect repellent, $10-$15 (£5-£7.50). www.advanceguardmilitaria.com

Tobacco/Smoking accessories

CAMEL CIGARETTES WITH MILITARY TAX STAMP

- Unopened pack of Camels with tax stamp "For use only of U.S. Military or Naval forces in Alaska or Hawaii, or for use outside the jurisdiction of the Internal Revenue laws of the United States..."................. **$75 (£40)**

LUCKY STRIKE CIGARETTES WITH WARTIME TAX STAMP AND INSCRIPTION

- Unopened pack of Lucky Strikes with tax stamp "For use only of U.S. Military or Naval forces in Alaska or Hawaii..."............................... **$65 (£35)**

SOLDIER'S BROWN BAKELITE CIGARETTE PACK CASE

- Brown Bakelite box sized to fit one pack of WWII era cigarettes, has decorative line design on the side and brand name "Johnny Box" on the lid .... **$25 (£15)**

SOLDIER'S "ZIPPO" STYLE LIGHTER

- Zippo style lighter with olive drab crinkle textured finish. Interior has "Zephyr" maker's name and address embossed into the lid .... **$65 (£35)**

USMC CIGARETTE LIGHTER

- Aluminum lighter with applied gilt EGA, marked "CREST CRAFT"......................... **$25 (£15)**

AAF ZIPPO LIGHTER

- Plain metal Zippo has side with bronze "U.S. Air Corps" and winged prop insignia, base has "Zippo" maker's stamp and 1937 patent number.............. **$75 (£40)**

ENGRAVED ALUMINUM LIGHTER

- Heavy-duty aluminum lighter has "USN" and fouled anchor engraved insignia .... **$90 (£45)**

ARMY MATCH SAFE WITH ORIGINAL ISSUE BOX

- Pasteboard carton printed "Box, Match, Waterproof" with August 1944 contract date. Contains olive drab plastic cylindrical match safe................ **$20 (£10)**

ARMY WATERPROOF MATCHES

- Pasteboard box of "kitchen" size matches with printed contract label marked "MATCHES, ORDINARY, WATER RESISTANT," with QMC stock numbers, side of container printed with "MOSQUITO BITES CAUSE MALARIA" warning .... **$8 (£4)**

Wings Cigarettes, $45-$65 (£20-£35). Charles D. Pautler

Wartime-pack of Camel cigarettes for domestic distribution, $45-$65 (£20-£35). Charles D. Pautler

Unopened carton of wartime Camels is prized today by collectors just as it was by soldiers during the war, $300-$400 (£150-£200). Charles D. Pautler

Chesterfield cigarettes from a K-Ration box, $15-$25 (£7-£12). Charles D. Pautler

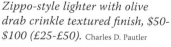

Zippo-style lighter with olive drab crinkle textured finish, $50-$100 (£25-£50). Charles D. Pautler

Philip Morris & Co. cigarettes with label indicating that they are not for sale and to be used only for distribution to the Armed Forces, $65-$85 (£30-£45). Charles D. Pautler

"Yankee Girl" chewing tobacco in leather carrying case, $45-$65 (£20-£35). Charles D. Pautler

Waterproof match safe in original carton, $20-$30 (£10-£15). Charles D. Pautler

A large variety of commercial hygiene products from the 1940s are readily available on the collector market today. The highest prices are paid for commercial items that are marked specifically for distribution to the armed forces. Charles D. Pautler

Toiletries/Personal Hygiene

ARMY BARBER FIELD KIT
- 15" x 9" x 7" olive drab metal carrying case with "U.S." stencil has footlocker-style latch closure. Opens to reveal instruction paper for care of tools labeled "KIT, BARBER, WITH CASE (M-1944)." Contents include barber shears, period comb, two barber clippers with extra blades, shaving brushes, straight razor, stop, one barber disinfecting tray, olive drab plastic soap dish with big embossed Army star in the center, and one can of lubricating oil . . . . **$325 (£165)**

WWII ARMY MARKED SOLDIER'S COMB
- 7" soldier's black composition comb with gilded "U.S. ARMY" inscription along spine. . . . . **$15 (£7)**

ARMY HAIR TONIC
- 4 oz. clear glass bottle of "Petro-Jeline" hair and scalp tonic with paper instruction label noting that this product is for sole distribution to the U.S. Army and Navy. . . . . **$25 (£12)**

BRITISH ARMY-ISSUE FOOT POWDER
- Small metal flask container retains gilt metallic finish with black lettering "FOOT POWDER / 1 3/4 oz". . . . . **$15 (£7)**

ARMY-ISSUE FOOT POWDER
- 5" OD metal can with shaker cap, marked "FOOT POWDER" with date "1942." Retains original contents. . . . . **$15 (£7)**

SOAP IN PX SOAP CASE
- Metal hinged-lid box has light olive finish with script "Soap." Interior has issue soap in original wrapper. . . . . **$20 (£10)**

NAVY SOAP DISH
- Blued metal soap kit with embossed "USN" on the top half . . . . **$15 (£7)**

GI PRO-KIT (PROPHYLACTIC)
- Paper wrapped kit includes soap impregnated cloth and ointment tube "For Army Use Only," with illustrated instruction sheet. . . . . **$55 (£25)**

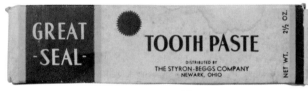

"Great Seal" toothpaste in original box, $12-$15 (£5-£7). Charles D. Pautler

Privately-purchased "trench mirror" in leather case, $15-$20 (£7-£10). Charles D. Pautler

"Let's clean up the Axis," soap, $15-$20 (£7-£10). Charles D. Pautler

Lifebuoy soap, $10-$15 (£5-£7). Charles D. Pautler

British Army issue foot powder, $15-$20 (£7-£10). www.advanceguardmilitaria.com

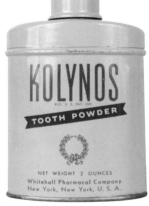

Kolynos tooth powder, $5-$10 (£2-£5). Charles D. Pautler

GI PROPHYLACTIC KIT

- "One Kit: Dough-Boy Prophylactic" box features image of US serviceman with rifle and bayonet. Contents include two condoms, soap-impregnated cloth, ointment, and a tube of Silver Picrate ointment . . . . **$75 (£35)**

ISSUE SOAP

- Unused bar of SOAP, GRIT, TYPE II, FOR SCOURING AND SCRUBBING, in original wrapping . . . . . . **$15 (£7)**

ISSUE TOILET PAPER

- Packet of toilet paper in a 5-1/2" x 3" waterproof envelope, came as part of the 10-in-1 ration . . . . **$12 (£5)**

PERSONAL ITEMS UTILITY KIT

- "BLITZ" MAKE UP ROLL AND UTILITY APRON, olive drab HBT personal items carry-all with 10 pockets for various toiletries can be conveniently worn like a tool belt when in use. . . . . **$35 (£17)**

SOLDIER'S HOLD-ALL

- Khaki cotton tri-fold hold-all with interior pockets, retains some contents including razor blades, shaving brush, housewife, mirror in case marked "Hoffman," etc. . . . . **$20 (£10)**

SOLDIER'S UNUSED RED CROSS GIFT BAG AND CONTENTS

- Olive drab cotton twill Red Cross soldier's gift bag with personal item hold-all of khaki cotton with olive drab edge binding and ties, also olive drab cotton twill housewife with card "With greetings from the Boston Metropolitan Chapter of the American Red Cross" . . **$45 (£25)**

GI Pro-Kit (prophylactic), $35-$55 (£15-£25). www. advanceguardmilitaria.com

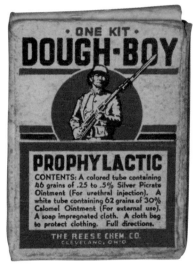

GI prophylactic kit, "One Kit: Dough-Boy Prophylactic," $50-$75 (£25-£40). www. advanceguardmilitaria.com

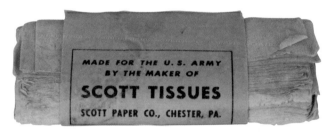

Packet of toilet paper in a 5-1/2" x 3" waterproof envelope, $10-$15 (£5-£7). Author's collection

Personal items utility kit with original box, $30-$50 (£15-£25). www.advanceguardmilitaria.com

Issue Gillette safety razor in box, $25-$35 (£12-£17). Charles D. Pautler

Privately purchased Gillette safety razor and blades, $25-$35 (£12-£17). Author's collection

Soldier's toiletry kit in zippered khaki cotton case, $25-$35 (£12-£15). Charles D. Pautler

Privately purchased leather toilet kit, $35-$65 (£15-£35). Author's collection

Individual's toiletry kit that includes a sewing kit, $55-$65 (£30-£35). Charles D. Pautler

SOLDIER'S RED CROSS PERSONAL EFFECTS BAG

- Olive drab cotton with white cotton label and red stamp "AMERICAN RED CROSS," white twill tape drawstring. .... **$10 (£5)**

PERSONAL KIT

- Complete ivory-colored celluloid set including brush, comb, nail file, curved scissors, toothbrush holder with toothbrush, soap dish, clothes brush, and mirror. Comes in light olive drab semi-waterproof carrier with nickeled closure buckle and retains original "ART IVORY" product card inside .... **$60 (£30)**

SOLDIER'S PERSONAL KIT

- Khaki canvas hold-all kit with olive drab tape binding and ties. Interior includes shaving mirror, towels, razor kit, issue ration soap, and razor blades. .... **$25 (£15)**

SOLDIER'S HBT PERSONAL KIT BAG

- 10" tall olive drab HBT personal bag has drawstring top closure, shows little use. .... **$10 (£5)**

HANDKERCHIEF WITH ORIGINAL PX TAG

- Olive drab hanky with original Camp Campbell Exchange price tag .... **$15 (£5)**

USMC AND GENERAL SERVICE PERSONAL ITEMS LOT

- Includes Squibb tooth powder, military-issue foot powder, Ammen's powder, "USMC" marked shoe brush, Gillette service razor kit and metal soap container, ... **$45 (£20)**

WAAC/WAC COMPACT

- Oval powder compact, 4" at the widest point, brass with black Japanned finish and raised WAAC eagle cap emblem finished in ivory applied to the lid. Interior has mirrored lid and powder puff with the "REX FIFTH AVENUE" distributor's label on the ribbon. .... **$195 (£100)**

Olive drab hankerchief, $5-$10 (£2-£5). Charles D. Pautler

Trunks, Suitcases, and Barracks Bags

WWII BARRACKS BAG

- Pieced construction khaki heavy cotton barracks bag with white cotton draw cord .... **$5 (£2)**

WWII AAF AVIATOR'S KIT BAG

- Olive canvas with white web reinforcement and handles, marked with "AN" proof and "AVIATOR'S KIT BAG / 0158791" nomenclature stamp .... **$75 (£40)**

SOLDIER'S WAR DIARY SATCHEL

- Light olive drab canvas satchel with brown leather trim, inscribed throughout with unit insignia, this man's name, and many place names in the Italian theater including "Anzio," "Rome," "Trieste," etc. .... **$35 (£20)**

ARMY OFFICER'S B-4 SUITCASE

- Light olive canvas and brown leather suitcase stenciled with officer's name and service number ..... **$40 (£20)**

FOOTLOCKER LOCK

- Yale footlocker lock assembly complete with attachment rivets and keys, brand new in the 1943-dated box.
  .... **$45 (£25)**

Round plastic compact with national symbol, $25-$50 (£12-£25). Charles D. Pautler

G.I. TRUNK LOCK UNISSUED IN ORIGINAL CARTON

- Replacement lock retains 99% olive drab finish, complete with mounting hardware, two keys, and original Quartermaster issue carton..................... **$50 (£25)**

NAVY FOOTLOCKER LOCK

Footlocker lock with "USN" designation....... **$40 (£20)**

NAVY OFFICER'S UNIFORM TRUNK

- 25" x 20" x 15" olive drab trunk is a cross between a footlocker and a suitcase, lid is stenciled with Navy Ensign's name and is decorated by several Navy stickers.
  .... **$40 (£20)**

NAVY SEABEE OFFICER'S DECORATED FOOTLOCKER

- Military-issue footlocker has large 7" diameter full-color Seabee insignia decal on the lid, stencil has officer's name, interior complete with tray........... **$95 (£50)**

RED CROSS CONVALESCENT KIT GIFT BAG

- 14" by 11" light blue cotton ditty bag with red twill drawstring closure, obverse with sewn label printed with a red cross and inscription "CONVALESCENT KIT / AMERICAN RED CROSS." Interior with woven label from the "BAYSIDE BRANCH / NORTH SHORE CHAPTER / NEW YORK". .... **$25 (£15)**

RED CROSS MEDICAL PACKAGE FOR U.S. PRISONERS OF WAR

- 10" x 10" x 5-1/2" unsealed pasteboard carton is printed with Red Cross insignia and green block letter inscription "AMERICAN RED CROSS / PRISONER OF WAR MEDICAL KIT NO. 4 / FOR DISTRIBUTION THROUGH / INTERNATIONAL RED CROSS COMMITTEE." Sealed and contents completely intact.
  .... **$385 (£195)**

WAAC/WAC oval powder compact with "REX FIFTH AVENUE" distributor's label, $150-$195 (£75-£95). www.advanceguardmilitaria.com

Normally, an Army suitcase would not garner too much interest. However, if it is decorated with a unit insignia such as this example, it quickly becomes a valued artifact, $75-$150 (£40-£75). Charles D. Pautler

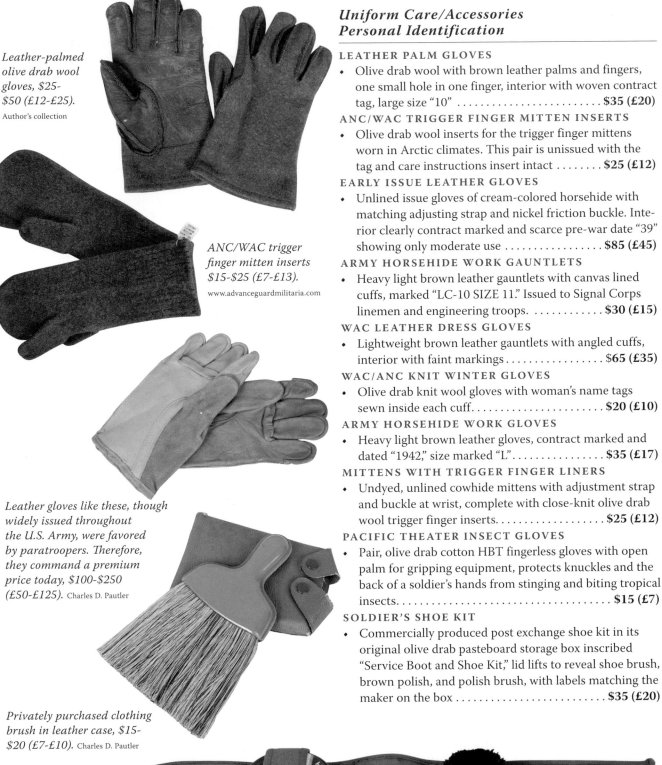

Leather-palmed olive drab wool gloves, $25-$50 (£12-£25).
Author's collection

ANC/WAC trigger finger mitten inserts $15-$25 (£7-£13).
www.advanceguardmilitaria.com

Leather gloves like these, though widely issued throughout the U.S. Army, were favored by paratroopers. Therefore, they command a premium price today, $100-$250 (£50-£125). Charles D. Pautler

Privately purchased clothing brush in leather case, $15-$20 (£7-£10). Charles D. Pautler

Uniform Care/Accessories
Personal Identification

LEATHER PALM GLOVES
- Olive drab wool with brown leather palms and fingers, one small hole in one finger, interior with woven contract tag, large size "10" . . . . **$35 (£20)**

ANC/WAC TRIGGER FINGER MITTEN INSERTS
- Olive drab wool inserts for the trigger finger mittens worn in Arctic climates. This pair is unissued with the tag and care instructions insert intact . . . . **$25 (£12)**

EARLY ISSUE LEATHER GLOVES
- Unlined issue gloves of cream-colored horsehide with matching adjusting strap and nickel friction buckle. Interior clearly contract marked and scarce pre-war date "39" showing only moderate use . . . . **$85 (£45)**

ARMY HORSEHIDE WORK GAUNTLETS
- Heavy light brown leather gauntlets with canvas lined cuffs, marked "LC-10 SIZE 11." Issued to Signal Corps linemen and engineering troops. . . . . **$30 (£15)**

WAC LEATHER DRESS GLOVES
- Lightweight brown leather gauntlets with angled cuffs, interior with faint markings . . . . **$65 (£35)**

WAC/ANC KNIT WINTER GLOVES
- Olive drab knit wool gloves with woman's name tags sewn inside each cuff. . . . . **$20 (£10)**

ARMY HORSEHIDE WORK GLOVES
- Heavy light brown leather gloves, contract marked and dated "1942," size marked "L". . . . . **$35 (£17)**

MITTENS WITH TRIGGER FINGER LINERS
- Undyed, unlined cowhide mittens with adjustment strap and buckle at wrist, complete with close-knit olive drab wool trigger finger inserts. . . . . **$25 (£12)**

PACIFIC THEATER INSECT GLOVES
- Pair, olive drab cotton HBT fingerless gloves with open palm for gripping equipment, protects knuckles and the back of a soldier's hands from stinging and biting tropical insects. . . . . **$15 (£7)**

SOLDIER'S SHOE KIT
- Commercially produced post exchange shoe kit in its original olive drab pasteboard storage box inscribed "Service Boot and Shoe Kit," lid lifts to reveal shoe brush, brown polish, and polish brush, with labels matching the maker on the box . . . . **$35 (£20)**

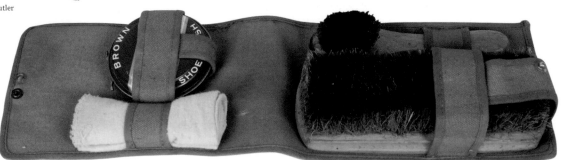

Shoe polishing kit in khaki cotton carrying case, $30-$50 (£15-£25). Charles D. Pautler

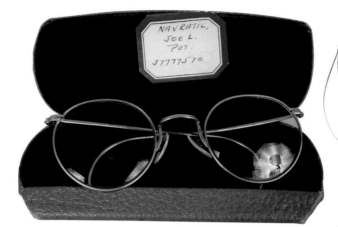

Army issue eyeglasses, with case, $35-$65 (£15-£35). Charles D. Pautler

U.S. Army Air Force aviator's sunglasses, $50-$75 (£25-£40).
Charles D. Pautler

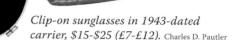

Clip-on sunglasses in 1943-dated carrier, $15-$25 (£7-£12). Charles D. Pautler

ANTI-GAS SHOE IMPREGNITE GREASE CAN

• Unopened metal can of "IMPREGNITE, SHOE, M1," gray painted finish . . . . **$10 (£5)**

SOLDIER'S MONEY BELT

• Khaki cotton money belt has one large pocket and two smaller ones, olive tape binding and strap . . . . . **$25 (£12)**

SOLDIER'S DISCHARGE WALLET

• Extra-quality grained leather trifold wallet for the soldier's discharge has a small service record diary, a frame for a photograph, and comes in the original pasteboard box. Includes letter from Thompson Products, Inc. of Cleveland "to the families of our men and women in service" presenting this as a gift for Christmas 1944. New, but the retaining strap on the exterior of the wallet is broken on one side. Gilt embossed cover . . . **$45 (£20)**

SOLDIER'S SCARF

• Olive drab scarf with faint stenciled number on the end. . . . . **$35 (£15)**

KNITTED WOOL TOQUE

• M1941 olive drab knitted wool toque or balaclava. . . . . **$25 (£12)**

AAF PILOT'S SUNGLASSES

• White metal wire frame sunglasses have tan plastic nose and brow rests and temples, comfort cable ear loops, complete with brown stiffened composite carrying case marked with winged star logo and "ROCKGLAS / ARMY AIR FORCE TYPE" . . . . **$75 (£40)**

AAF FLYER'S SUNGLASSES

• Gilt-metal wire-frame green-tinted sunglasses have comfort cable ear loops, complete with brown stiffened composite carrying case marked with wing logo and "AVIATION" . . . . **$75 (£40)**

IDENTIFICATION TAGS

• Pair, on original chain inscribed to GI . . . . **$25 (£12)**

Pair of identification tags (also known as "dog tags"), $15-$30 (£7-£15).
www.advanceguardmilitaria.com

Dog tags on handmade thong with religious medal ("God protect me" in German), $35-$50 (£15-£25).
Charles D. Pautler

Privately purchased identification bracelet, $15-$25 (£7-£15). Author's collection

Identification tag for a Navy WAVE, $25-$40 (£12-£20).

www.advanceguardmilitaria.com

Hamilton military wristwatch marked "U.S. / No. / GRADE WG," $100-$150 (£50-£75).

www.advanceguardmilitaria.com

USMC IDENTIFICATION TAG

- Oval nickel tag pierced with two holes for neck chain, stamped with Marine's name, number, date "1/42," blood type and "USMC"..........................**$25 (£15)**

CLOTHES MARKING KIT

- Complete kit with letters and numbers, stamps pads, and ink for marking clothes and equipment of members of the Armed Forces," dated 1944 ....**$25 (£15)**

ACCOUTERMENT STAMPING KIT

- Essentially the same as the WWI ID tag and equipment metal stamp kit but with no provision for ID tags, as these were marked by machine during WWII. The set comes in an olive wood case marked "U.S." with 1942-dated maker's stamp, and is complete with all letters, metal hammer, bronze anvil, and template jigs for meat can, fork, spoon, and knife, as well as locking nut.
....**$225 (£115)**

Watches

HAMILTON MILITARY WRISTWATCH

- Military wristwatch has luminous numerals and hands, 60 second sweep, and "Hamilton" maker. Reverse has "U.S. / No. / GRADE WG." Includes a later olive drab cotton wristband ....**$125 (£65)**

ARMY WALTHAM WRISTWATCH

- Waltham Co. Type A-17 watch, military face with 24 hour display, wind button with "hack" feature, reverse with "U.S. PROPERTY" military contract stamping, and complete with original olive cotton band.
....**$225 (£115)**

ARMY ELGIN WRISTWATCH

- Nickel case Elgin wristwatch has age-toned face with 60 second sweep, numerals and hands with radium finish, reverse with "ORD. DEPT. / U.S.A. / OG-180418".
....**$135 (£70)**

USMC WRISTWATCH STRAP, NEW ON MANUFACTURER'S CARD

- Brown nylon watch strap has nickeled frame buckle, maker's card printed "U.S. MARINE CORPS Wrist-Watch Strap" with manufacturer's information.
....**$30 (£15)**

Bulova Mil-W-3818A watch with military time face, $100-$200 (£50-£100). www.advanceguardmilitaria.com

> *"My first censored letter home prompted my mother to ask in her return letter what I possibly could have written to have so many words cut out!"*
>
> PRIVATE GENE GARRISON, 87TH U.S. INFANTRY DIVISION

Writing Materials

SOLDIER'S CORRESPONDENCE KIT

- 12" x 9" when folded, brown leather correspondence kit has stationery wallet from Ft. Benning, several postcards and letters, several pages of Camp Butler stationary. Interior has empty notebook and address book. . . . .**$25 (£12)**

V-MAIL INK

- Two bottles of ink with the specific designation "for V-mail" on the label, one retains liquid contents . . **$15 (£7)**

NAVY SPILLPROOF INK WELL

- Glass inkwell with ribbed concentric ring design and black plastic screw-on lid with a bulbous glass funnel inside that acts as a baffle. In original box with the Navy contract number on the side . . . . **$20 (£10)**

ARMY PORTABLE TYPEWRITER

- "Corona Zephyr" brand typewriter, 12" x 11" x 3" metal housing and removable cover with olive drab finish. Metal handle probably lacks a leather cover . . . **$75 (£40)**

AAF DIARY

- Brown leatherbound journal with a locking tab, cover with gold embossed winged propeller and inscription "AIR CORPS DAYS". . . . .**$45 (£20)**

Personal diary with base identification, $15-$35 (£7-£20). Author's collection

Auction Houses

BOSLEYS MILITARY AUCTION
The White House, Marlow
Buckinghamshire SL7 1AH, England
www.bosleys.co.uk

HERMANN HISTORICA OHG
Linprunstr. 16
D-80335 Munich, Germany
www.hermann-historica.com

JAMES D. JULIA, INC.
P.O. Box 830
Fairfield, ME 04937
www.juliaauctions.com

MANION'S INTERNATIONAL AUCTION
P.O. Box 122144
Kansas City, KS 66112
www.manions.com

MOWHAWK ARMS INC.
P.O. Box 157
Bouckville, NY 13310
www.militaryrelics.com

ROCK ISLAND AUCTION COMPANY
4507 49th Avenue
Moline, IL 61265
www.rockislandauction.com

WALLIS & WALLIS
West Street Auction Galleries
Lewes, Sussex
BN7 2NJ England
www.wallisandwallis.com.uk

Dealers

ADVANCE GUARD MILITARIA
270 State Hwy HH
Burfordville, MO 63739
www.advanceguardmilitaria.com

ATLANTIC CROSSROADS, INC.
P.O. Box 144
Tenafly, NJ 07670
www.collectrussia.com

BAY STATE MILITARY ANTIQUES
Phone: (978) 870-2944
www.baystatemilitaria.com

BROCK'S
5742 Bostwick Hwy
Bostwick, GA 30623
www.brocksguns.com

BUNKER MILITARIA
P.O. Box 1531
Claremore, OK 74018
www.bunkermilitaria.com

**HELMUT WEITZE FINE
MILITARY ANTIQUES**
Neuer Wall 18, 2nd Floor
20354 Hamburg, Germany
www.weitze.net

JASON BURMEISTER MILITARIA
Phone: (419) 665-2060
Email:militaryantiques@msn.com

JOHNSON REFERENCE BOOKS & MILITARIA
#403 Chatham Square
Fredericksburg, VA 22405
www.ww2daggers.com

THE RUPTURED DUCK
51 Morgan Road
Hubbardston, MA 01452-1602
www.therupturedduck.com

MICHAEL A. MORRIS
40 West 25th St.
New York, NY 10021
www.morrismilitaria.com

STEWART'S MILITARY ANTIQUES
P.O. Box 1492
Mesa, AZ 85211
www.stewartsmilitaryantiques.com

WARTIME COLLECTABLES
P.O. Box 165
Camden, SC 29020
www.wartimecollectables.com

WITTMAN ANTIQUE MILITARIA
P.O. Box 350
Moorestown, NY 08057
www.wwiidaggers.com

WORLD WIDE MILITARY EXCHANGE
P.O. Box 745
Batavia, IL 60510
www.wwmeinc.com

AAC-U.S. Army Air Corps

AAF-U.S. Army Air Force

AFB-U.S. Air Force base

ANC-U.S. Army Nurse Corps

ATS-British Auxiliary Territorial Service

AVG-American Volunteer Group

BAR-Browning Automatic Rifle

BeVo-Badfabrik Ewald Vorsteher, the major manufacturer of German cloth insignia. Today, collectors use the term to describe smooth, tightly woven cloth insignia

CAC-U.S. Coastal Artillery Corps

CBI-China-Burma-India theater of operations

CPO-U.S. Chief Petty Officer

CWAC- Canadian Women's Army Corps

DAF-Deutsche Arbeitsfront, the German Labor Front

DAK-Deutsches Afrikakorps, the German Africa Corps

DI- Distinctive Insignia, usually U.S.

DLV-Deutsche Luftsport-Verband, German Air Sports Formation

DRGM-Deutsches Reichsgebrauchsmuster, German nationally used pattern

EGA-"Eagle, Globe and Anchor" the insignia of the United States Marine Corps

EM-Enlisted Man

ETO-European Theater of Operations

Ges. Gesch.-Gesetzlich Geschutzt, "legally protected"

Gestapo-GeheimeStaatspolizei, German Secret State Police

GHQ-General Headquarters, U.S. Army

GI-Government Issue

GPO-Government Printing Office

HBT-Herringbone Twill

HMAS-His Majesty's Australian Ship

HMCS-His Majesty's Canadian Ship

HMNZS-His Majesty's New Zealand Ship

HMS-His Majesty's Ship

HMSO-His Majesty's Stationery Office

HQ-Headquarters

Id'ed-Identified

IJA-Imperial Japanese Army

IJN-Imperial Japanese Navy

JAG-U.S. Judge Advocate General

KIA-Killed in Action

LDO-Leistungsgemeinschaft der Deutschen Ordenhersteller, German Administration of German Manufacturers

MIA-Missing in Action

MK-Mark

MTO-Mediterranean Theater of Operations

NAS-U.S. Naval Air Station

NCO-Noncommissioned Officer

NSBO-Nationalsozialistische Betriebsorganisation, German National Socialist Factory Organization

NSDAP-Nationalsozialistische Deutsche Arbeiterpartei, the German Nazi Party

NSFK-Nationalsozialistisches Fliegerkorps, German National Socialist Flying Corps

NSKK-Nationalsozialistisches Kraftfahrkorps, German National Socialist Motor Corps

OD-Olive Drab

OCD-Office of Civilian Defense

OCS-Officer Candidate School

OSS-Office of Strategic Services, U.S. organization to support underground operations

OT-Organization Todt

OWI-Office of War Information

POW-Prisoner of War

PFR-Partito Fascista Repubblicano, Fascist Republican Party, the political arm of the RSI (q.v.)

PTO-Pacific Theater of Operations

PX-Post exchange

QMB-U.S. Quartermaster Board

QMC-U.S. Quartermaster Corps

RAD-Reichsarbeitsdienst, German National Labor Service

RAF-British Royal Air Force

RAAF-Royal Australian Air Force

RAN-Royal Australian Navy

RCAF-Royal Canadian Air Force

RCN-Royal Canadian Navy

RCT-U.S. Regimental Combat Team

RB-Nr.-Reichsbetriebsnummer, German National Factory Code Number

RLB-Reichsluftschutzbund, German National Air Raid Protection Force

RM-Royal Marine(s)

RMA-Royal Marine Artillery

RN-Royal Navy

ROTC-U.S. Reserve Officer Training Corps

RSI-Repubblica Sociale Italiana, Italian Social Republic, the government established in north Italy by Mussolini after Italy capitulated in 1943

RZM-Reichszeugmeisterie, German National Material Control Board

SA-Sturmabteilung, Nazi party "assault detachment," also known as the "Brown Shirts"

SOS-U.S. Service of Supply

SS-Schutzstaffel, the Nazi "protection squad"

SHAEF-Supreme Headquarters, Allied Expeditionary Force, Eisenhower's headquarters for D-Day

Showa-reign title used by Japanese Emperor Hirohito, 1926-1989

SOE-Special Operations Executive, British organization to support underground operations

SNLF-Japanese Special Naval Landing Force ("marines")

SPARS-U.S. Coast Guard Women's Reserve

TENO-Technische Nothilfe, German Technical Emergency Service

UDT-Underwater Demolition Team

USA-United States Army

USAAC-United States Army Air Corps

USAAF-United States Army Air Force

USAFFE-United States Army Forces in the Far East

USAFISPA-U.S. Army Forces in the South Pacific Area

USCG-United State Coast Guard

USCGR-United State Coast Guard Reserve

USFIP-United States Forces in the Philippines

USMC-United States Marine Corps

USMCR-United States Marine Corps Reserve

USMCWR- United States Marine Corps Women's Reserve

USN-United States Navy

USNR-United State Navy Reserves

USO-United States Service Organization

USQMC-United States Quartermaster Corps

USS-United States Ship

VB-U.S. Bomber plane or squadron

VC-U.S. Composite plane or squadron

VF-U.S. Fighter plane or squadron

VMF-U.S. Marine Fighter Squadron

VMJ-U.S. Marine Utility Squadron

VMSB-U.S. Marine Scout-Bomber Squadron

VP-U.S. Navy Patrol Squadron

VS-U.S. Navy Scouting Squadron

VT-U.S. Torpedo plane or squadron

VOS-U.S. Observation-Scout plane or squadron

WBA-Wehrmachtbekleidungsamt, German Armed Forces Clothing Office

WAAC-U.S. Women's Army Auxiliary Corps, created on May 14, 1942. Evolved into the Women's Army Corp (WAC) in July 1943

WAC-U.S. Women's Army Corps, created in July 1943

WAFS-U.S. Women's Auxiliary Ferrying Squadron

WASP-U.S. Women's Airforce Service Pilot

WAVES-U.S. Women Accepted for Volunteer Emergency Service

WIA-Wounded in Action

WD-U.S. War Department

WR-U.S. Women Reservist, USMC

World War II collectors are very fortunate. Thousands of volumes have been published on the myriad of collecting interests. The following is just a brief list of books that new collectors will find beneficial.

Ailsby, Christopher J. *A Collector's Guide to the Luftwaffe.* Hersham, Surrey, UK: Ian Allan Publishing, 2006.

Angolia, LTC John R. *For Führer and Fatherland: Military Awards of the Third Reich,* 2nd ed. San Jose, CA: R. James Bender Publishing, 1985.

———*For Führer and Fatherland: Political & Civil Awards of the Third Reich.* San Jose, CA: R. James Bender Publishing, 1978.

Armold, Chris. *Steel Pots: The History of America's Steel Combat Helmets.* San Jose, CA: R. James Bender Publishing, 1997.

———*Painted Steel: Steel Pots, Volume II.* San Jose, CA: R. James Bender Publishing, 2000.

Ball, Robert W.D. *Collector's Guide to British Army Campaign Medals.* Dubuque, IA: Antique Trader Books, 1996.

Beadle, Alan. *German Combat Awards, 1935-45.* Bridport, Dorset, UK: Alan Beadle Ltd., 2004.

Beaver, Michal D. with Kelly Hicks, *SS Helmets: The History and Decoration of the Helmets of the Black Corps.* Atglen, PA: Schiffer Military History, 2006.

Békési, László. *Stalin's War: Soviet Uniforms & Militaria, 1941-45 in Colour Photographs.* Ramsbury, Marlborough, Wiltshire, UK: The Crowood Press, Ltd. 2006.

Bouchery, Jean. *From D-Day to VE-Day: The Canadian Soldier.* Paris: Histoire & Collections, 2003.

Bouchery, Jean and Philippe Charbonnier. *D-Day Paratroopers: The British, The Canadians, The French.* Paris: Histoire & Collections, 2004.

Brayley, Martin J. *Bayonets: An Illustrated History.* Iola, WI: KP Books, 2004.

———*American Web Equipment, 1910-1967.* Ramsbury, Marlborough, Wiltshire, UK: The Crowood Press, Ltd., 2006.

———*British Web Equipment of the Two World Wars.* Ramsbury, Marlborough, Wiltshire, UK: The Crowood Press, Ltd., 2005.

Brayley, Martin J. and Richard Ingram. *Khaki Drill & Jungle Green: British Tropical Uniforms, 1939-45 in Colour Photographs.* Ramsbury, Marlborough, Wiltshire, UK: The Crowood Press, Ltd., 2000.

———*The World War II Tommy: British Army Uniforms European Theatre 1939-45 in Colour Photographs.* Ramsbury, Marlborough,

Wiltshire, UK: The Crowood Press, Ltd.. 1998.

Brown, Christopher P. *U.S. Military Patches of World War II.* Paducah, KY: Turner Publishing Co., 2002.

Canfield, Bruce N. *U.S. Infantry Weapons of World War II.* Lincoln, RI: Andrew Mowbray Publishers, 1994.

Clark, Jeff. *Uniforms of the NSDAP: Uniforms, Headgear, Insignia of the Nazi Party.* Atglen, PA: Schiffer Military History, 2007.

Clawson, Robert W. *Russian Helmets: From Kaska to Stalshlyem, 1916-2001.* San Jose, CA: R. James Bender Publishing, 2002.

Curley, Timothy J. and Neil G. Stewart. *Waffenrock: Parade Uniforms of the German Army.* San Jose, CA: R. James Bender Publishing, 2006.

Davis, Aaron, *Standard Catalog of Luger: Identification & Pricing for all Models, Every Variation.* Iola, WI: Gun Digest Books, 2006.

Davis, Brian L. *Badges & Insignia of the Third Reich, 1933-1945.* Poole, Dorset, England: Blandford Books, Ltd., 1983.

———*German Army Uniforms and Insignia, 1933-1945.* London: Arms and Armour Press, 1971.

Dawson, Jim. *Swords of Imperial Japan, 1868-1945.* Newnan, GA: Stenger-Scott Publishing Co., 1996.

DeSchodt, Christophe and Laurent Rouger. *D-Day Paratroopers: The Americans.* Paris: Histoire & Collections, 2004.

de LaGarde, Jean. *German Soldiers of World War Two.* Paris: Histoire & Collections, 2005.

de Quesada, Alejandro M. *Uniforms of the German Soldier: An Illustrated History from World War II to the Present Day.* London: Greenhill Books, 2006.

Dorosh, Michael A. *Dressed to Kill.* Ottawa, Ontario, Canada: Service Publications, 2001.

Dorsey, R. Stephen. *U.S. Martial Web Belts and Bandoliers: 1903-1981.* Eugene, OR: Collector's Library, 1993.

Emerson, William K. *Encyclopedia of United Staes Army Insignia and Uniforms.* Norman, OK: University of Oklahoma Press, 1996

Enjames, Henri-Paul: *Government Issue: U.S. Army European Theater of Operations Collector Guide.* Paris: Histoire & Collections, 2003.

Fisch, Robert. *Field Equipment of the Infantry, 1914-1945*. Sykesville, MD: Greenberg Publishing Company, Inc., 1989.

Foster, Col. Frank C. *Complete Guide to United States Army Medals, Badges and Insignia, World War II to Present*. Fountain Inn, SC: Medals of America Press, 2004.

Gordon, David B. *Equipment of the WWII Tommy*. Missoula, MT: Pictorial Histories Publishing Co., Inc., 2004.

Hertfurth, Dietrich. *Sowjetische Auszeichnungen, 1918-1991*, 3rd ed. Berlin: Dietrich Hertfurth, 1999.

Hewitt, Mike. *Uniforms and Equipment of the Imperial Japanese Army in World War II*. Atglen, PA: Schiffer Military History, 2002.

Hicks, Kelly. *SS-Steel: Parade and Combat Helmets of Germany's Third Reich Elite*. San Jose, CA: R. James Bender Publishing, 2004.

Hogg, Ian V. and John S. Weeks. *Military Small Arms of the 20th Century*, 7th ed. Iola, WI: Krause Publications, 2000.

Hughes, Gordon, Barry Jenkins, and Robert A. Buerlein, *Knives of War: An International Guide to Military Knives from World War I to the Present*. Boulder, CO: Paladin Press, 2006.

Kibler, Thomas. *Combat Helmets of the Third Reich: A Study in Photographs*. Pottsboro, TX: Reddick Enterprises, 2003.

Kibler, Thomas and Robert Igbal. *Combat Helmets of the Third Reich, Vol. II*. Pottsboro, TX: Reddick Enterprises, 2005.

Lewis, Kenneth. *Doughboy to GI: U.S. Army Clothing and Equipment, 1900-1945*. Winton, Bournemouth, UK: Norman D. Landing Books, 2002.

Lucy, Roger V. *Tin Lids: Canadian Combat Helmets, 2nd ed.* Ottawa, Ontario, Canada: Service Publications, 2000.

Johnson, Thomas M. *Collecting the Edged Weapons of the Third Reich, Volume I*. Columbia, SC: LTC Thomas M. Johnson, 1977.

Lumsden, Robin. *Medals and Decorations of Hitler's Germany*. Shrewsbury: Airlife Publishing, Ltd., 2001.

Maguire, Jon A. and John P. Conway, *American Flight Jackets: A History of U.S. Flyers' Jackets from World War I to Desert Storm*. Atglen, PA: Schiffer Military History, 1994.

Manion, Ron. *American Military Collectibles Price Guide*. Dubuque, IA: Antique Trader Books, 1995.

———*German Military Collectibles Price Guide*. Dubuque, IA: Antique Trader Books, 1995.

———*Japanese & Other Foreign Military Collectibles Price Guide*. Dubuque, IA: Antique Trader Books, 1996.

Mason, Chris. *Paramarine: Uniforms and Equipment of Marine Corps Parachute Units in World War II*. Atglen, PA: Schiffer Military History, 2004.

Mirouze, Laurent. *World War II Infantry in Color Photographs*. London: Windrow & Greene Ltd., 1990.

Nakata, Tadao and Thomas B. Nelson. *Imperial Japanese Army and Navy Uniforms and Equipment*, Revised ed., Alexandria, VA: Ironside International Publishers, Inc., 1997.

Nash, Peter. *German Belt Buckles, 1845-1945*. Atglen, PA: Schiffer Military History, 2003.

Nelson, Derek and Dave Parson. *A-2 & G-1 Flight Jackets: Hell-Bent for Leather*. St. Paul, MN: MBI Publishing, 2002.

Rentz, Bill. *Geronimo! U.S. Airborne Uniforms, Insignia & Equipment in World War II*. Atglen, PA: Schiffer Military History, 1999.

Schwan, C. Frederick and Joseph E. Boling. *World War II Remembered: History in Your Hands: A Numismatic Study*. Port Clinton, OH: BNR Press, 1995.

Schwing, Ned. *Standard Catalog of Military Firearms: The Collector's Price and Reference Guide*, 3rd ed. Iola, WI: Gun Digest Books, 2005.

Silvey, M.W., Gary D. Boyd & Frank Trzaska. *U.S. Military Knives, Bayonets and Machetes Price Guide*, 4th ed. Knoxville, TN: Knife World Publications, 2000.

Stanton, Shelby. *U.S. Army Uniforms of World War II*. Harrisburg, PA: Stackpole Books, 1991.

Stein, Barry Jason. *U.S. Army Patches, Flashes and Ovals: An Illustrated Encyclopedia of Cloth Unit Insignia*. Insignia Ventures, 2007.

Strandberg, LTC John E. and Roger James Bender. *The Call of Duty: Military Awards and Decorations of the United States of America*, 2nd ed. San Jose, CA: R. James Bender Publishing, 2004.

Storey, Ed. *'37 Web: Equipping the Canadian Soldier*. Ottawa, Ontario, Canada: Service Publications, 2003.

Suermont, Jan. *Infantry Weapons of World War II*. Iola, WI: Krause Publications, 2004.

Sweeting, C.G. *Combat Flying Clothing: Army Air Forces Clothing During World War II*. Washington, DC: Smithsonian Institution Press, 1984.

Tulkoff, Alec S. *Grunt Gear: USMC Combat Infantry Equipment of World War II*. San Jose, CA: R. James Bender Publishing, 2003.

Vernon, Sydney B. *Vernon's Collectors' Guide to Orders, Medals & Decorations*, 4th ed. Temecula, CA: Sydney B. Vernon, 2004.

Warner, Jeff. *Sailors in Forest Green: USN Personnel Attached to the USMC*. Atglen, PA: Schiffer Military History, 2006.

Windrow, Richard and Tim Hawkins. *The World War II GI: U.S. Army Uniform, 1941-45 in Color Photographs*. Ramsbury, Marlborough, Wiltshire, UK: The Crowood Press, Ltd., 1993.

Jason Burmeister
MILITARIA

Orders & Decorations, Documents, Embroidered Flags & Pennants,
Uniforms, Insignia, Headgear, Helmets & Edged Weapons

Preserving Minnesota's Military History

Minnesota Military Museum
15000 Highway 115
Little Falls, MN 56345-417
(320) 632-7374
mnmuseum@brainerd.net

—WANTED—
Donations of objects, photographs
and archival material related to
Minnesota's military past

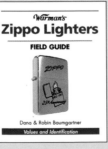